Kimi Shiruya-
Dost thou Know?

by
Satoru Ishihara

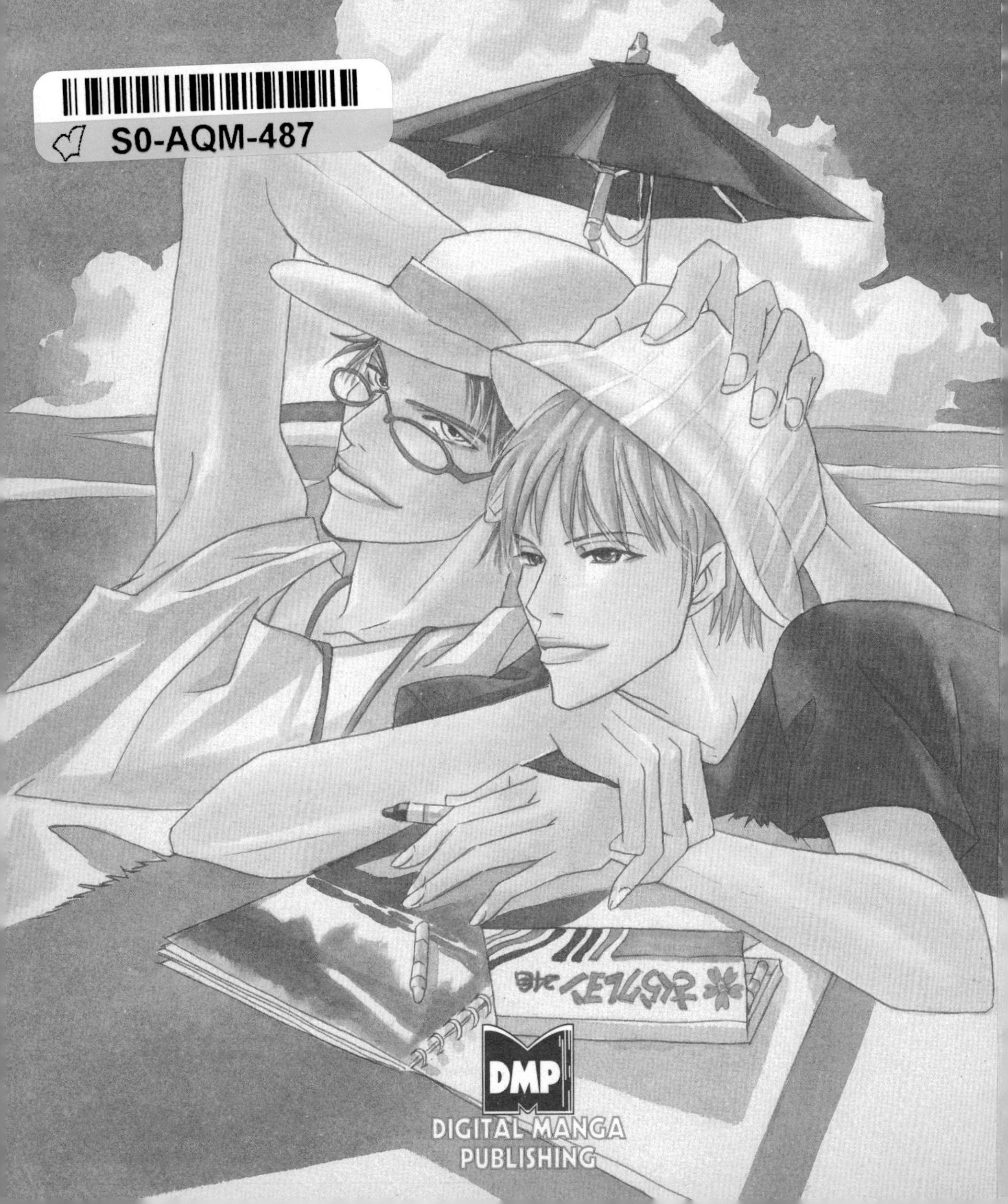

DMP
DIGITAL MANGA PUBLISHING

Kimi Shiruya- Dost thou Know?

Translation	**Sachiko Sato**
Lettering	**Melanie Lewis**
Graphic Design	**Eric Rosenberger**
Editing	**Stephanie Donnelly**
Editor in Chief	**Fred Lui**
Publisher	**Hikaru Sasahara**

English Edition Published by
DIGITAL MANGA PUBLISHING
A division of DIGITAL MANGA, Inc.
1487 W 178th Street, Suite 300
Gardena, CA 90248

www.dmpbooks.com

First Edition: October 2005
ISBN: 1-56970-934-3

1 3 5 7 9 10 8 6 4 2

Printed in China

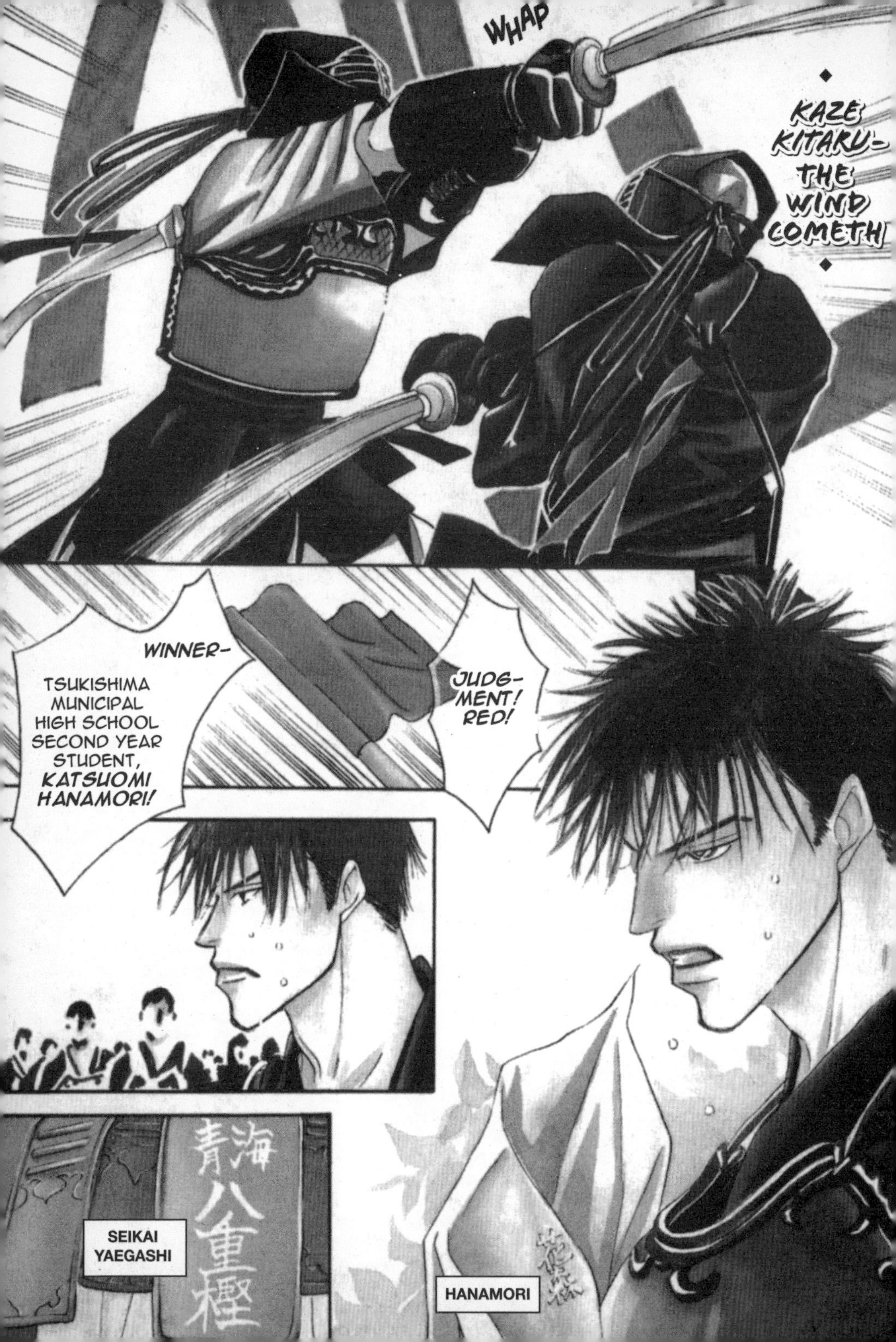
WHAP
KAZE KITARU- THE WIND COMETH
JUDG-MENT! RED!
WINNER-
TSUKISHIMA MUNICIPAL HIGH SCHOOL SECOND YEAR STUDENT, KATSUOMI HANAMORI!
HANAMORI
青海 八重樫
SEIKAI YAEGASHI

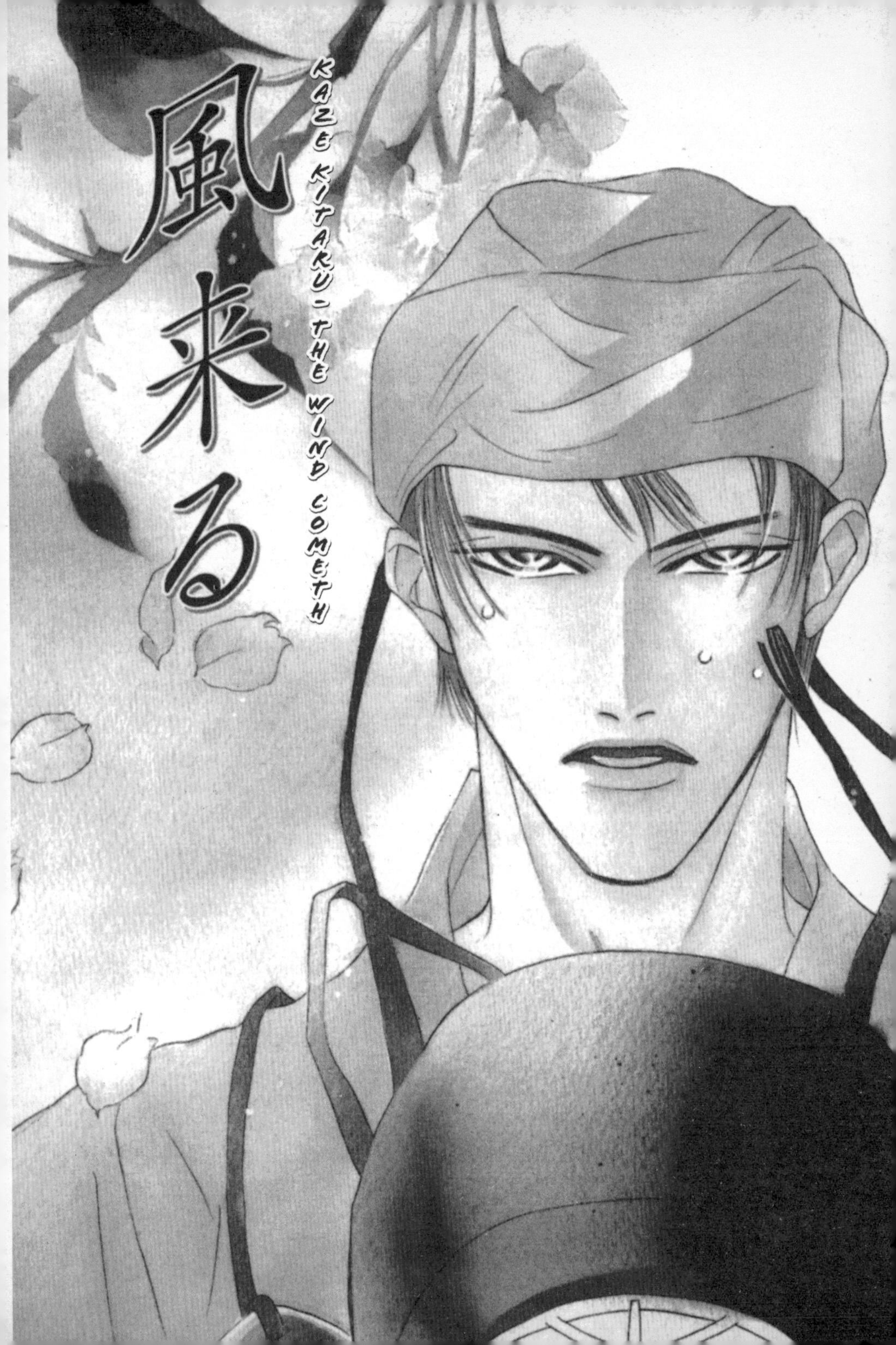
風来る
KAZE KITARU- THE WIND COMETH

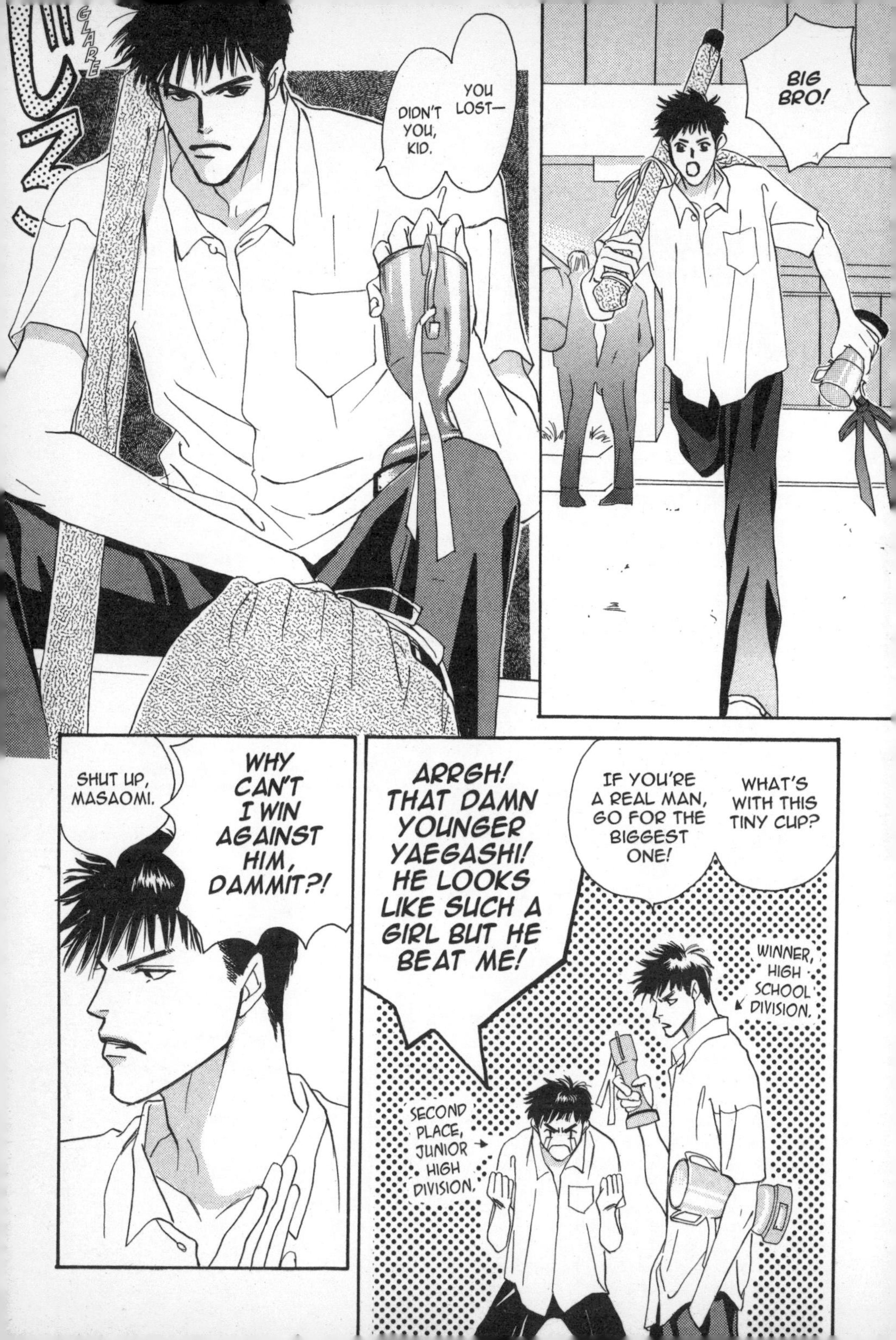
BIG BRO!
GLARE
YOU LOST— DIDN'T YOU, KID.
WHAT'S WITH THIS TINY CUP?
IF YOU'RE A REAL MAN, GO FOR THE BIGGEST ONE!
ARRGH! THAT DAMN YOUNGER YAEGASHI! HE LOOKS LIKE SUCH A GIRL BUT HE BEAT ME!
WINNER, HIGH SCHOOL DIVISION.
SECOND PLACE, JUNIOR HIGH DIVISION.
WHY CAN'T I WIN AGAINST HIM, DAMMIT?!
SHUT UP, MASAOMI.

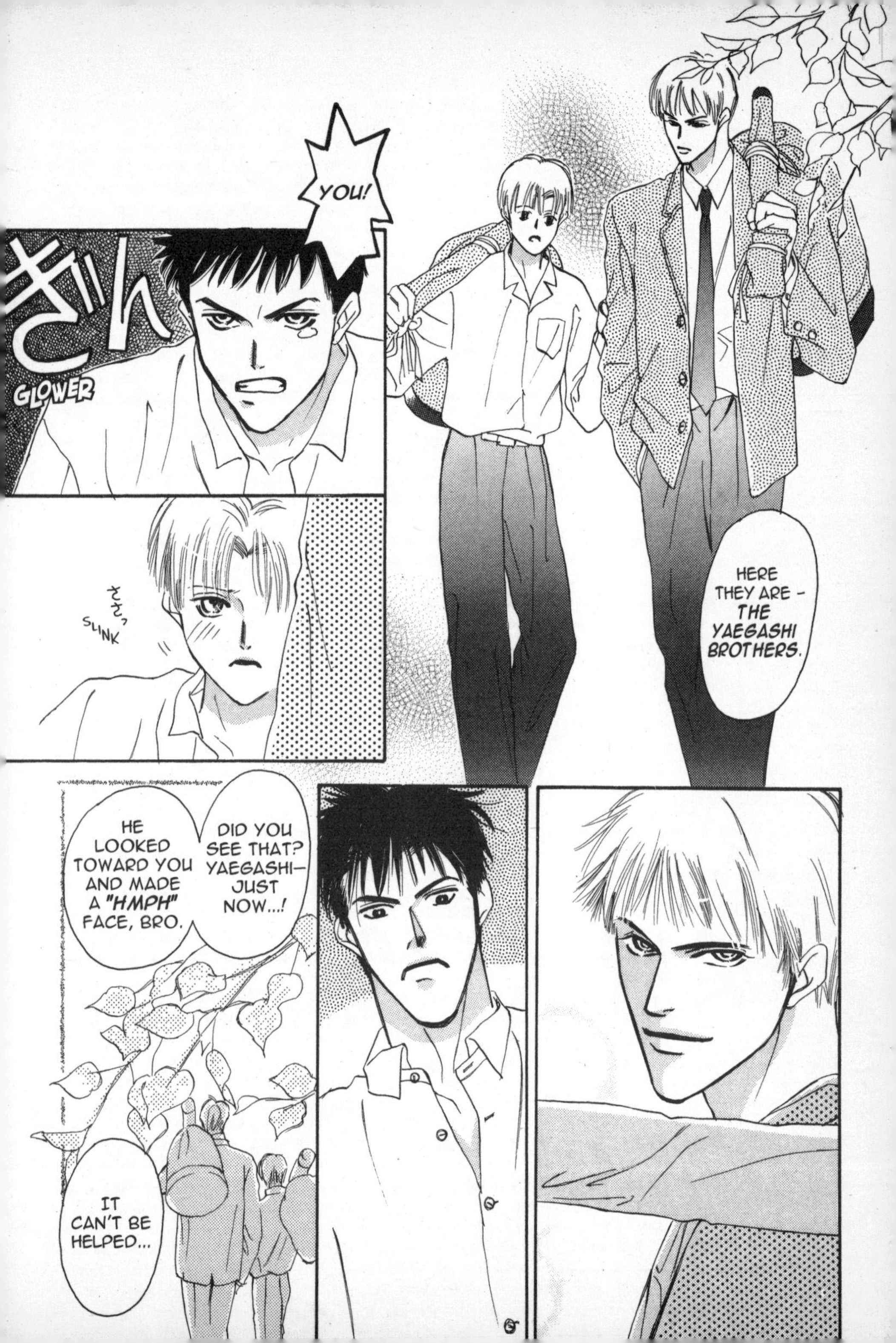
HERE THEY ARE - THE YAEGASHI BROTHERS.
YOU!
きぃん
GLOWER
ささっ
SLINK
DID YOU SEE THAT? YAEGASHI— JUST NOW...!
HE LOOKED TOWARD YOU AND MADE A "HMPH" FACE, BRO.
IT CAN'T BE HELPED...

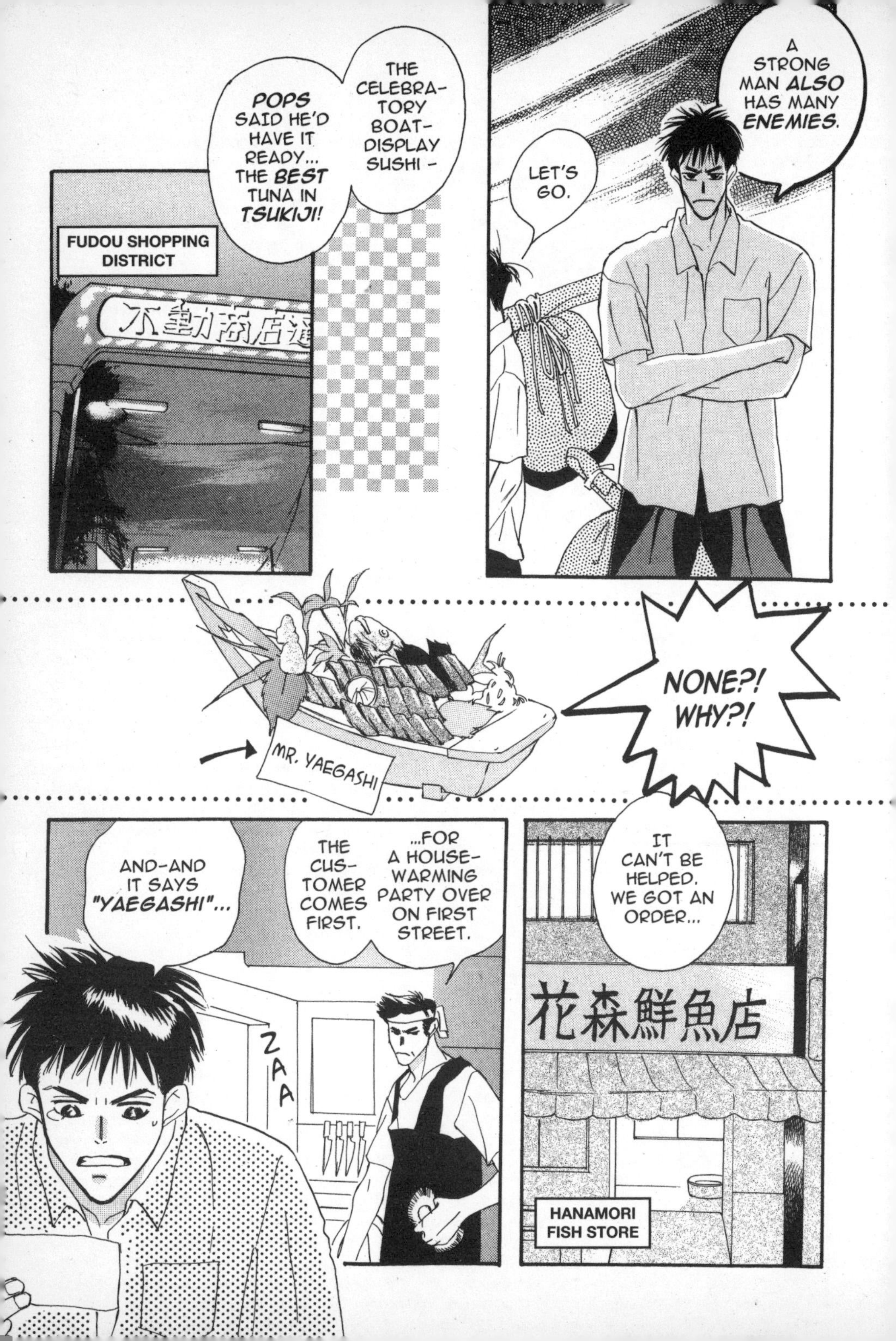
A STRONG MAN **ALSO** HAS MANY **ENEMIES**.
LET'S GO.
THE CELEBRATORY BOAT-DISPLAY SUSHI -
POPS SAID HE'D HAVE IT READY... THE **BEST** TUNA IN **TSUKIJI**!
FUDOU SHOPPING DISTRICT
不動商店
NONE?! WHY?!
MR. YAEGASHI
IT CAN'T BE HELPED. WE GOT AN ORDER...
花森鮮魚店
HANAMORI FISH STORE
...FOR A HOUSE-WARMING PARTY OVER ON FIRST STREET.
THE CUSTOMER COMES FIRST.
AND-AND IT SAYS ***"YAEGASHI"***...
ZAA

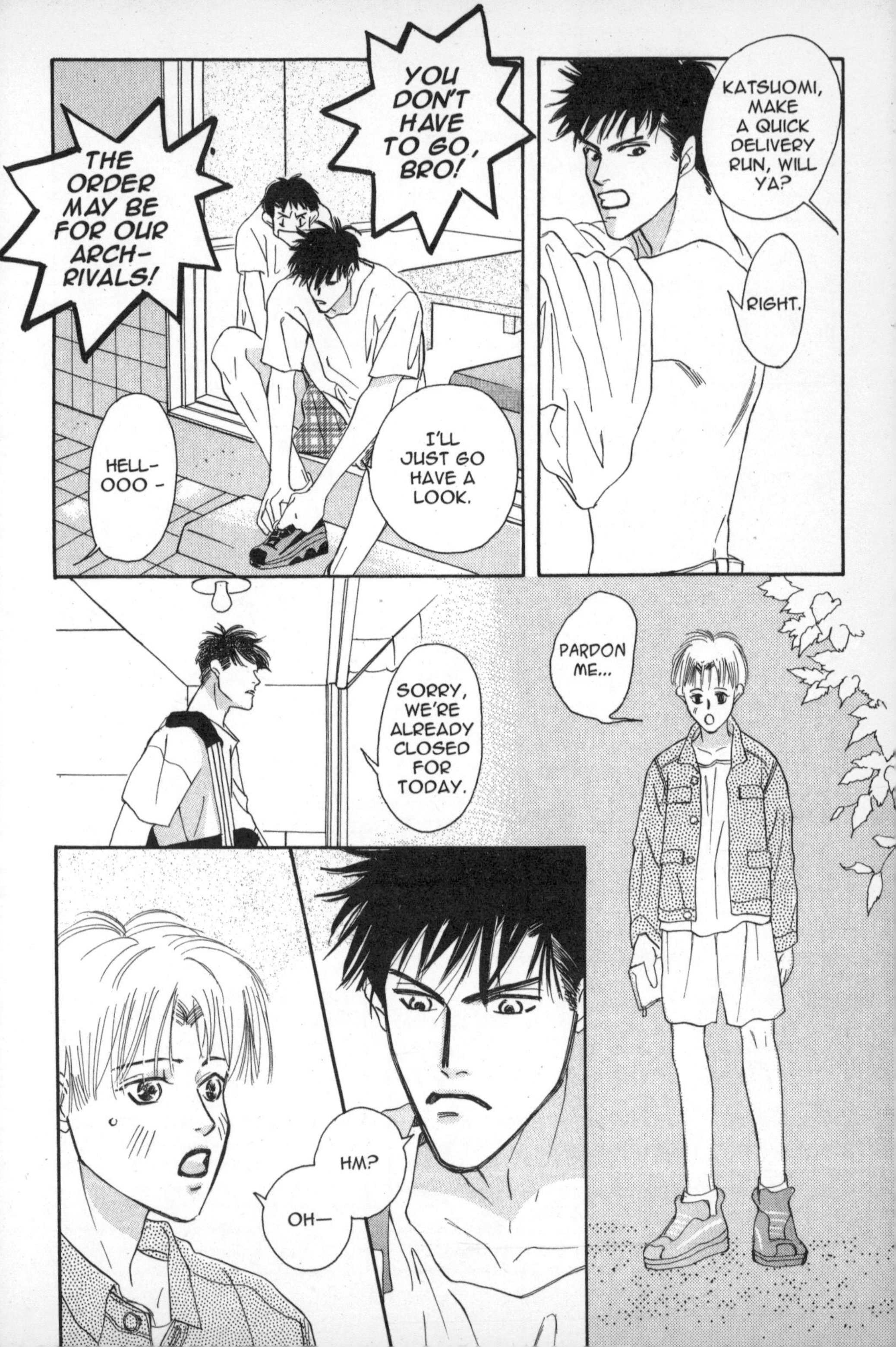
KATSUOMI, MAKE A QUICK DELIVERY RUN, WILL YA?
RIGHT.
YOU DON'T HAVE TO GO, BRO!
THE ORDER MAY BE FOR OUR ARCH-RIVALS!
I'LL JUST GO HAVE A LOOK.
HELL-OOO -
PARDON ME...
SORRY, WE'RE ALREADY CLOSED FOR TODAY.
HM?
OH—

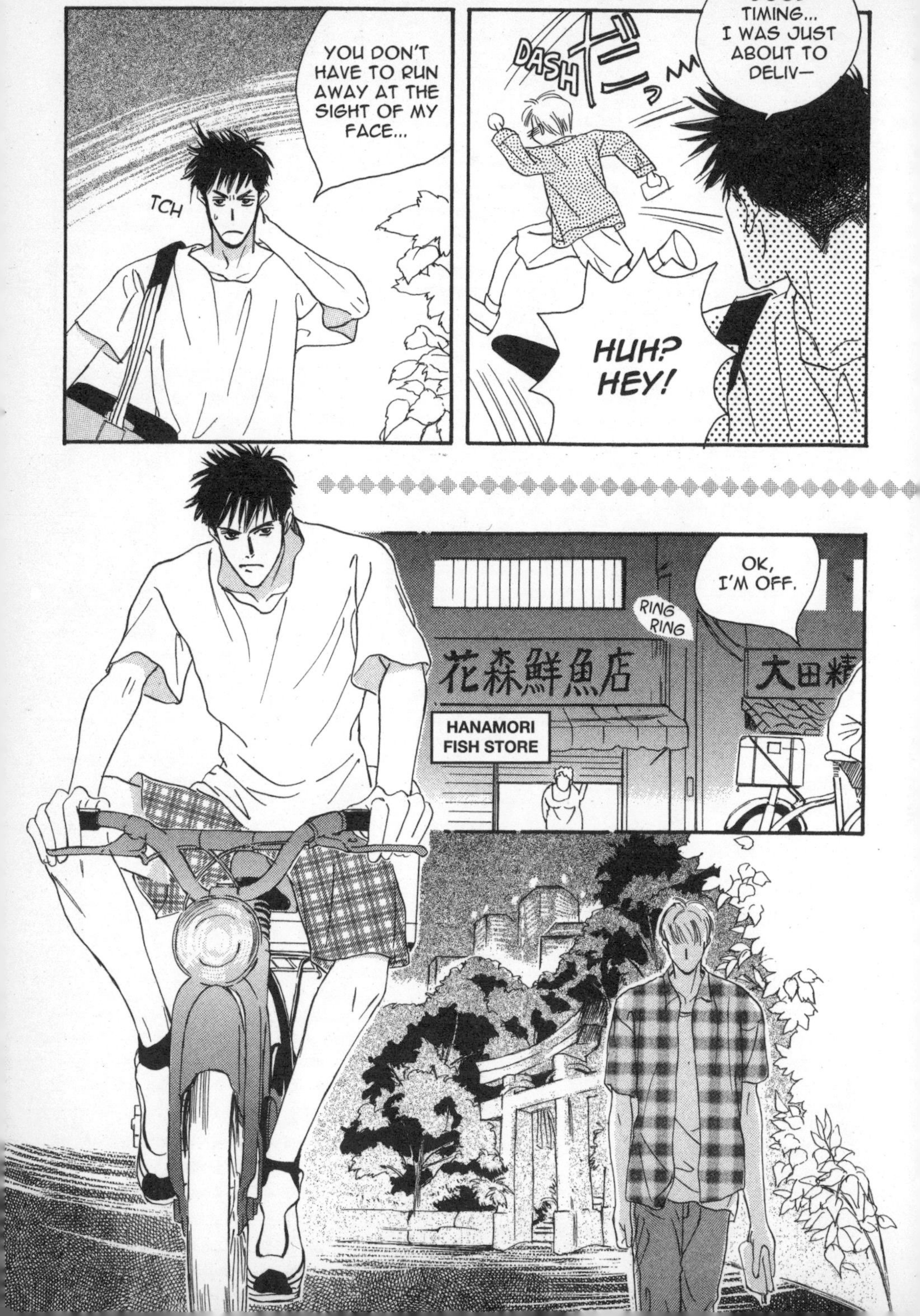
GOOD TIMING... I WAS JUST ABOUT TO DELIV—
DASH
HUH? HEY!
YOU DON'T HAVE TO RUN AWAY AT THE SIGHT OF MY FACE...
TCH
OK, I'M OFF.
RING RING
大田精
花森鮮魚店
HANAMORI FISH STORE

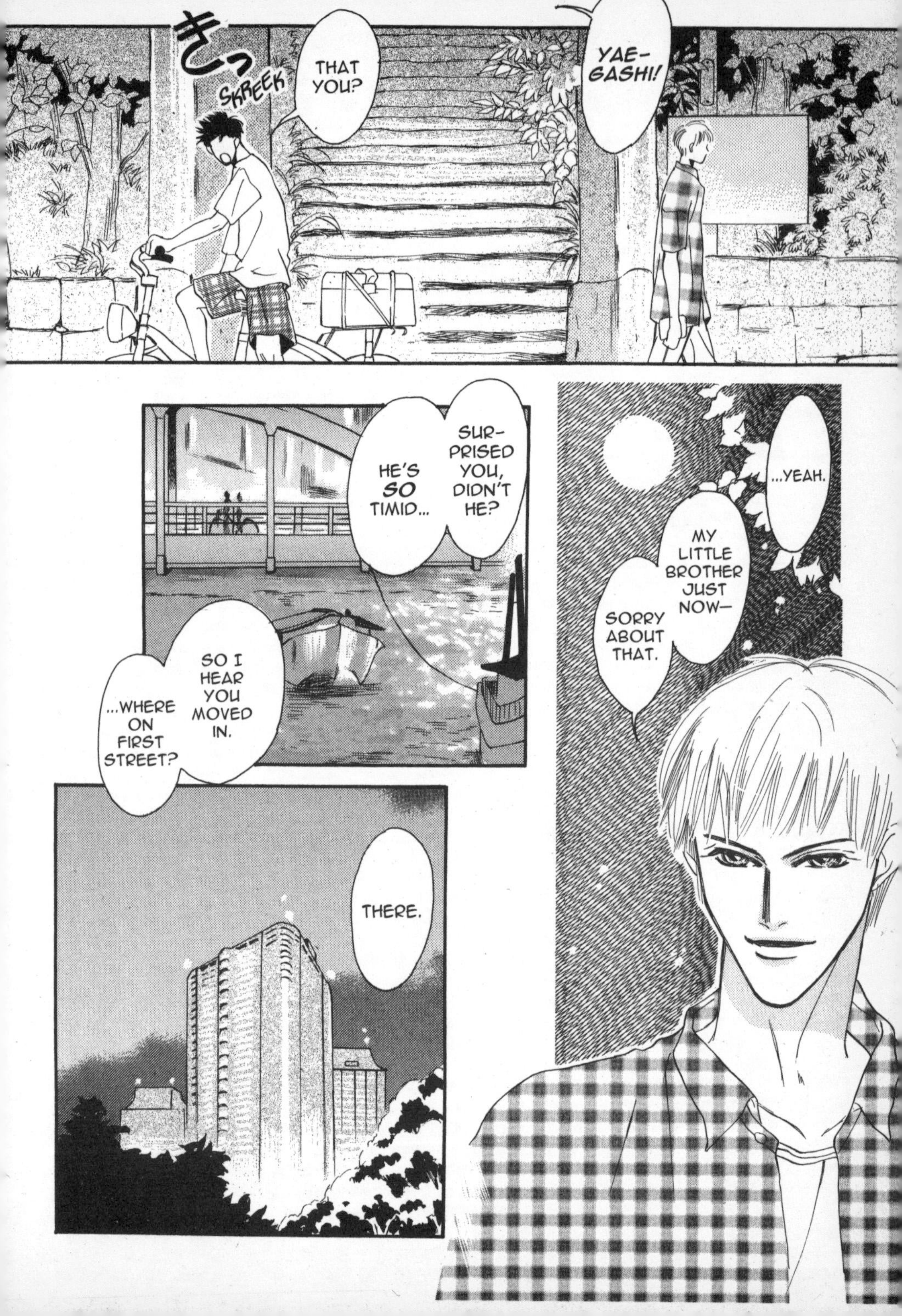
YAE-GASHI!
THAT YOU?
きっ
SKREEK
...YEAH.
MY LITTLE BROTHER JUST NOW—
SORRY ABOUT THAT.
SUR-PRISED YOU, DIDN'T HE?
HE'S SO TIMID...
SO I HEAR YOU MOVED IN.
...WHERE ON FIRST STREET?
THERE.

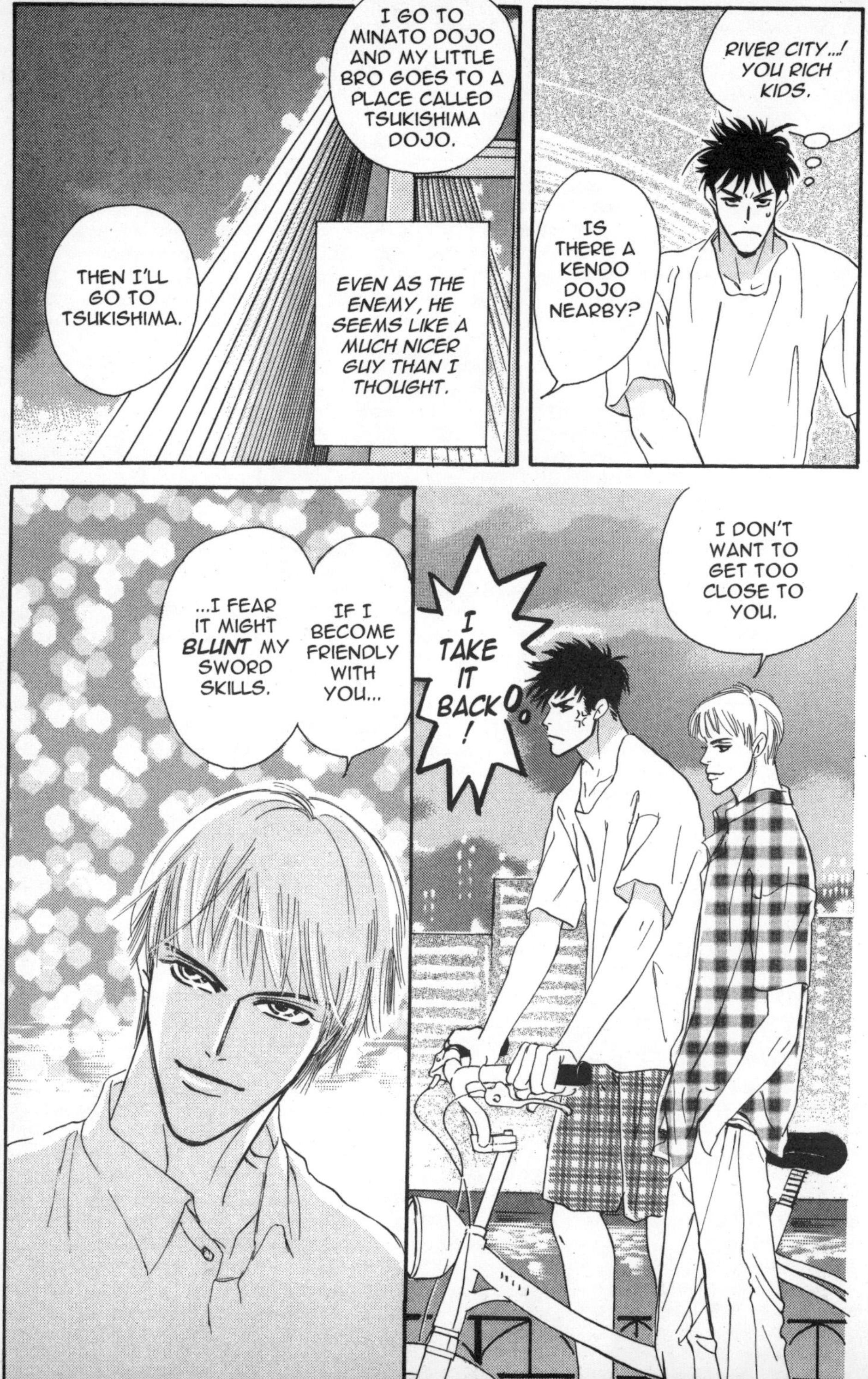

RIVER CITY...! YOU RICH KIDS.
IS THERE A KENDO DOJO NEARBY?
I GO TO MINATO DOJO AND MY LITTLE BRO GOES TO A PLACE CALLED TSUKISHIMA DOJO.
EVEN AS THE ENEMY, HE SEEMS LIKE A MUCH NICER GUY THAN I THOUGHT.
THEN I'LL GO TO TSUKISHIMA.
I DON'T WANT TO GET TOO CLOSE TO YOU.
I TAKE IT BACK!
IF I BECOME FRIENDLY WITH YOU...
...I FEAR IT MIGHT BLUNT MY SWORD SKILLS.

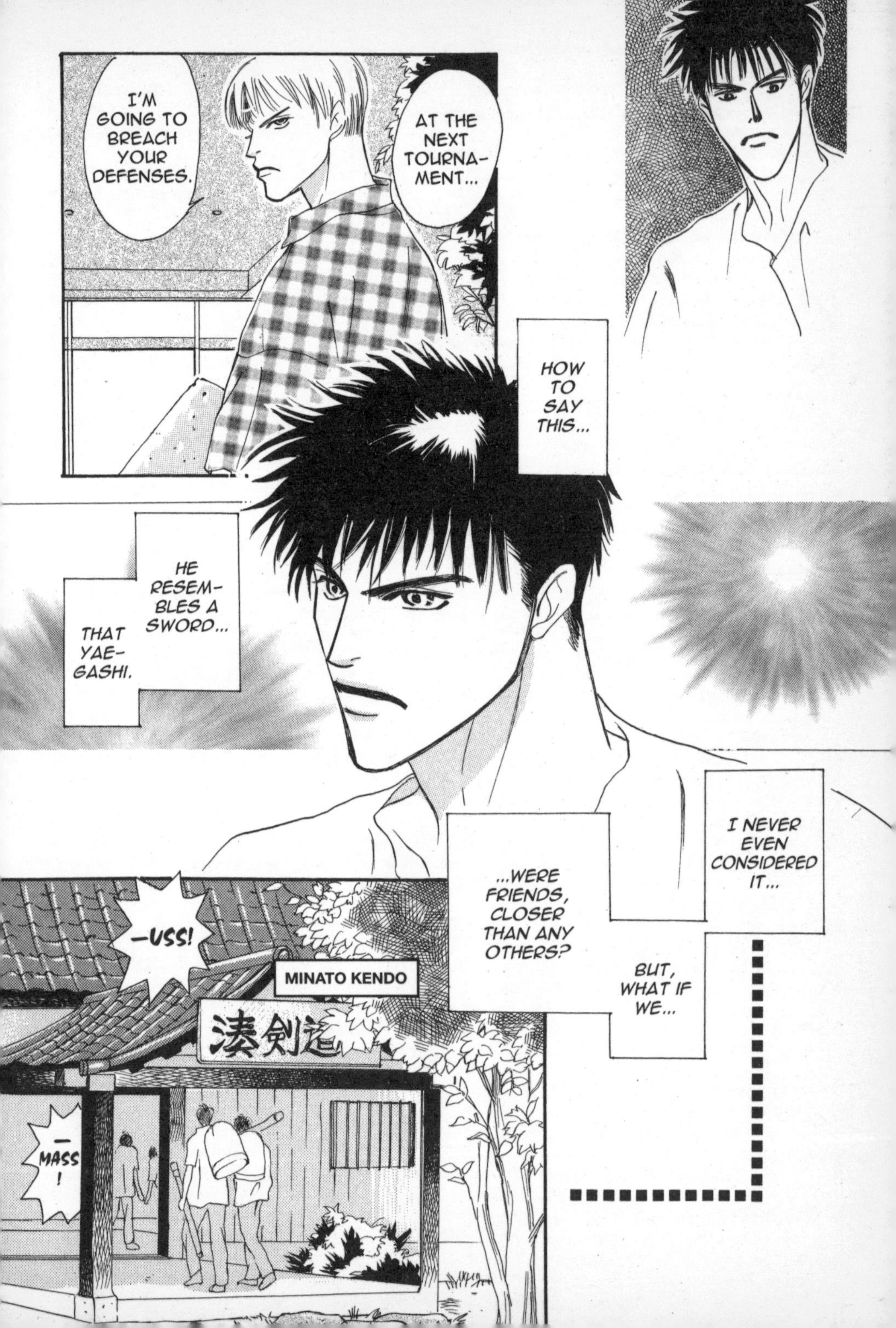
AT THE NEXT TOURNAMENT...
I'M GOING TO BREACH YOUR DEFENSES.
HOW TO SAY THIS...
HE RESEMBLES A SWORD...
THAT YAEGASHI.
I NEVER EVEN CONSIDERED IT...
BUT, WHAT IF WE...
...WERE FRIENDS, CLOSER THAN ANY OTHERS?
—USS!
MINATO KENDO
湊剣道
—MASS!

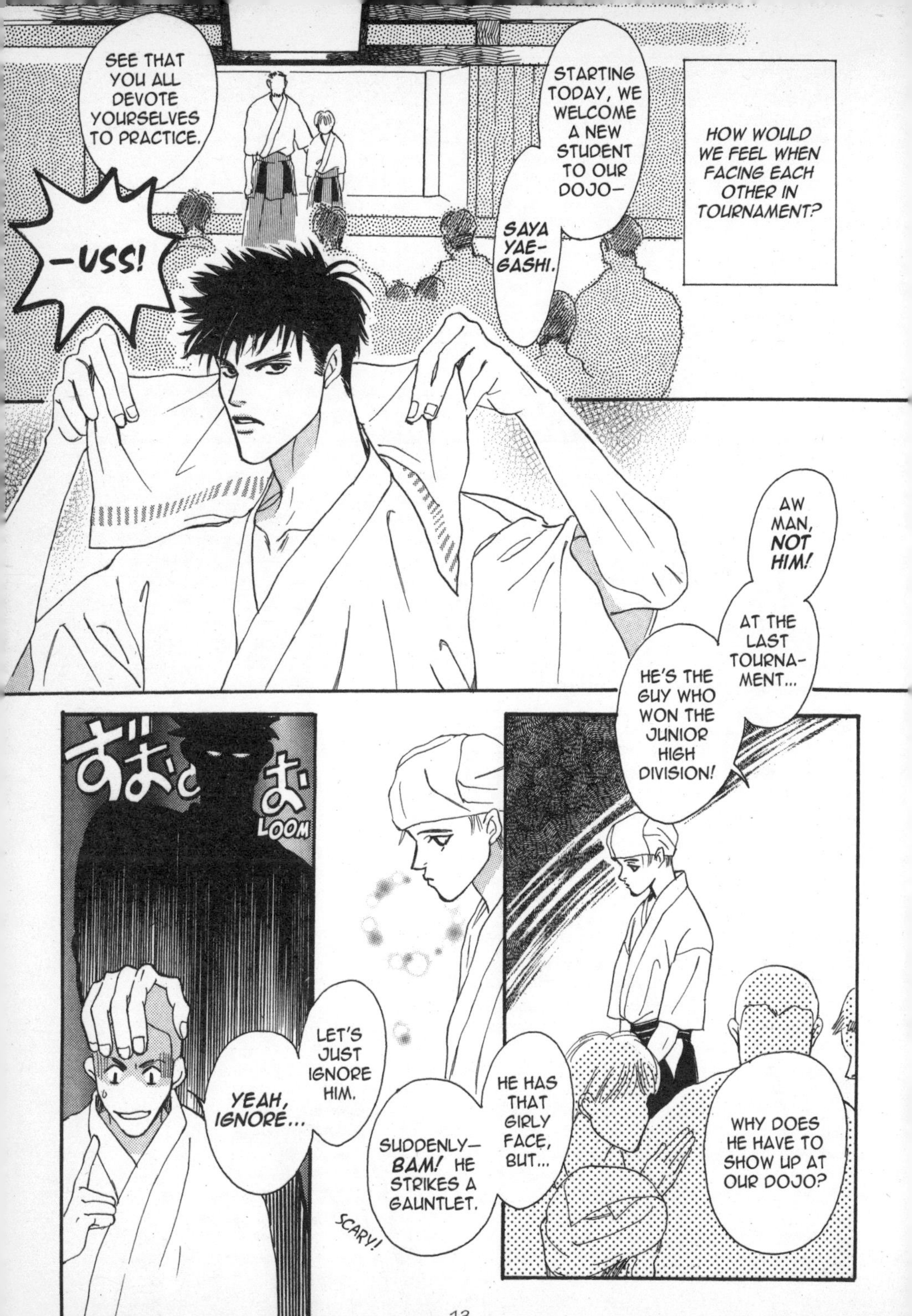
HOW WOULD WE FEEL WHEN FACING EACH OTHER IN TOURNAMENT?
STARTING TODAY, WE WELCOME A NEW STUDENT TO OUR DOJO—
SAYA YAE-GASHI.
SEE THAT YOU ALL DEVOTE YOURSELVES TO PRACTICE.
—USS!
AW MAN, NOT HIM!
AT THE LAST TOURNA-MENT...
HE'S THE GUY WHO WON THE JUNIOR HIGH DIVISION!
WHY DOES HE HAVE TO SHOW UP AT OUR DOJO?
HE HAS THAT GIRLY FACE, BUT...
SUDDENLY— BAM! HE STRIKES A GAUNTLET.
SCARY!
LET'S JUST IGNORE HIM.
LOOM
YEAH, IGNORE...

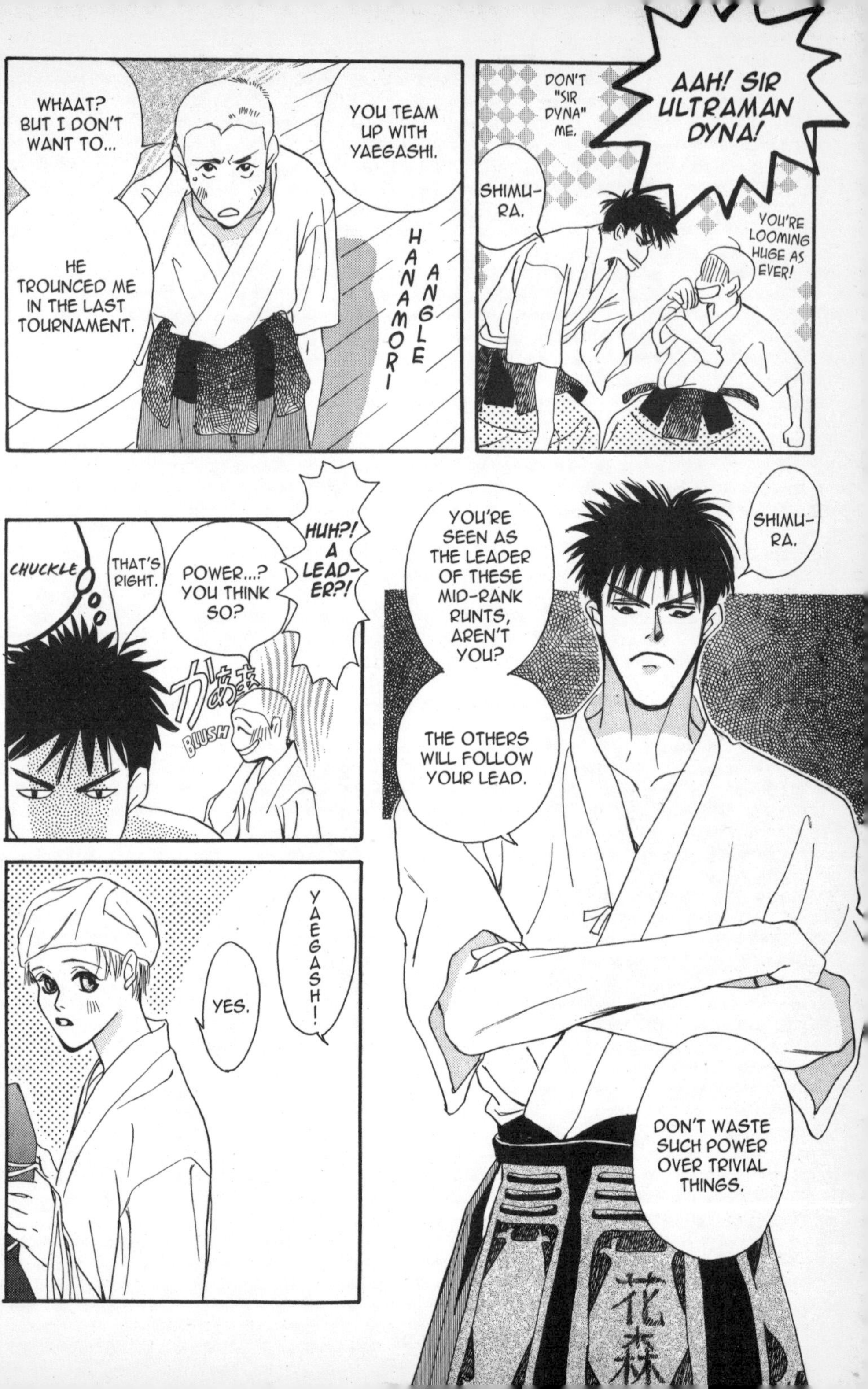
AAH! SIR ULTRAMAN DYNA!
DON'T "SIR DYNA" ME.
SHIMU-RA.
YOU'RE LOOMING HUGE AS EVER!
YOU TEAM UP WITH YAEGASHI.
HANAMORI ANGLE
WHAAT? BUT I DON'T WANT TO...
HE TROUNCED ME IN THE LAST TOURNAMENT.
SHIMU-RA.
YOU'RE SEEN AS THE LEADER OF THESE MID-RANK RUNTS, AREN'T YOU?
THE OTHERS WILL FOLLOW YOUR LEAD.
DON'T WASTE SUCH POWER OVER TRIVIAL THINGS.
花森
HUH?! A LEAD-ER?!
POWER...? YOU THINK SO?
THAT'S RIGHT.
CHUCKLE
BLUSH
YAEGASHI!
YES.

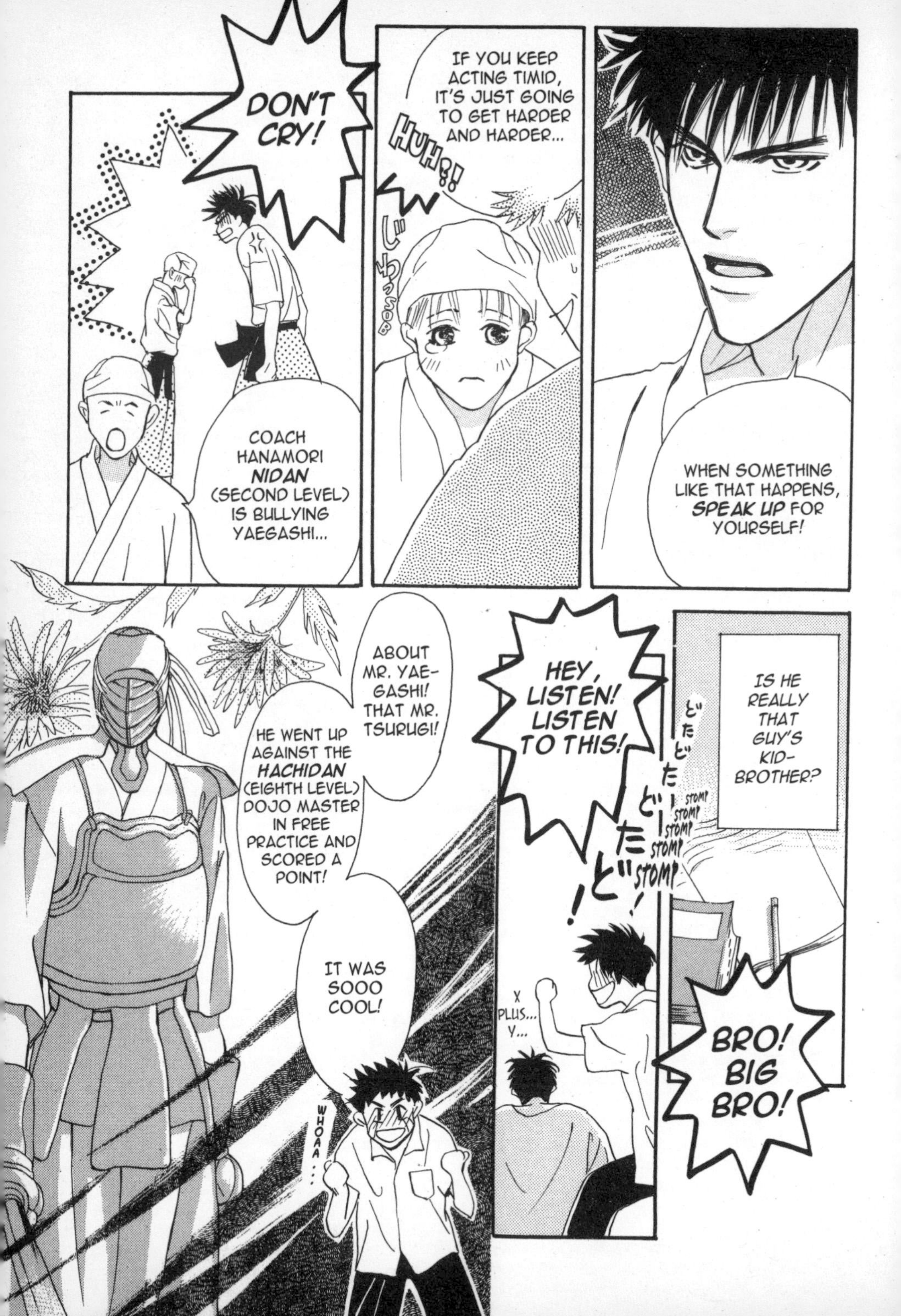
WHEN SOMETHING LIKE THAT HAPPENS, SPEAK UP FOR YOURSELF!
IF YOU KEEP ACTING TIMID, IT'S JUST GOING TO GET HARDER AND HARDER...
HUH?!
じわっ
DON'T CRY!
COACH HANAMORI NIDAN (SECOND LEVEL) IS BULLYING YAEGASHI...
IS HE REALLY THAT GUY'S KID-BROTHER?
HEY, LISTEN! LISTEN TO THIS!
STOMP STOMP STOMP STOMP STOMP
BRO! BIG BRO!
X PLUS... Y...
ABOUT MR. YAE-GASHI! THAT MR. TSURUGI!
HE WENT UP AGAINST THE HACHIDAN (EIGHTH LEVEL) DOJO MASTER IN FREE PRACTICE AND SCORED A POINT!
IT WAS SOOO COOL!
WHOAA...

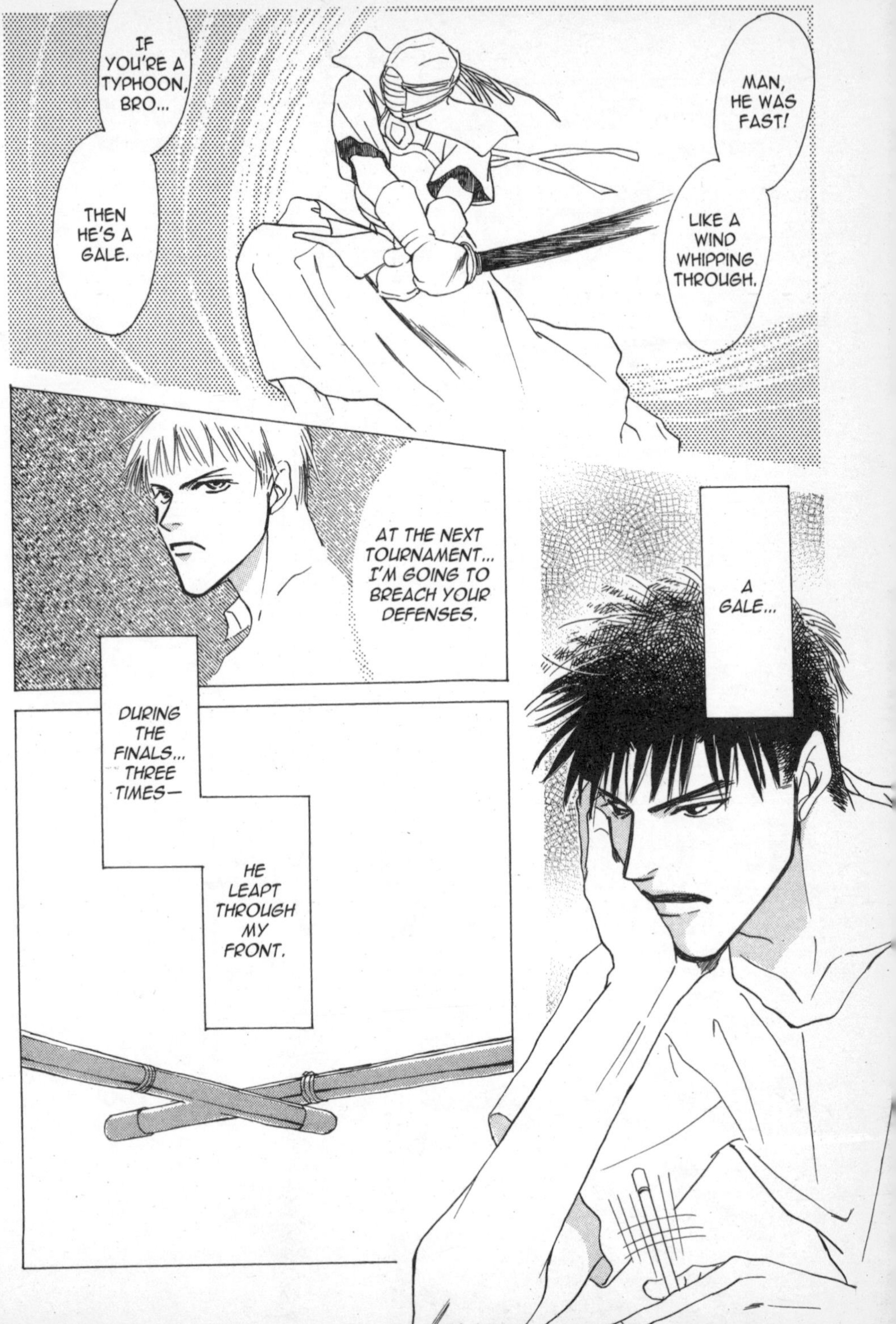
MAN, HE WAS FAST!
LIKE A WIND WHIPPING THROUGH.
IF YOU'RE A TYPHOON, BRO...
THEN HE'S A GALE.
A GALE...
AT THE NEXT TOURNAMENT... I'M GOING TO BREACH YOUR DEFENSES.
DURING THE FINALS... THREE TIMES—
HE LEAPT THROUGH MY FRONT.

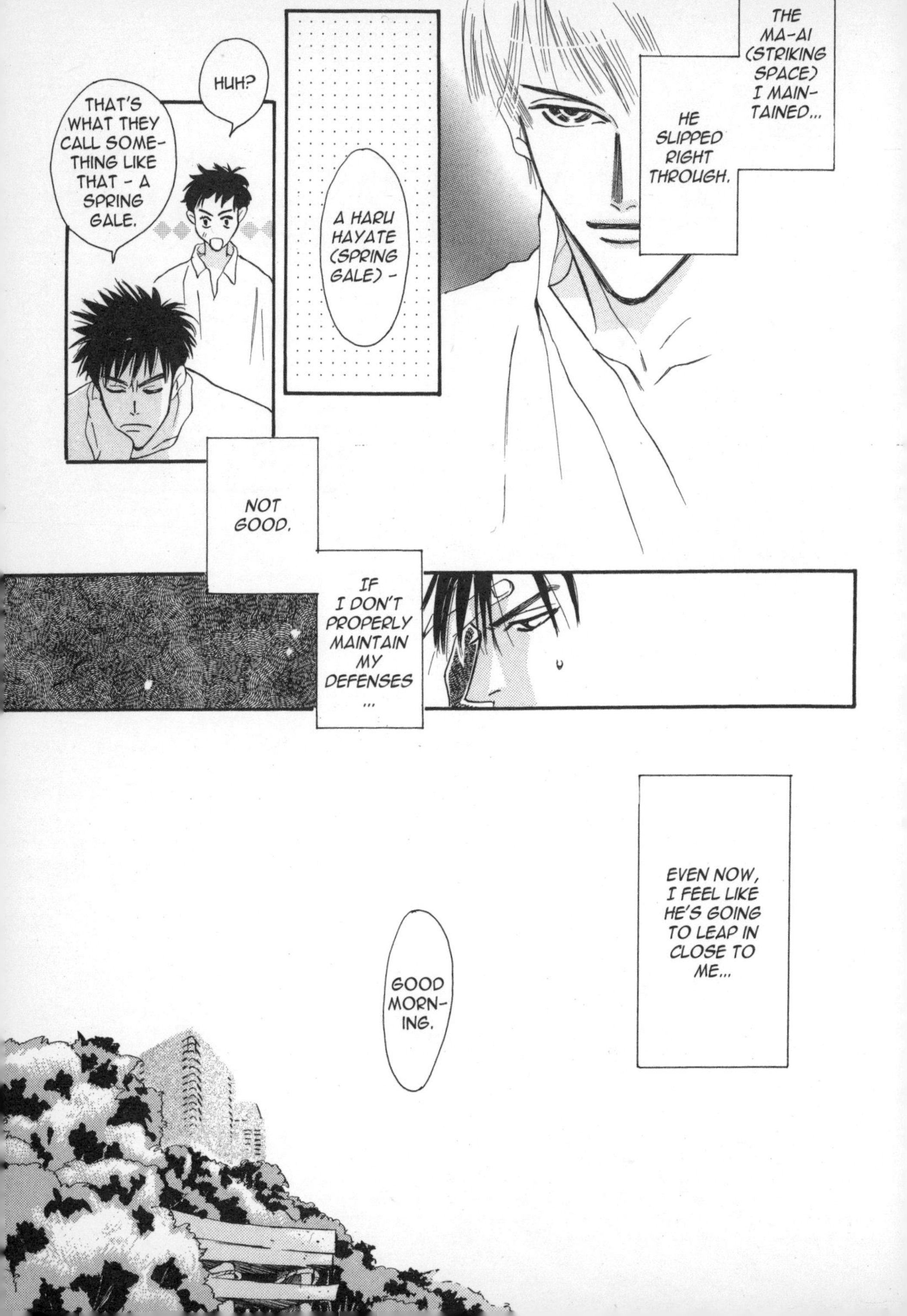
THE MA-AI (STRIKING SPACE) I MAINTAINED...
HE SLIPPED RIGHT THROUGH.
A HARU HAYATE (SPRING GALE) -
HUH?
THAT'S WHAT THEY CALL SOMETHING LIKE THAT - A SPRING GALE.
NOT GOOD.
IF I DON'T PROPERLY MAINTAIN MY DEFENSES ...
EVEN NOW, I FEEL LIKE HE'S GOING TO LEAP IN CLOSE TO ME...
GOOD MORNING.

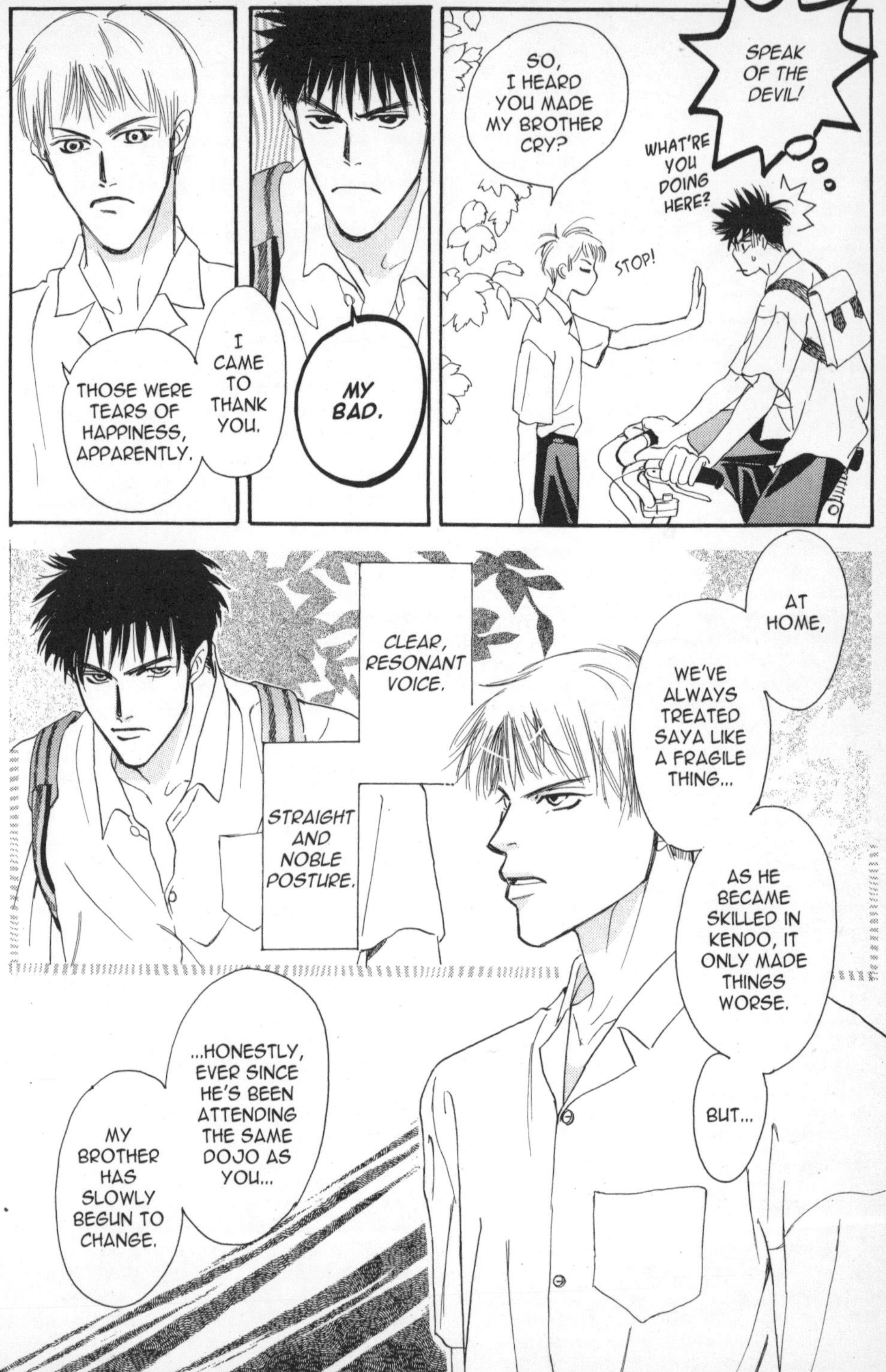
SPEAK OF THE DEVIL!
WHAT'RE YOU DOING HERE?
SO, I HEARD YOU MADE MY BROTHER CRY?
STOP!
MY BAD.
I CAME TO THANK YOU.
THOSE WERE TEARS OF HAPPINESS, APPARENTLY.
AT HOME,
WE'VE ALWAYS TREATED SAYA LIKE A FRAGILE THING...
AS HE BECAME SKILLED IN KENDO, IT ONLY MADE THINGS WORSE.
CLEAR, RESONANT VOICE.
STRAIGHT AND NOBLE POSTURE.
BUT...
...HONESTLY, EVER SINCE HE'S BEEN ATTENDING THE SAME DOJO AS YOU...
MY BROTHER HAS SLOWLY BEGUN TO CHANGE.

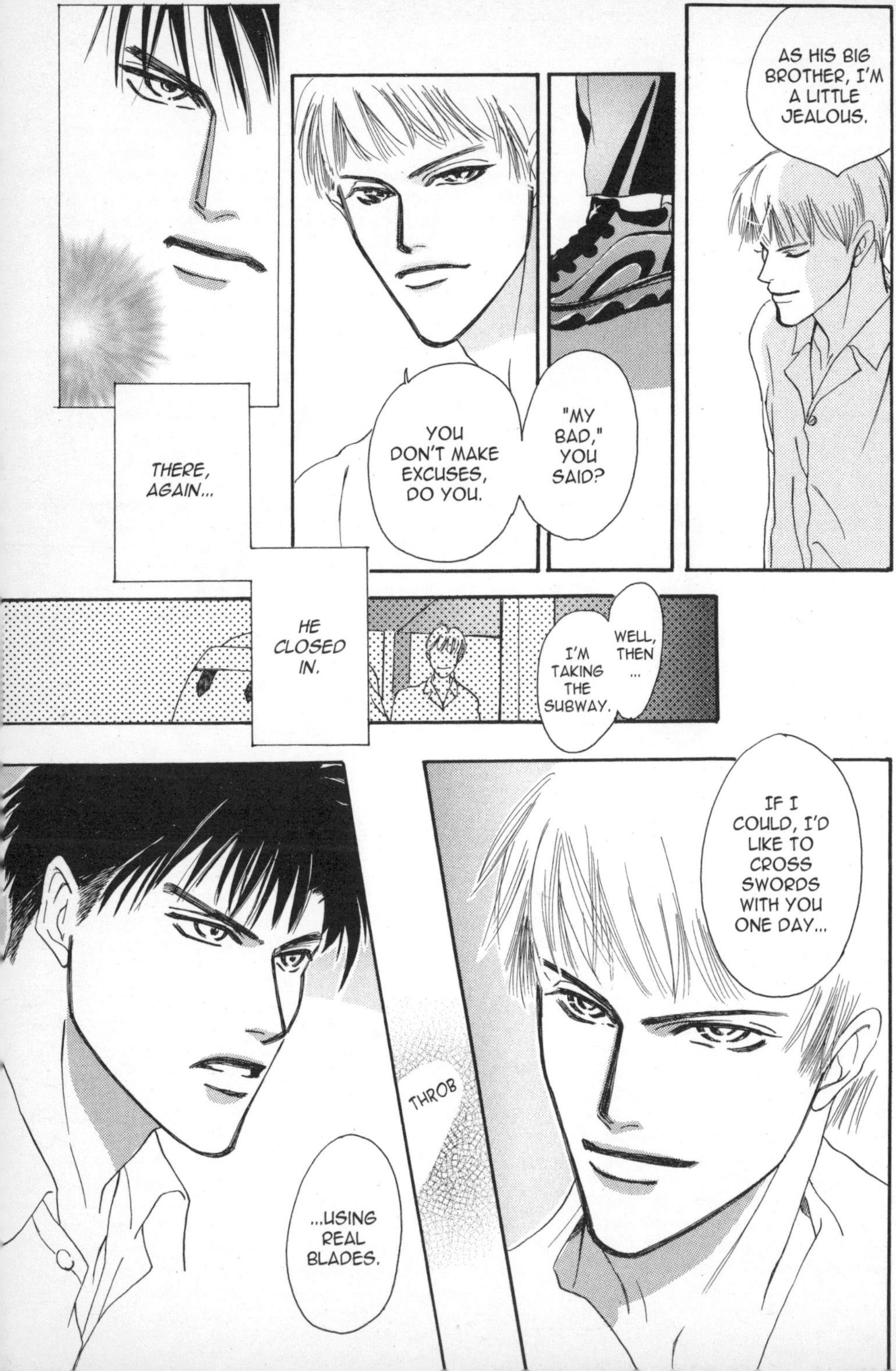
AS HIS BIG BROTHER, I'M A LITTLE JEALOUS.
"MY BAD," YOU SAID?
YOU DON'T MAKE EXCUSES, DO YOU.
THERE, AGAIN...
WELL, THEN ...
I'M TAKING THE SUBWAY.
HE CLOSED IN.
IF I COULD, I'D LIKE TO CROSS SWORDS WITH YOU ONE DAY...
THROB
...USING REAL BLADES.

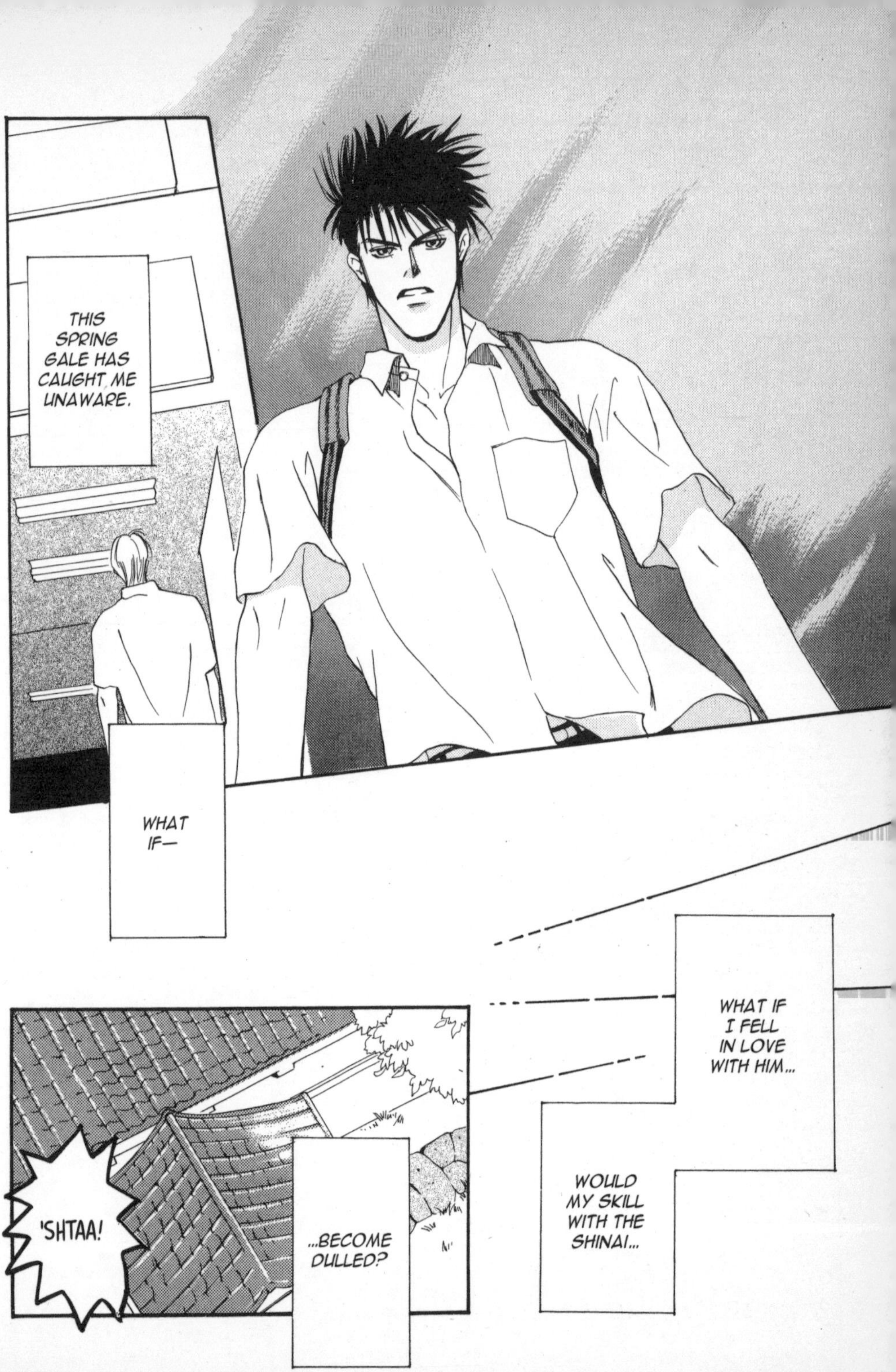
THIS SPRING GALE HAS CAUGHT ME UNAWARE.
WHAT IF—
WHAT IF I FELL IN LOVE WITH HIM...
WOULD MY SKILL WITH THE SHINAI...
...BECOME DULLED?
'SHTAA!

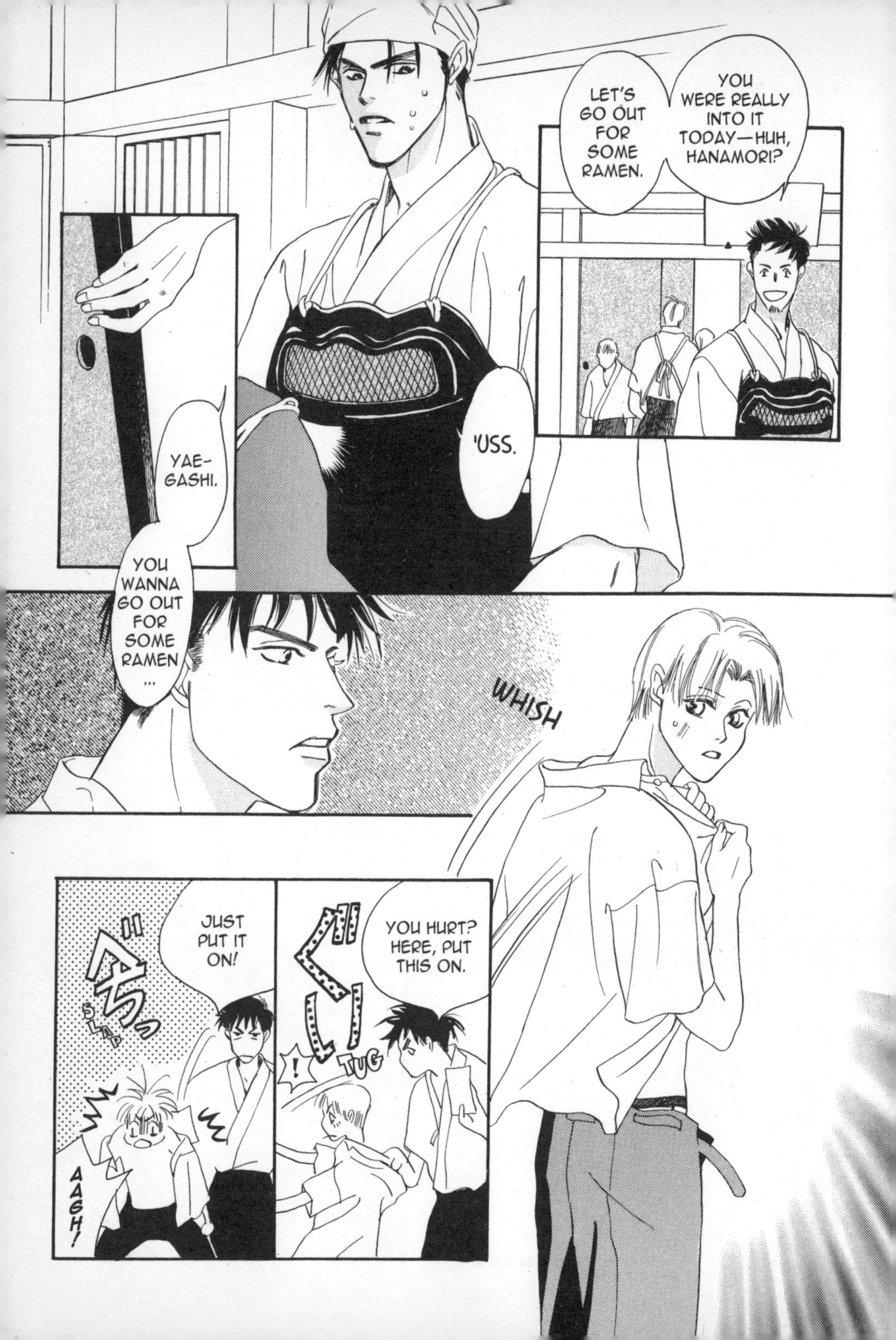
YOU WERE REALLY INTO IT TODAY—HUH, HANAMORI?
LET'S GO OUT FOR SOME RAMEN.
'USS.
YAE-GASHI.
YOU WANNA GO OUT FOR SOME RAMEN ...
WHISH
YOU HURT? HERE, PUT THIS ON.
TUG
JUST PUT IT ON!
SLAP
AAGH!

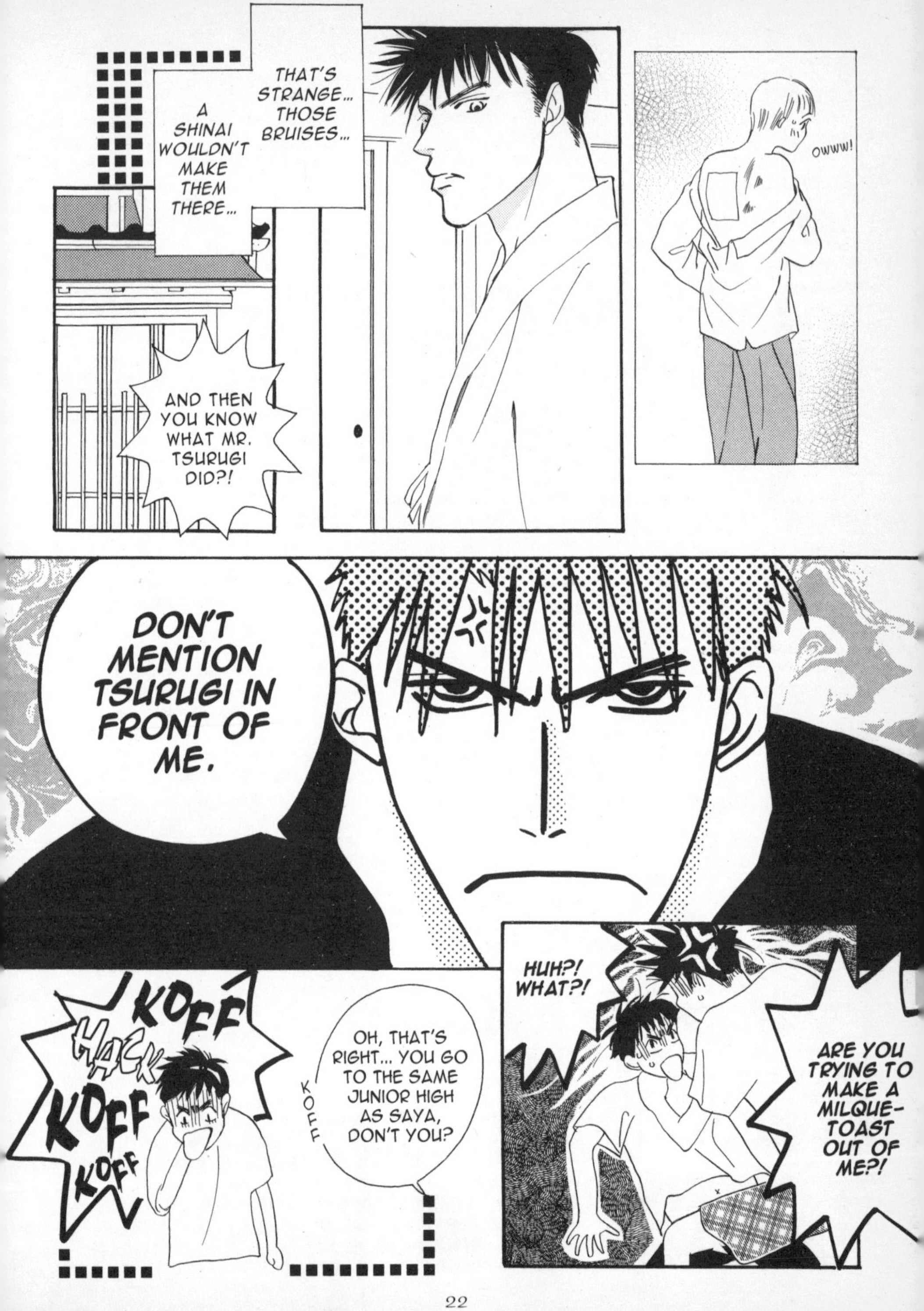
OWWW!
THAT'S STRANGE... THOSE BRUISES...
A SHINAI WOULDN'T MAKE THEM THERE...
AND THEN YOU KNOW WHAT MR. TSURUGI DID?!
DON'T MENTION TSURUGI IN FRONT OF ME.
ARE YOU TRYING TO MAKE A MILQUE-TOAST OUT OF ME?!
HUH?! WHAT?!
OH, THAT'S RIGHT... YOU GO TO THE SAME JUNIOR HIGH AS SAYA, DON'T YOU?
KOFF
KOFF
HACK
KOFF
KOFF

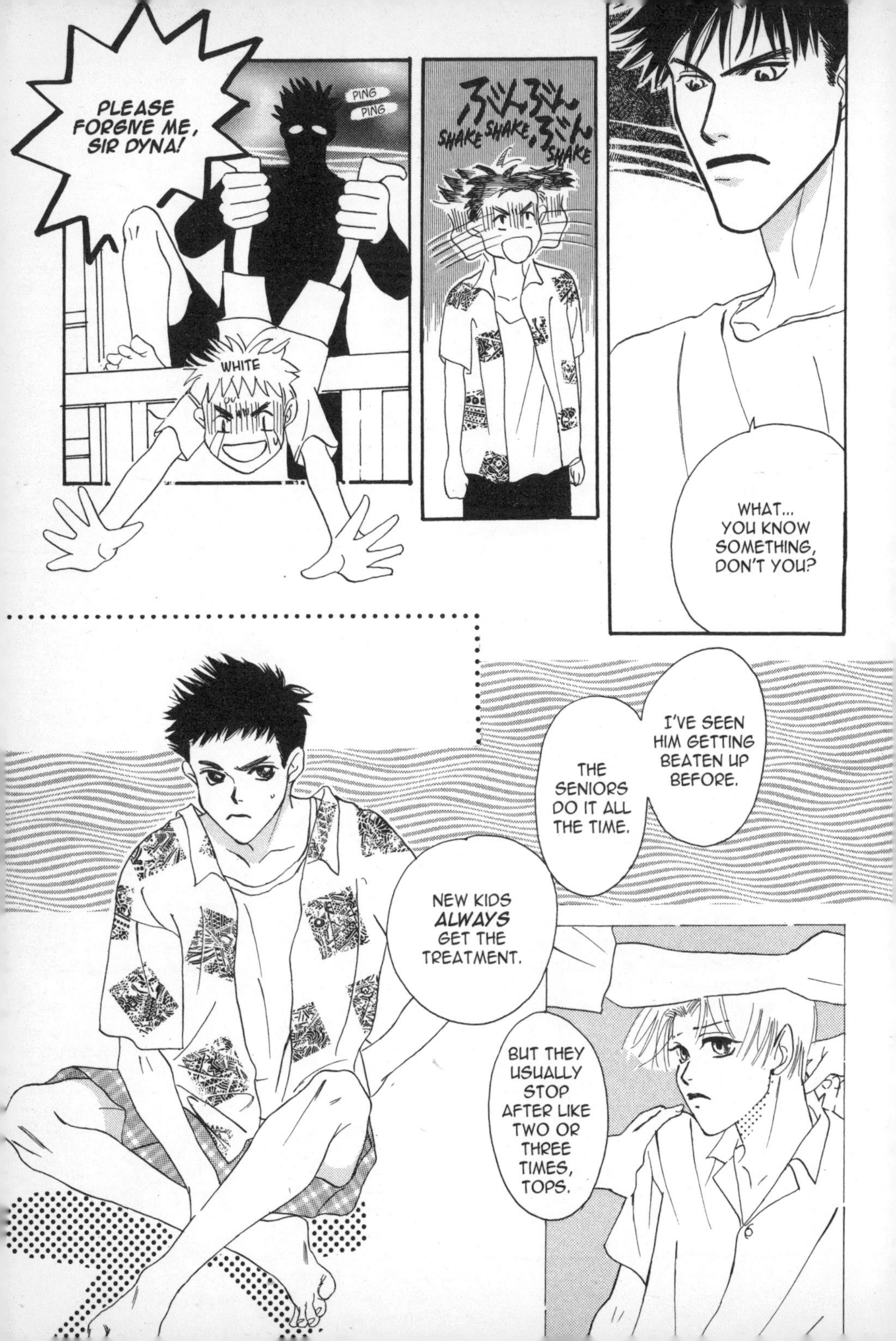
WHAT... YOU KNOW SOMETHING, DON'T YOU?
ぶんぶん、ぶん
SHAKE SHAKE SHAKE
PLEASE FORGIVE ME, SIR DYNA!
PING PING
WHITE
I'VE SEEN HIM GETTING BEATEN UP BEFORE.
THE SENIORS DO IT ALL THE TIME.
NEW KIDS ALWAYS GET THE TREATMENT.
BUT THEY USUALLY STOP AFTER LIKE TWO OR THREE TIMES, TOPS.

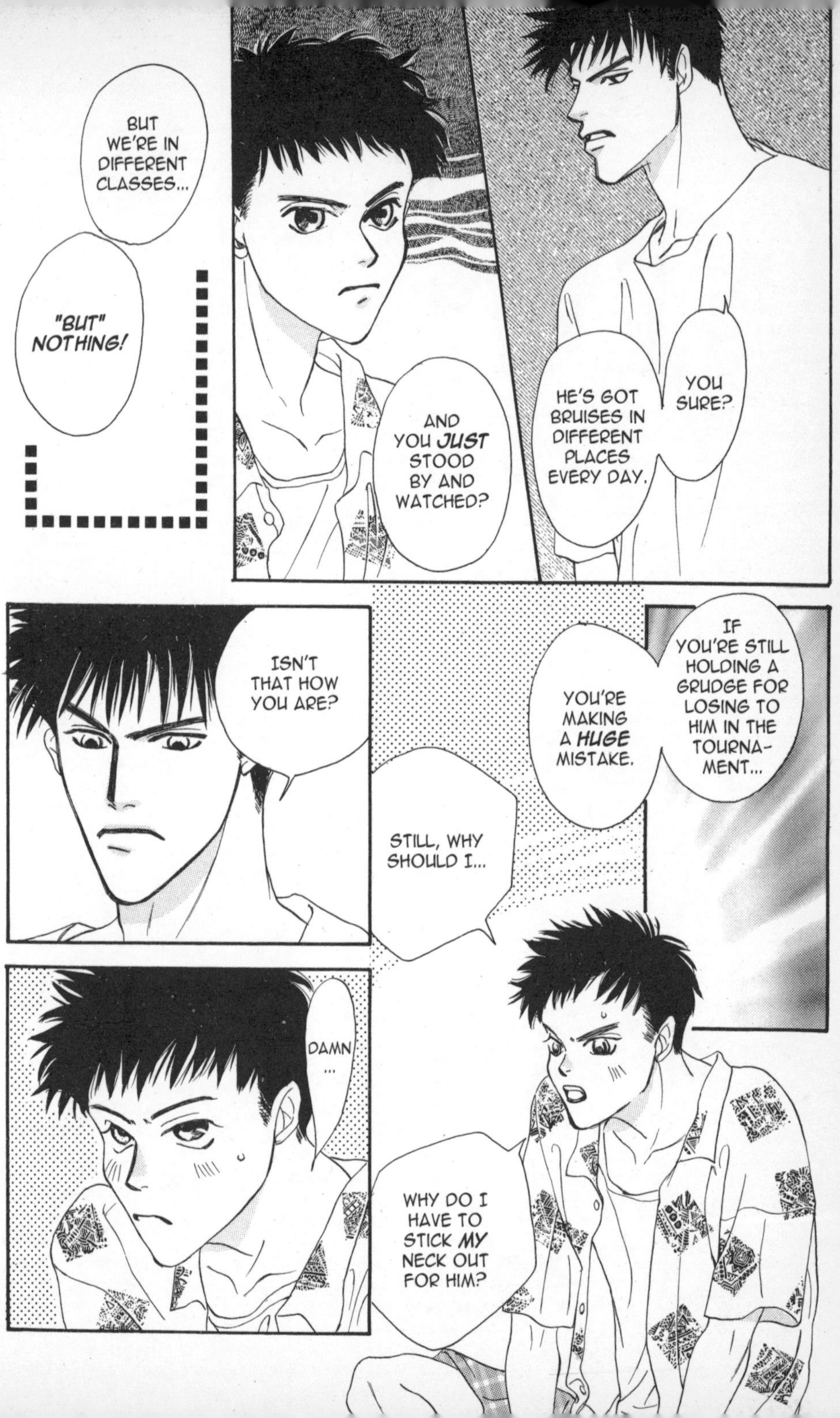
YOU SURE?
HE'S GOT BRUISES IN DIFFERENT PLACES EVERY DAY.
AND YOU JUST STOOD BY AND WATCHED?
BUT WE'RE IN DIFFERENT CLASSES...
"BUT" NOTHING!
IF YOU'RE STILL HOLDING A GRUDGE FOR LOSING TO HIM IN THE TOURNA-MENT...
YOU'RE MAKING A HUGE MISTAKE.
ISN'T THAT HOW YOU ARE?
STILL, WHY SHOULD I...
WHY DO I HAVE TO STICK MY NECK OUT FOR HIM?
DAMN...

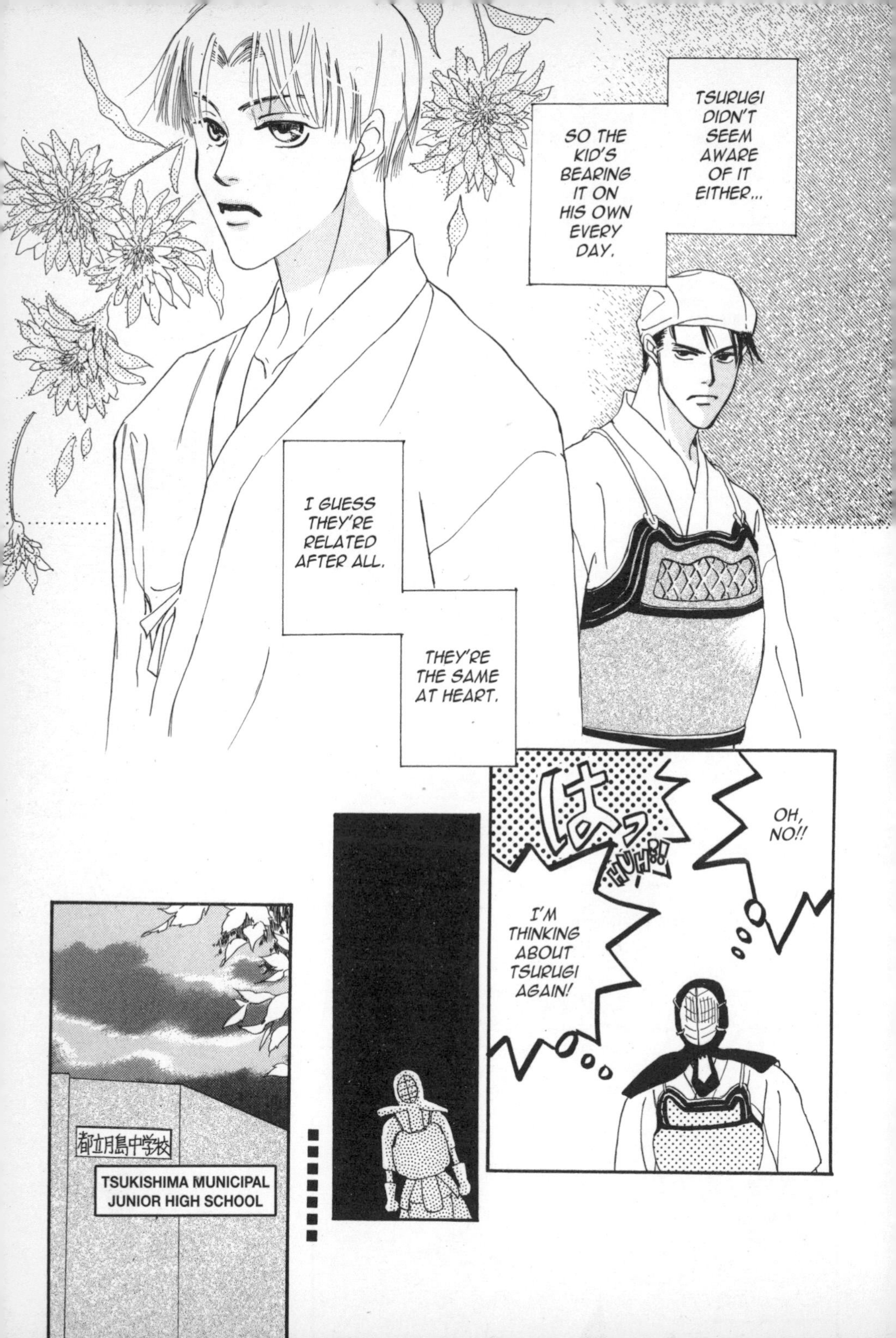
TSURUGI DIDN'T SEEM AWARE OF IT EITHER...
SO THE KID'S BEARING IT ON HIS OWN EVERY DAY.
I GUESS THEY'RE RELATED AFTER ALL.
THEY'RE THE SAME AT HEART.
はっ
HUH!!
OH, NO!!
I'M THINKING ABOUT TSURUGI AGAIN!
都立月島中学校
TSUKISHIMA MUNICIPAL JUNIOR HIGH SCHOOL

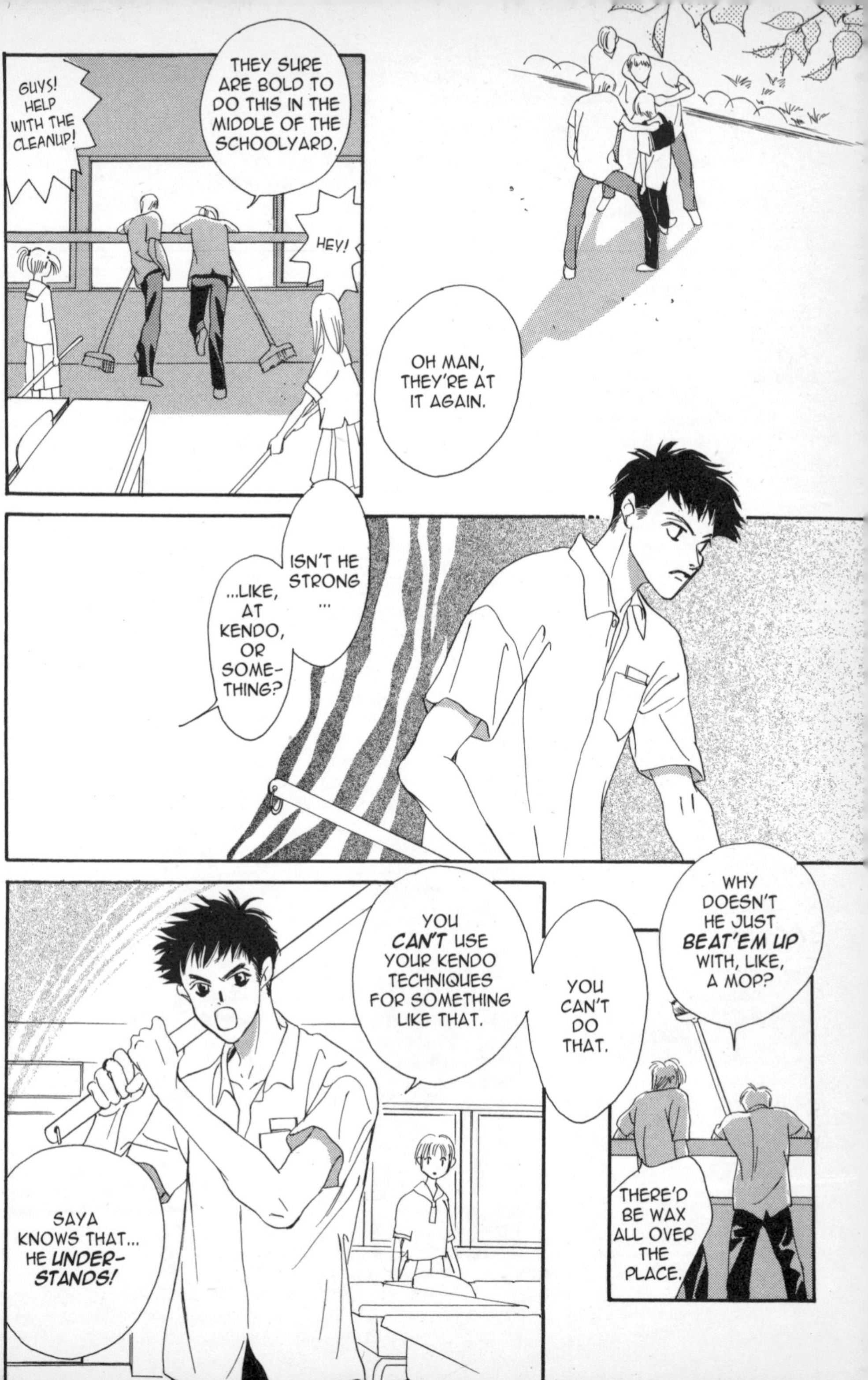

OH MAN, THEY'RE AT IT AGAIN.
THEY SURE ARE BOLD TO DO THIS IN THE MIDDLE OF THE SCHOOLYARD.
GUYS! HELP WITH THE CLEANUP!
HEY!
ISN'T HE STRONG...
...LIKE, AT KENDO, OR SOME-THING?
WHY DOESN'T HE JUST BEAT'EM UP WITH, LIKE, A MOP?
THERE'D BE WAX ALL OVER THE PLACE.
YOU CAN'T DO THAT.
YOU CAN'T USE YOUR KENDO TECHNIQUES FOR SOMETHING LIKE THAT.
SAYA KNOWS THAT... HE UNDER-STANDS!

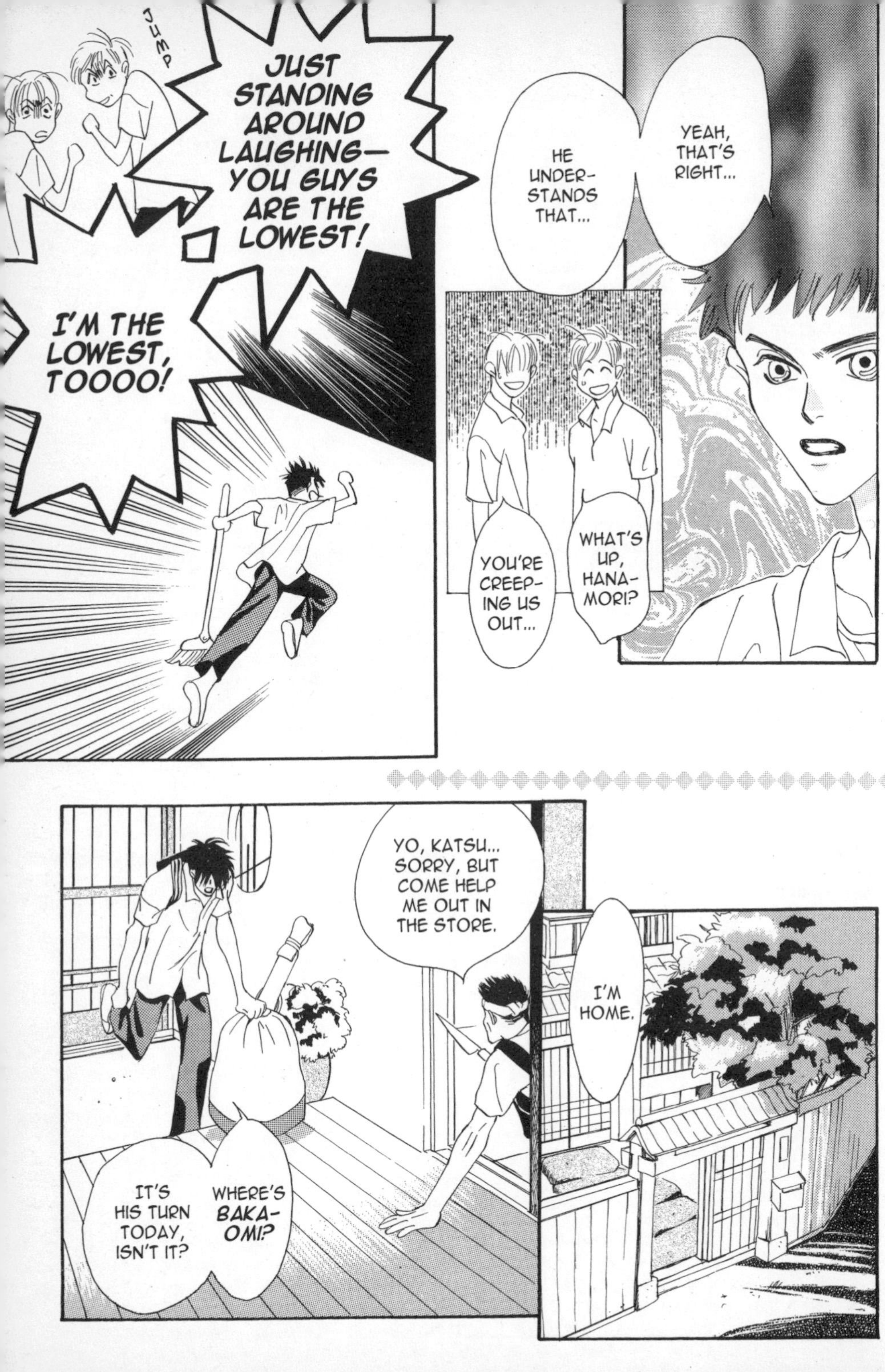
YEAH, THAT'S RIGHT...
HE UNDER-STANDS THAT...
WHAT'S UP, HANA-MORI?
YOU'RE CREEP-ING US OUT...
JUMP
JUST STANDING AROUND LAUGHING— YOU GUYS ARE THE LOWEST!
I'M THE LOWEST, TOOOO!
I'M HOME.
YO, KATSU... SORRY, BUT COME HELP ME OUT IN THE STORE.
WHERE'S BAKA-OMI?
IT'S HIS TURN TODAY, ISN'T IT?

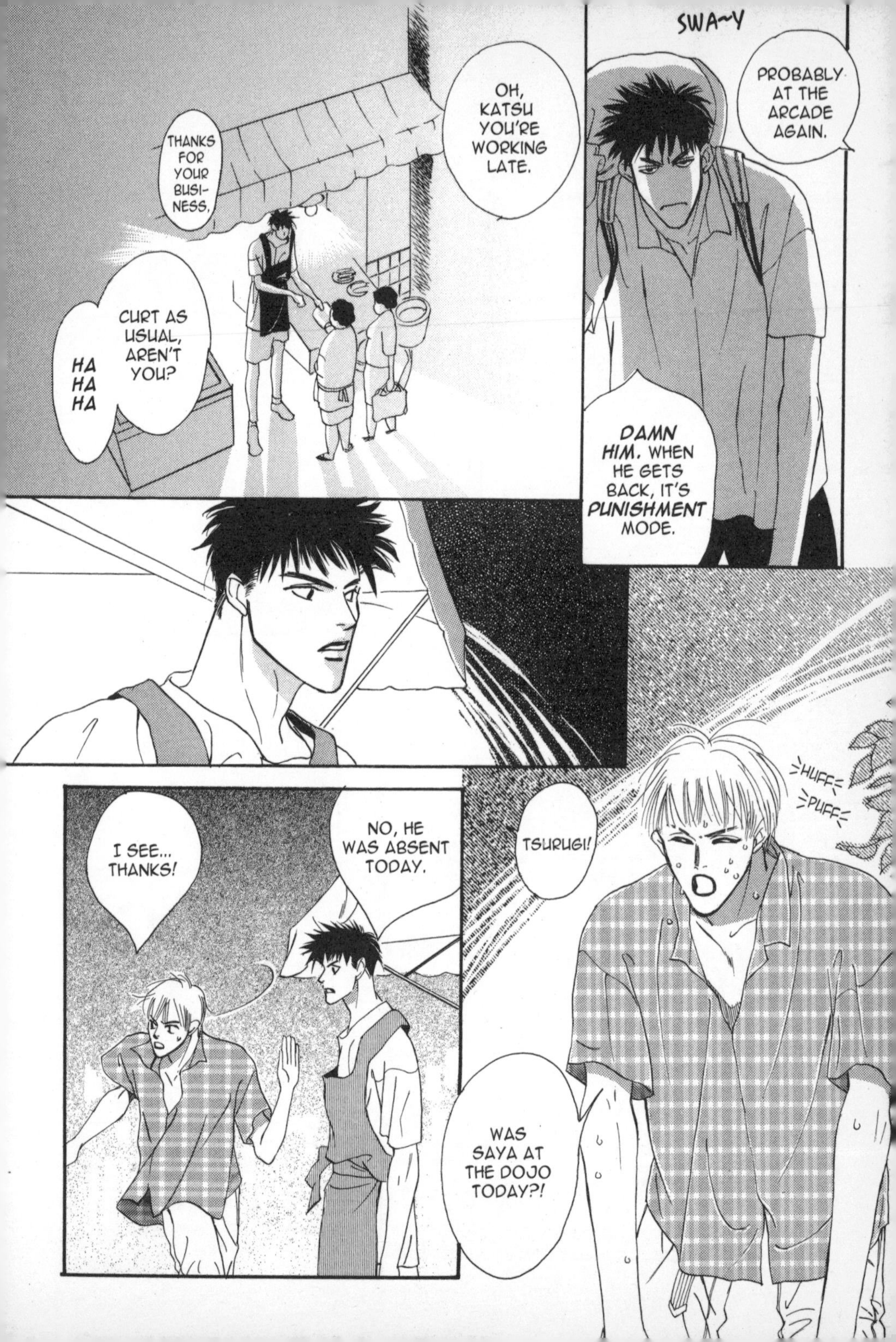
SWA~Y
PROBABLY AT THE ARCADE AGAIN.
DAMN HIM. WHEN HE GETS BACK, IT'S PUNISHMENT MODE.
OH, KATSU YOU'RE WORKING LATE.
THANKS FOR YOUR BUSI-NESS,
CURT AS USUAL, AREN'T YOU?
HA HA HA
HUFF
PUFF
TSURUGI!
WAS SAYA AT THE DOJO TODAY?!
NO, HE WAS ABSENT TODAY.
I SEE... THANKS!

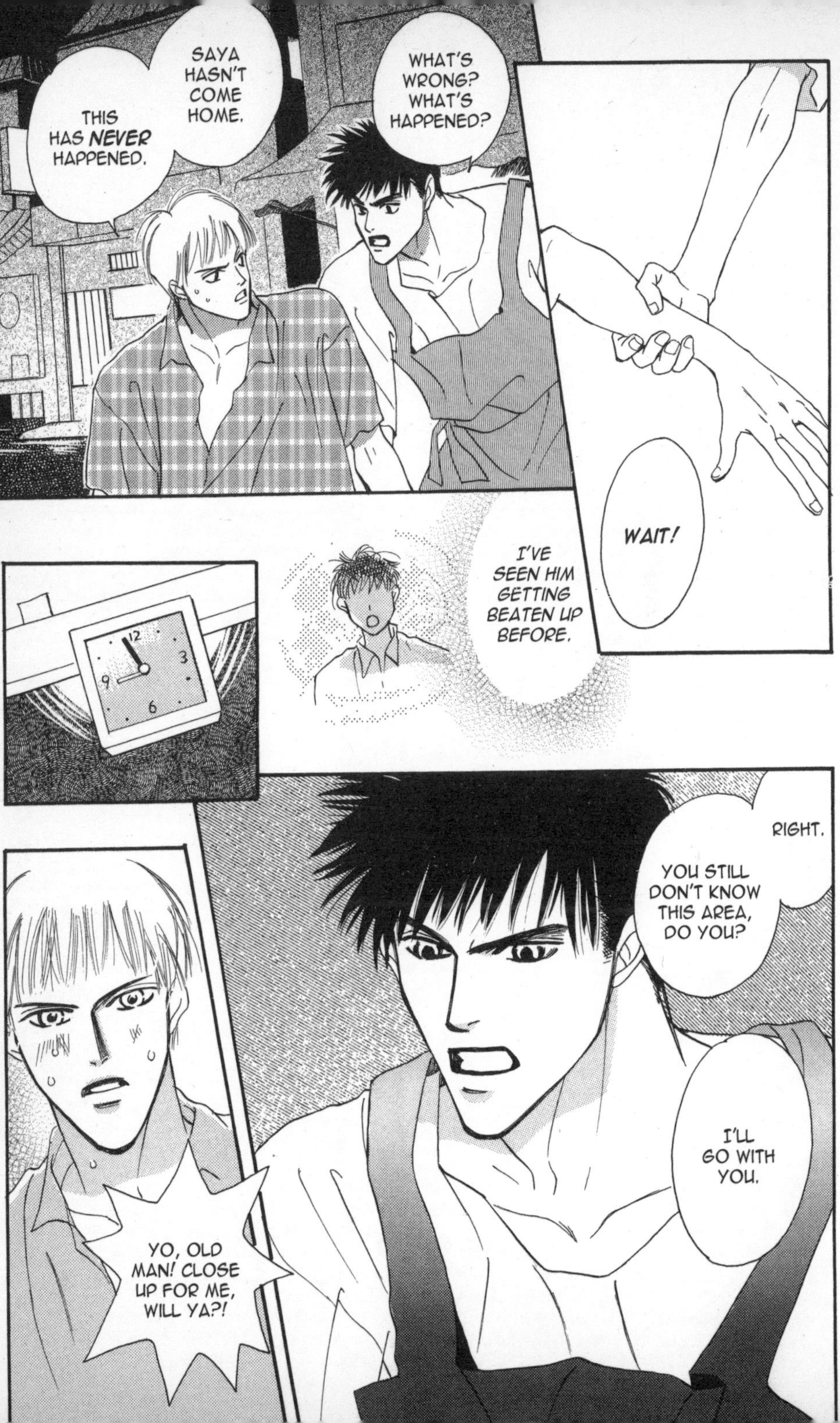
WAIT!
WHAT'S WRONG? WHAT'S HAPPENED?
SAYA HASN'T COME HOME.
THIS HAS ***NEVER*** HAPPENED.
I'VE SEEN HIM GETTING BEATEN UP BEFORE.
RIGHT.
YOU STILL DON'T KNOW THIS AREA, DO YOU?
I'LL GO WITH YOU.
YO, OLD MAN! CLOSE UP FOR ME, WILL YA?!

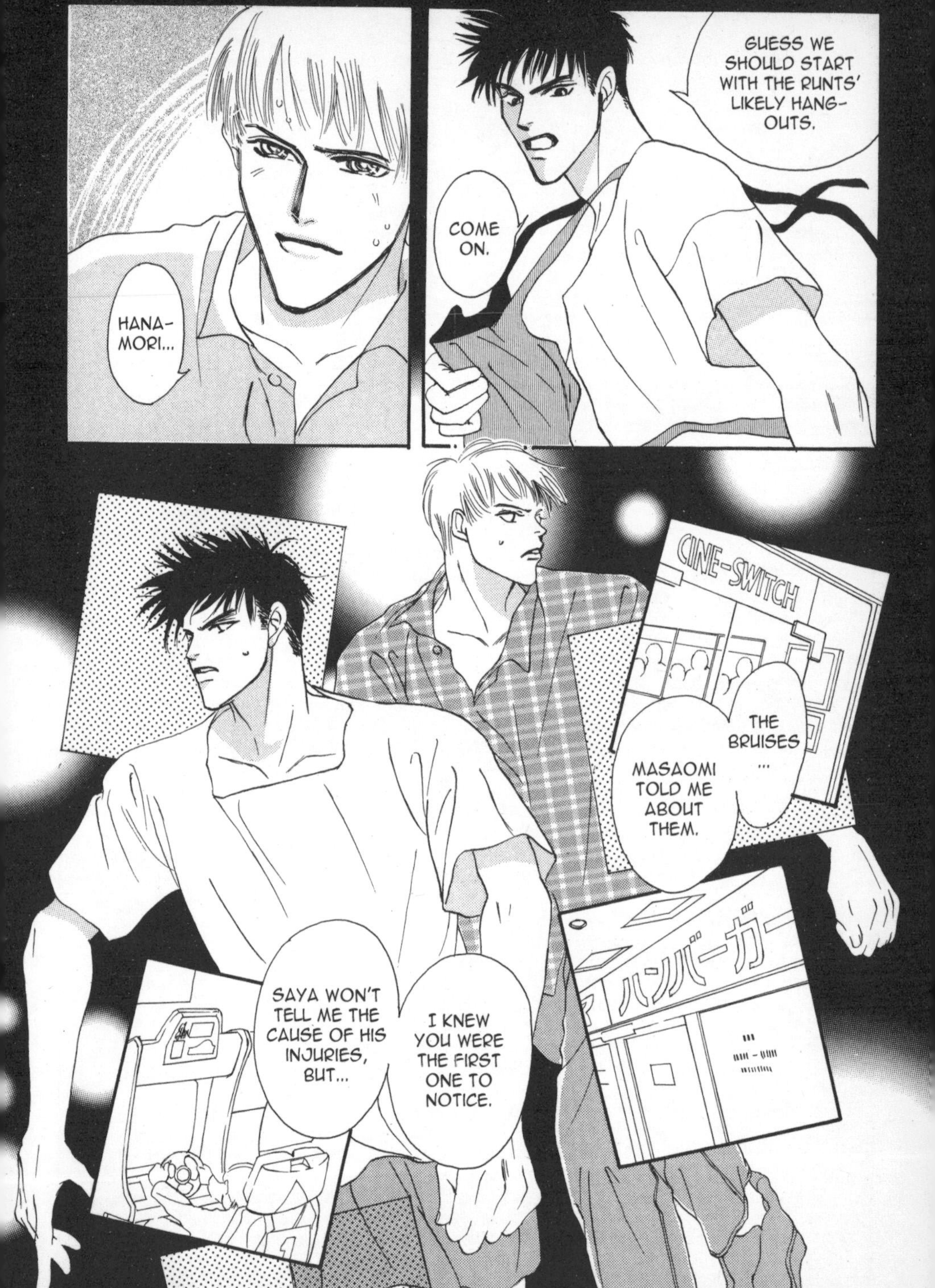
GUESS WE SHOULD START WITH THE RUNTS' LIKELY HANG-OUTS.
COME ON.
HANA-MORI...
CINE-SWITCH
THE BRUISES ...
MASAOMI TOLD ME ABOUT THEM.
ハンバーガー
I KNEW YOU WERE THE FIRST ONE TO NOTICE.
SAYA WON'T TELL ME THE CAUSE OF HIS INJURIES, BUT...

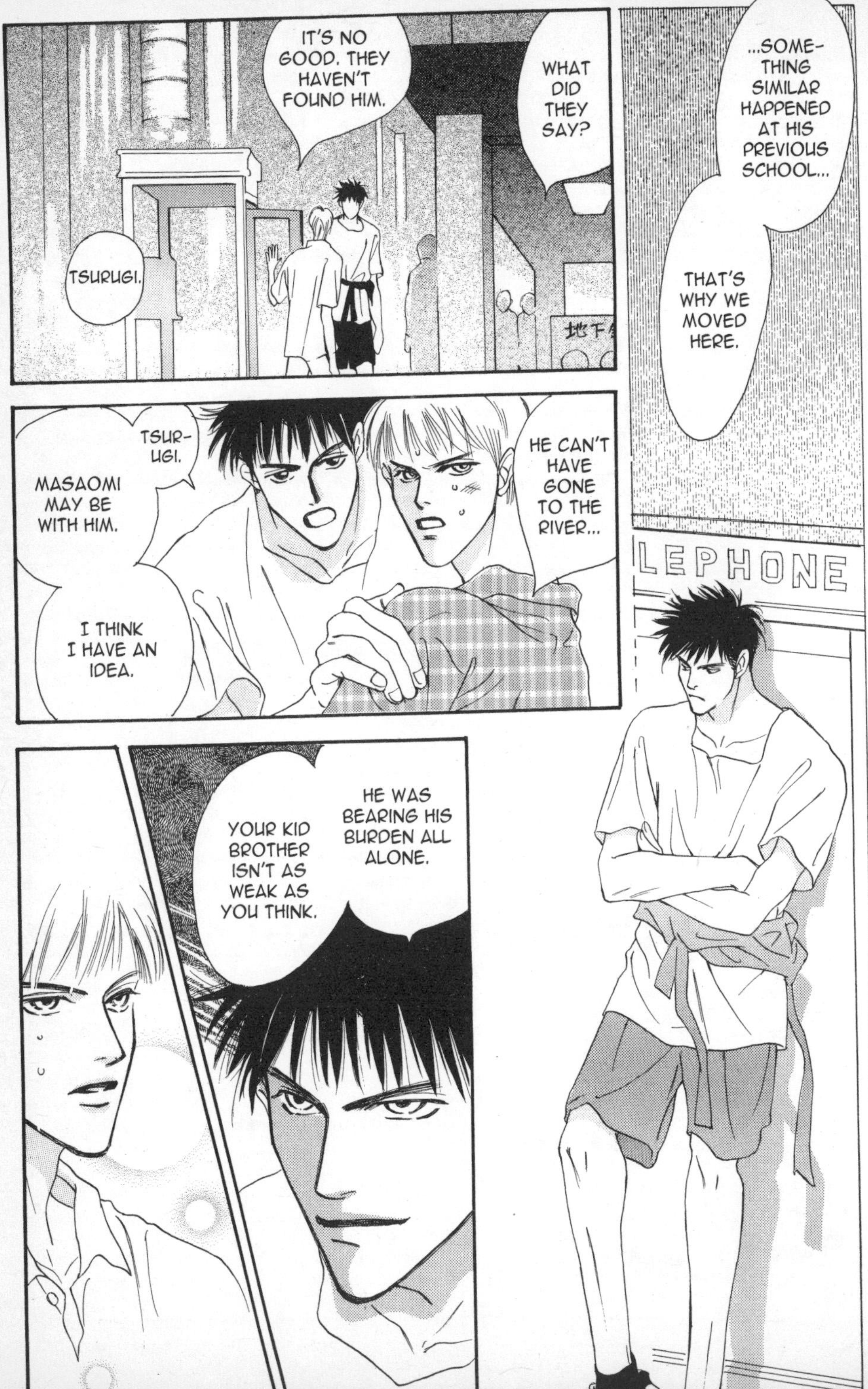
...SOME-THING SIMILAR HAPPENED AT HIS PREVIOUS SCHOOL...
THAT'S WHY WE MOVED HERE.
LEPHONE
WHAT DID THEY SAY?
IT'S NO GOOD. THEY HAVEN'T FOUND HIM.
TSURUGI.
地下
HE CAN'T HAVE GONE TO THE RIVER...
TSUR-UGI.
MASAOMI MAY BE WITH HIM.
I THINK I HAVE AN IDEA.
HE WAS BEARING HIS BURDEN ALL ALONE.
YOUR KID BROTHER ISN'T AS WEAK AS YOU THINK.

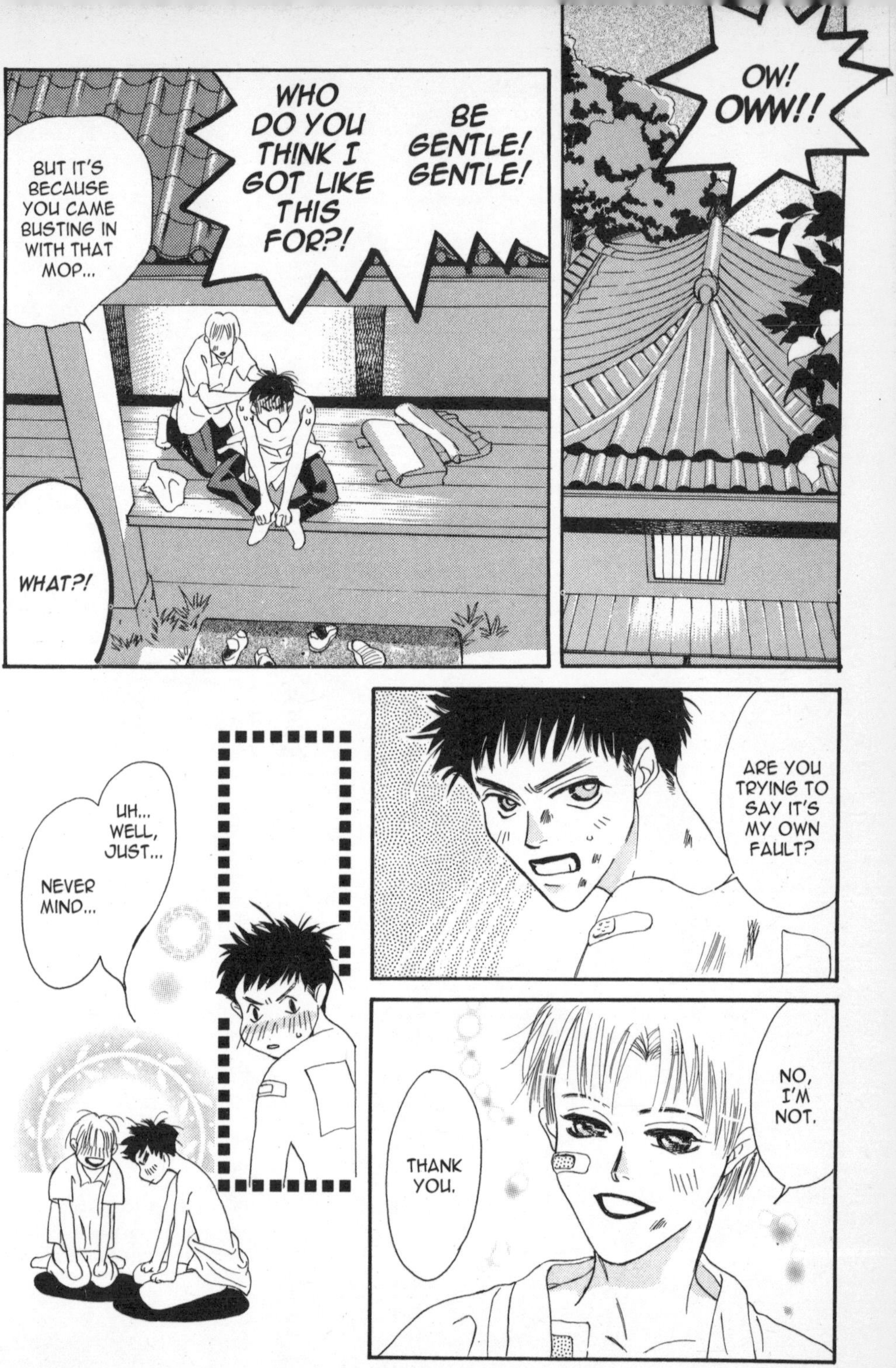
OW! OWW!!
BE GENTLE! GENTLE!
WHO DO YOU THINK I GOT LIKE THIS FOR?!
BUT IT'S BECAUSE YOU CAME BUSTING IN WITH THAT MOP...
WHAT?!
ARE YOU TRYING TO SAY IT'S MY OWN FAULT?
NO, I'M NOT.
THANK YOU.
UH... WELL, JUST...
NEVER MIND...

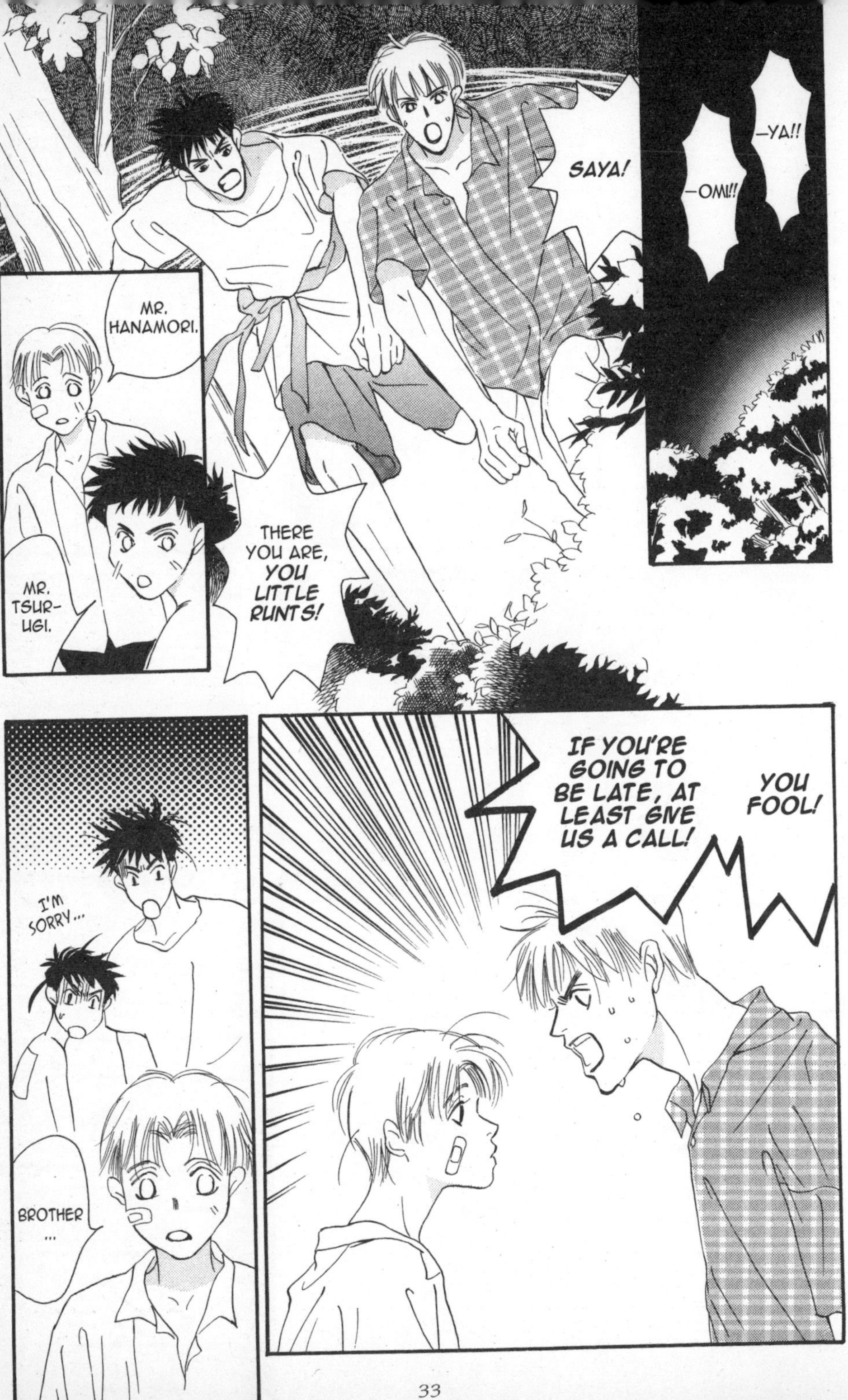
—YA!!
—OMI!!
SAYA!
THERE YOU ARE, YOU LITTLE RUNTS!
MR. HANAMORI.
MR. TSURU-UGI.
YOU FOOL!
IF YOU'RE GOING TO BE LATE, AT LEAST GIVE US A CALL!
I'M SORRY...
BROTHER ...

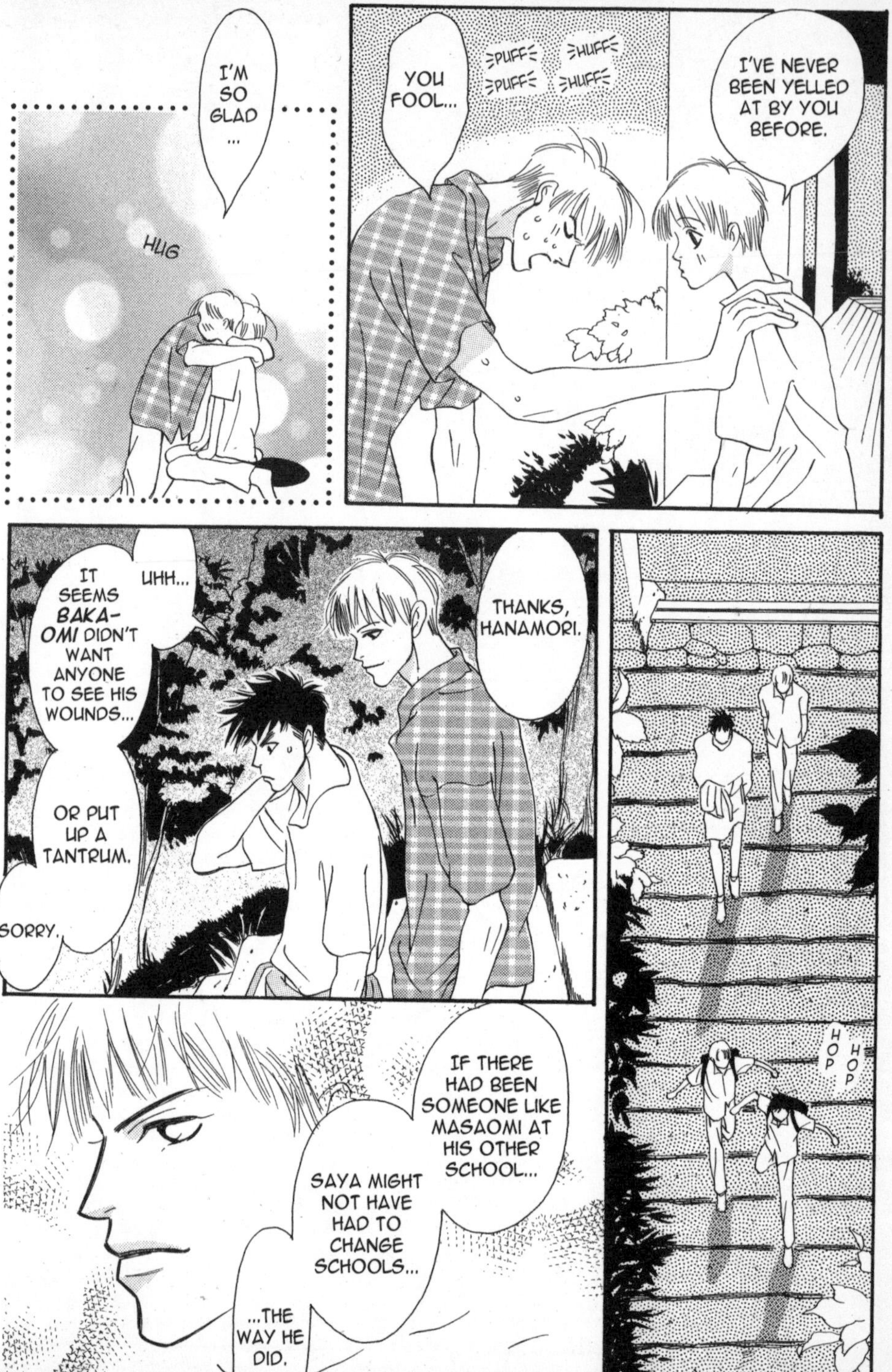
I'VE NEVER BEEN YELLED AT BY YOU BEFORE.
PUFF PUFF
HUFF HUFF
YOU FOOL...
I'M SO GLAD ...
HUG
HOP HOP
THANKS, HANAMORI.
UHH...
IT SEEMS BAKA-OMI DIDN'T WANT ANYONE TO SEE HIS WOUNDS...
OR PUT UP A TANTRUM.
SORRY.
IF THERE HAD BEEN SOMEONE LIKE MASAOMI AT HIS OTHER SCHOOL...
SAYA MIGHT NOT HAVE HAD TO CHANGE SCHOOLS...
...THE WAY HE DID.

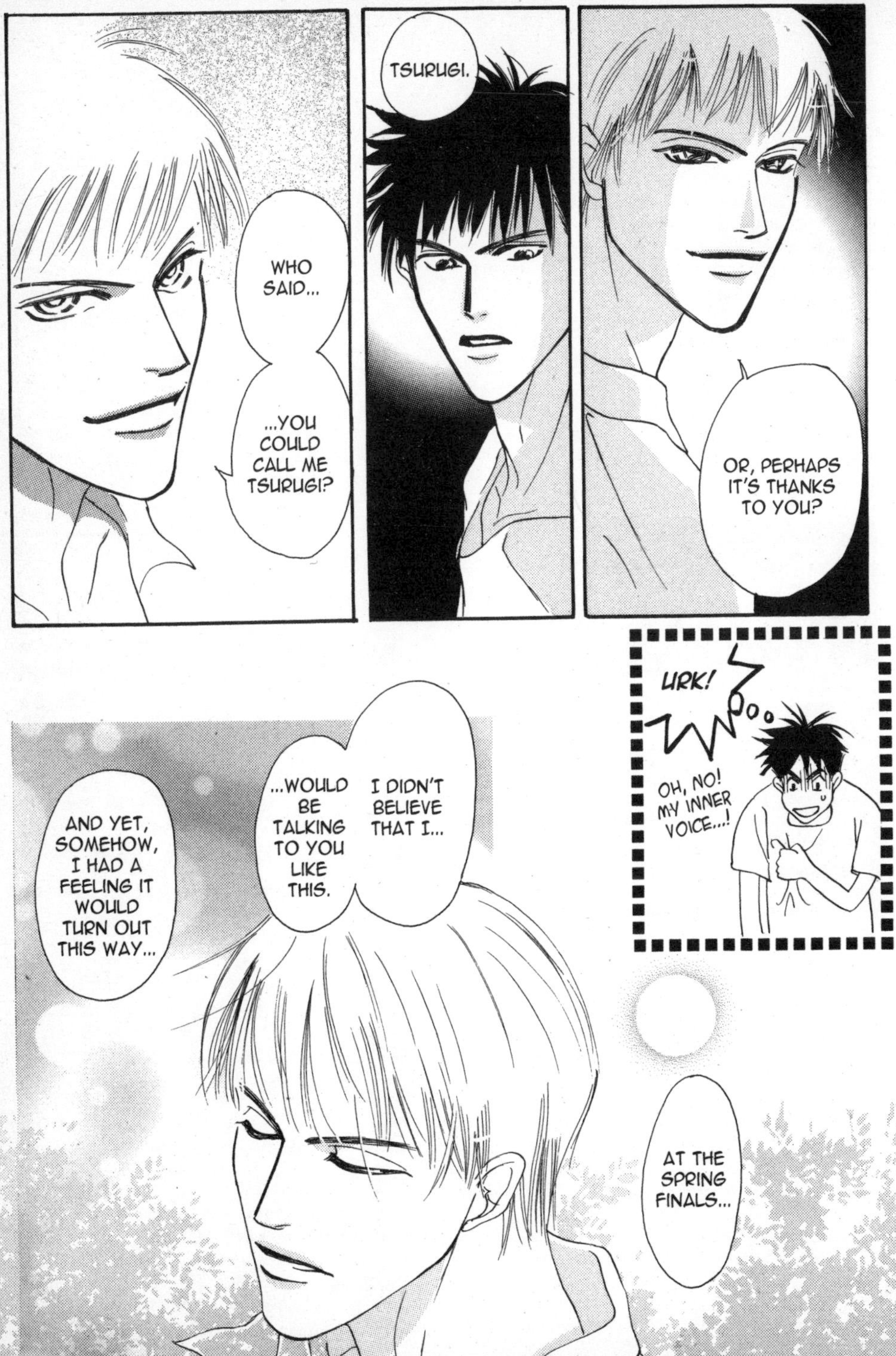
OR, PERHAPS IT'S THANKS TO YOU?
TSURUGI.
WHO SAID...
...YOU COULD CALL ME TSURUGI?
URK!
OH, NO! MY INNER VOICE...!
I DIDN'T BELIEVE THAT I...
...WOULD BE TALKING TO YOU LIKE THIS.
AND YET, SOMEHOW, I HAD A FEELING IT WOULD TURN OUT THIS WAY...
AT THE SPRING FINALS...

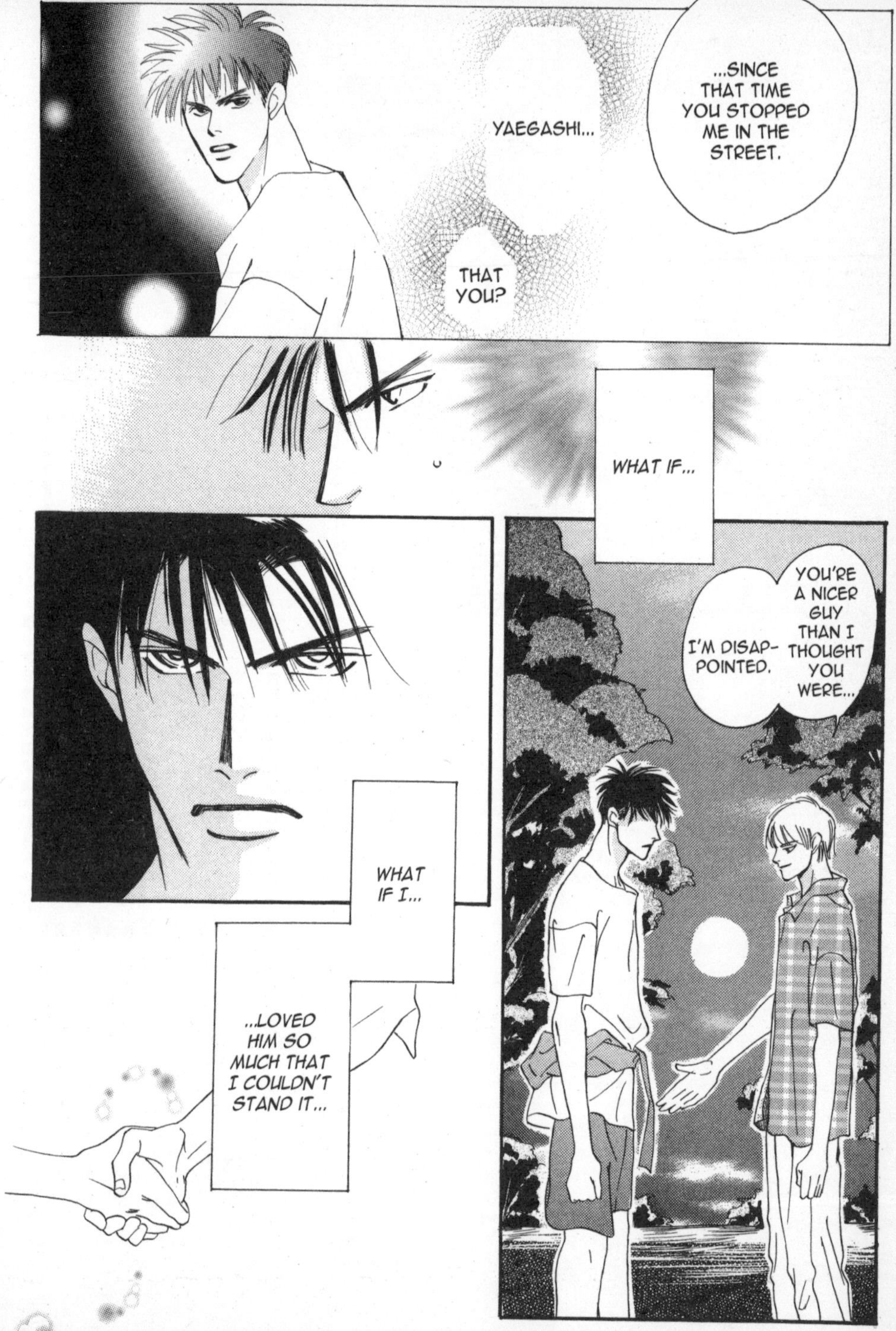
...SINCE THAT TIME YOU STOPPED ME IN THE STREET.
YAEGASHI...
THAT YOU?
WHAT IF...
YOU'RE A NICER GUY THAN I THOUGHT YOU WERE...
I'M DISAP-POINTED.
WHAT IF I...
...LOVED HIM SO MUCH THAT I COULDN'T STAND IT...

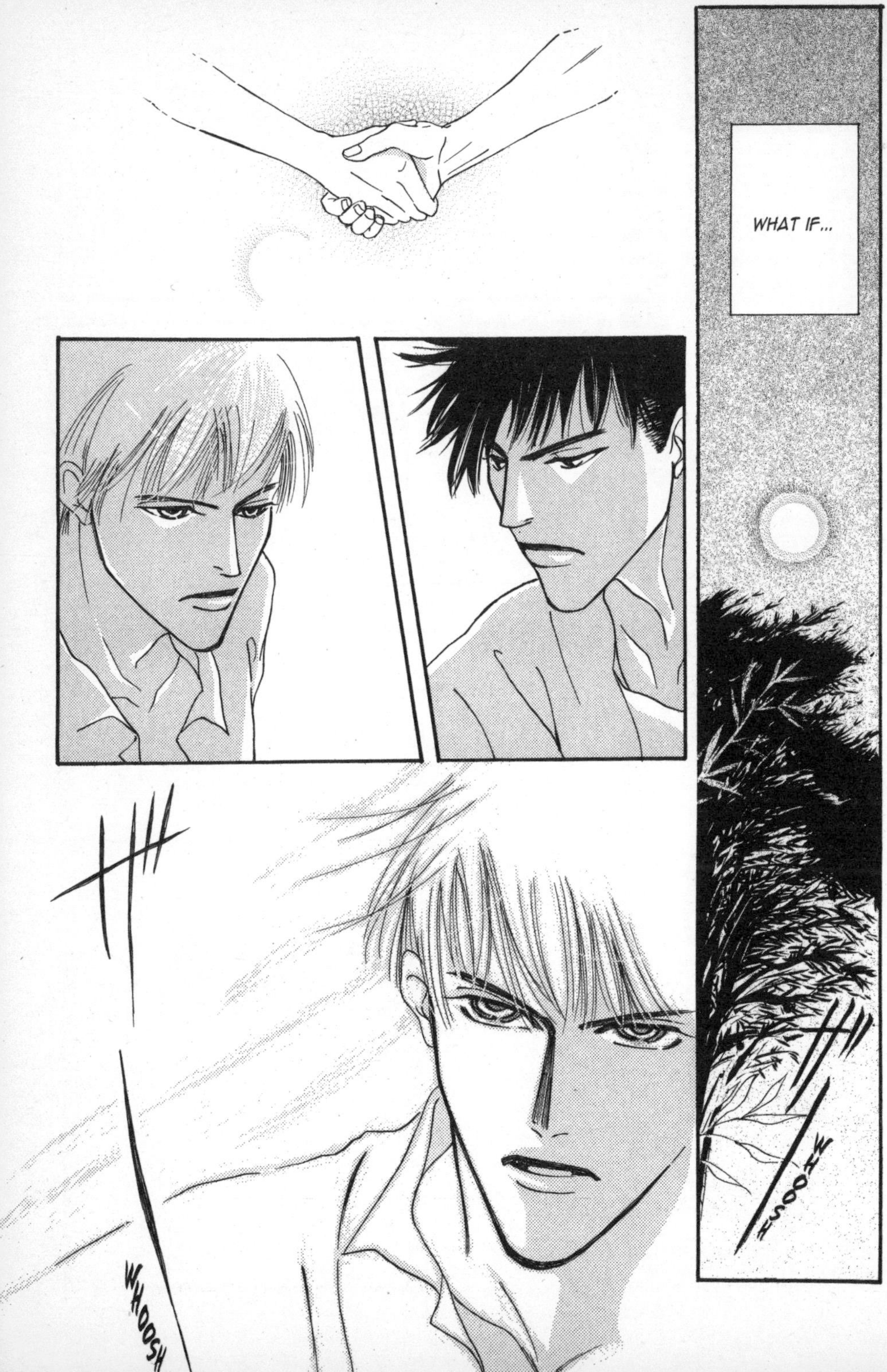
WHAT IF...
WHOOSH
WHOOSH

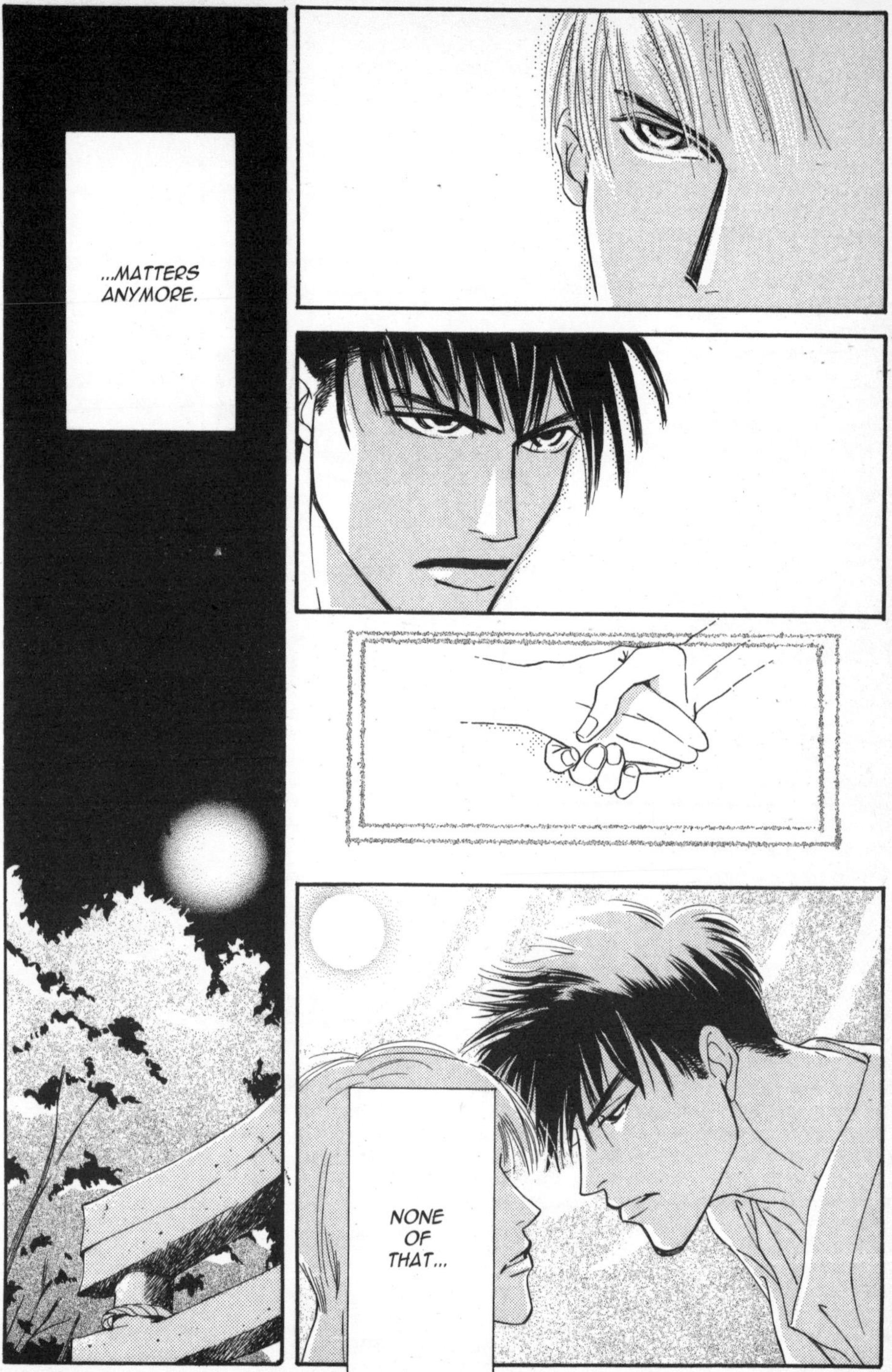
NONE OF THAT...
...MATTERS ANYMORE.

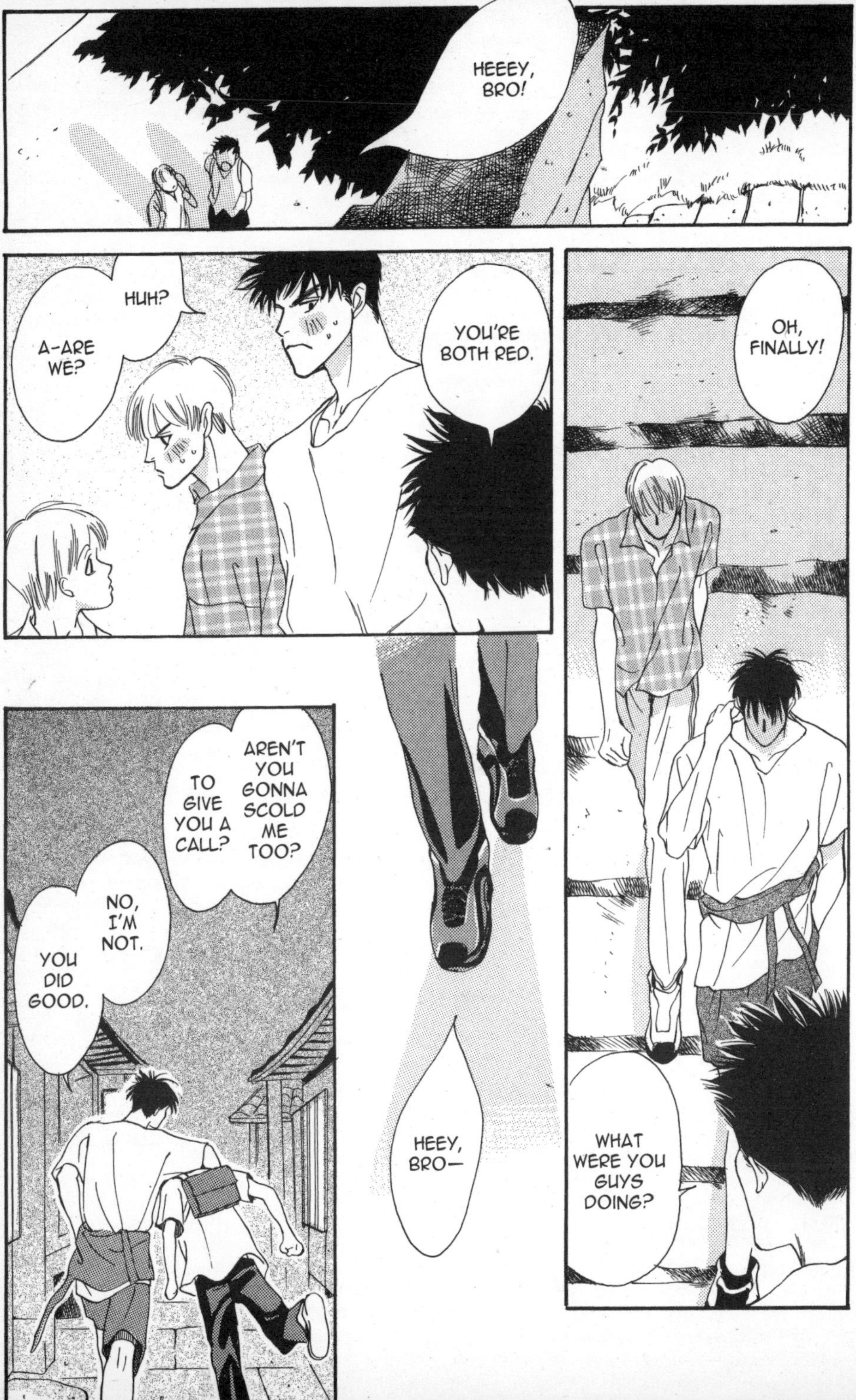
HEEEY, BRO!
OH, FINALLY!
WHAT WERE YOU GUYS DOING?
YOU'RE BOTH RED.
HUH?
A-ARE WE?
HEEY, BRO—
AREN'T YOU GONNA SCOLD ME TOO?
TO GIVE YOU A CALL?
NO, I'M NOT.
YOU DID GOOD.

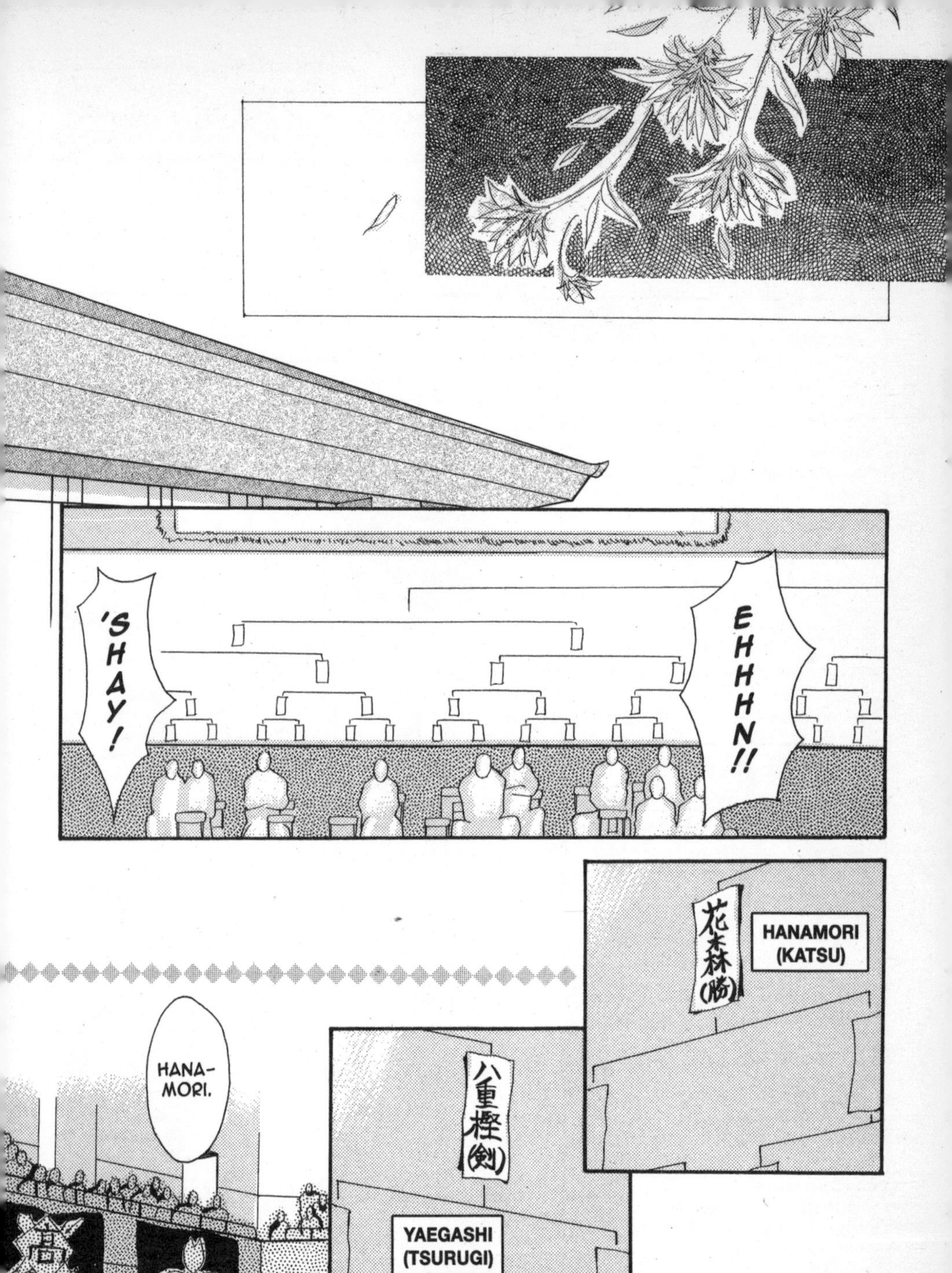
EHHHHN!!
'SHAY!
花森(勝)
HANAMORI (KATSU)
八重樫(剣)
YAEGASHI (TSURUGI)
HANA-MORI.

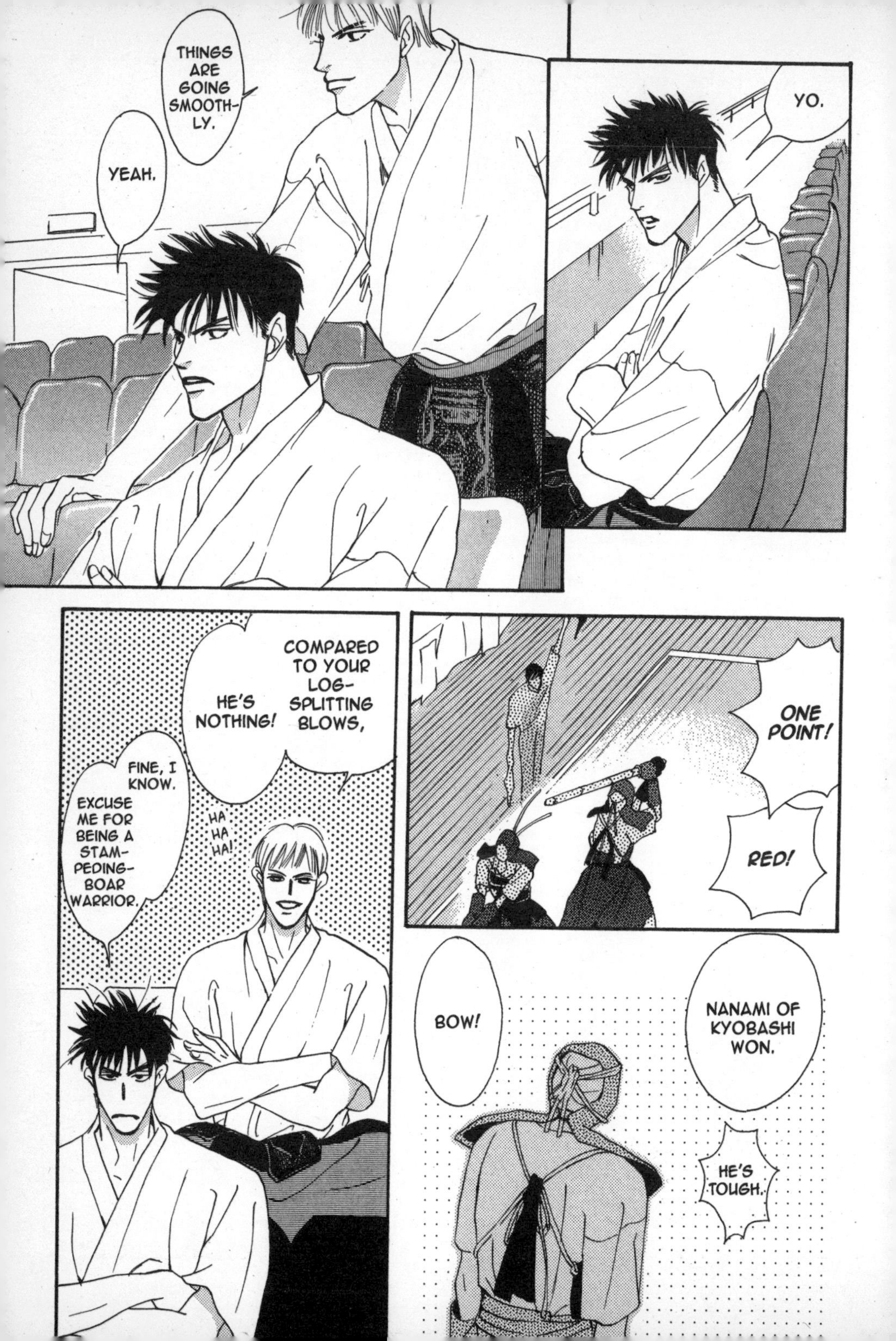
YO.
THINGS ARE GOING SMOOTHLY.
YEAH.
ONE POINT!
RED!
NANAMI OF KYOBASHI WON.
BOW!
HE'S TOUGH.
COMPARED TO YOUR LOG-SPLITTING BLOWS,
HE'S NOTHING!
FINE, I KNOW. EXCUSE ME FOR BEING A STAMPEDING-BOAR WARRIOR.
HA HA HA!

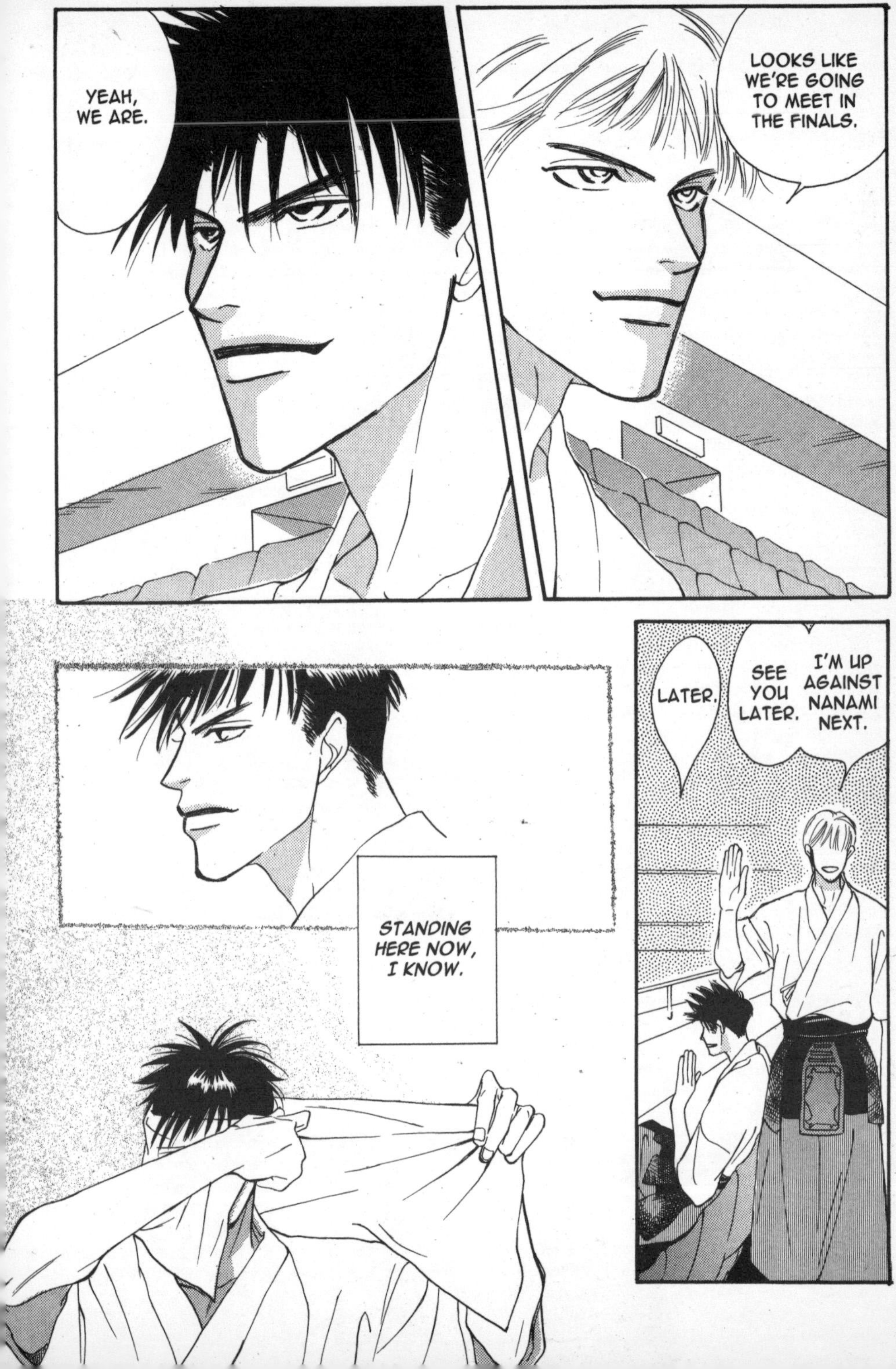
LOOKS LIKE WE'RE GOING TO MEET IN THE FINALS.
YEAH, WE ARE.
I'M UP AGAINST NANAMI NEXT.
SEE YOU LATER.
LATER.
STANDING HERE NOW, I KNOW.

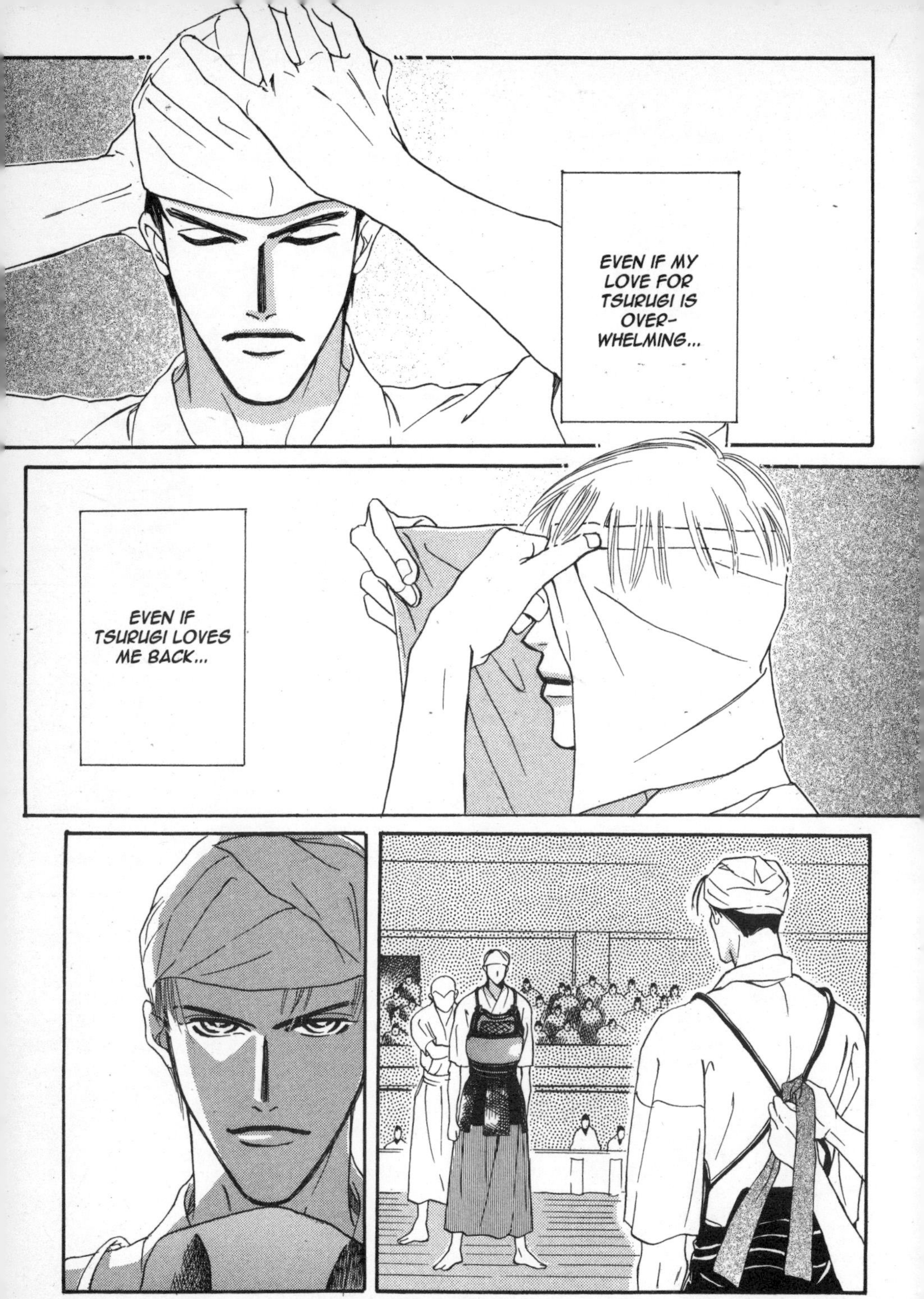
EVEN IF MY LOVE FOR TSURUGI IS OVER-WHELMING...
EVEN IF TSURUGI LOVES ME BACK...

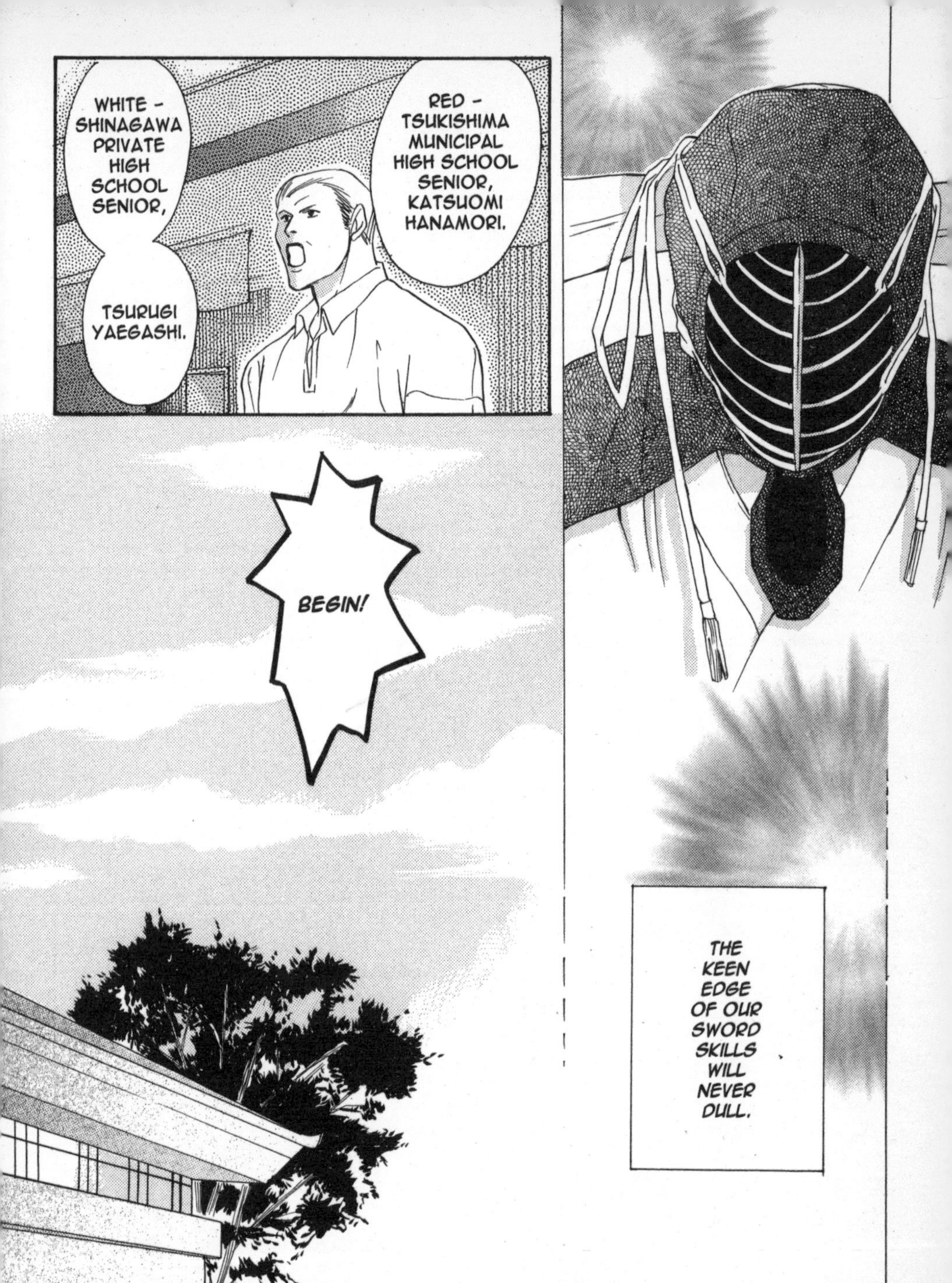
THE KEEN EDGE OF OUR SWORD SKILLS WILL NEVER DULL.
RED - TSUKISHIMA MUNICIPAL HIGH SCHOOL SENIOR, KATSUOMI HANAMORI.
WHITE - SHINAGAWA PRIVATE HIGH SCHOOL SENIOR,
TSURUGI YAEGASHI.
BEGIN!

KAZE KITARU - THE WIND COMETH • END

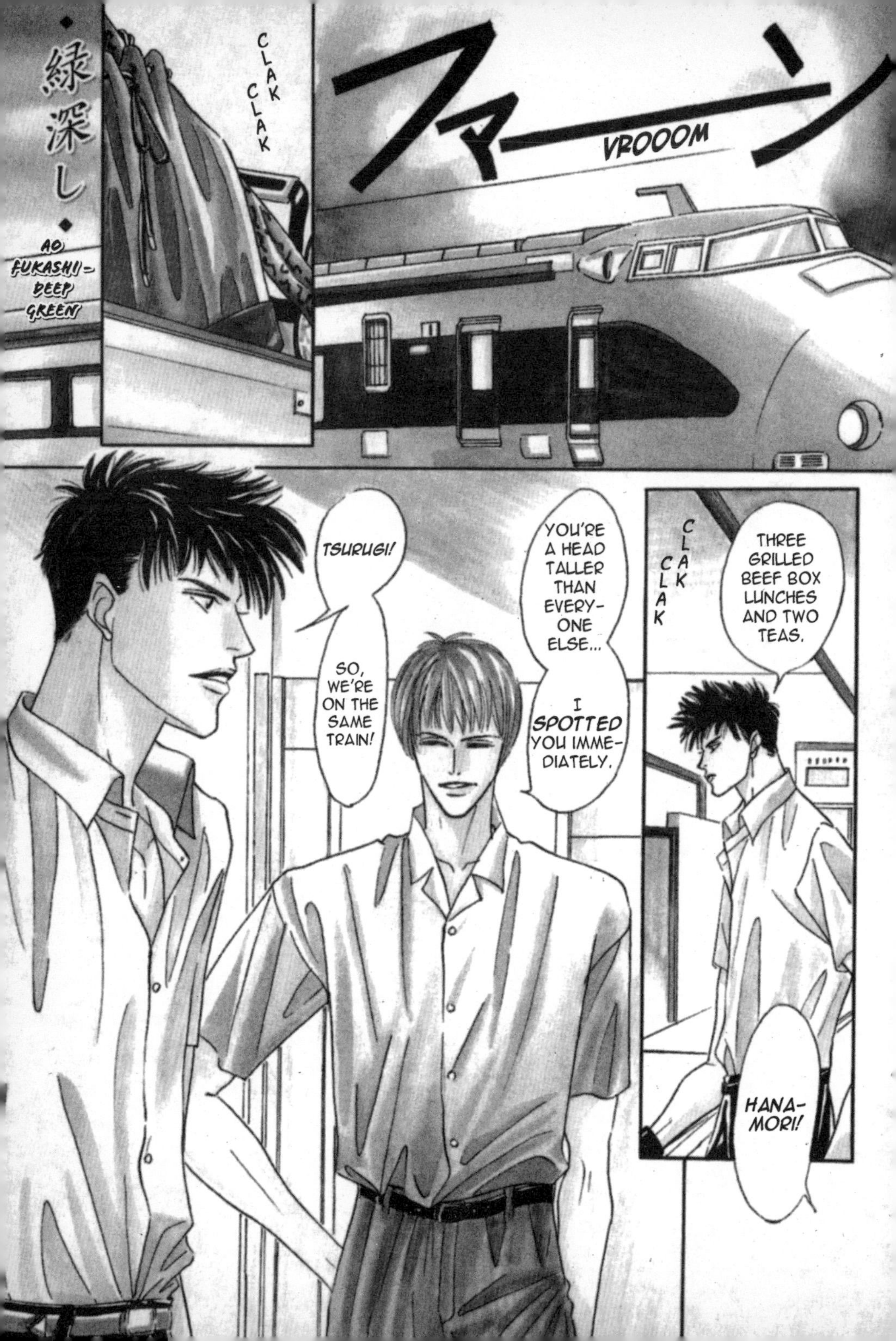
ファーン
VROOOM
CLAK CLAK CLAK
・緑深し・
AO FUKASHI - DEEP GREEN
CLAK CLAK
THREE GRILLED BEEF BOX LUNCHES AND TWO TEAS.
HANA-MORI!
YOU'RE A HEAD TALLER THAN EVERY-ONE ELSE...
I ***SPOTTED*** YOU IMME-DIATELY.
TSURUGI!
SO, WE'RE ON THE SAME TRAIN!

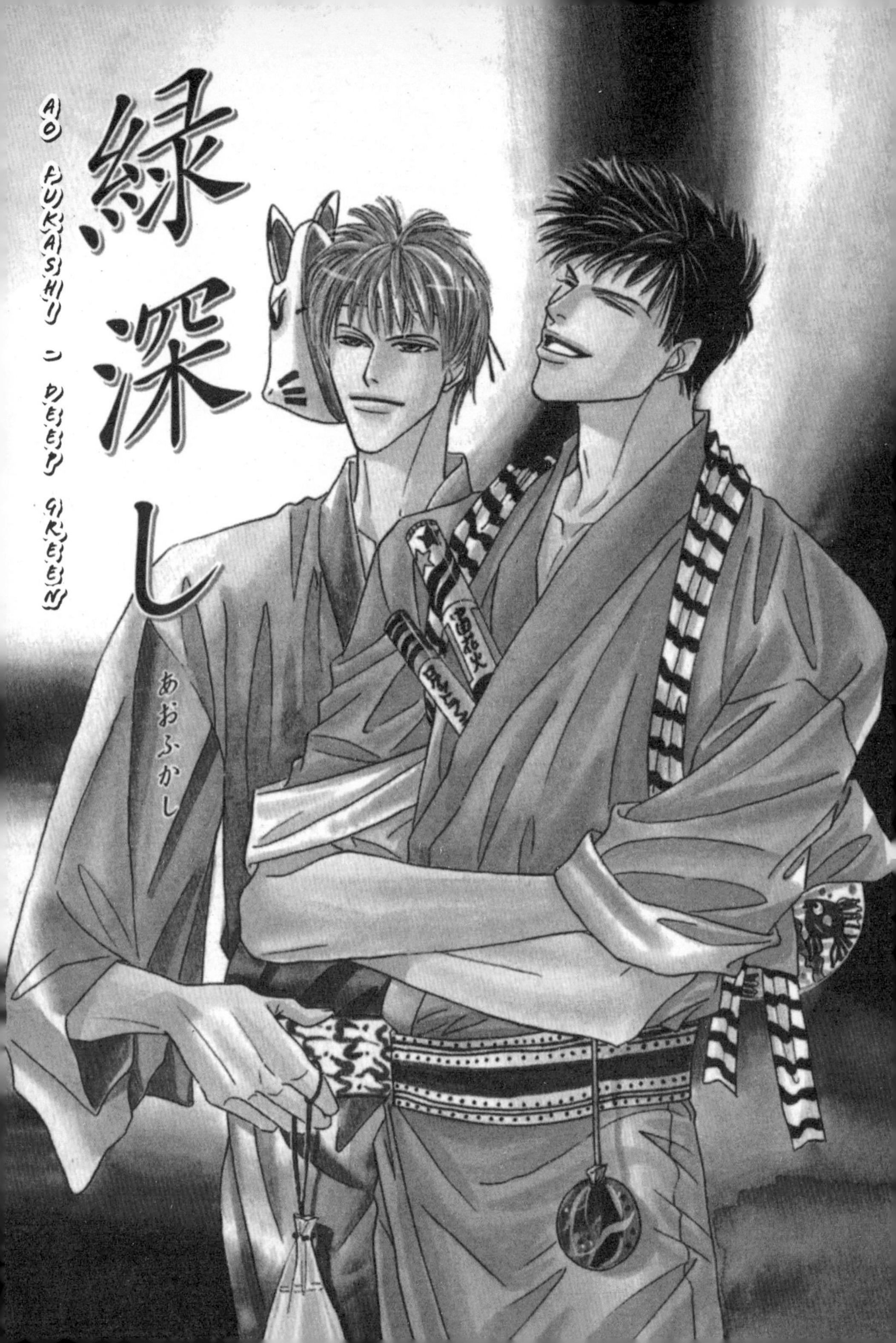
緑深し
AO FUKASHI — DEEP GREEN
あおふかし

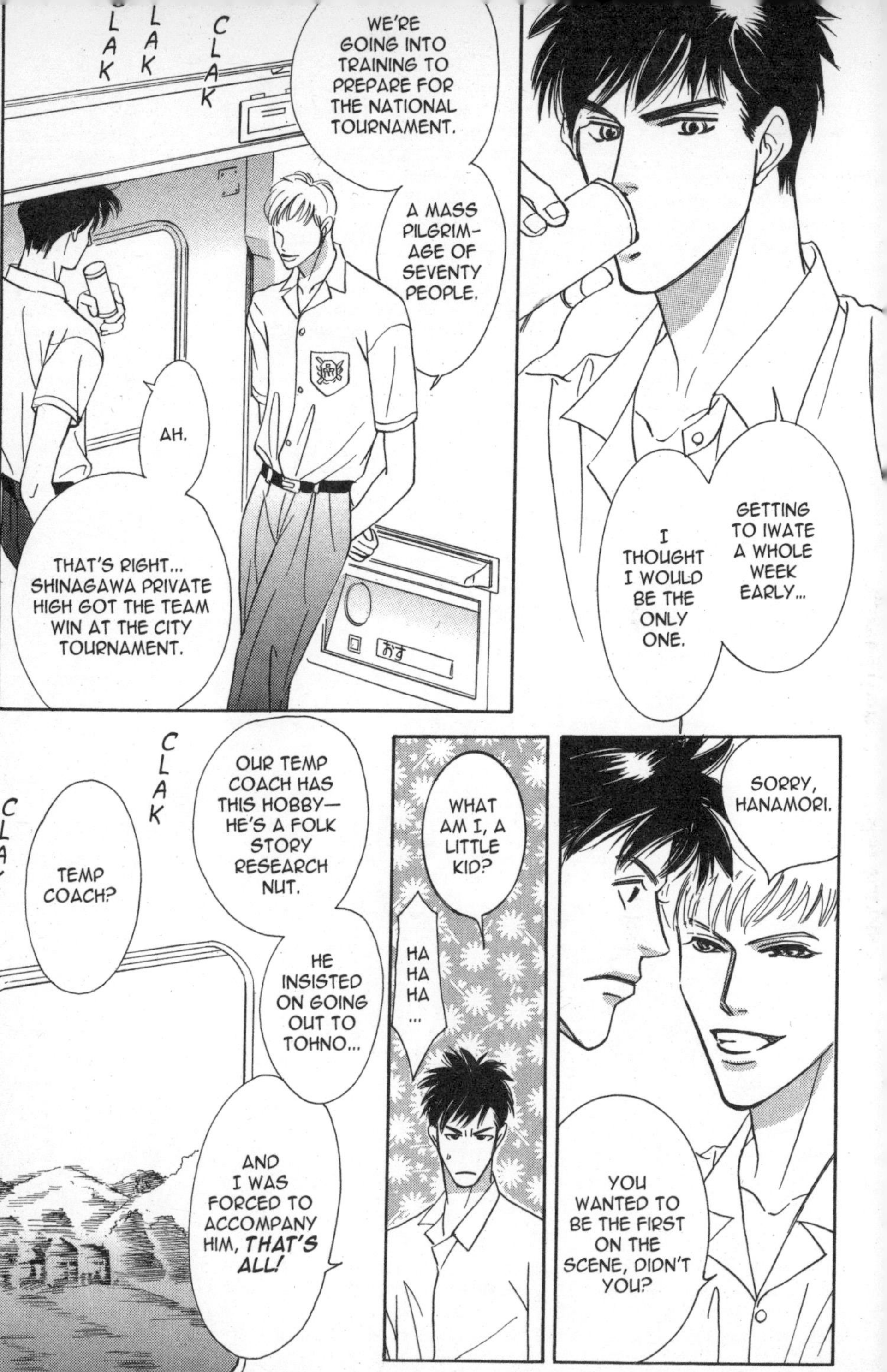
GETTING TO IWATE A WHOLE WEEK EARLY...
I THOUGHT I WOULD BE THE ONLY ONE.
CLAK
CLAK
CLAK
WE'RE GOING INTO TRAINING TO PREPARE FOR THE NATIONAL TOURNAMENT.
A MASS PILGRIMAGE OF SEVENTY PEOPLE.
AH.
THAT'S RIGHT... SHINAGAWA PRIVATE HIGH GOT THE TEAM WIN AT THE CITY TOURNAMENT.
SORRY, HANAMORI.
YOU WANTED TO BE THE FIRST ON THE SCENE, DIDN'T YOU?
WHAT AM I, A LITTLE KID?
HA HA HA ...
CLAK
OUR TEMP COACH HAS THIS HOBBY—HE'S A FOLK STORY RESEARCH NUT.
CLAK
TEMP COACH?
HE INSISTED ON GOING OUT TO TOHNO...
AND I WAS FORCED TO ACCOMPANY HIM, ***THAT'S ALL!***

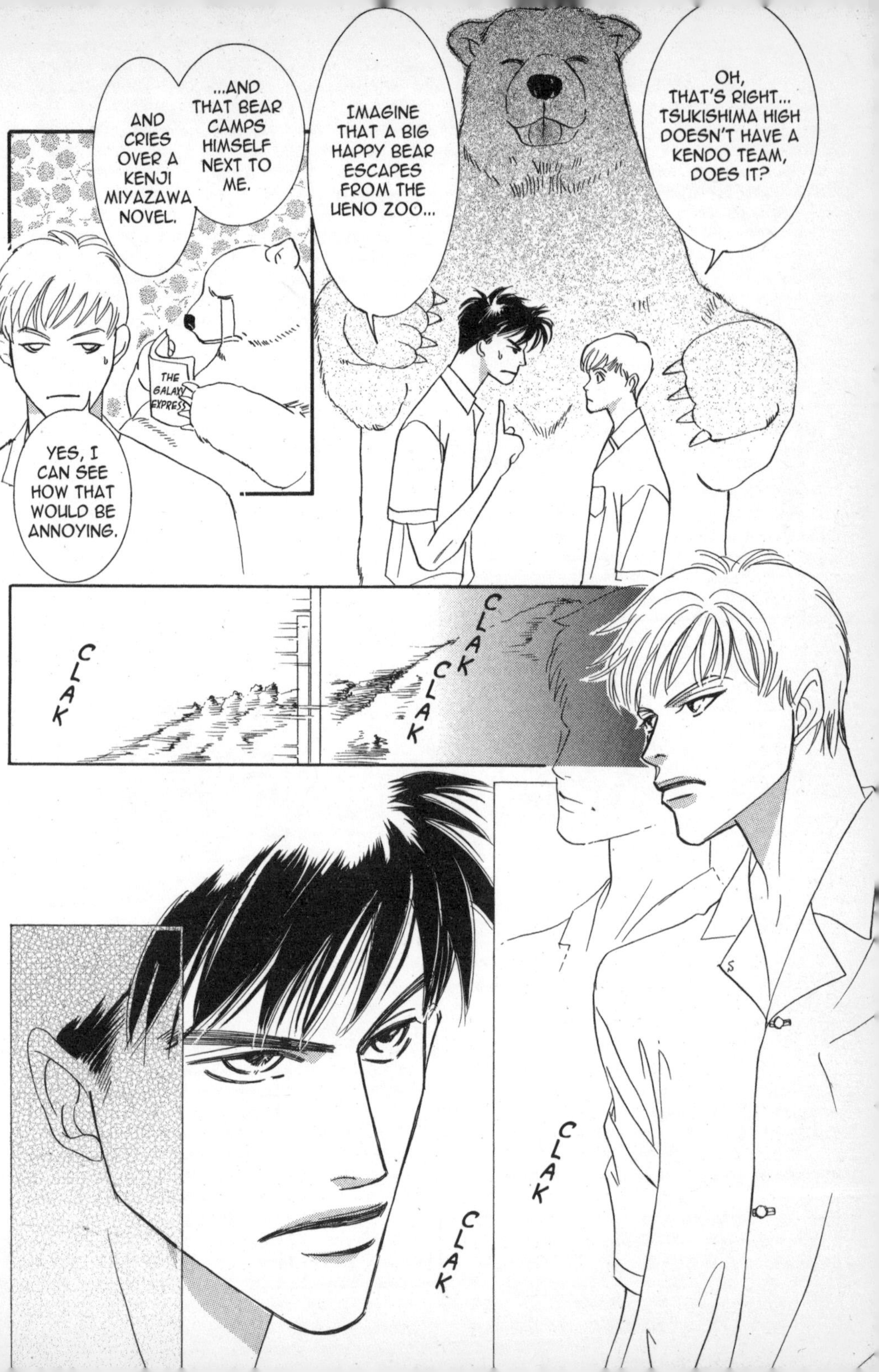
OH, THAT'S RIGHT... TSUKISHIMA HIGH DOESN'T HAVE A KENDO TEAM, DOES IT?
IMAGINE THAT A BIG HAPPY BEAR ESCAPES FROM THE UENO ZOO...
...AND THAT BEAR CAMPS HIMSELF NEXT TO ME.
AND CRIES OVER A KENJI MIYAZAWA NOVEL.
THE GALAXY EXPRESS
YES, I CAN SEE HOW THAT WOULD BE ANNOYING.
CLAK
CLAK
CLAK
CLAK
CLAK

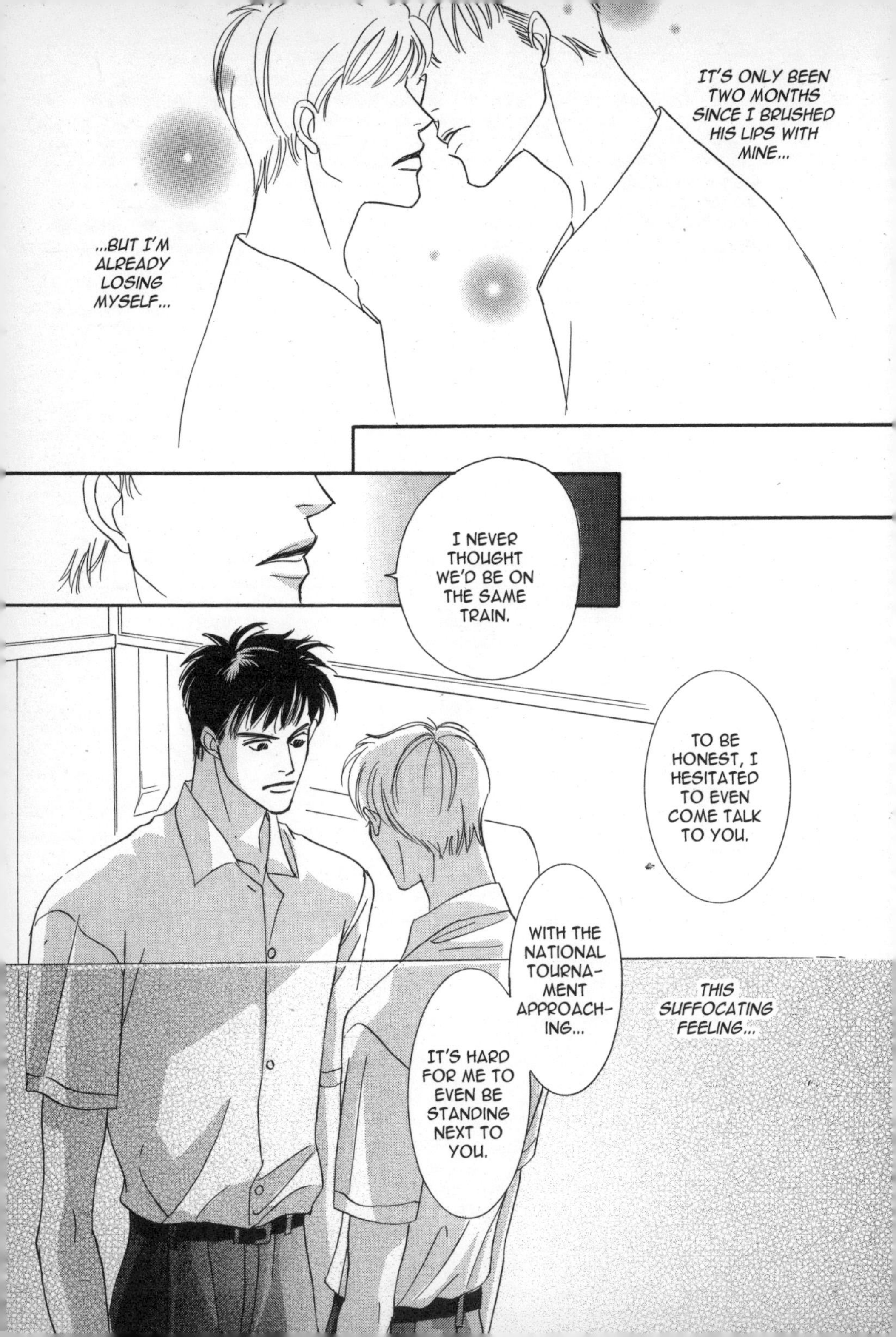
IT'S ONLY BEEN TWO MONTHS SINCE I BRUSHED HIS LIPS WITH MINE...
...BUT I'M ALREADY LOSING MYSELF...
I NEVER THOUGHT WE'D BE ON THE SAME TRAIN.
TO BE HONEST, I HESITATED TO EVEN COME TALK TO YOU.
WITH THE NATIONAL TOURNA-MENT APPROACH-ING...
IT'S HARD FOR ME TO EVEN BE STANDING NEXT TO YOU.
THIS SUFFOCATING FEELING...

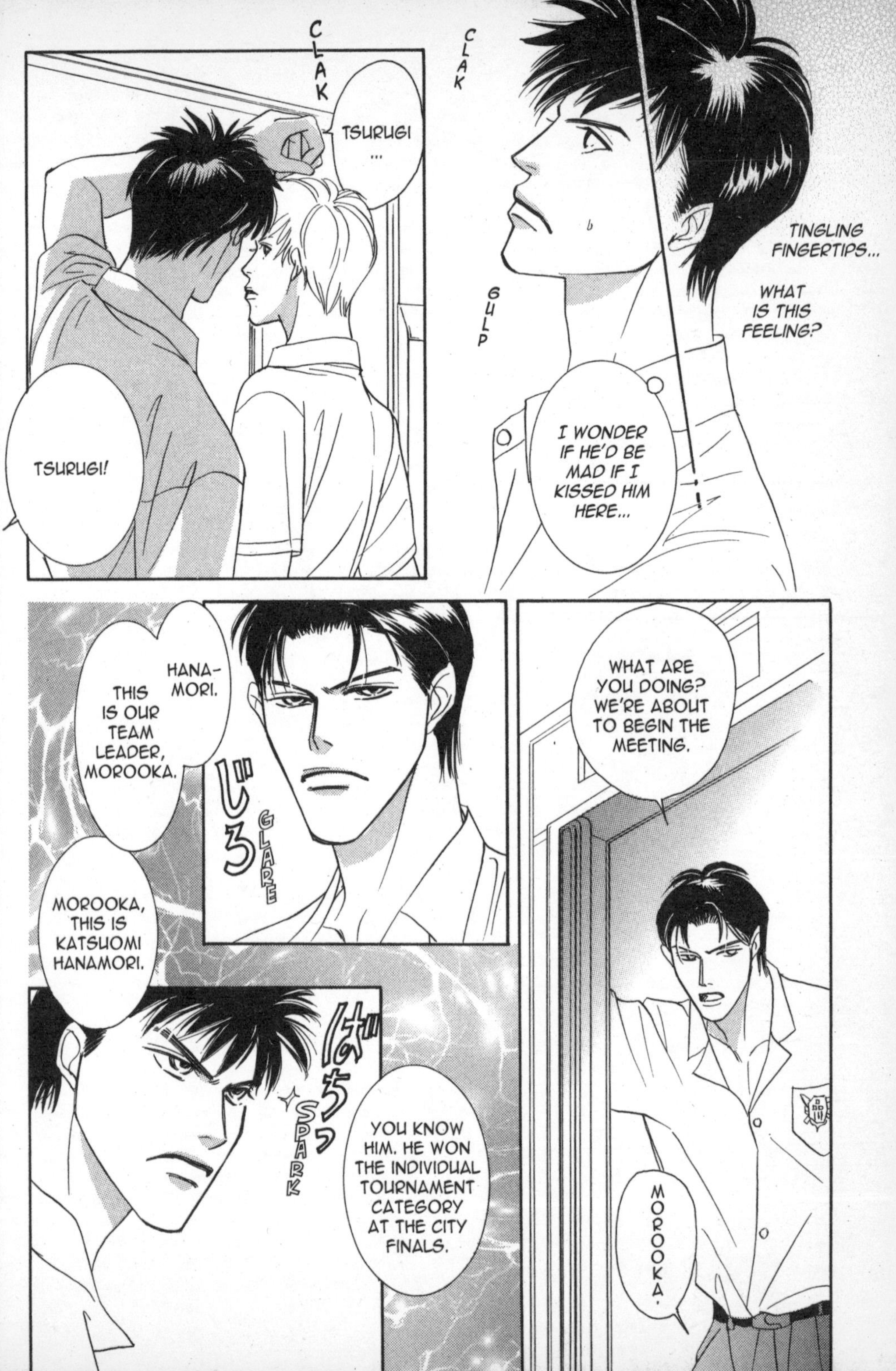
TINGLING FINGERTIPS...
WHAT IS THIS FEELING?
GULP
I WONDER IF HE'D BE MAD IF I KISSED HIM HERE...
CLAK
CLAK
TSURUGI ...
TSURUGI!
WHAT ARE YOU DOING? WE'RE ABOUT TO BEGIN THE MEETING.
MOROOKA.
HANAMORI. THIS IS OUR TEAM LEADER, MOROOKA.
じろ
GLARE
MOROOKA, THIS IS KATSUOMI HANAMORI.
ばちっ
SPARK
YOU KNOW HIM. HE WON THE INDIVIDUAL TOURNAMENT CATEGORY AT THE CITY FINALS.

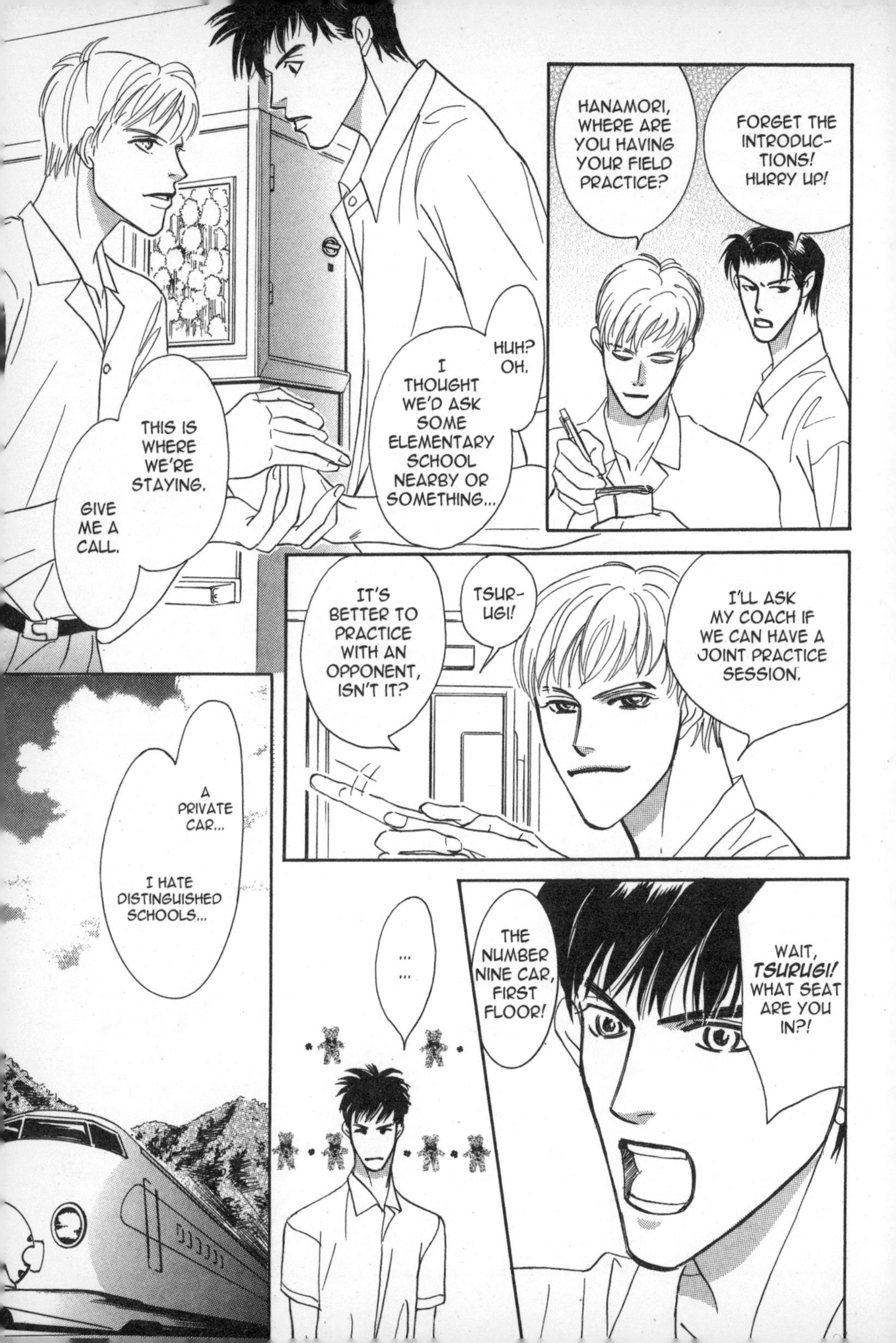
FORGET THE INTRODUCTIONS! HURRY UP!
HANAMORI, WHERE ARE YOU HAVING YOUR FIELD PRACTICE?
HUH? OH.
I THOUGHT WE'D ASK SOME ELEMENTARY SCHOOL NEARBY OR SOMETHING...
THIS IS WHERE WE'RE STAYING.
GIVE ME A CALL.
I'LL ASK MY COACH IF WE CAN HAVE A JOINT PRACTICE SESSION.
TSURUGI!
IT'S BETTER TO PRACTICE WITH AN OPPONENT, ISN'T IT?
WAIT, TSURUGI! WHAT SEAT ARE YOU IN?!
THE NUMBER NINE CAR, FIRST FLOOR!
... ...
A PRIVATE CAR...
I HATE DISTINGUISHED SCHOOLS...

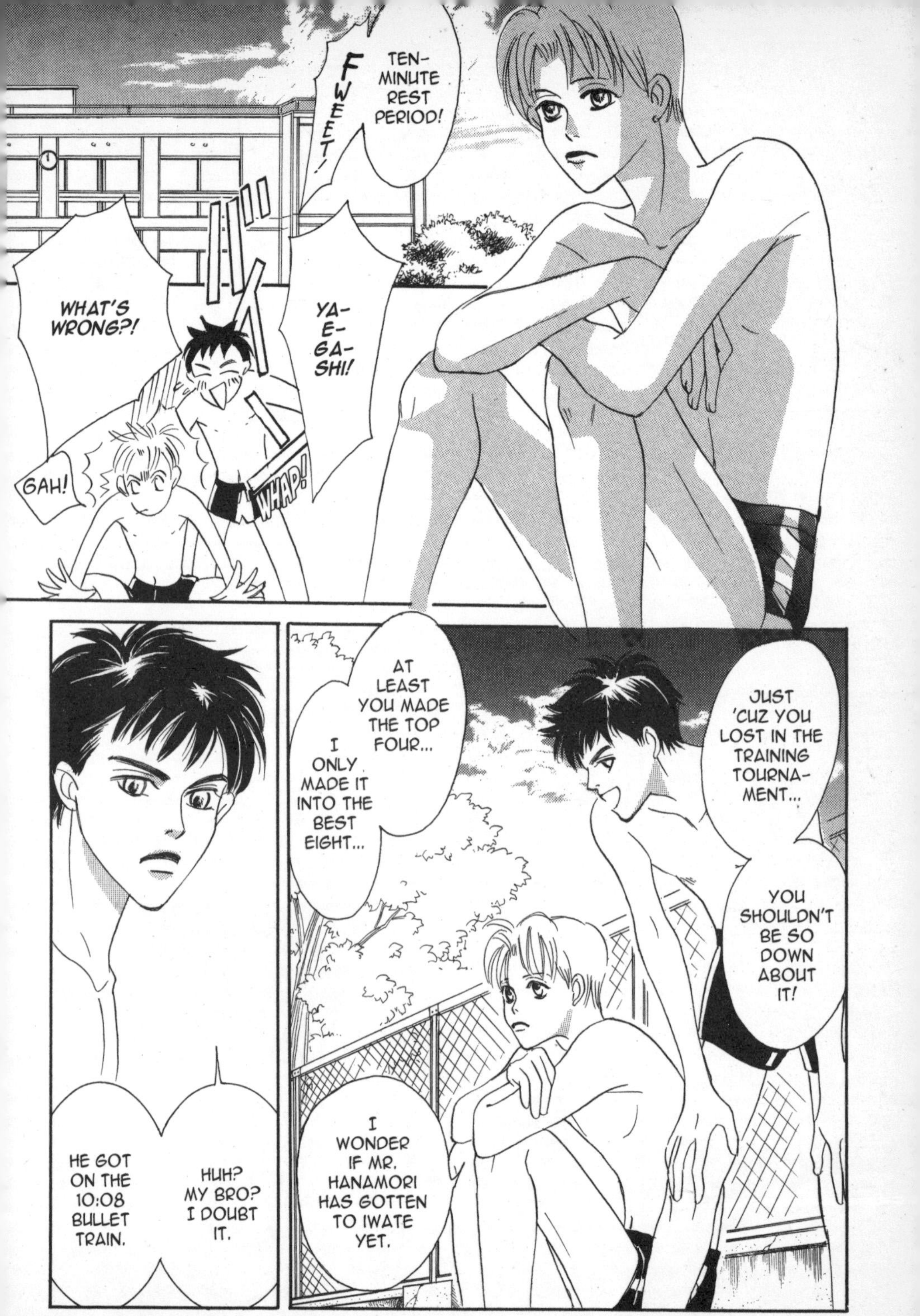
FWEET!
TEN-MINUTE REST PERIOD!
!!
YA-E-GA-SHI!
WHAT'S WRONG?!
WHAP!
GAH!
JUST 'CUZ YOU LOST IN THE TRAINING TOURNAMENT...
YOU SHOULDN'T BE SO DOWN ABOUT IT!
AT LEAST YOU MADE THE TOP FOUR...
I ONLY MADE IT INTO THE BEST EIGHT...
I WONDER IF MR. HANAMORI HAS GOTTEN TO IWATE YET.
HUH? MY BRO? I DOUBT IT.
HE GOT ON THE 10:08 BULLET TRAIN.

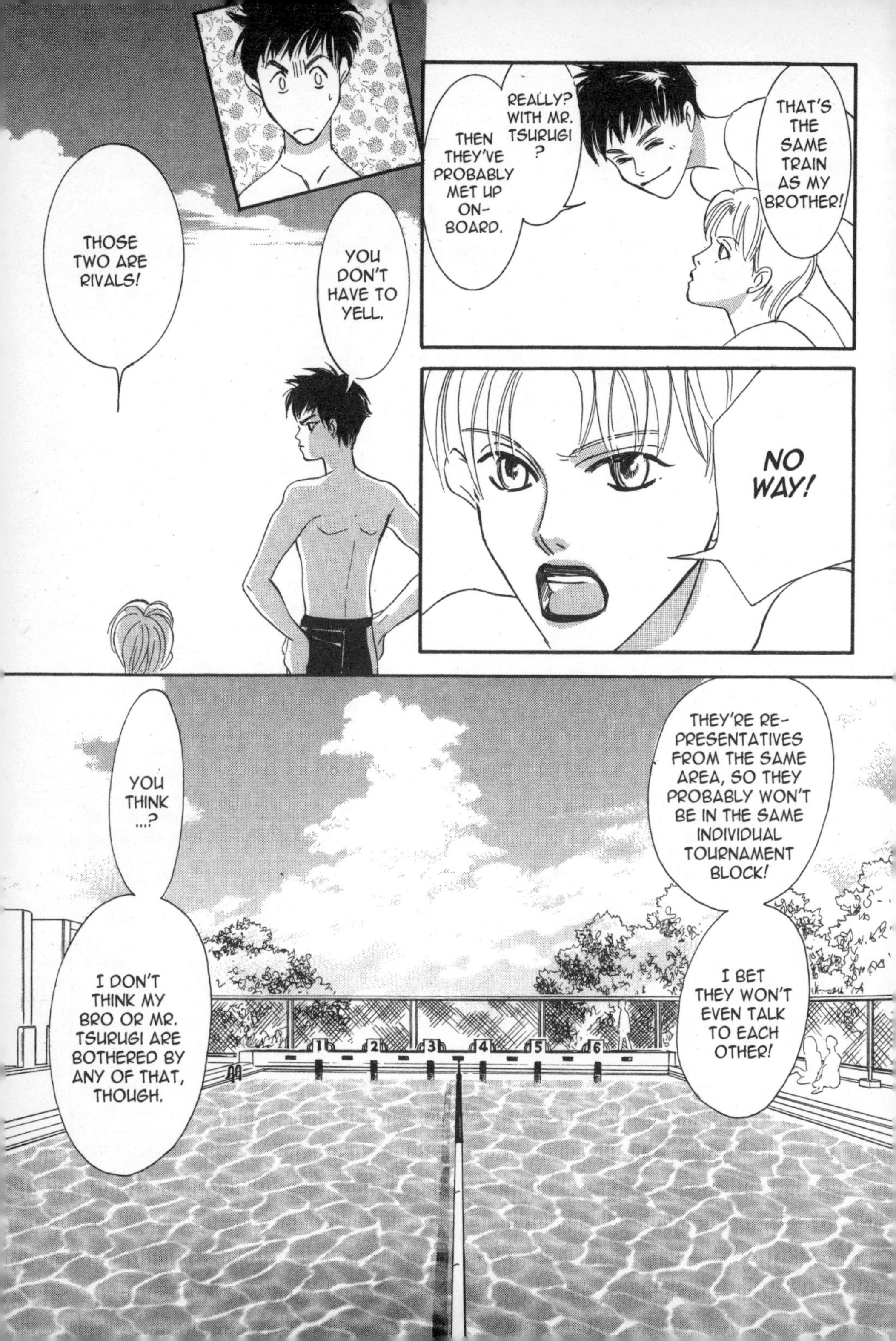
THAT'S THE SAME TRAIN AS MY BROTHER!
REALLY? WITH MR. TSURUGI?
THEN THEY'VE PROBABLY MET UP ON-BOARD.
NO WAY!
YOU DON'T HAVE TO YELL.
THOSE TWO ARE RIVALS!
THEY'RE RE-PRESENTATIVES FROM THE SAME AREA, SO THEY PROBABLY WON'T BE IN THE SAME INDIVIDUAL TOURNAMENT BLOCK!
I BET THEY WON'T EVEN TALK TO EACH OTHER!
YOU THINK ...?
I DON'T THINK MY BRO OR MR. TSURUGI ARE BOTHERED BY ANY OF THAT, THOUGH.

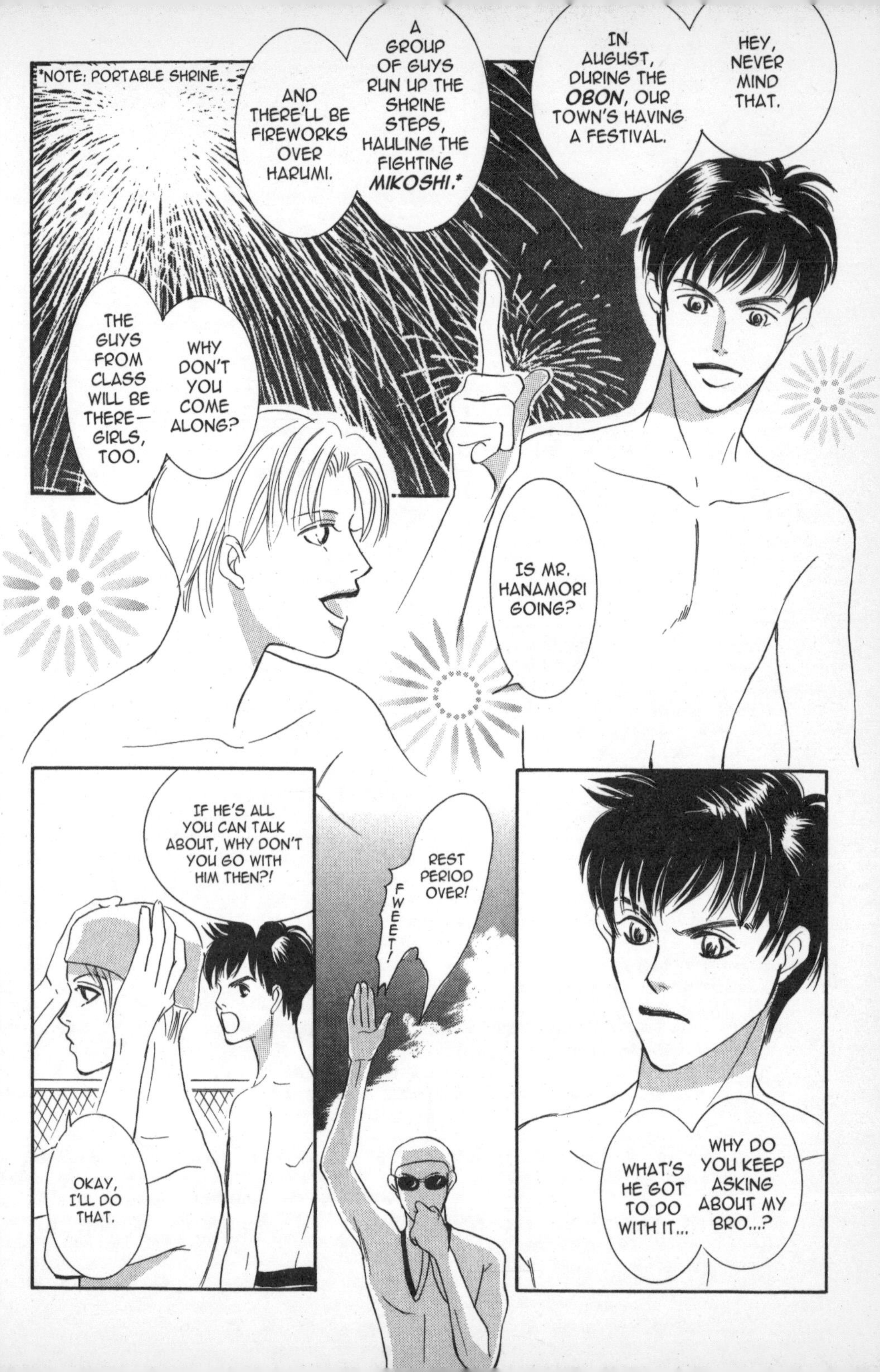
HEY, NEVER MIND THAT.
IN AUGUST, DURING THE *OBON*, OUR TOWN'S HAVING A FESTIVAL.
A GROUP OF GUYS RUN UP THE SHRINE STEPS, HAULING THE FIGHTING *MIKOSHI*.*
AND THERE'LL BE FIREWORKS OVER HARUMI.
*NOTE: PORTABLE SHRINE.
WHY DON'T YOU COME ALONG?
THE GUYS FROM CLASS WILL BE THERE—GIRLS, TOO.
IS MR. HANAMORI GOING?
WHY DO YOU KEEP ASKING ABOUT MY BRO...?
WHAT'S HE GOT TO DO WITH IT...
IF HE'S ALL YOU CAN TALK ABOUT, WHY DON'T YOU GO WITH HIM THEN?!
OKAY, I'LL DO THAT.
FWEET!
REST PERIOD OVER!

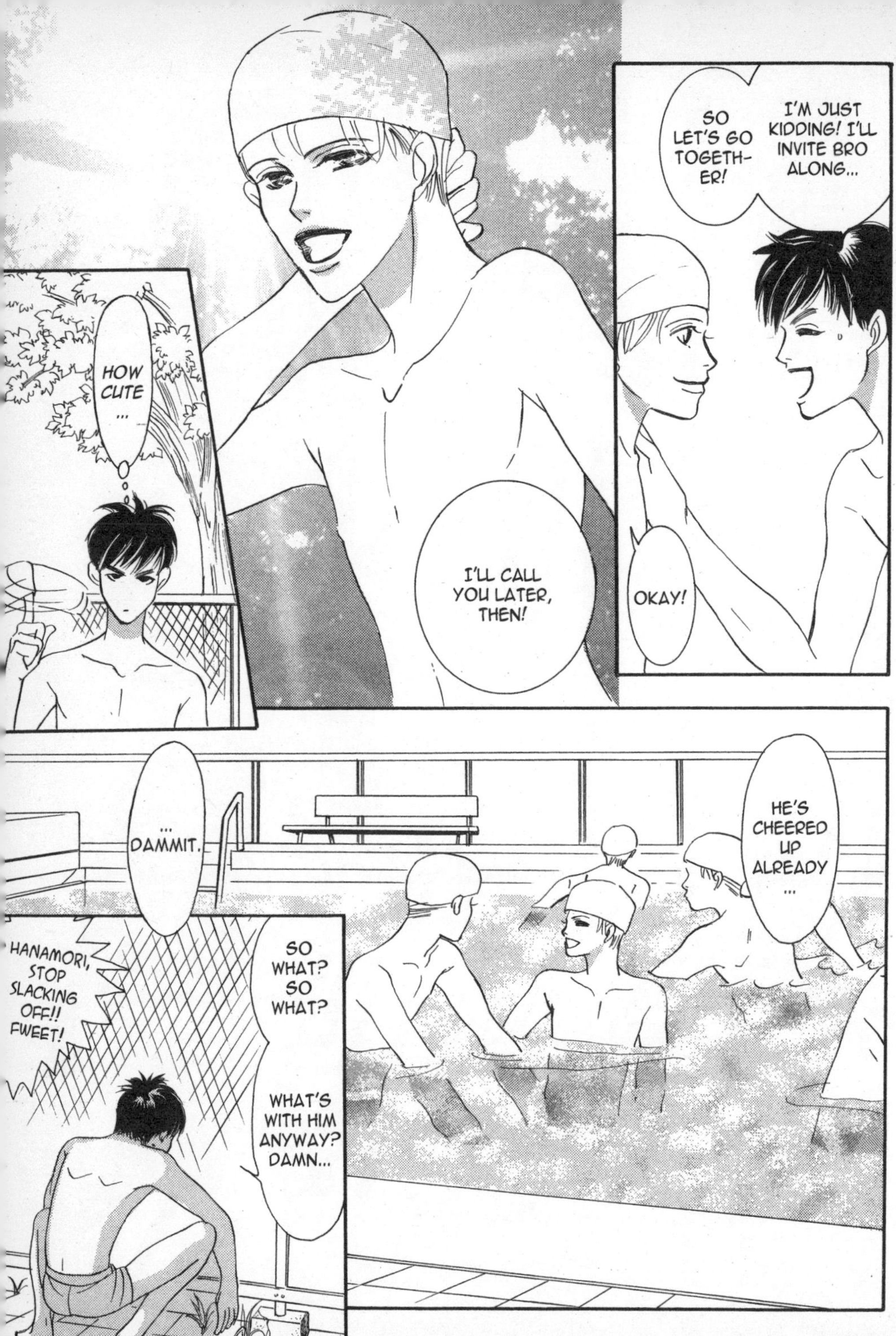
I'M JUST KIDDING! I'LL INVITE BRO ALONG...
SO LET'S GO TOGETH-ER!
OKAY!
I'LL CALL YOU LATER, THEN!
HOW CUTE ...
HE'S CHEERED UP ALREADY ...
... DAMMIT.
SO WHAT? SO WHAT?
WHAT'S WITH HIM ANYWAY? DAMN...
HANAMORI, STOP SLACKING OFF!! FWEET!

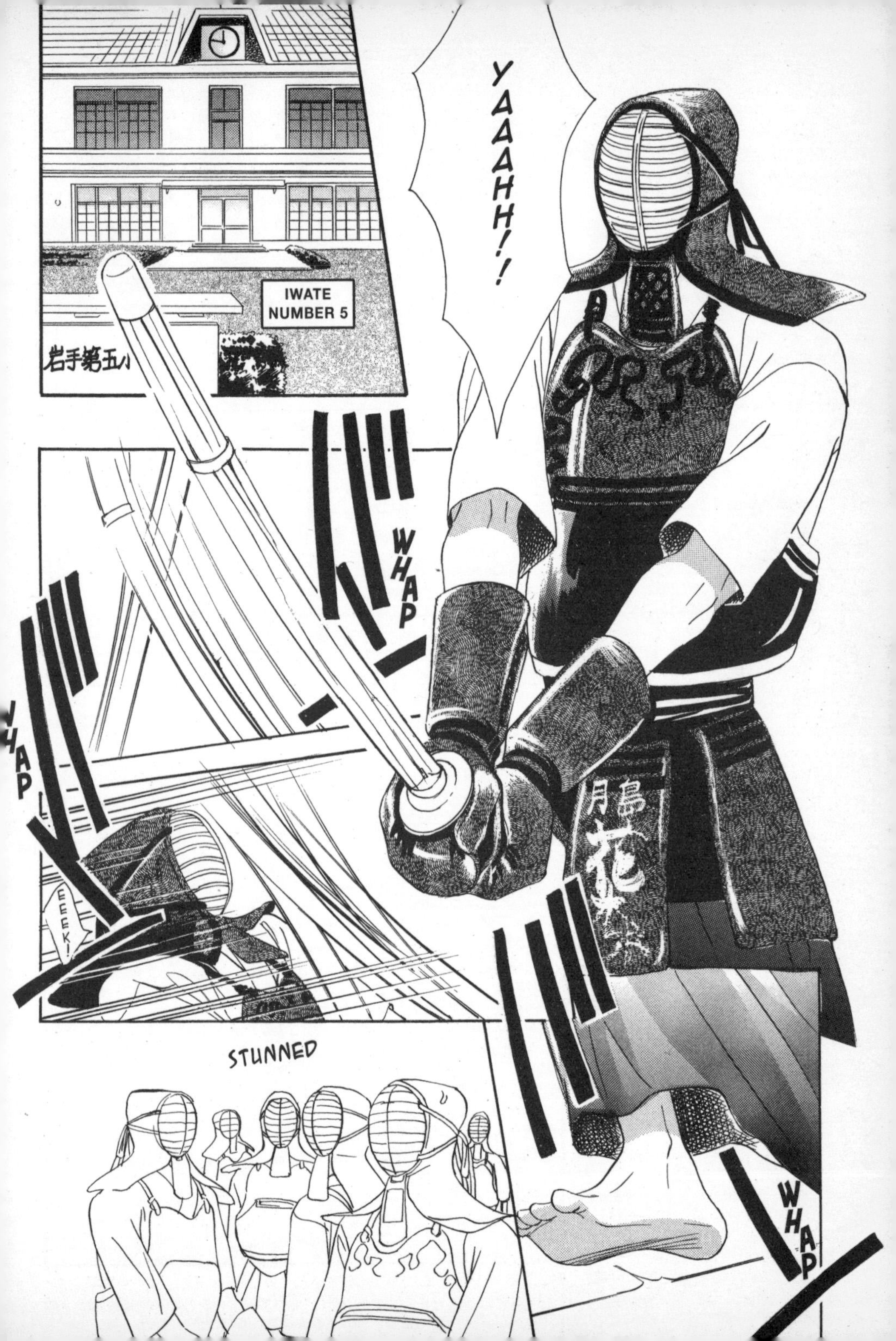

YAAAAHH!!
WHAP
WHAP
IWATE NUMBER 5
岩手第五小
WHAP
WHAP
EEEK!
STUNNED

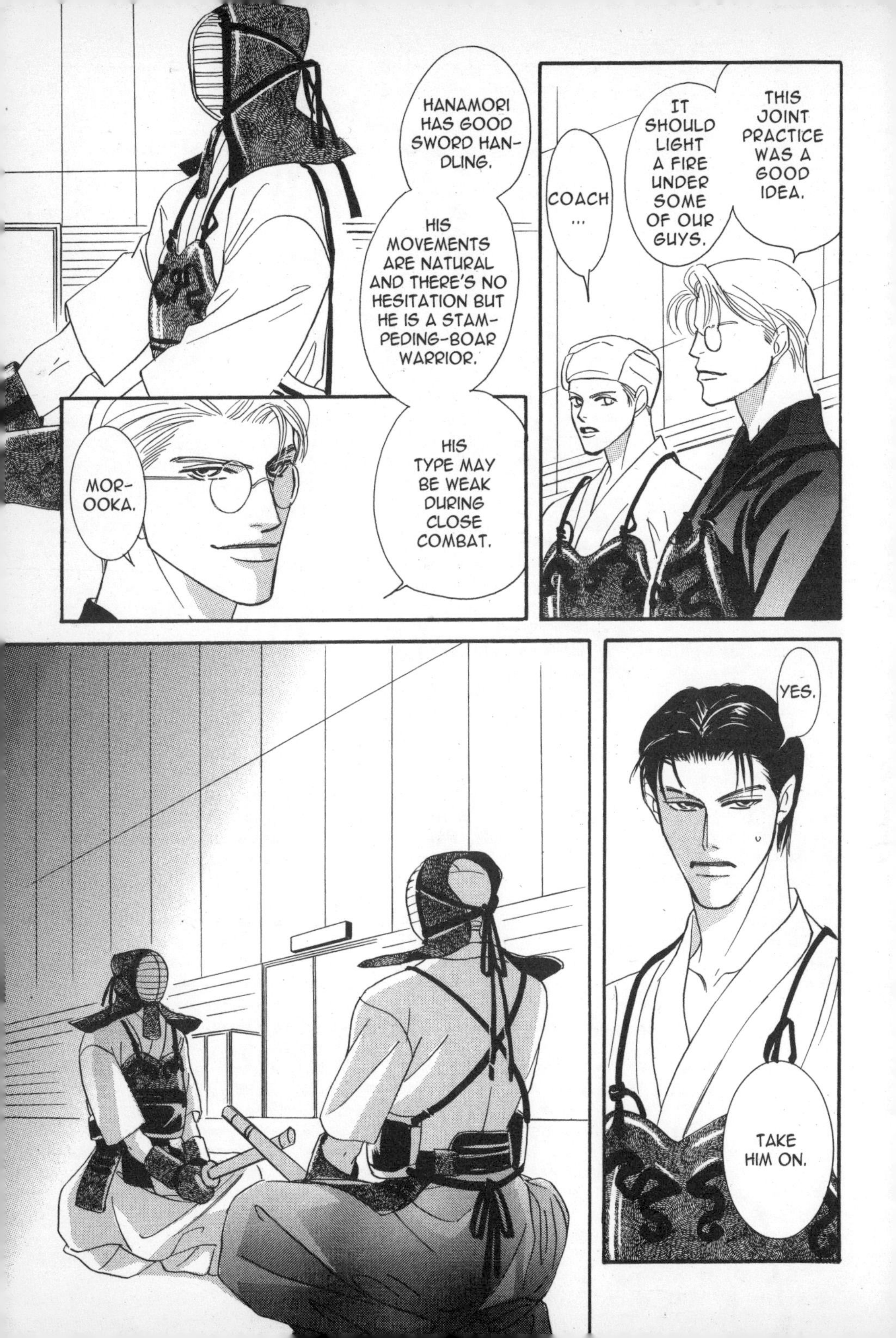
THIS JOINT PRACTICE WAS A GOOD IDEA.
IT SHOULD LIGHT A FIRE UNDER SOME OF OUR GUYS.
COACH ...
HANAMORI HAS GOOD SWORD HAN-DLING.
HIS MOVEMENTS ARE NATURAL AND THERE'S NO HESITATION BUT HE IS A STAMPEDING-BOAR WARRIOR.
HIS TYPE MAY BE WEAK DURING CLOSE COMBAT.
MOR-OOKA.
YES.
TAKE HIM ON.

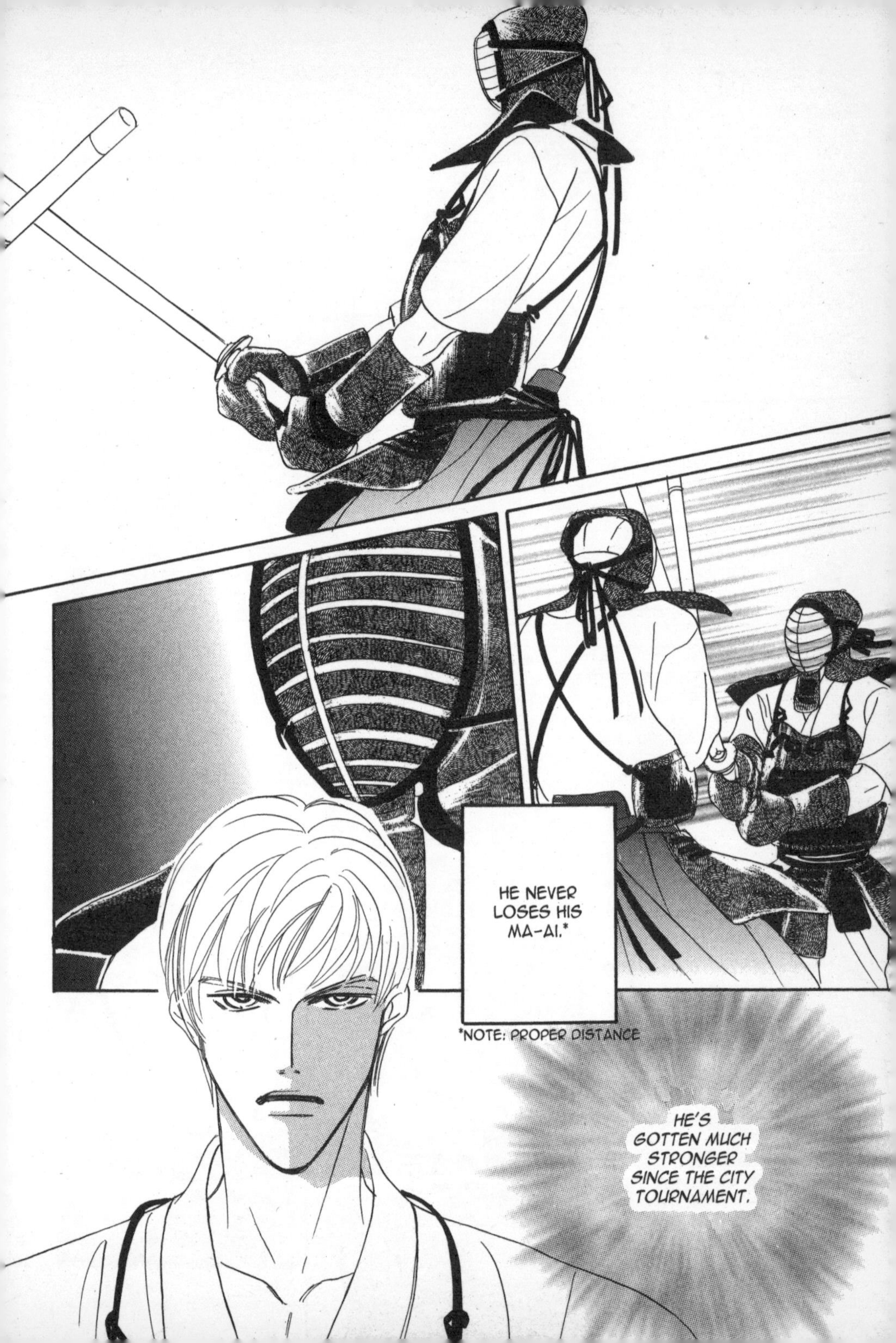
HE NEVER LOSES HIS MA-AI.*
*NOTE: PROPER DISTANCE
HE'S GOTTEN MUCH STRONGER SINCE THE CITY TOURNAMENT.

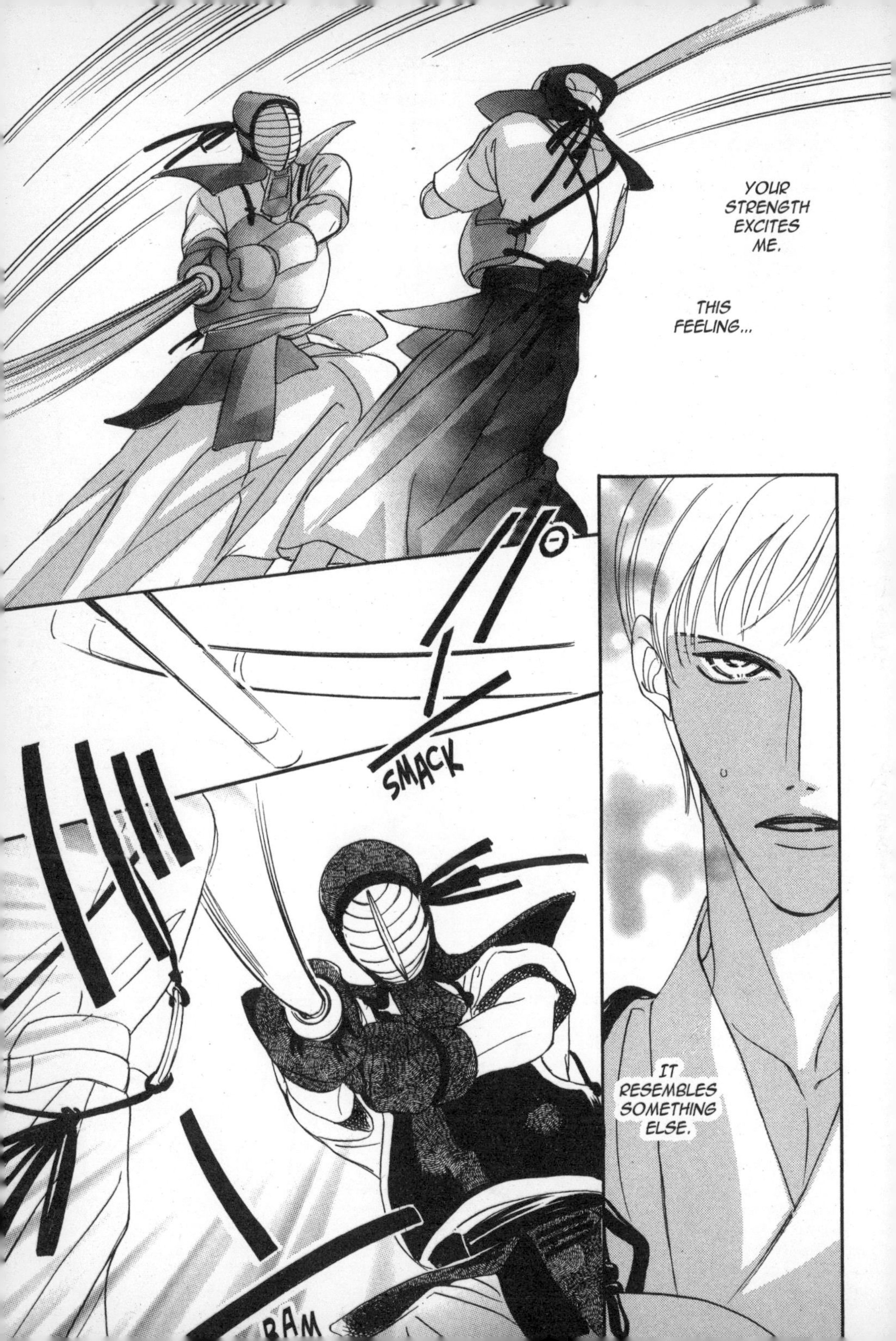
YOUR STRENGTH EXCITES ME.
THIS FEELING...
IT RESEMBLES SOMETHING ELSE.
SMACK
BAM

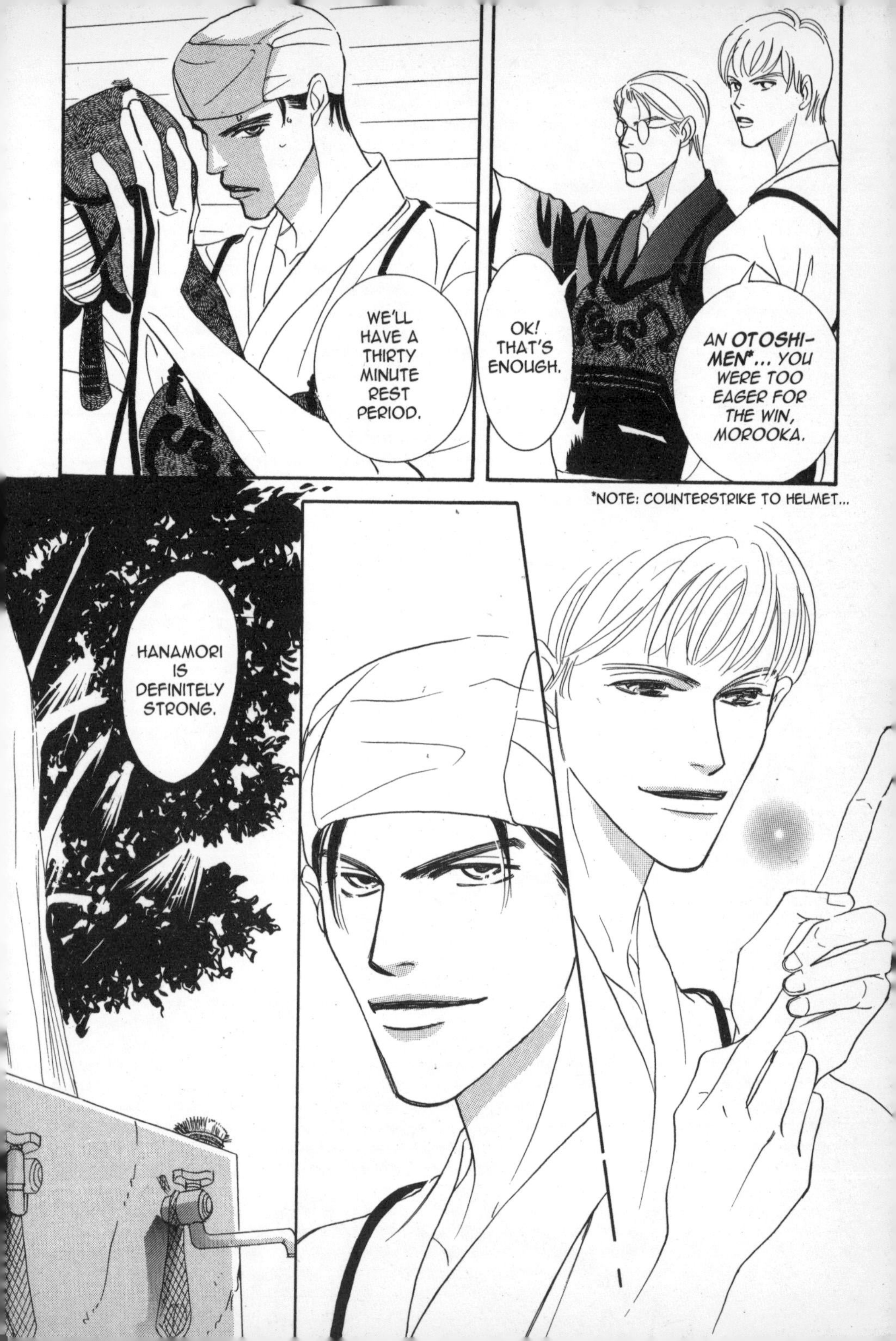
AN OTOSHI-MEN*... YOU WERE TOO EAGER FOR THE WIN, MOROOKA.
OK! THAT'S ENOUGH.
WE'LL HAVE A THIRTY MINUTE REST PERIOD.
*NOTE: COUNTERSTRIKE TO HELMET...
HANAMORI IS DEFINITELY STRONG.

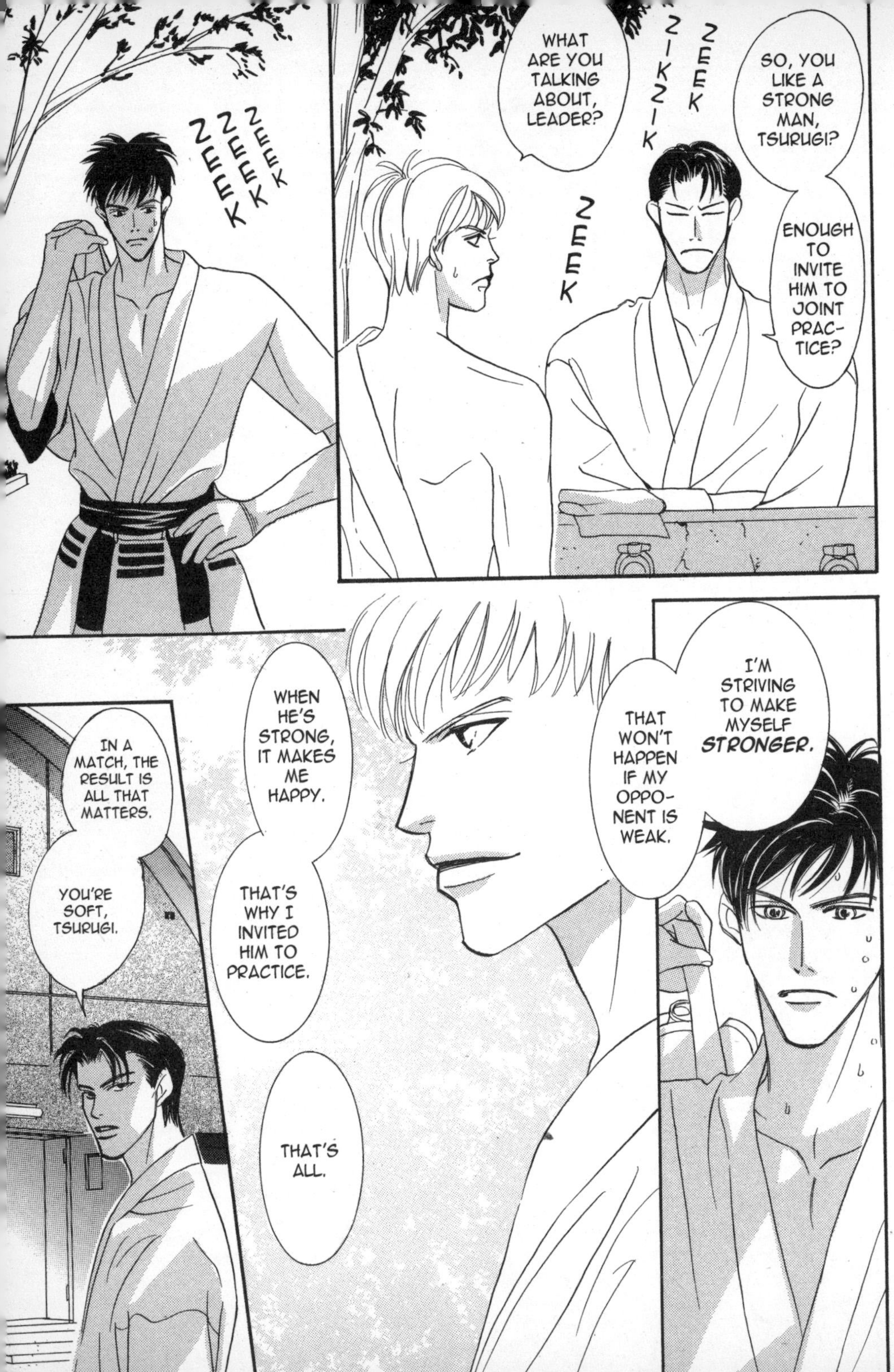
SO, YOU LIKE A STRONG MAN, TSURUGI?
ZEEK
ZIKZIK
WHAT ARE YOU TALKING ABOUT, LEADER?
ENOUGH TO INVITE HIM TO JOINT PRAC-TICE?
ZEEK
ZEEK ZEEK ZEEK
I'M STRIVING TO MAKE MYSELF **STRONGER.**
THAT WON'T HAPPEN IF MY OPPO-NENT IS WEAK.
WHEN HE'S STRONG, IT MAKES ME HAPPY.
THAT'S WHY I INVITED HIM TO PRACTICE.
THAT'S ALL.
IN A MATCH, THE RESULT IS ALL THAT MATTERS.
YOU'RE SOFT, TSURUGI.

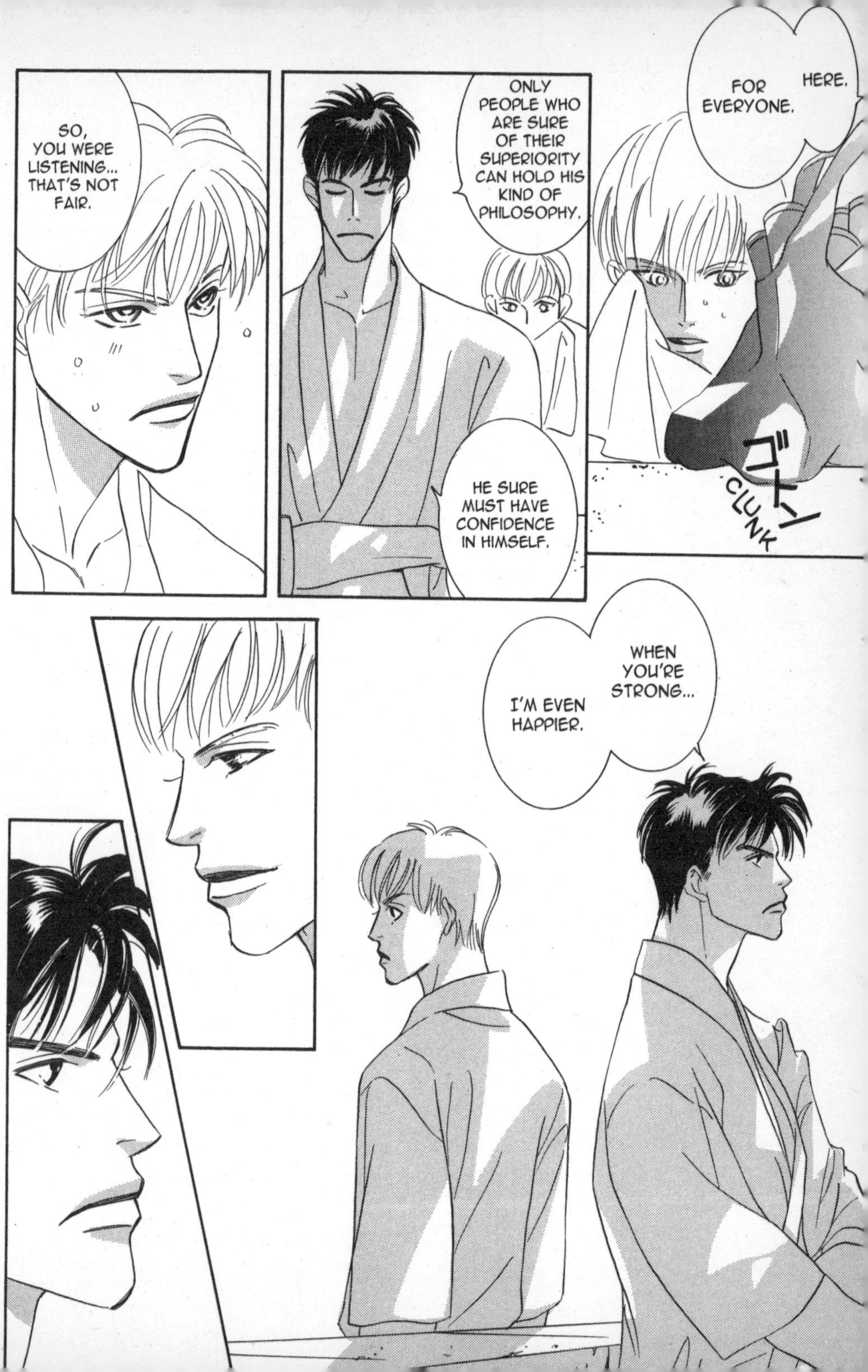
HERE.
FOR EVERYONE.
CLUNK
ONLY PEOPLE WHO ARE SURE OF THEIR SUPERIORITY CAN HOLD HIS KIND OF PHILOSOPHY.
HE SURE MUST HAVE CONFIDENCE IN HIMSELF.
SO, YOU WERE LISTENING... THAT'S NOT FAIR.
WHEN YOU'RE STRONG...
I'M EVEN HAPPIER.

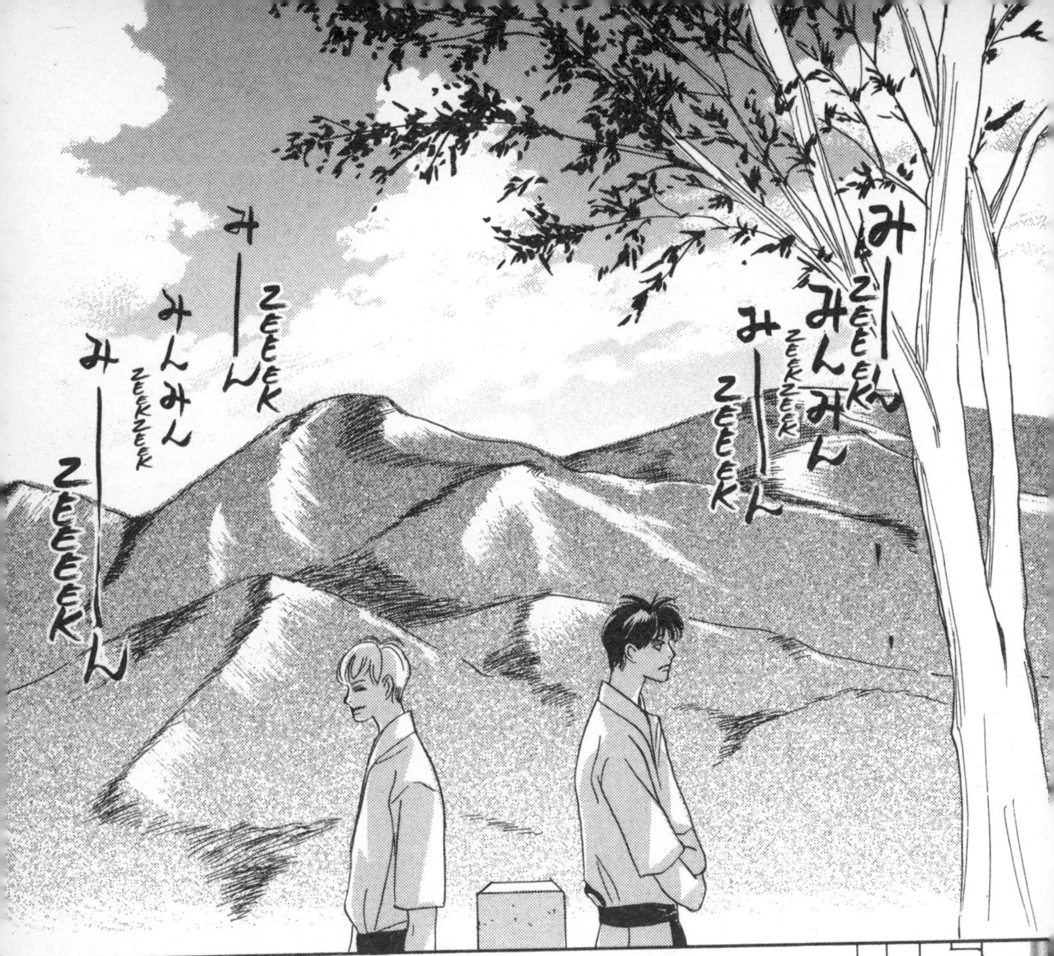

みーーん
ZEEEK
みんみん
ZEEKZEEK
みーーん
ZEEEK
みーーん
ZEEEK
みんみん
ZEEKZEEK
みーーーん
ZEEEEEK

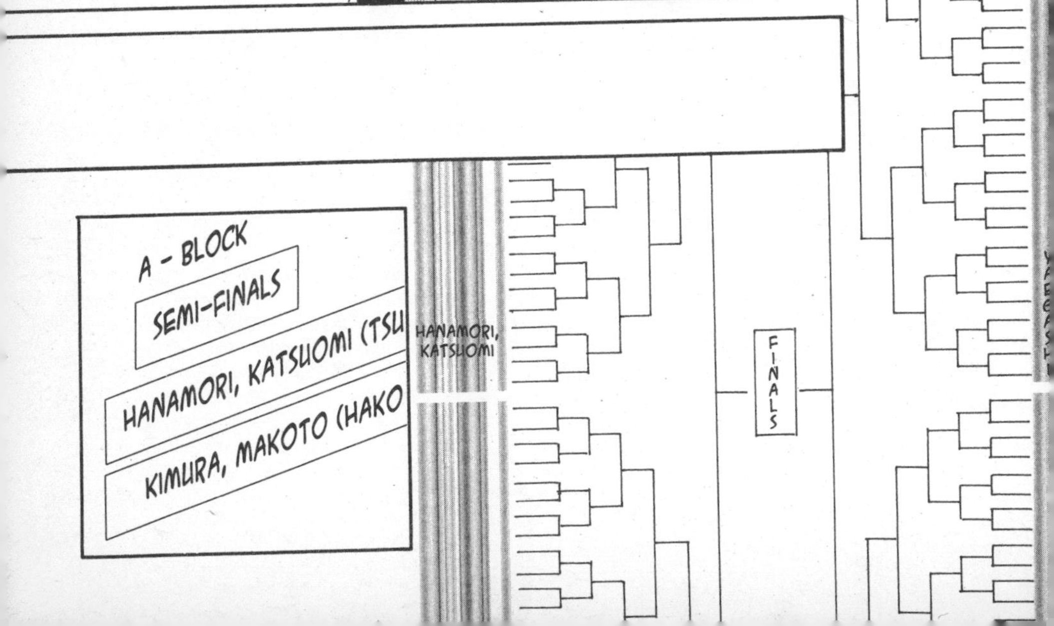

A - BLOCK
SEMI-FINALS
HANAMORI, KATSUOMI (TSU
KIMURA, MAKOTO (HAKO
HANAMORI, KATSUOMI
FINALS

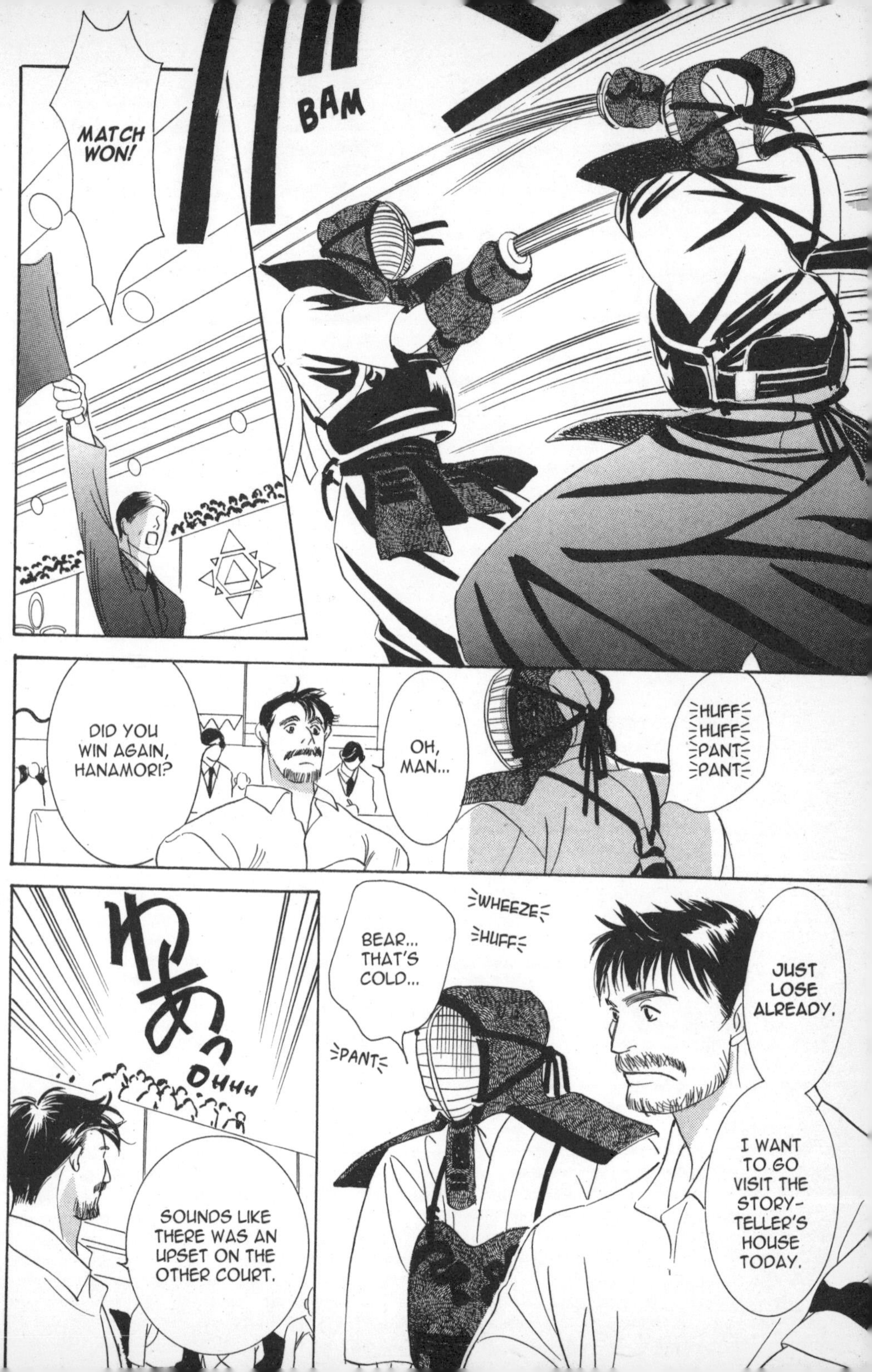
BAM
MATCH WON!
HUFF HUFF PANT PANT
OH, MAN...
DID YOU WIN AGAIN, HANAMORI?
JUST LOSE ALREADY.
I WANT TO GO VISIT THE STORY-TELLER'S HOUSE TODAY.
WHEEZE
HUFF
BEAR... THAT'S COLD...
PANT
わあっ
OHHH
SOUNDS LIKE THERE WAS AN UPSET ON THE OTHER COURT.

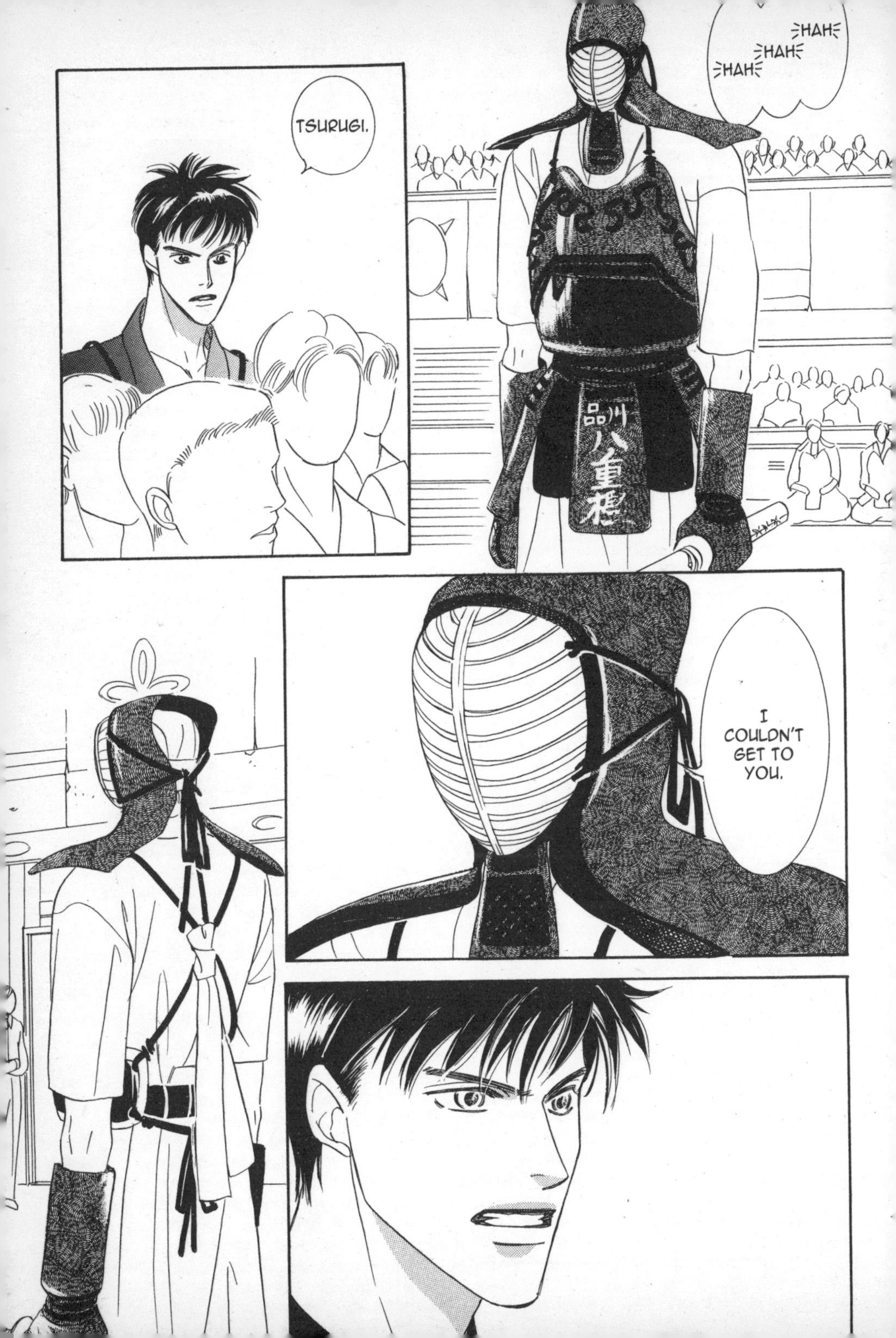
HAH HAH HAH
品川 八重樫
TSURUGI.
I COULDN'T GET TO YOU.

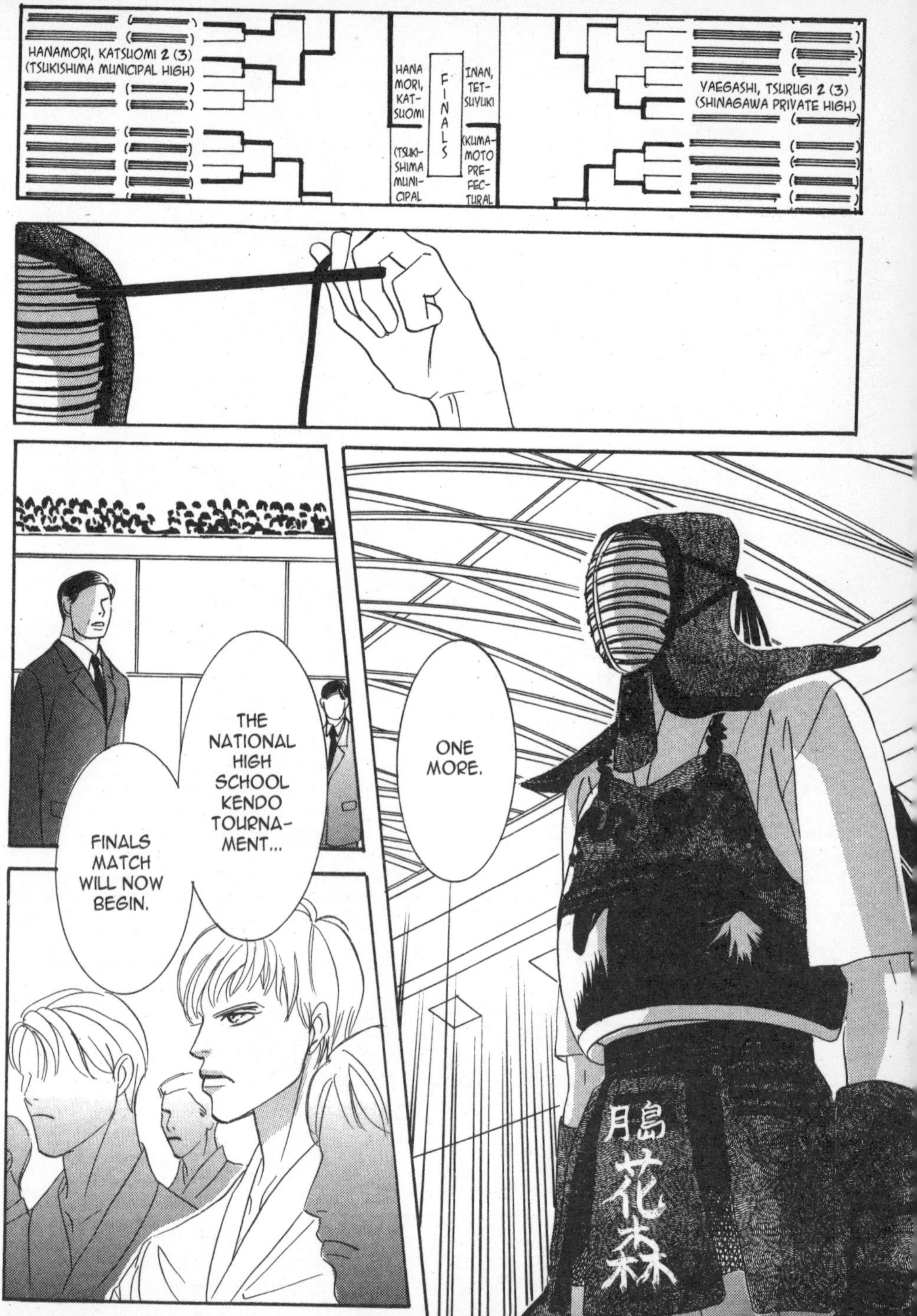
HANAMORI, KATSUOMI 2 (3)
(TSUKISHIMA MUNICIPAL HIGH)
HANA-MORI, KAT-SUOMI
(TSUKI-SHIMA MUNI-CIPAL
FINALS
INAN, TET-SUYUKI
(KUMA-MOTO PRE-FEC-TURAL
YAEGASHI, TSURUGI 2 (3)
(SHINAGAWA PRIVATE HIGH)
月島
花森
ONE MORE.
THE NATIONAL HIGH SCHOOL KENDO TOURNAMENT...
FINALS MATCH WILL NOW BEGIN.

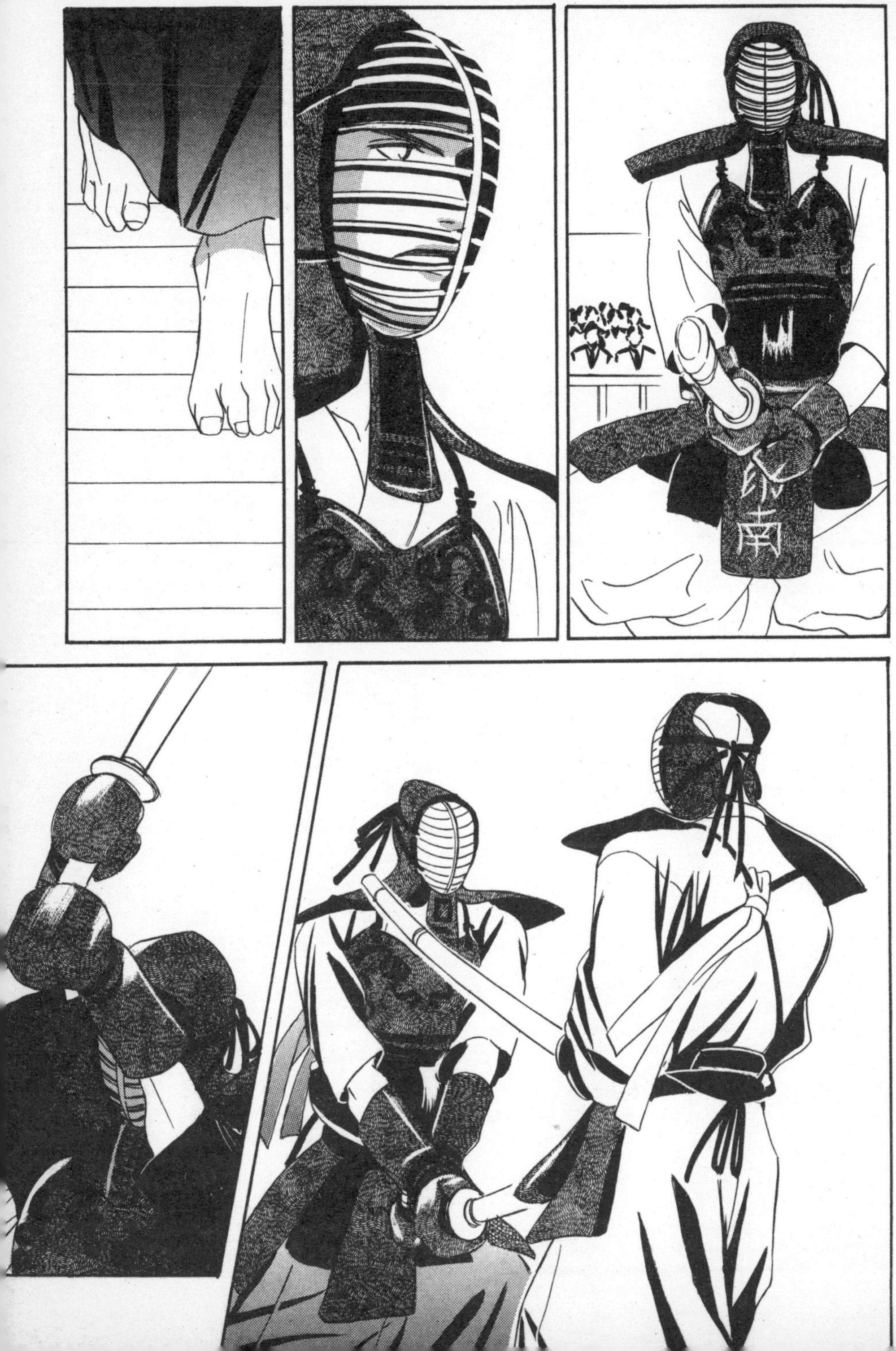

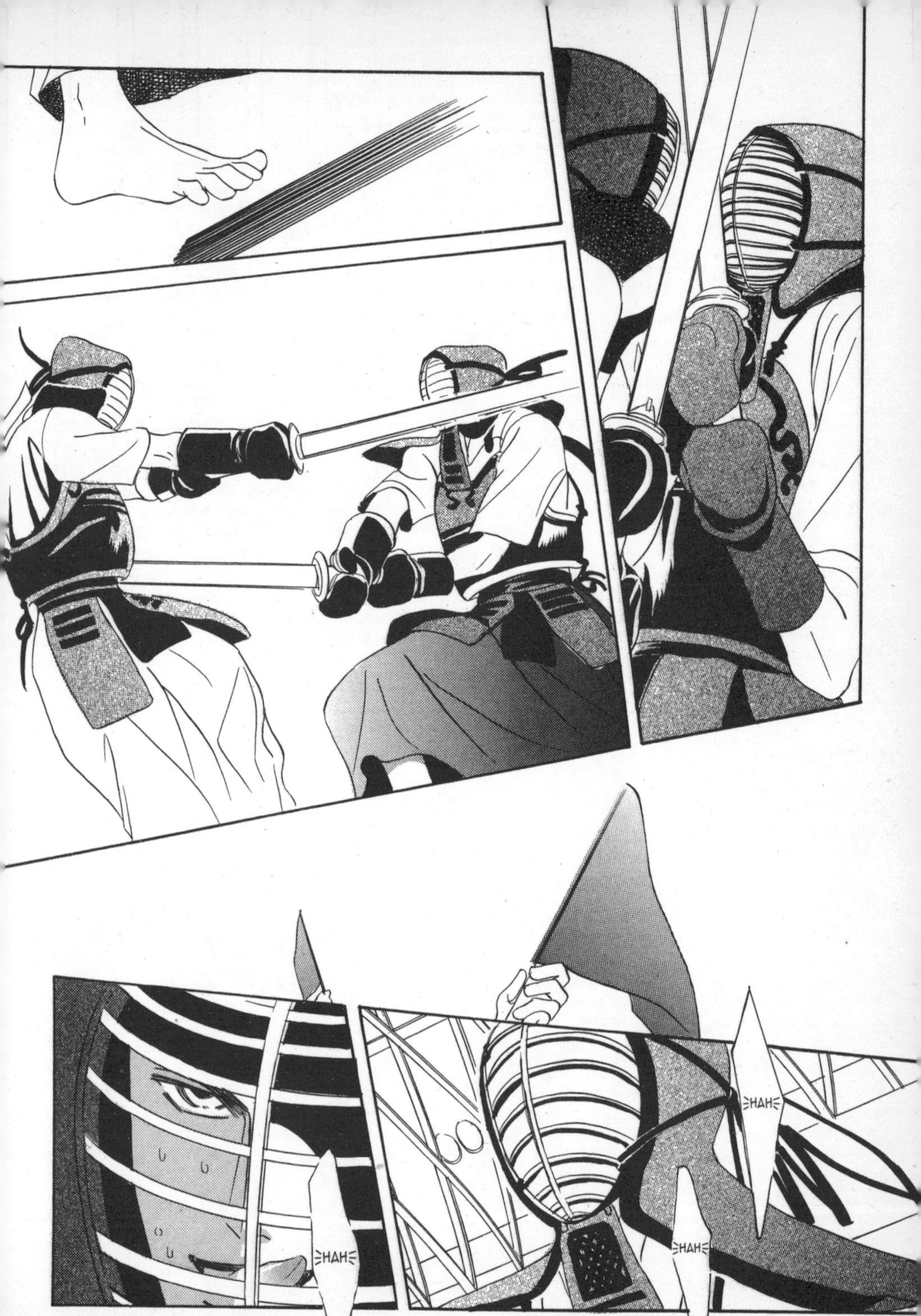
HAH
HAH
HAH

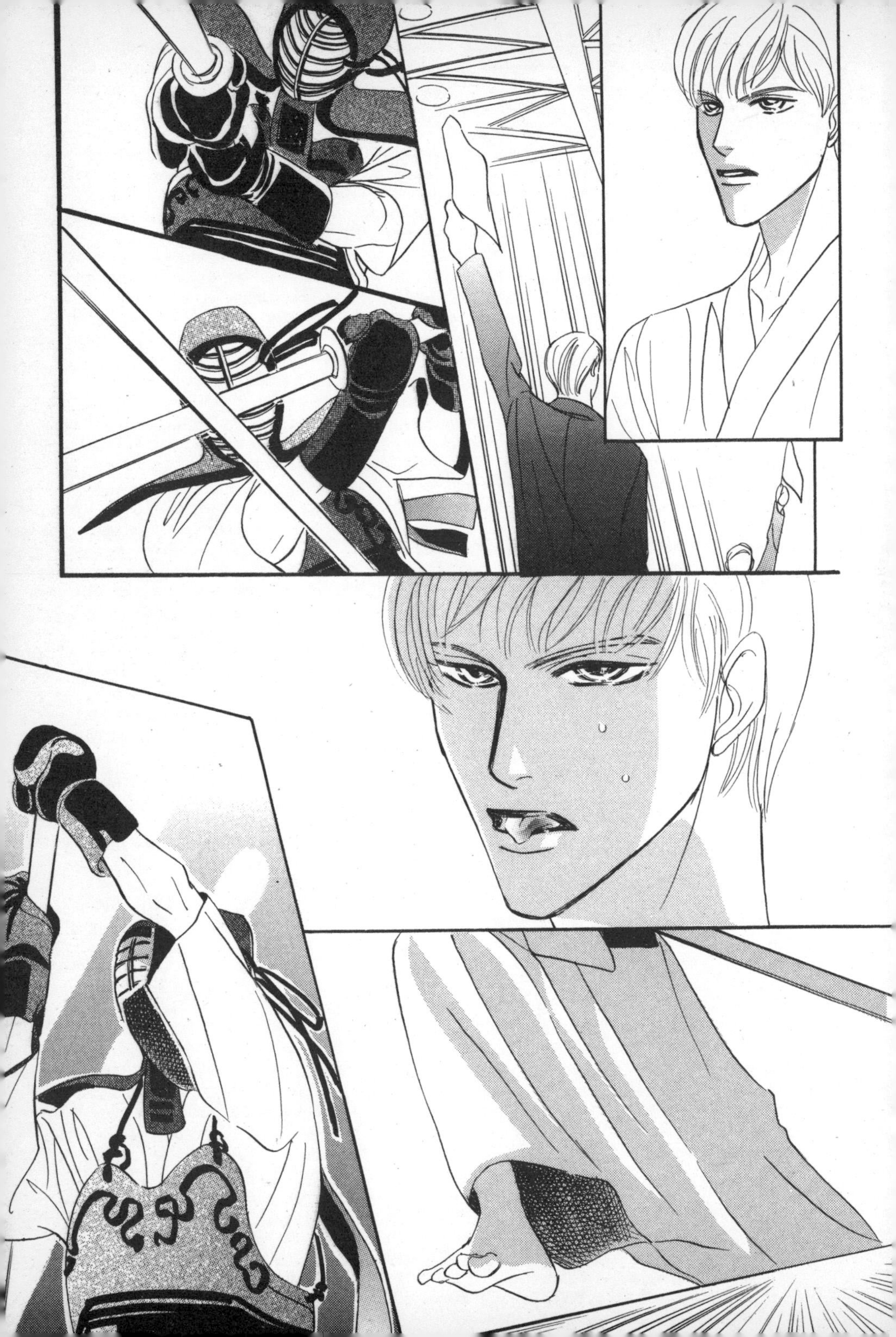

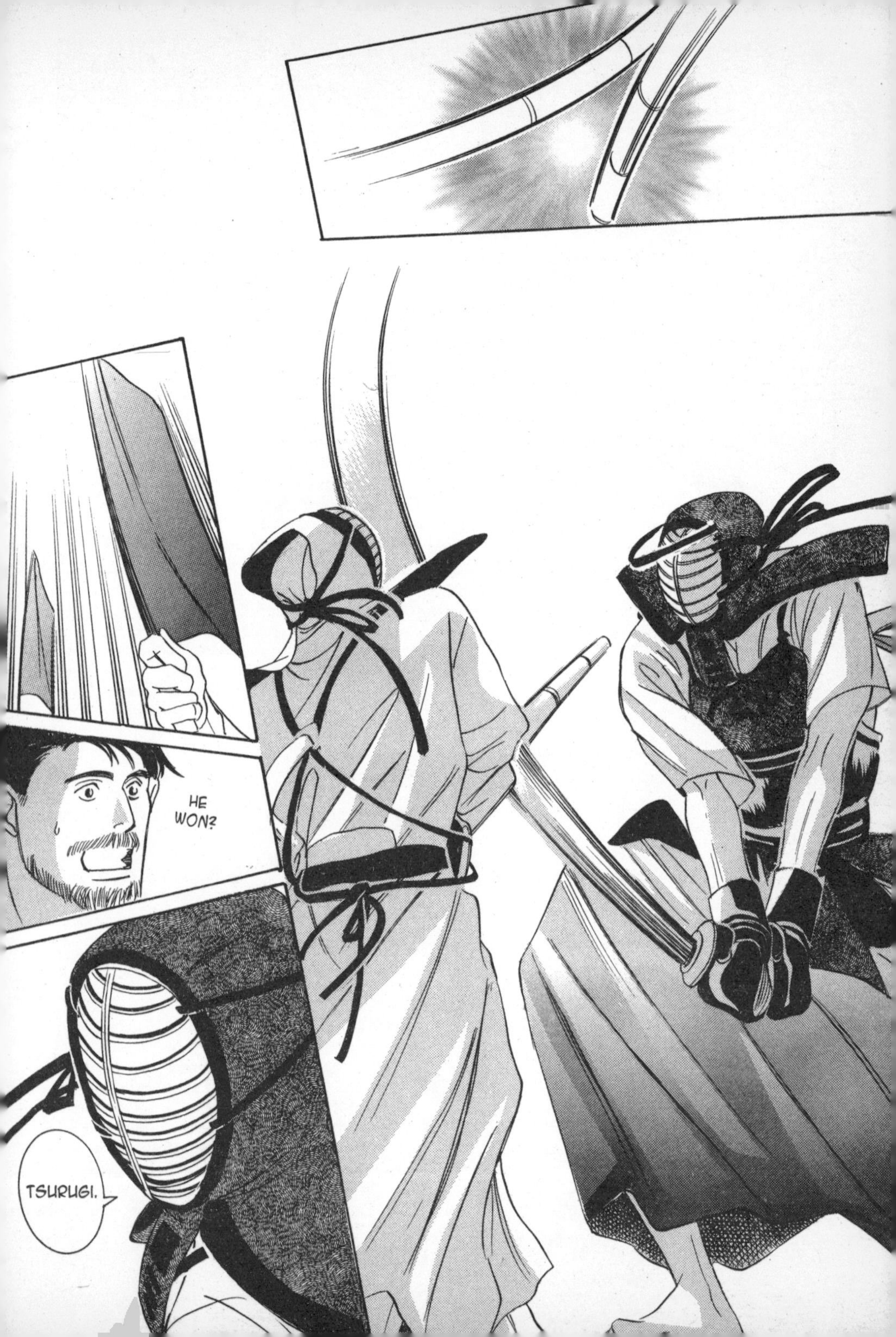
HE WON?
TSURUGI.

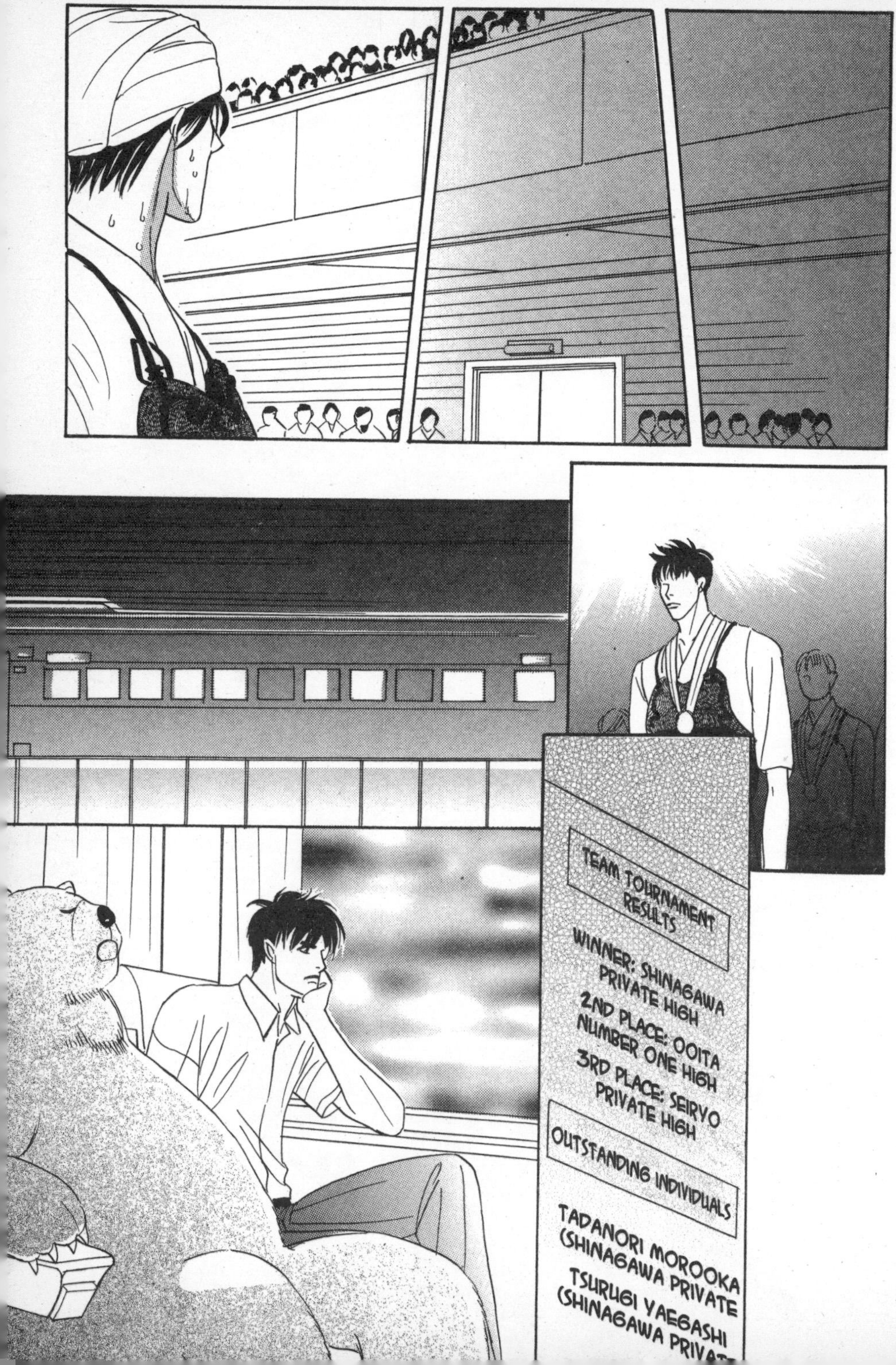

TEAM TOURNAMENT RESULTS
WINNER: SHINAGAWA PRIVATE HIGH
2ND PLACE: OOITA NUMBER ONE HIGH
3RD PLACE: SEIRYO PRIVATE HIGH
OUTSTANDING INDIVIDUALS
TADANORI MOROOKA (SHINAGAWA PRIVATE
TSURUGI YAEGASHI (SHINAGAWA PRIVAT

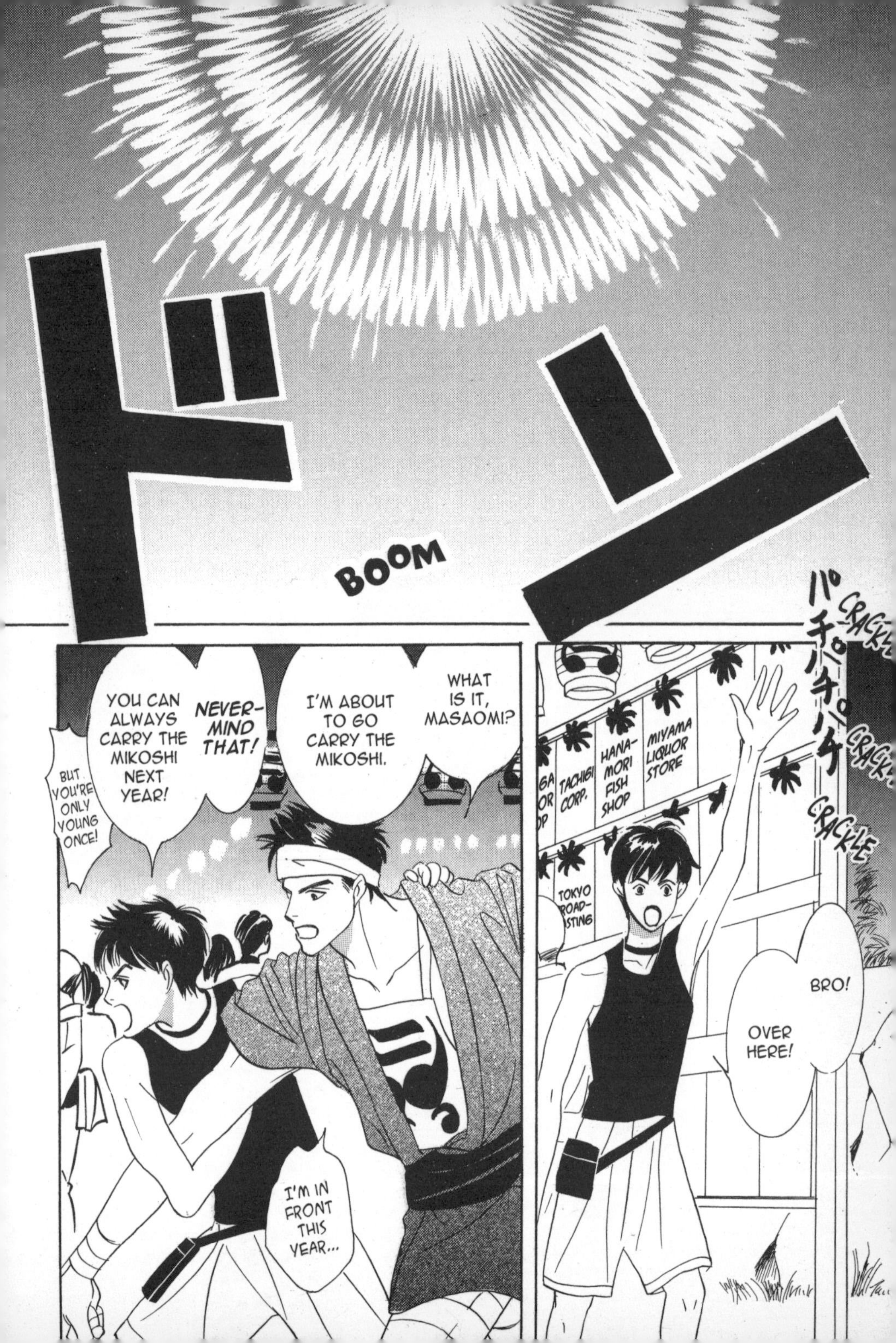
ドーン
BOOM
パチパチパチ
CRACKLE
CRACKLE
CRACKLE
MIYAMA LIQUOR STORE
HANA-MORI FISH SHOP
TACHIGI CORP.
BRO!
OVER HERE!
WHAT IS IT, MASAOMI?
I'M ABOUT TO GO CARRY THE MIKOSHI.
NEVER-MIND THAT!
YOU CAN ALWAYS CARRY THE MIKOSHI NEXT YEAR!
BUT YOU'RE ONLY YOUNG ONCE!
I'M IN FRONT THIS YEAR...

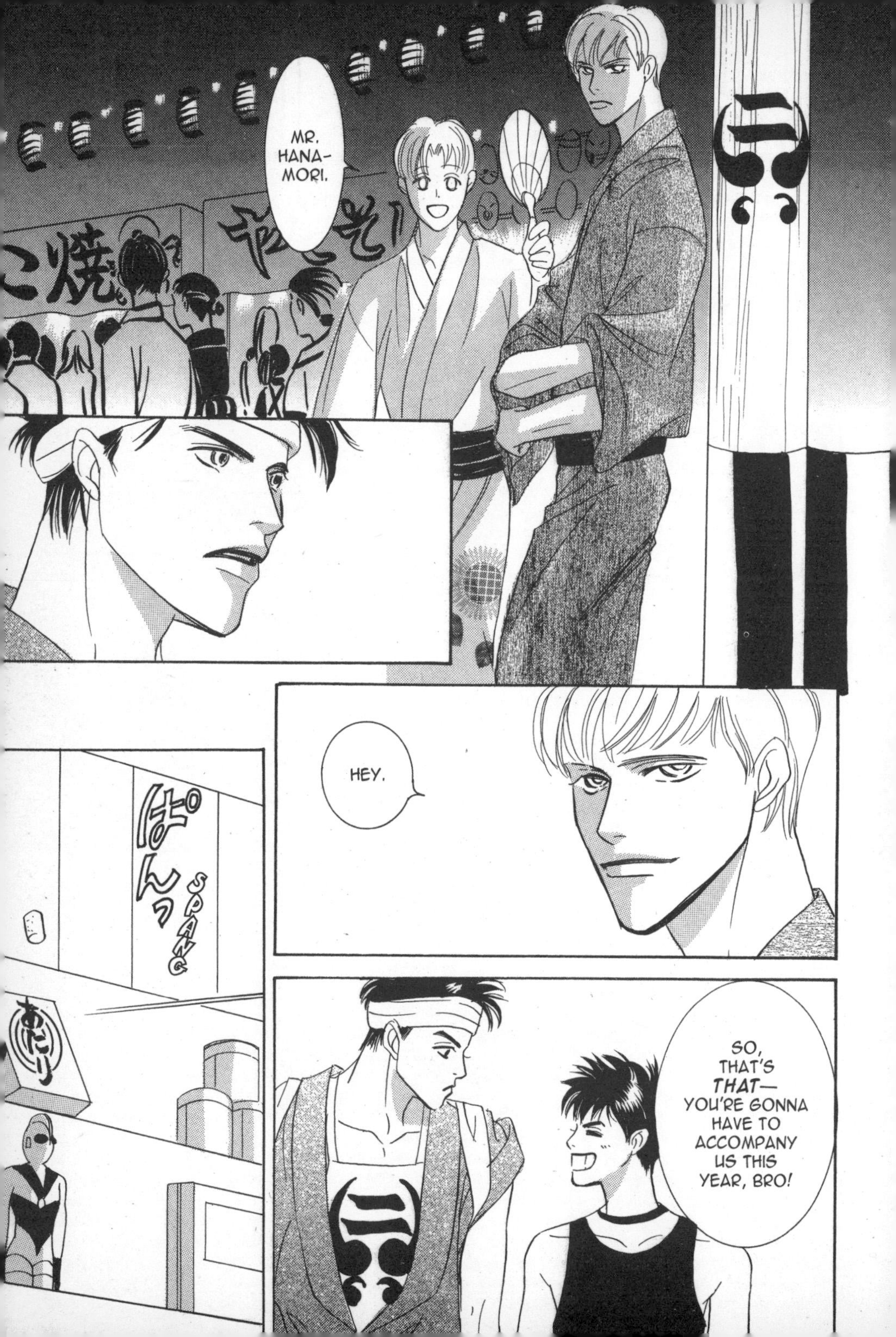
MR. HANAMORI.
HEY.
SO, THAT'S *THAT*— YOU'RE GONNA HAVE TO ACCOMPANY US THIS YEAR, BRO!
ぱんっ
SPANG
あたり

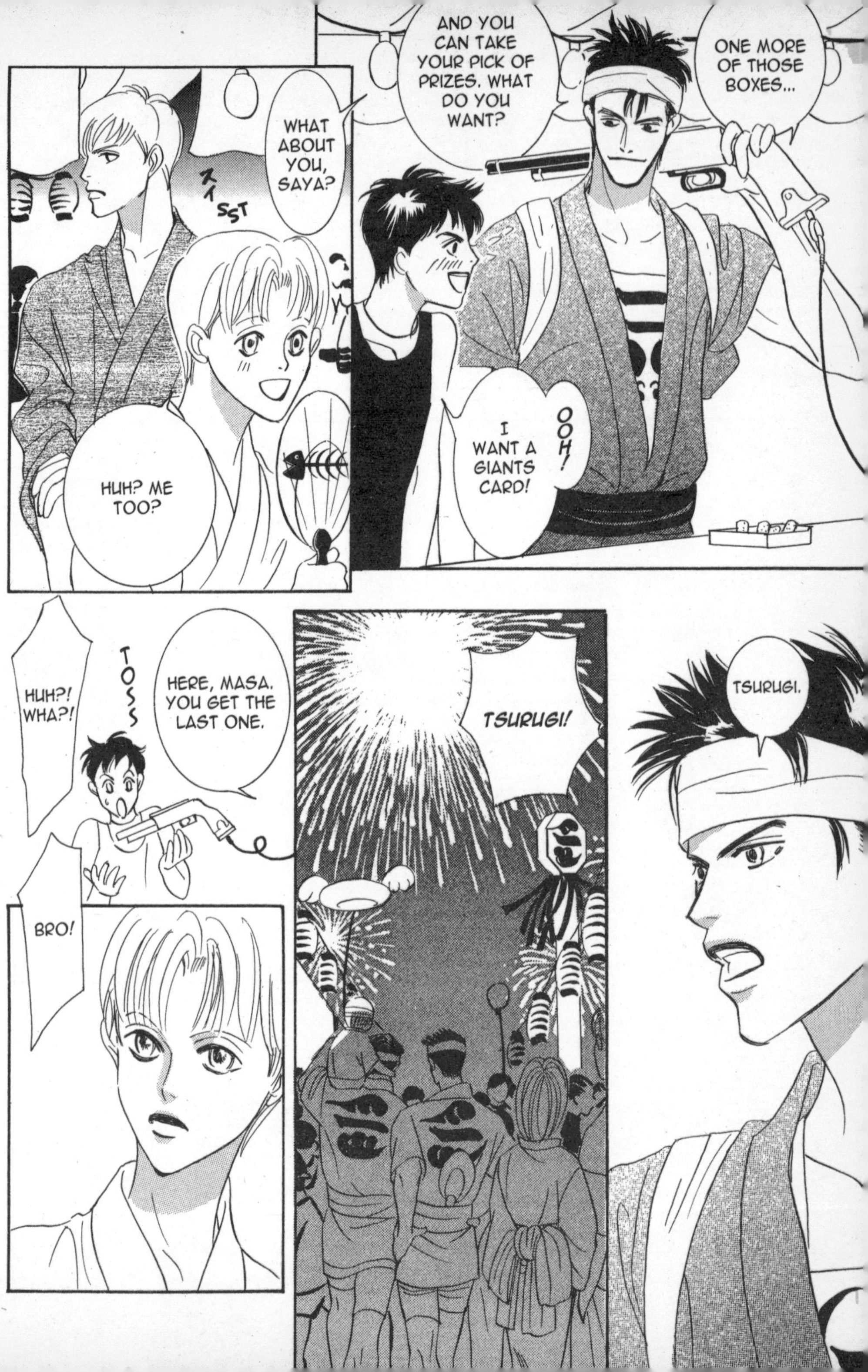
ONE MORE OF THOSE BOXES...
AND YOU CAN TAKE YOUR PICK OF PRIZES. WHAT DO YOU WANT?
OOH!
I WANT A GIANTS CARD!
WHAT ABOUT YOU, SAYA?
SST
HUH? ME TOO?
TSURUGI.
TSURUGI!
HERE, MASA. YOU GET THE LAST ONE.
TOSS
HUH?! WHA?!
BRO!

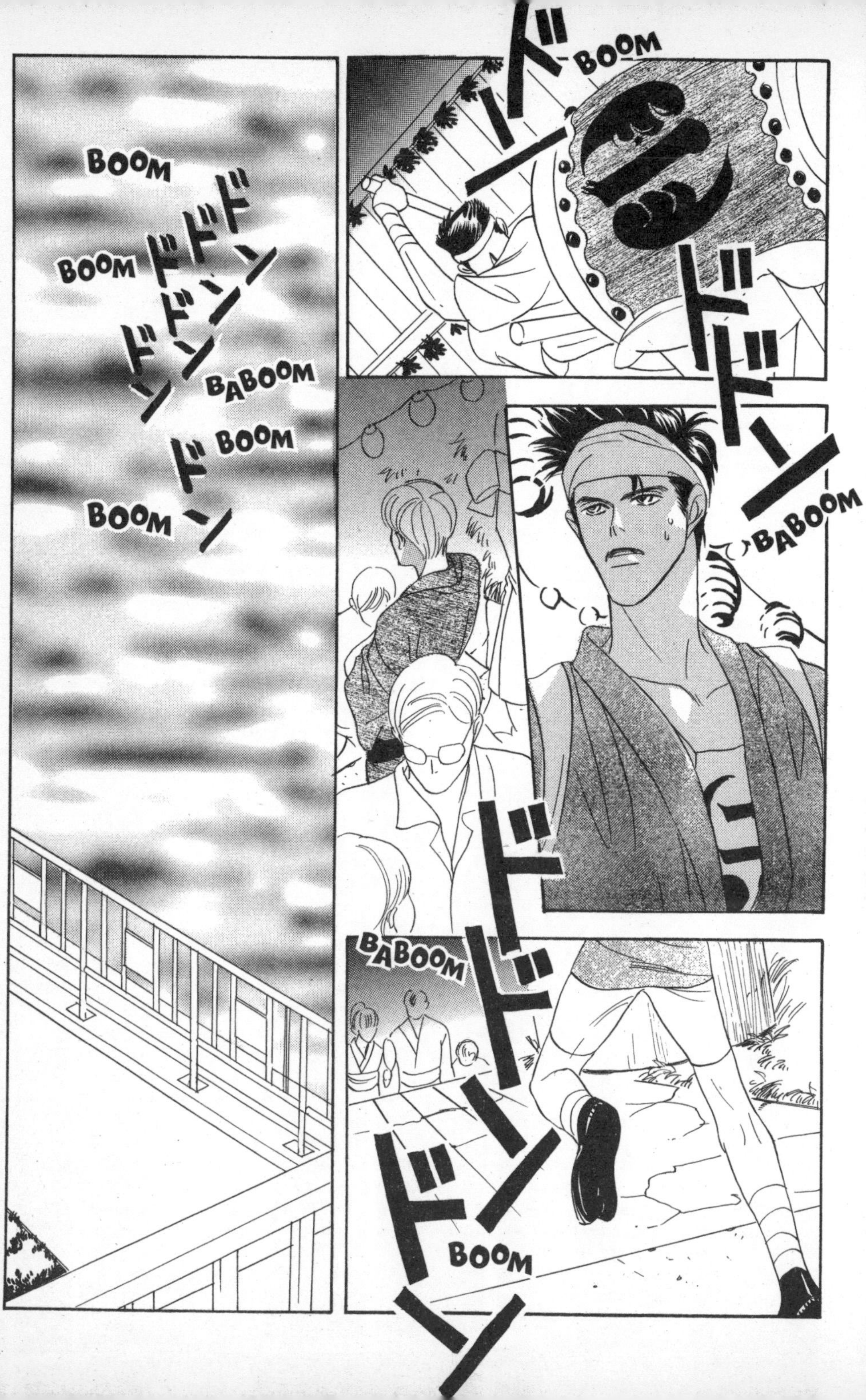

ドーン
BOOM
ドドーン
BABOOM
BABOOM
ドドドーン
BOOM
BOOM
BOOM
ドドドーン
BABOOM
BOOM
ドーン
BOOM

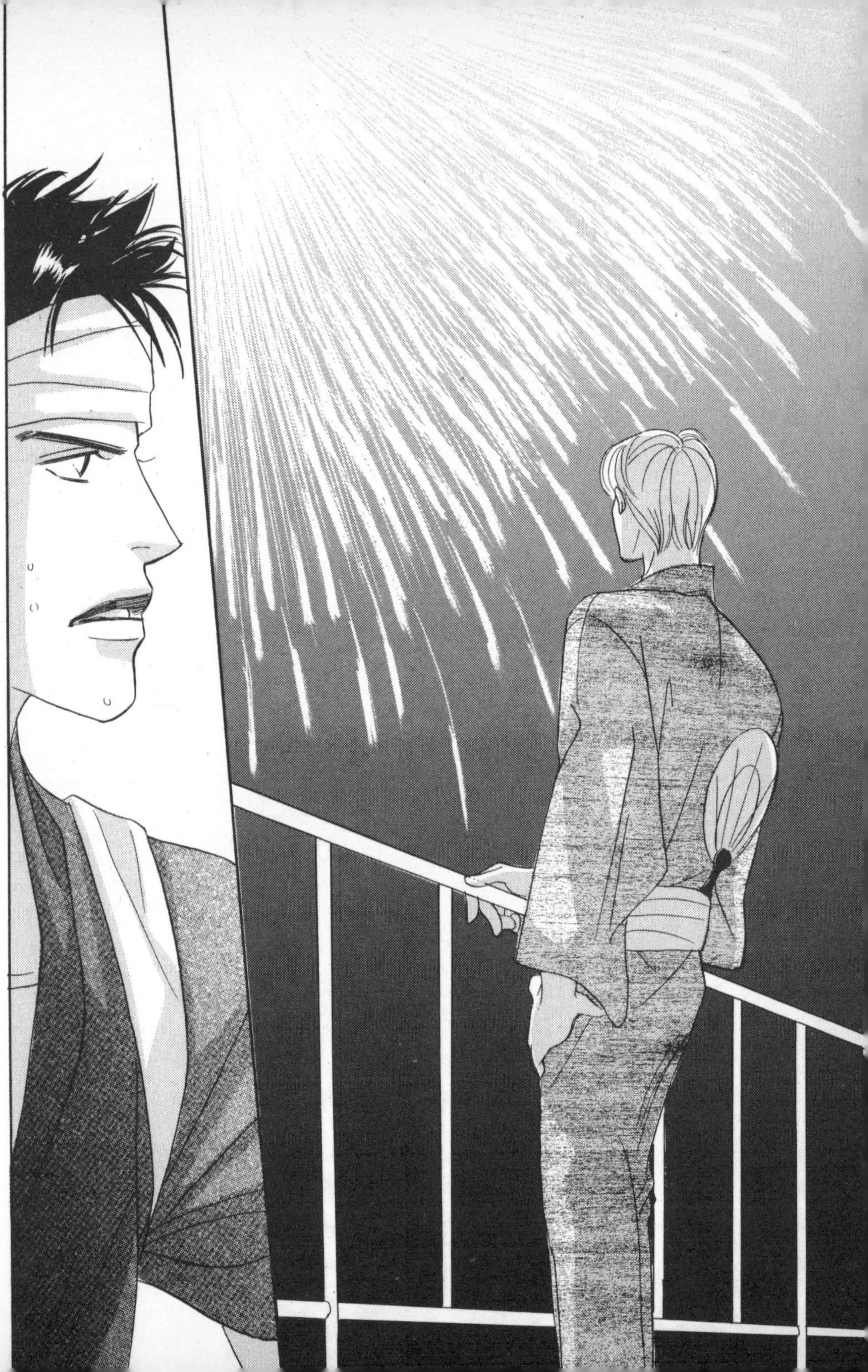

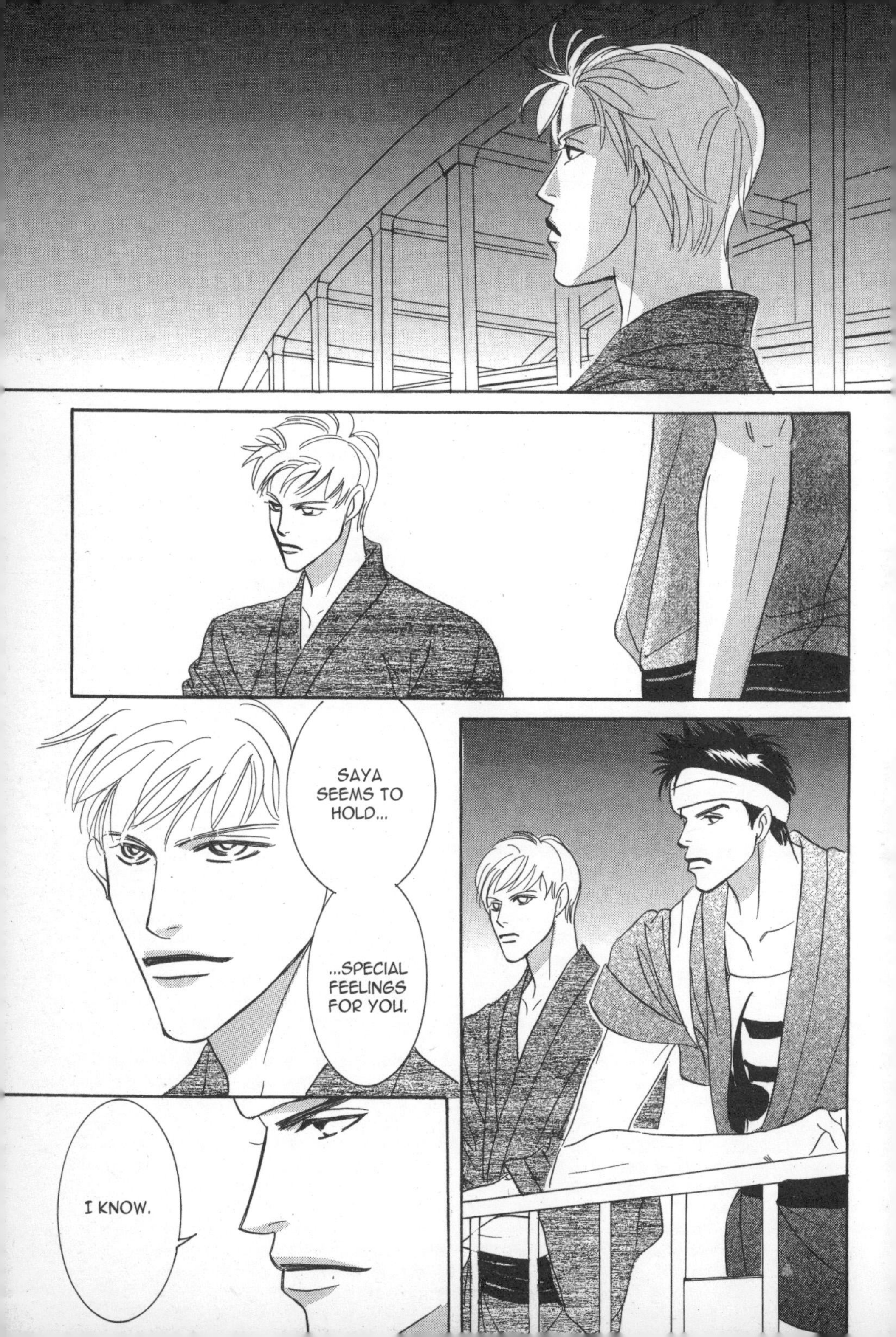
SAYA SEEMS TO HOLD...
...SPECIAL FEELINGS FOR YOU.
I KNOW.

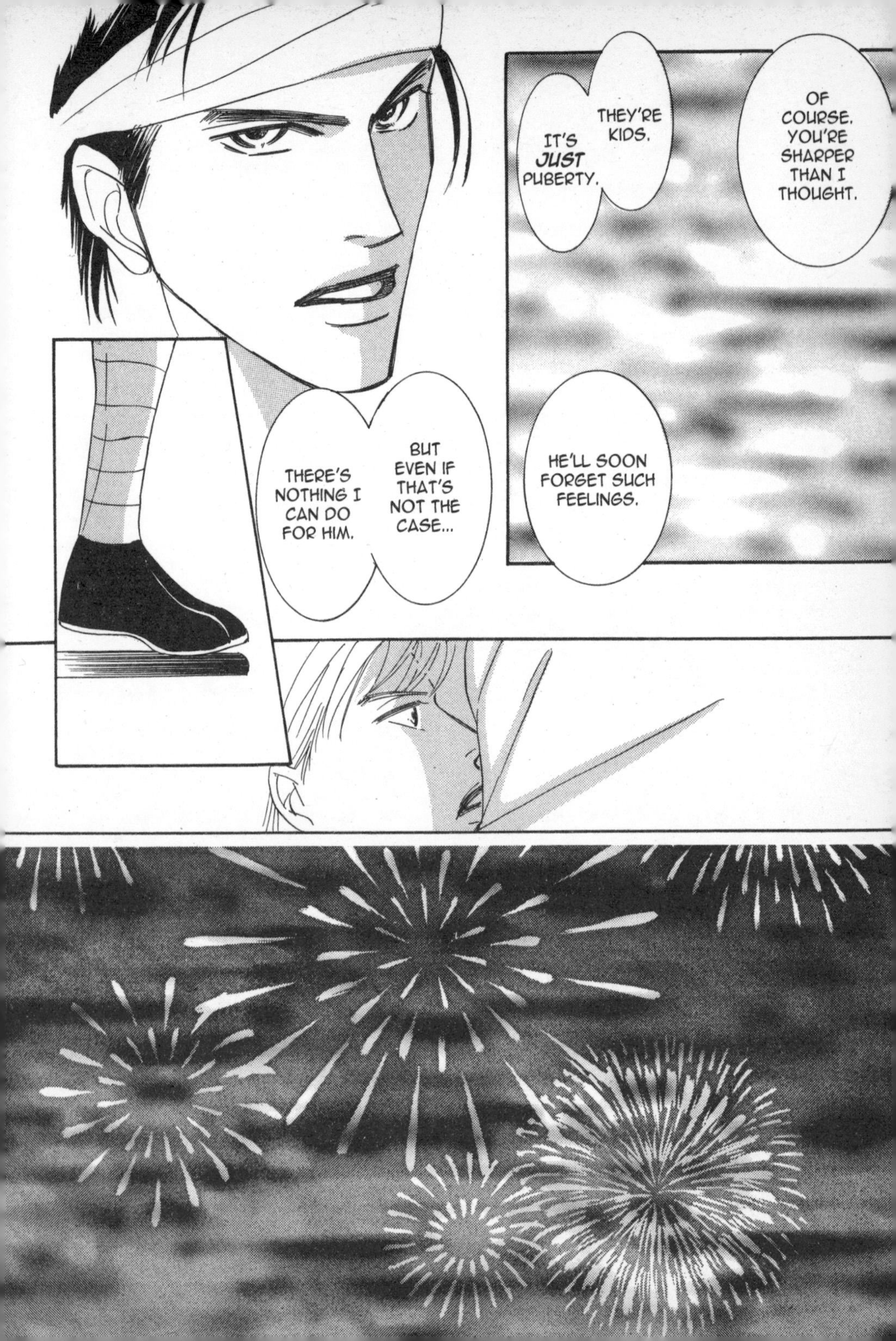
OF COURSE. YOU'RE SHARPER THAN I THOUGHT.
THEY'RE KIDS.
IT'S *JUST* PUBERTY.
HE'LL SOON FORGET SUCH FEELINGS.
BUT EVEN IF THAT'S NOT THE CASE...
THERE'S NOTHING I CAN DO FOR HIM.

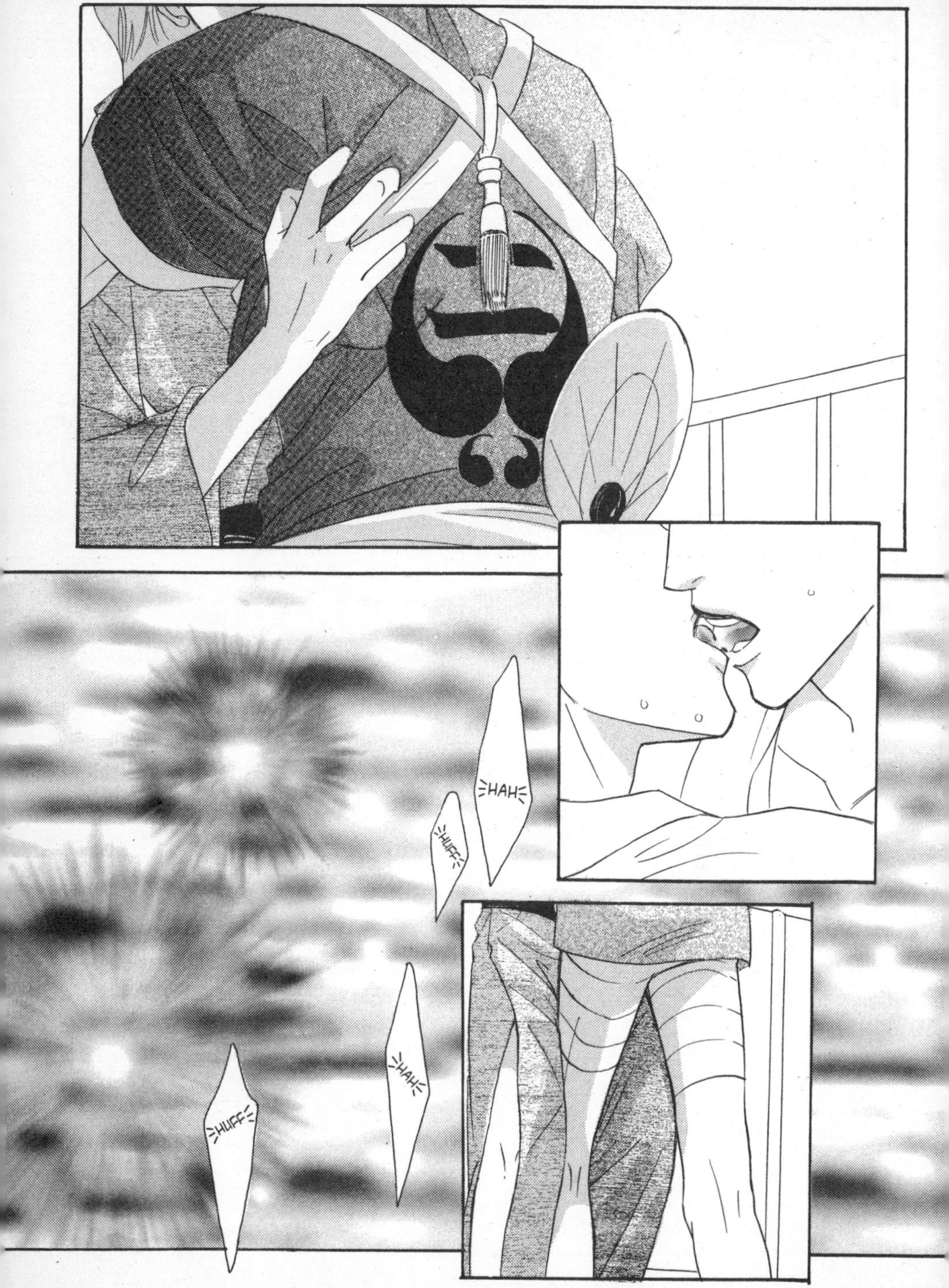
HAH
HUFF
HAH
HUFF

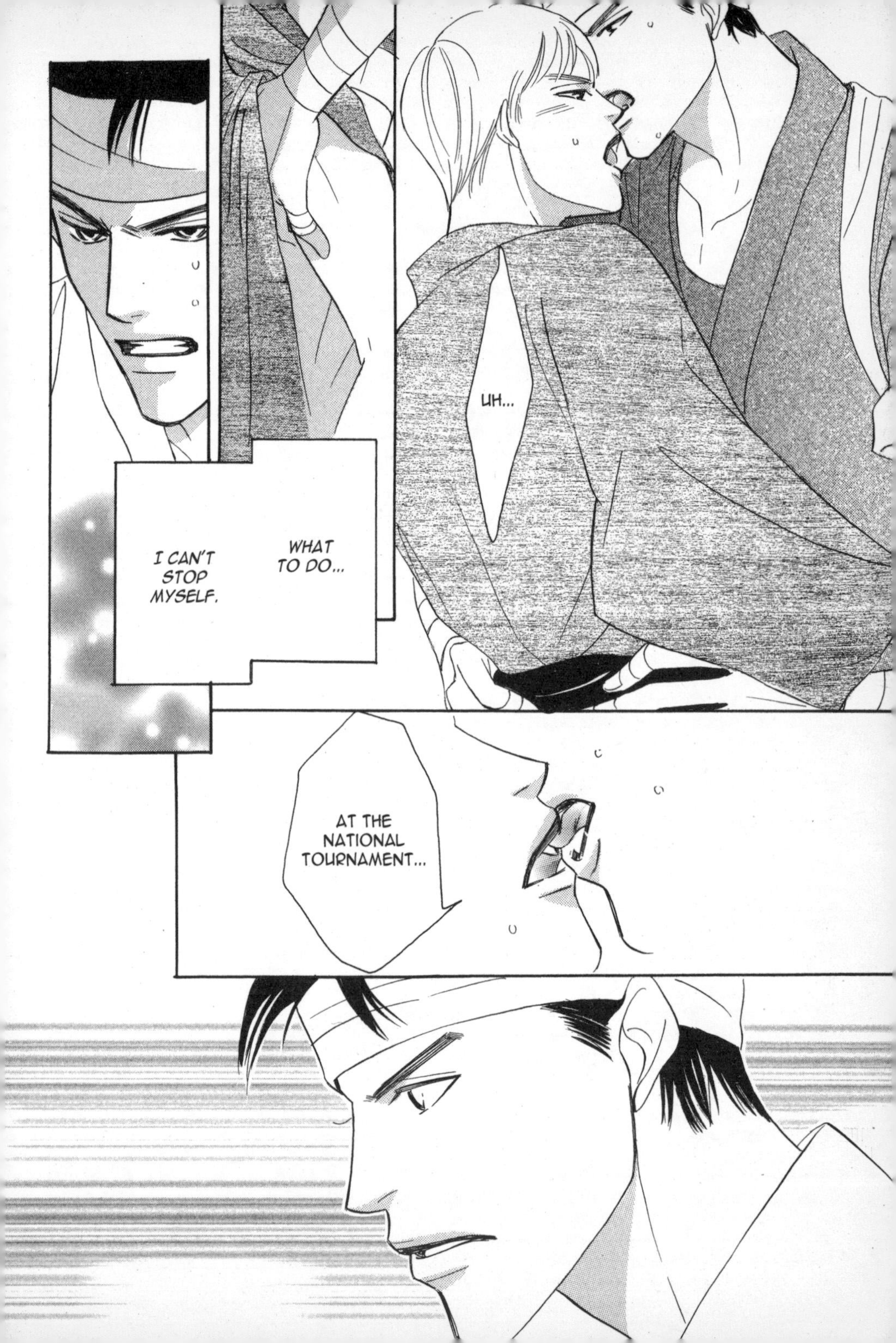
UH...
WHAT TO DO...
I CAN'T STOP MYSELF.
AT THE NATIONAL TOURNAMENT...

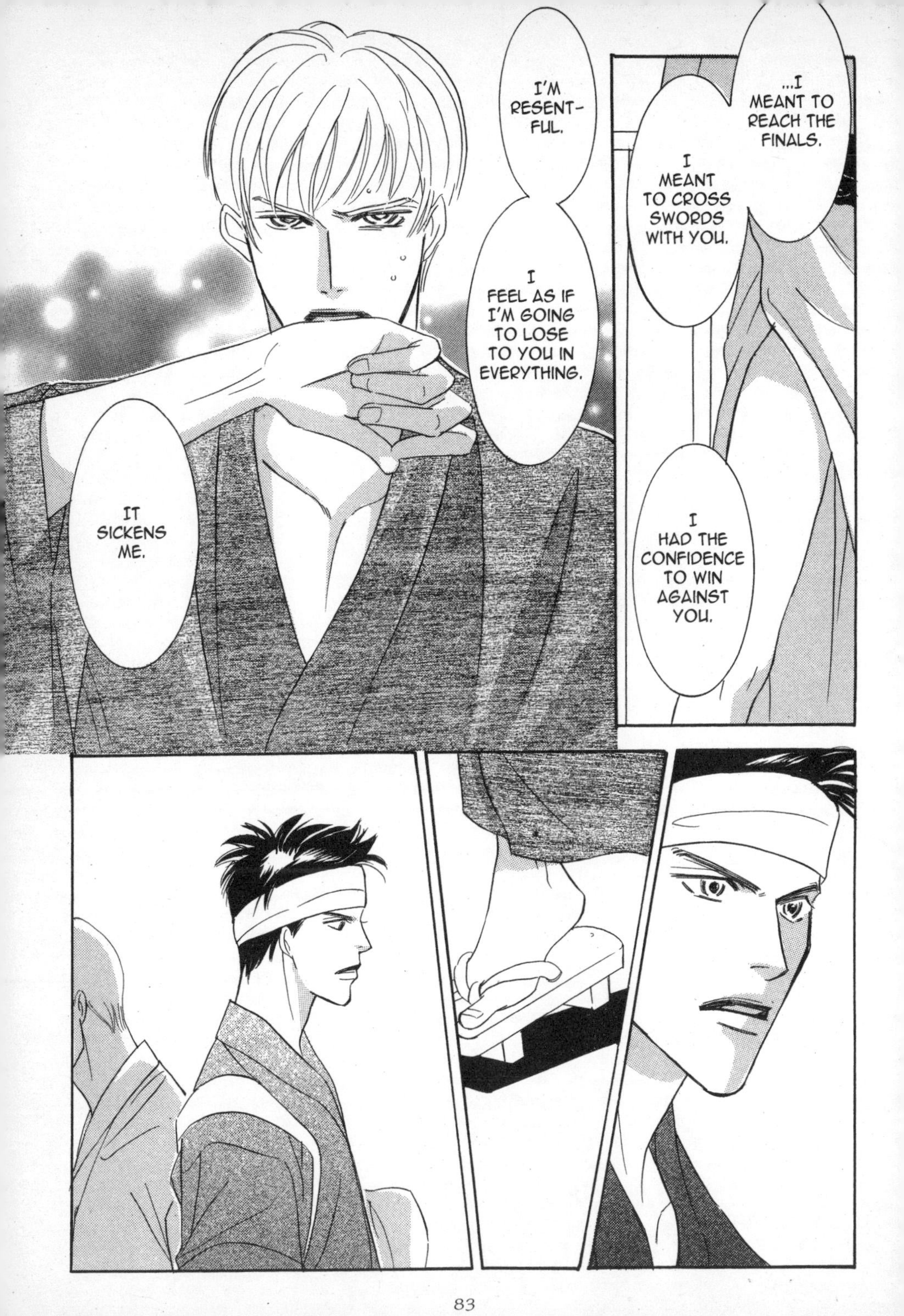
...I MEANT TO REACH THE FINALS.
I MEANT TO CROSS SWORDS WITH YOU.
I HAD THE CONFIDENCE TO WIN AGAINST YOU.
I'M RESENT-FUL.
I FEEL AS IF I'M GOING TO LOSE TO YOU IN EVERYTHING.
IT SICKENS ME.

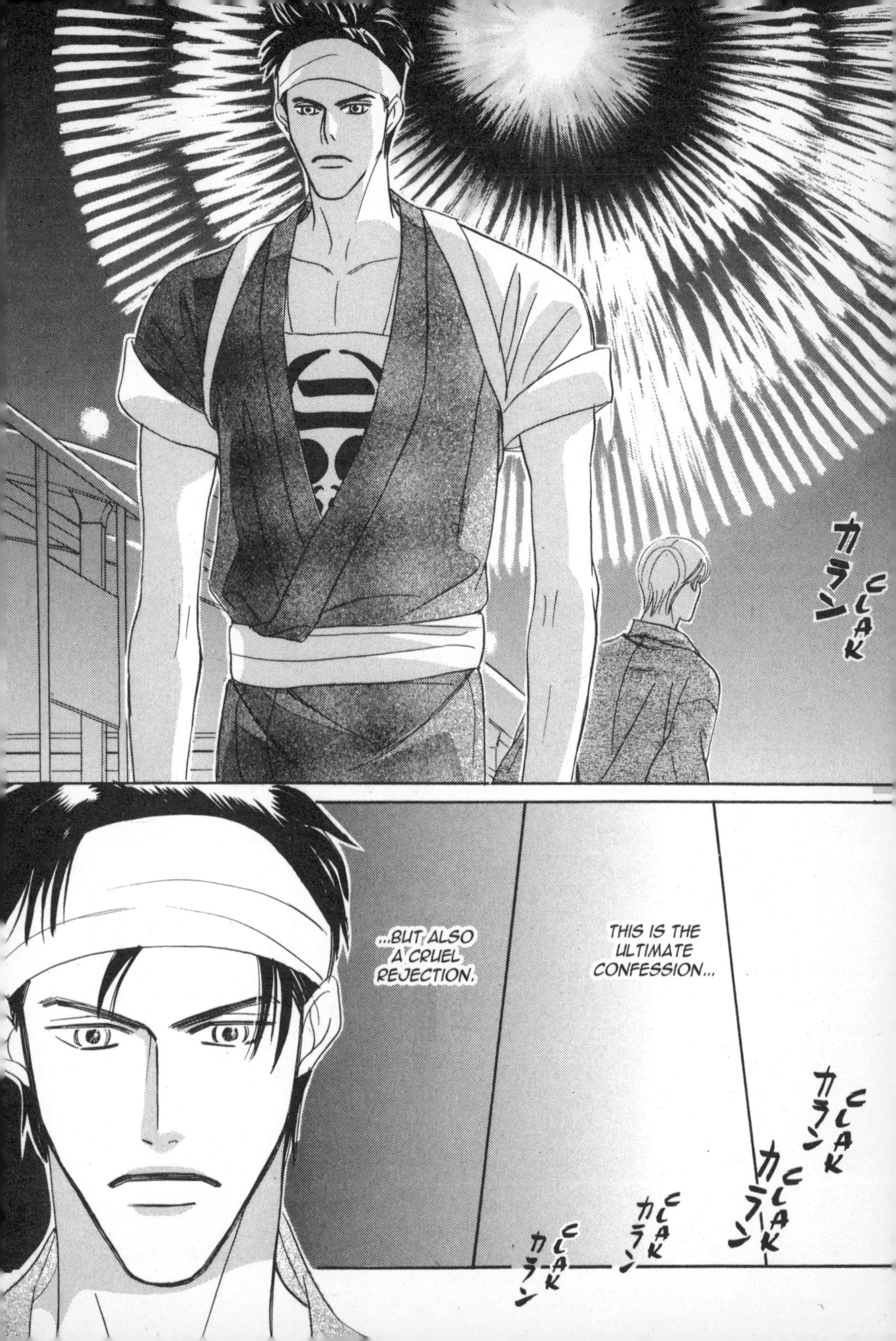
カラン CLAK
THIS IS THE ULTIMATE CONFESSION...
...BUT ALSO A CRUEL REJECTION.
カラン CLAK
カラン CLAK
カラン CLAK
カラン CLAK

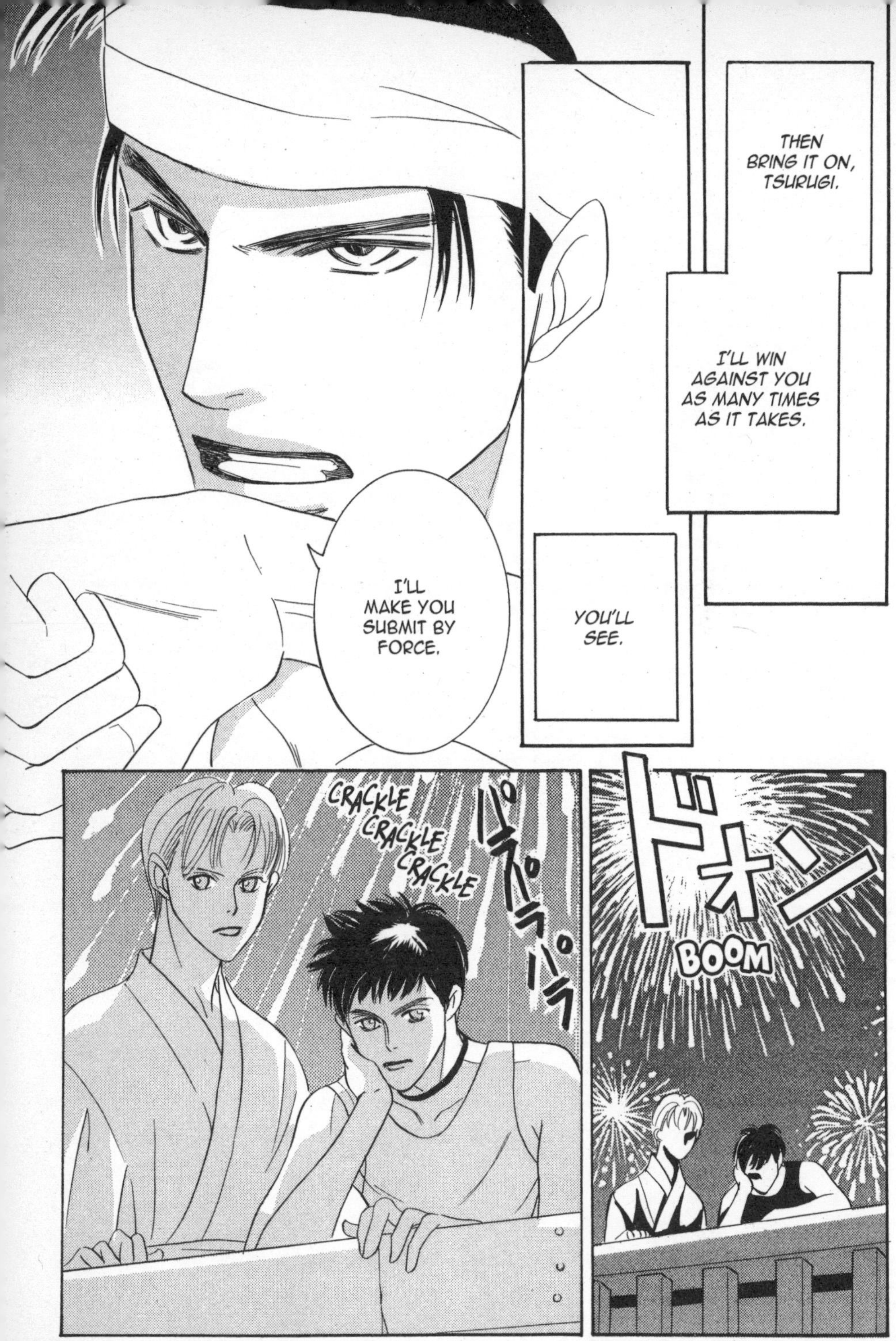
THEN BRING IT ON, TSURUGI.
I'LL WIN AGAINST YOU AS MANY TIMES AS IT TAKES.
YOU'LL SEE.
I'LL MAKE YOU SUBMIT BY FORCE.
ドォン
BOOM
パラパラ
CRACKLE CRACKLE CRACKLE

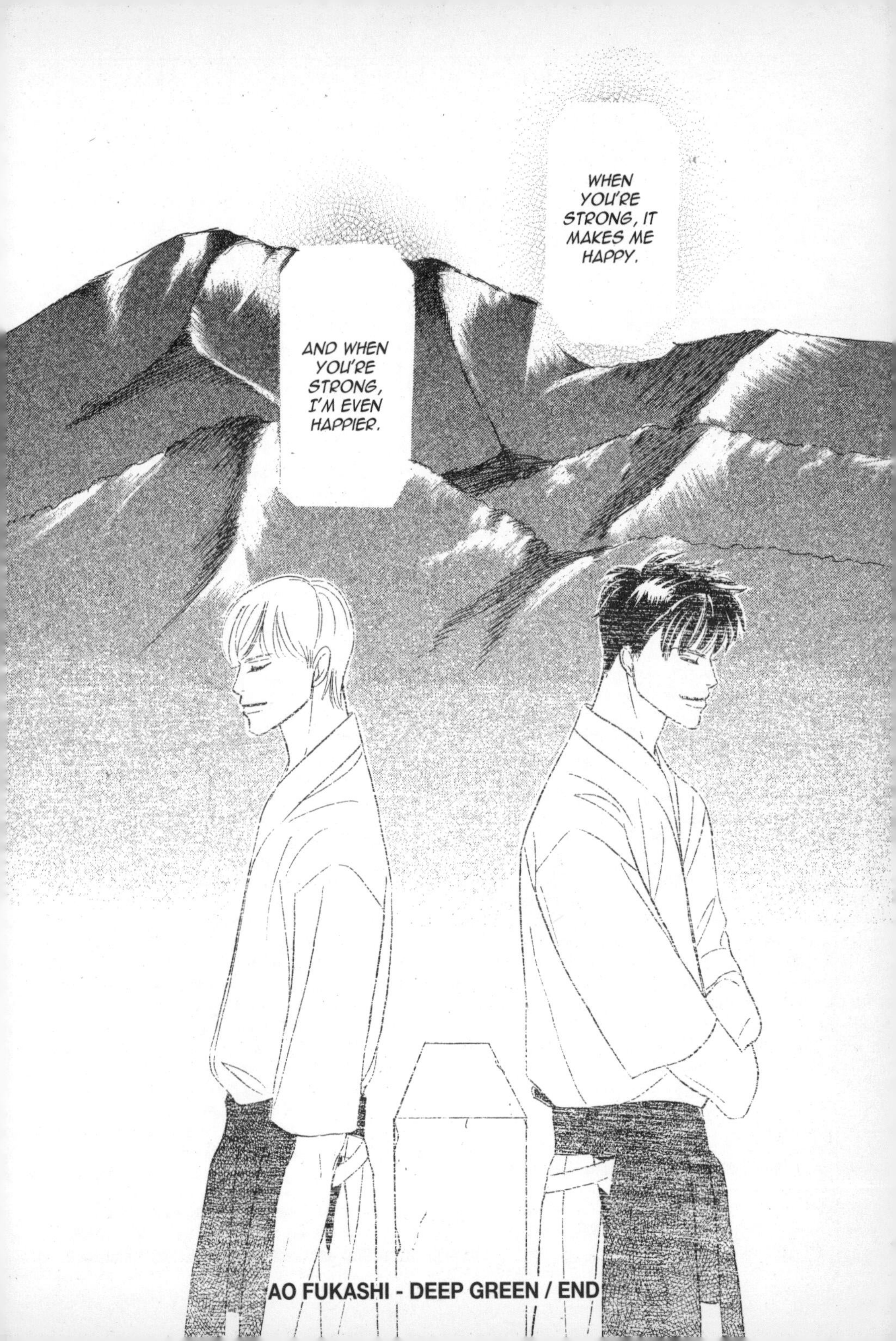
WHEN YOU'RE STRONG, IT MAKES ME HAPPY.
AND WHEN YOU'RE STRONG, I'M EVEN HAPPIER.
AO FUKASHI - DEEP GREEN / END

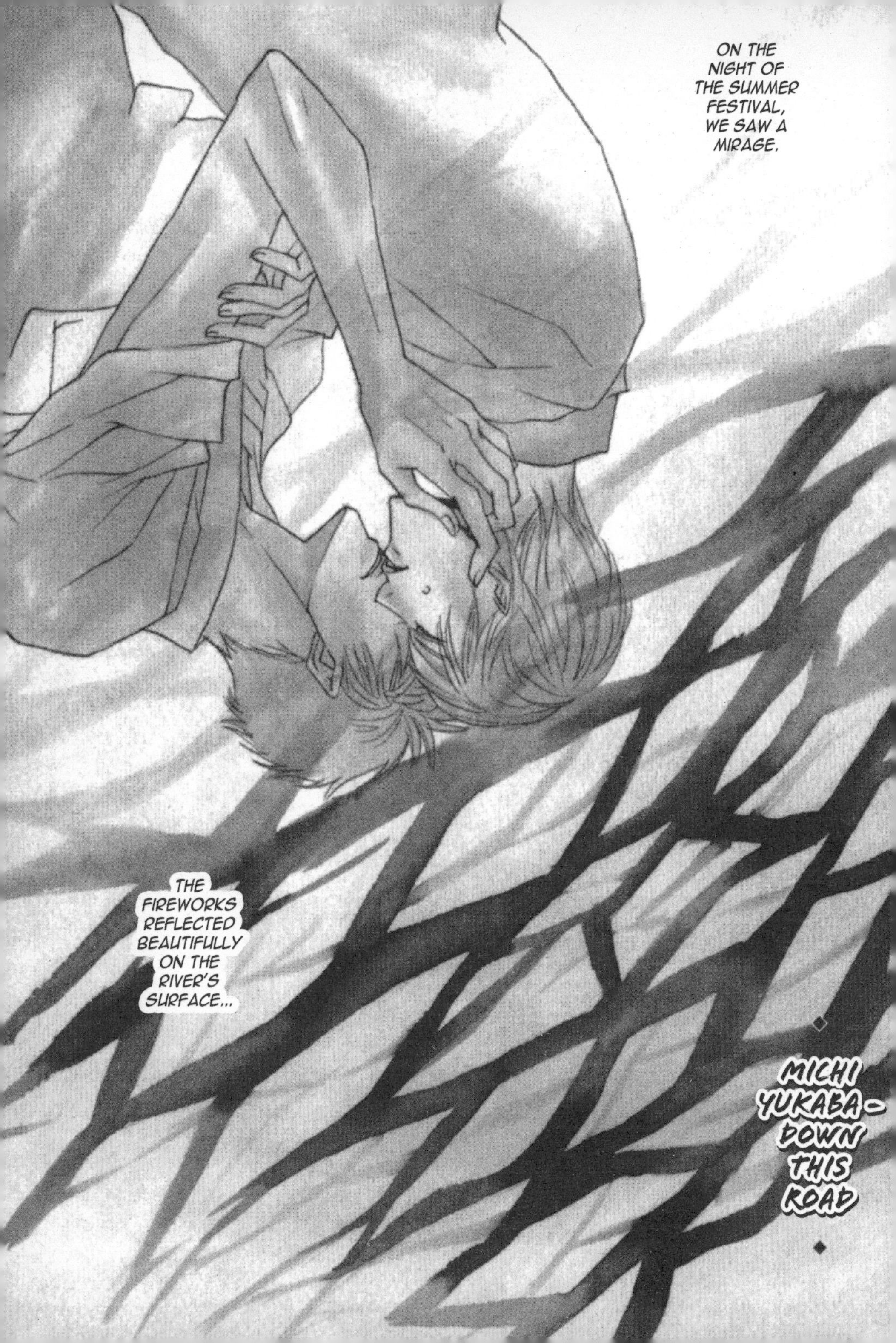
ON THE NIGHT OF THE SUMMER FESTIVAL, WE SAW A MIRAGE.
THE FIREWORKS REFLECTED BEAUTIFULLY ON THE RIVER'S SURFACE...
MICHI YUKABA-DOWN THIS ROAD

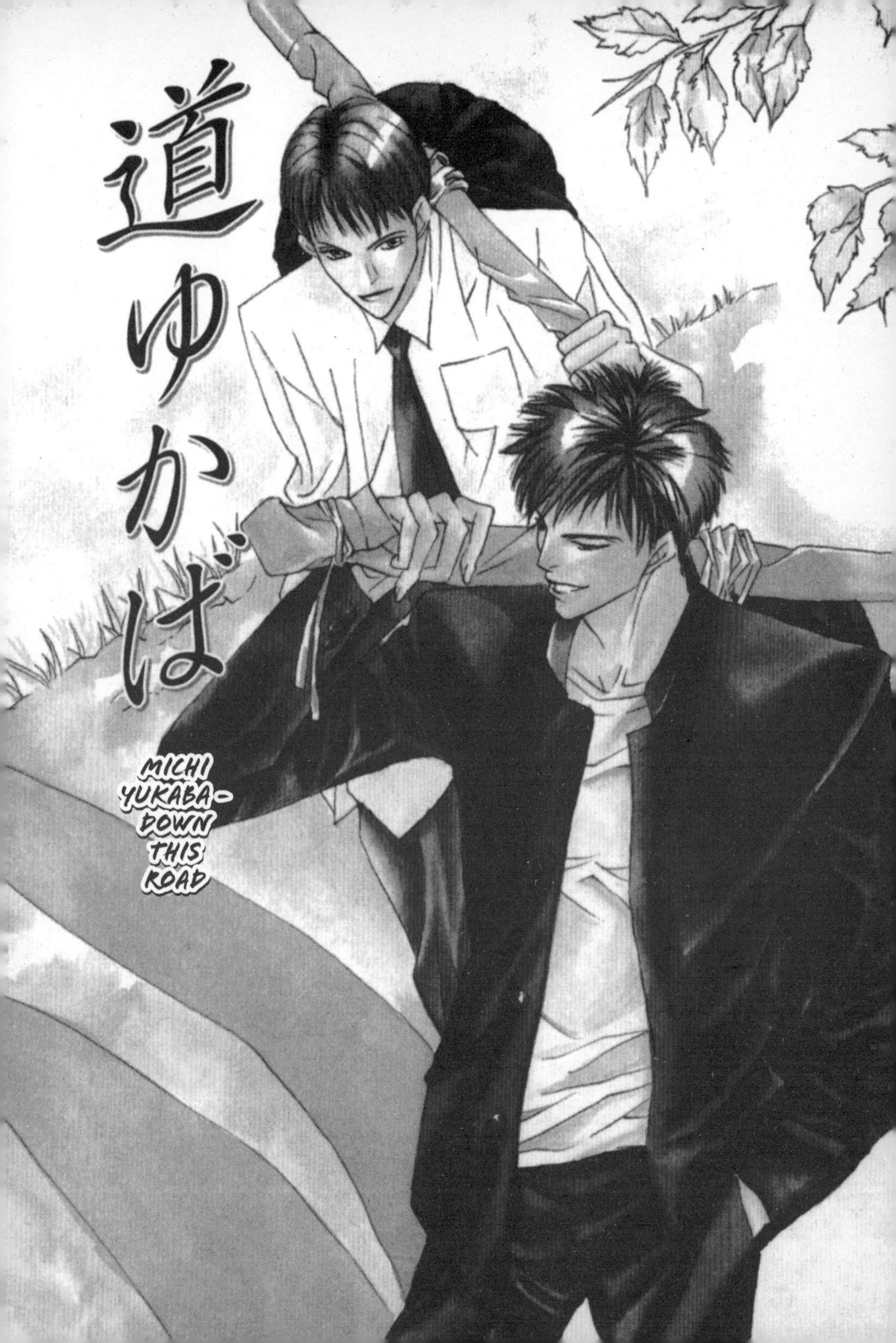
道ゆかば
MICHI YUKABA-
DOWN THIS ROAD

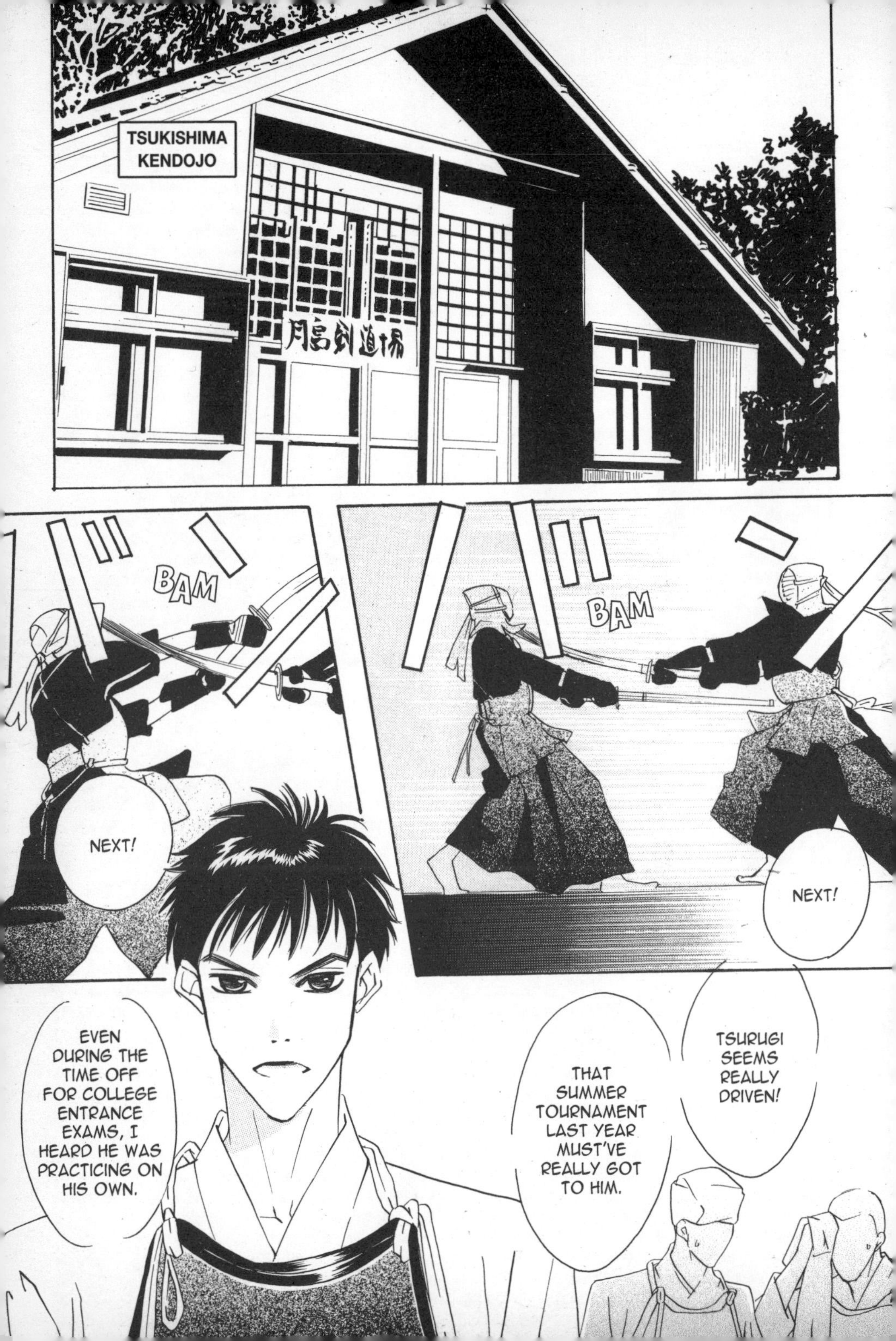
TSUKISHIMA KENDOJO
BAM
NEXT!
BAM
NEXT!
TSURUGI SEEMS REALLY DRIVEN!
THAT SUMMER TOURNAMENT LAST YEAR MUST'VE REALLY GOT TO HIM.
EVEN DURING THE TIME OFF FOR COLLEGE ENTRANCE EXAMS, I HEARD HE WAS PRACTICING ON HIS OWN.

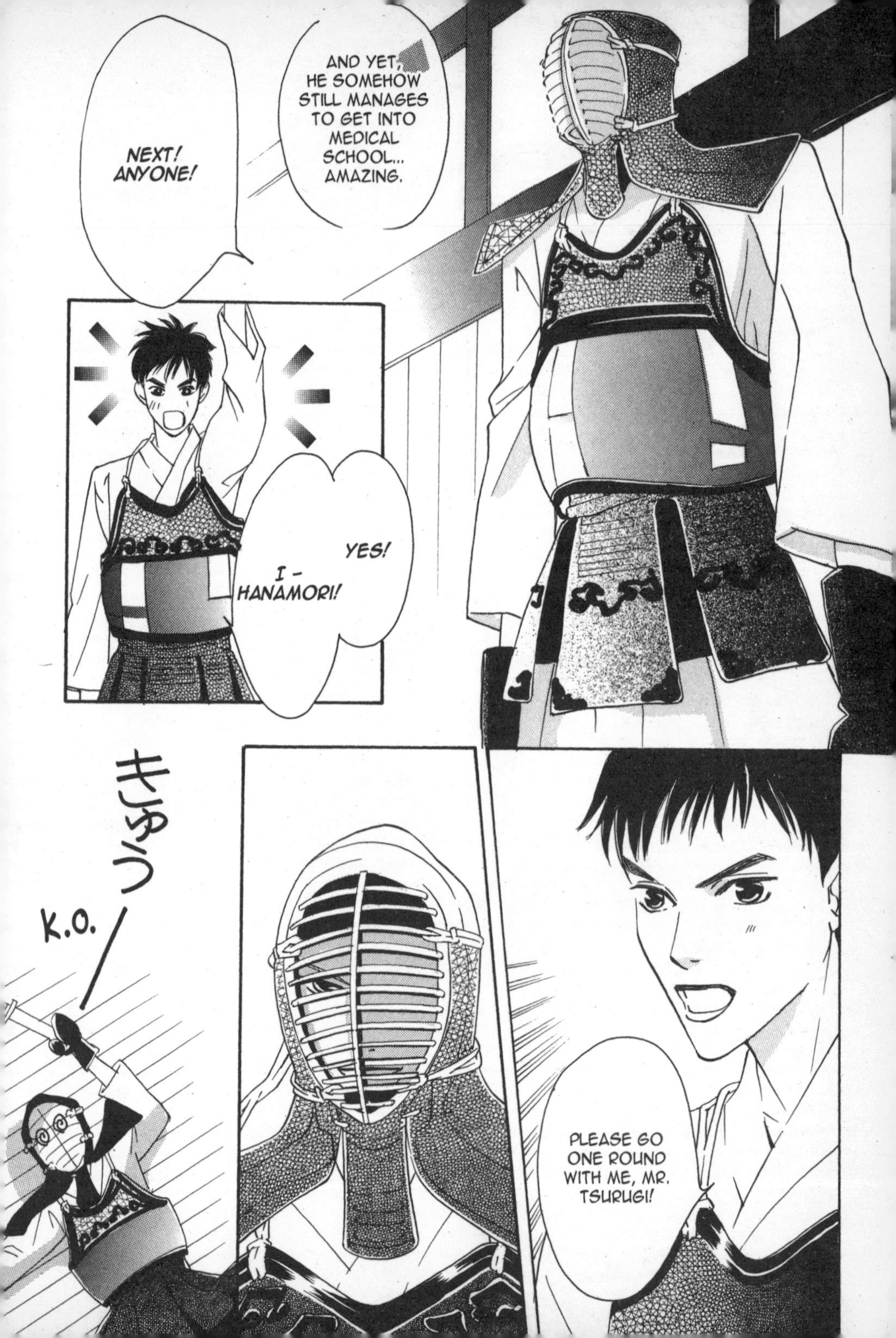
AND YET, HE SOMEHOW STILL MANAGES TO GET INTO MEDICAL SCHOOL... AMAZING.
NEXT! ANYONE!
YES! I - HANAMORI!
PLEASE GO ONE ROUND WITH ME, MR. TSURUGI!
きゅう
K.O.

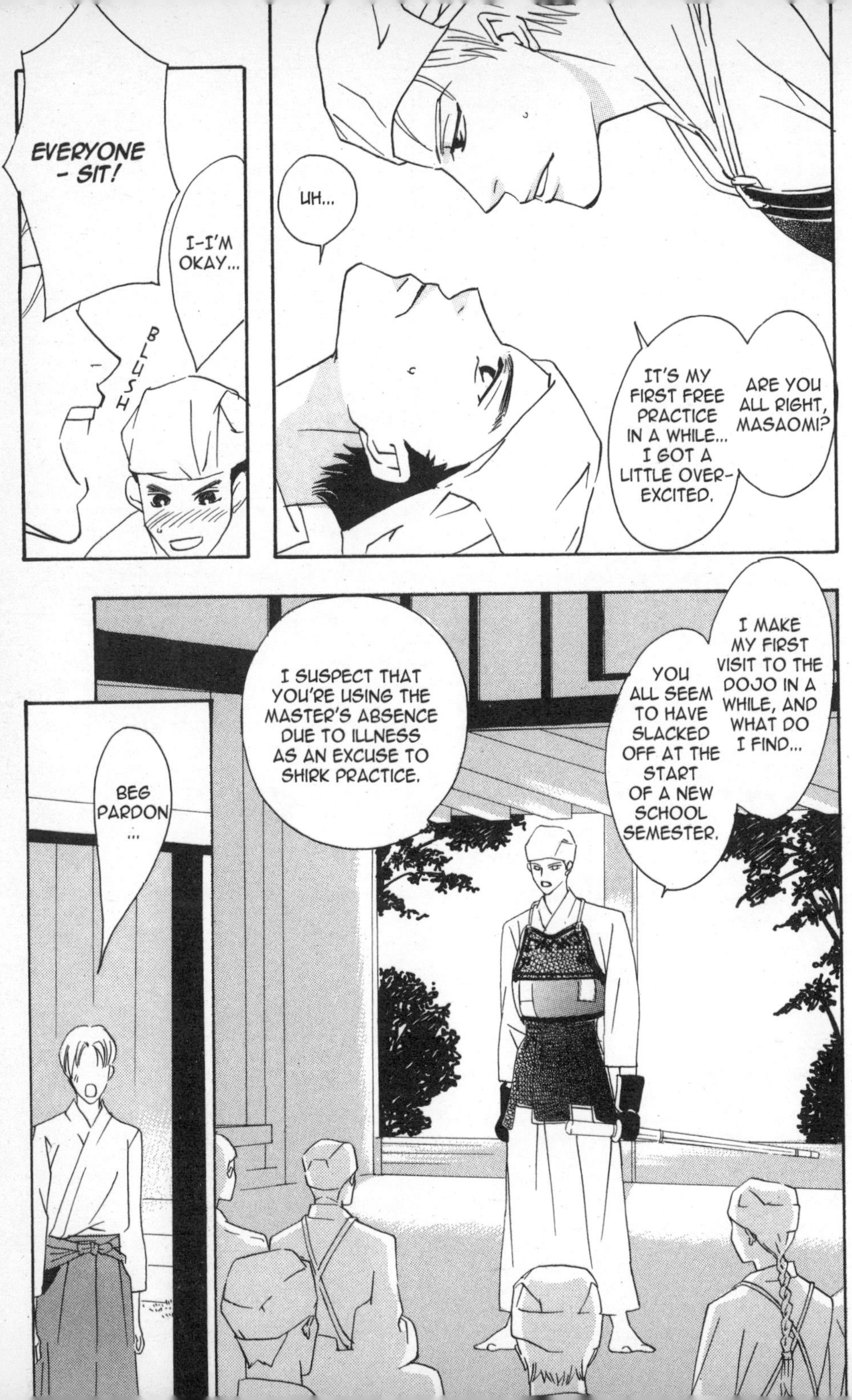
ARE YOU ALL RIGHT, MASAOMI?
UH...
IT'S MY FIRST FREE PRACTICE IN A WHILE... I GOT A LITTLE OVER-EXCITED.
I-I'M OKAY...
BLUSH
EVERYONE - SIT!
I MAKE MY FIRST VISIT TO THE DOJO IN A WHILE, AND WHAT DO I FIND...
YOU ALL SEEM TO HAVE SLACKED OFF AT THE START OF A NEW SCHOOL SEMESTER.
I SUSPECT THAT YOU'RE USING THE MASTER'S ABSENCE DUE TO ILLNESS AS AN EXCUSE TO SHIRK PRACTICE.
BEG PARDON ...

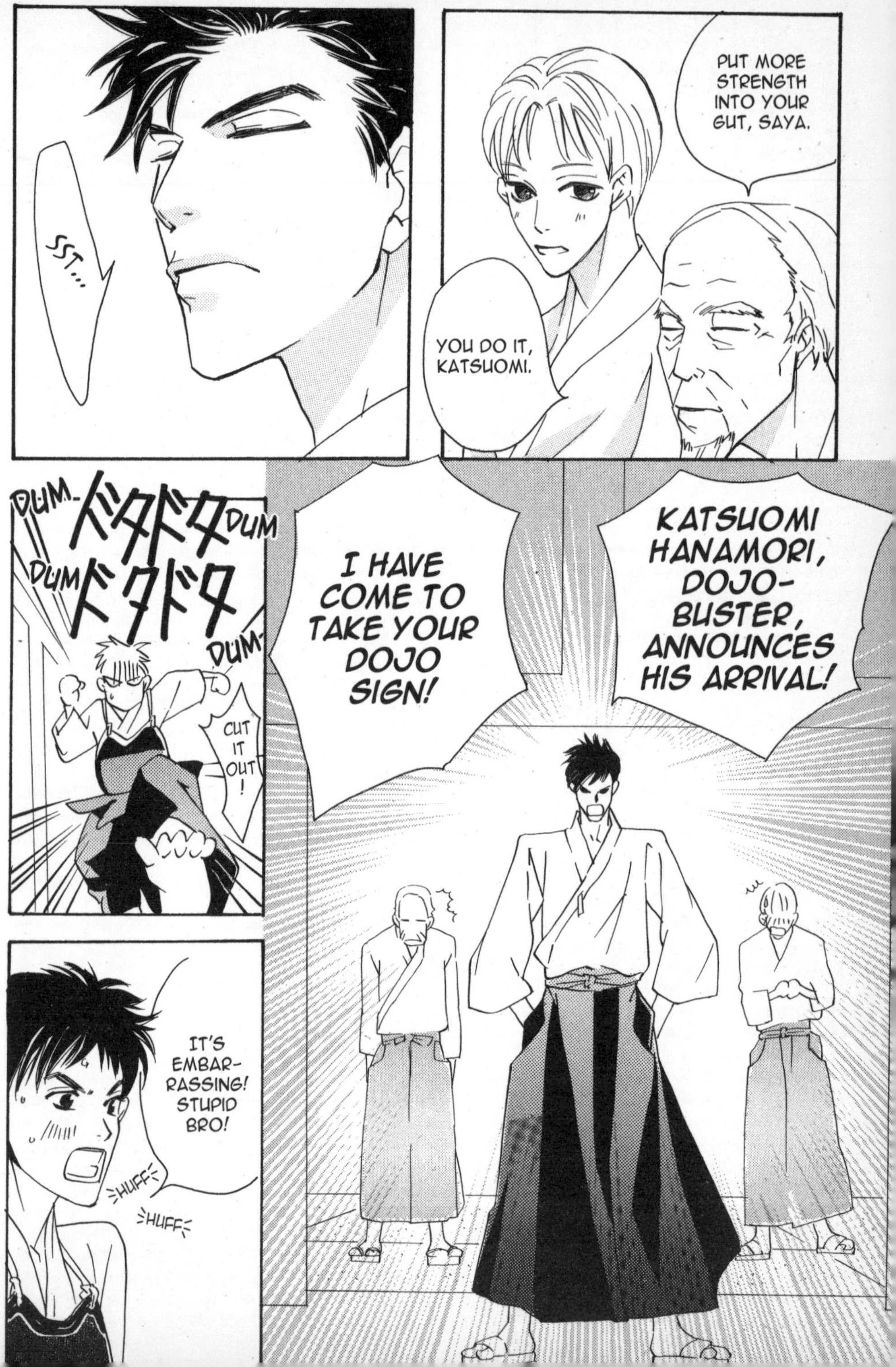
PUT MORE STRENGTH INTO YOUR GUT, SAYA.
YOU DO IT, KATSUOMI.
SST...
KATSUOMI HANAMORI, DOJO-BUSTER, ANNOUNCES HIS ARRIVAL!
I HAVE COME TO TAKE YOUR DOJO SIGN!
DUM-ドタドタDUM
DUMドタドタ
DUM-
CUT IT OUT!
IT'S EMBARRASSING! STUPID BRO!
HUFF
HUFF

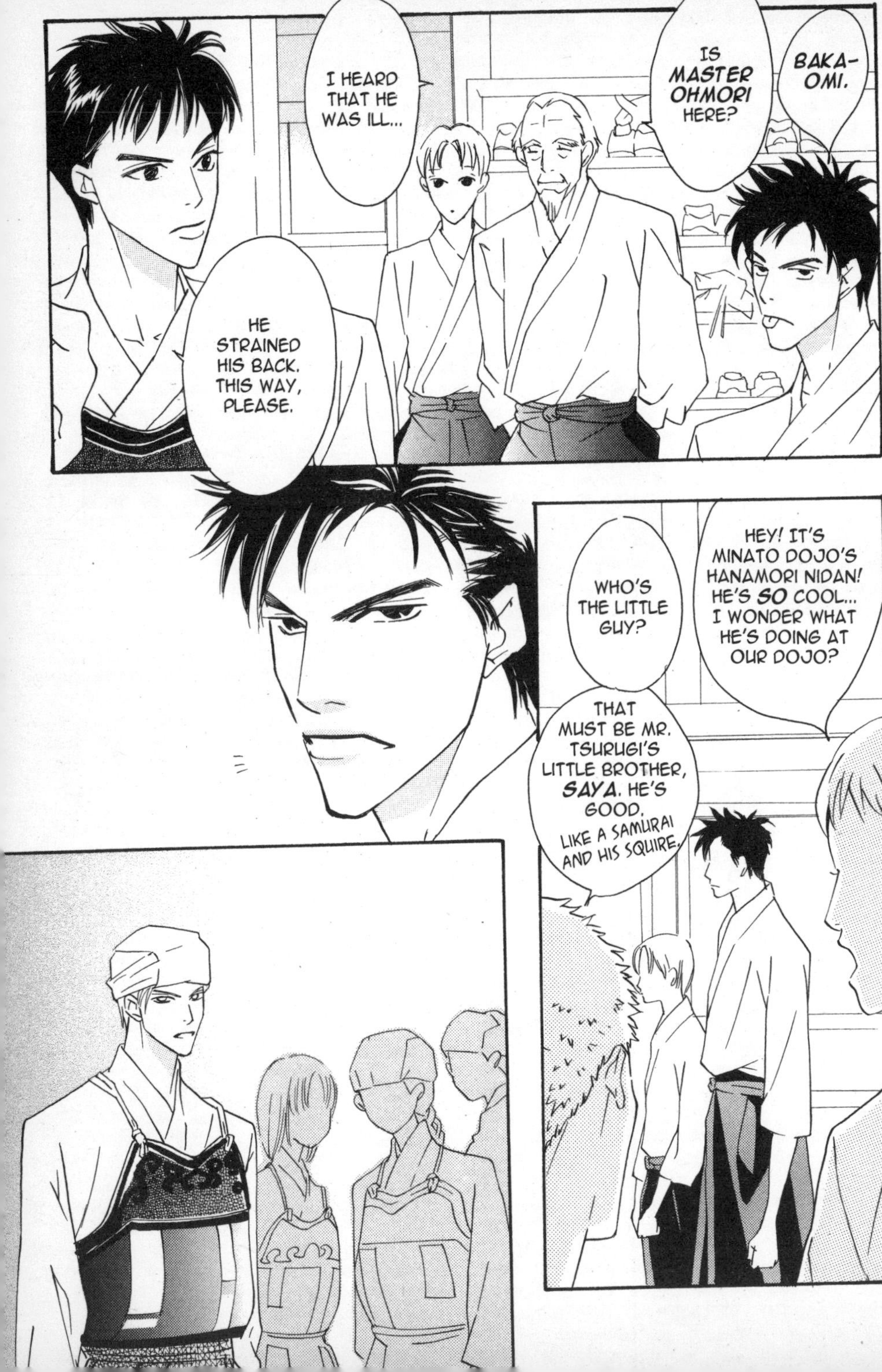
BAKA-OMI.
IS MASTER OHMORI HERE?
I HEARD THAT HE WAS ILL...
HE STRAINED HIS BACK. THIS WAY, PLEASE.
HEY! IT'S MINATO DOJO'S HANAMORI NIDAN! HE'S SO COOL... I WONDER WHAT HE'S DOING AT OUR DOJO?
WHO'S THE LITTLE GUY?
THAT MUST BE MR. TSURUGI'S LITTLE BROTHER, SAYA. HE'S GOOD. LIKE A SAMURAI AND HIS SQUIRE.

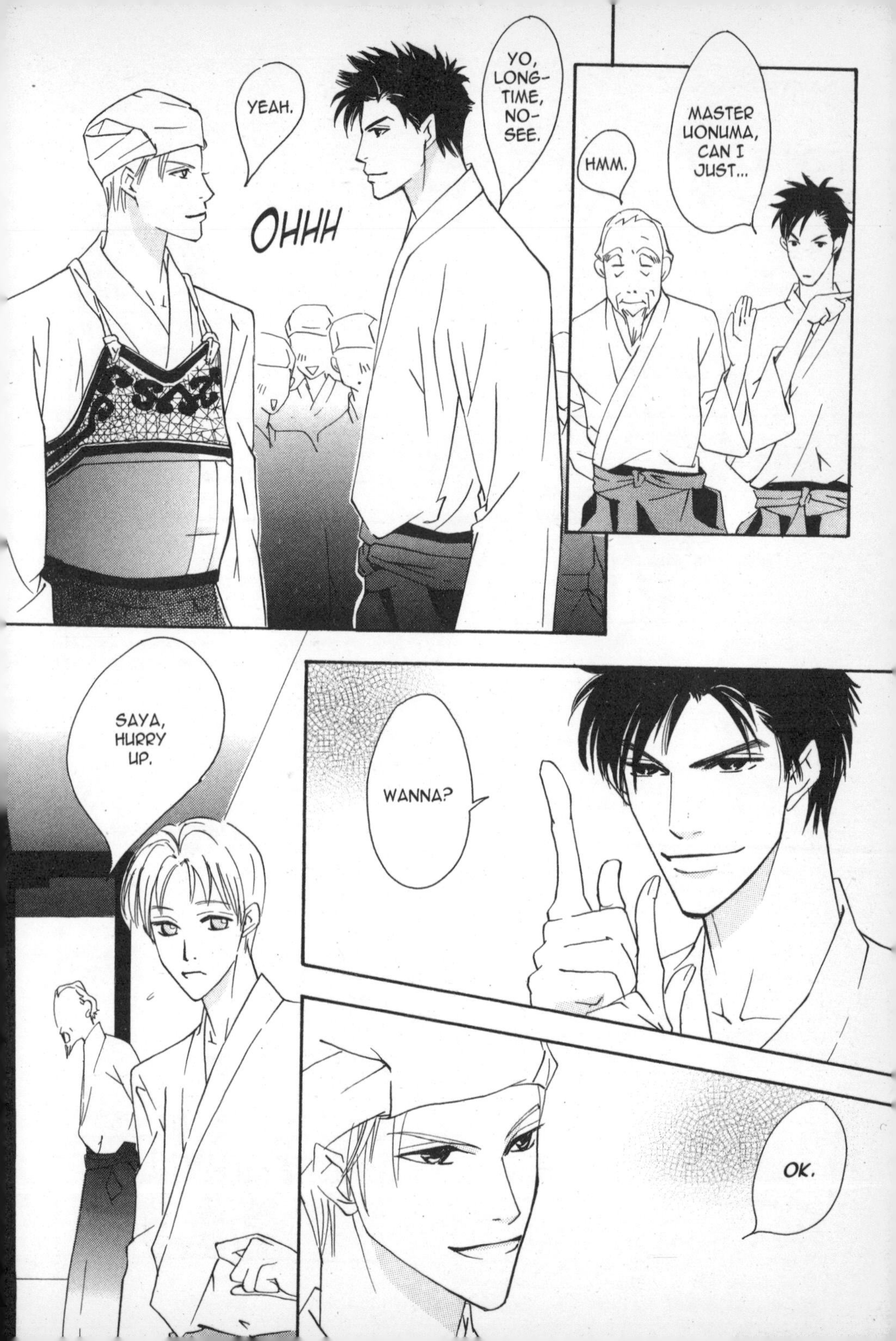
MASTER UONUMA, CAN I JUST...
HMM.
YO, LONG-TIME, NO-SEE.
YEAH.
OHHH
WANNA?
OK.
SAYA, HURRY UP.

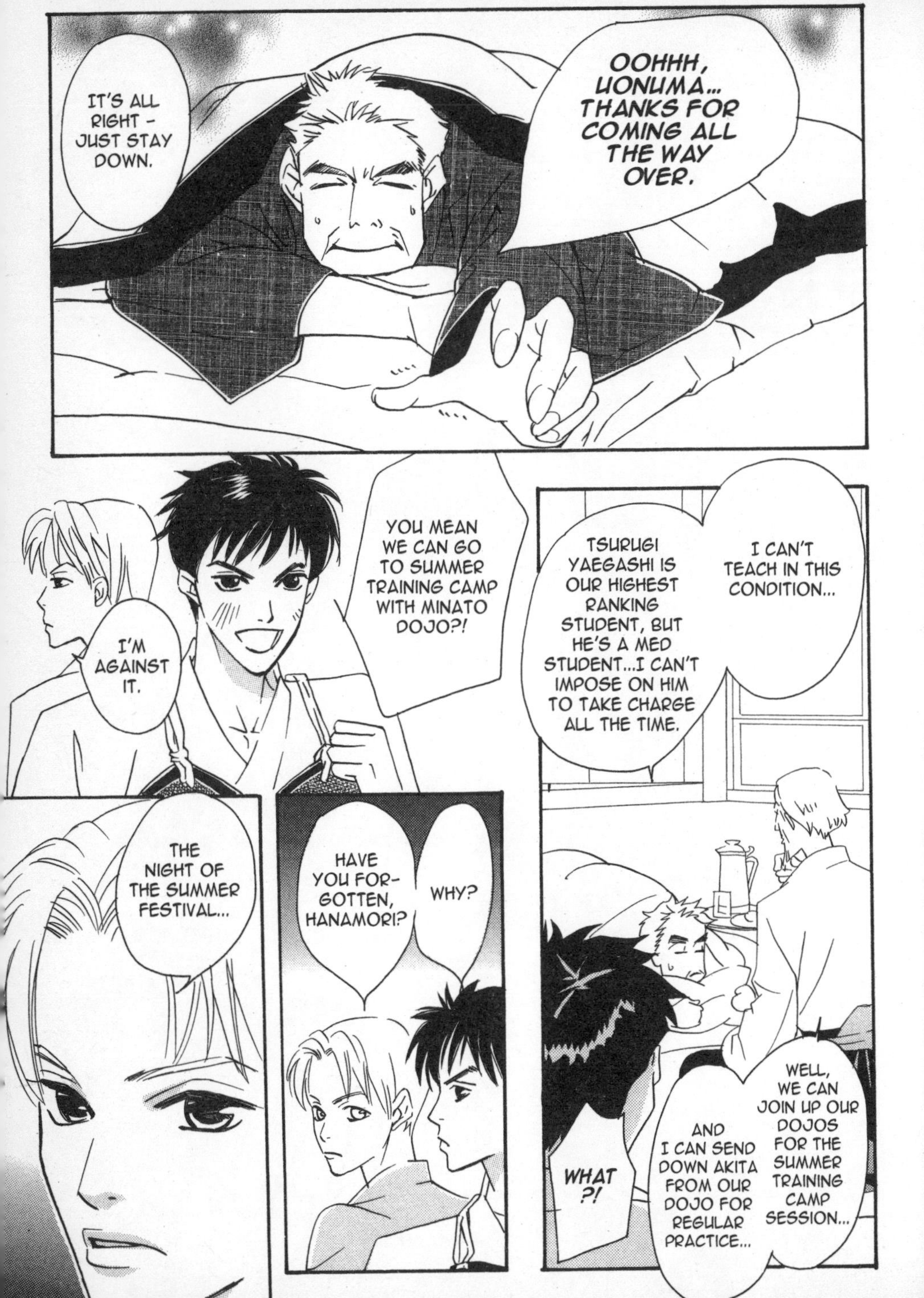
OOHHH, UONUMA... THANKS FOR COMING ALL THE WAY OVER.
IT'S ALL RIGHT - JUST STAY DOWN.
I CAN'T TEACH IN THIS CONDITION...
TSURUGI YAEGASHI IS OUR HIGHEST RANKING STUDENT, BUT HE'S A MED STUDENT...I CAN'T IMPOSE ON HIM TO TAKE CHARGE ALL THE TIME.
WELL, WE CAN JOIN UP OUR DOJOS FOR THE SUMMER TRAINING CAMP SESSION...
AND I CAN SEND DOWN AKITA FROM OUR DOJO FOR REGULAR PRACTICE...
WHAT?!
YOU MEAN WE CAN GO TO SUMMER TRAINING CAMP WITH MINATO DOJO?!
I'M AGAINST IT.
WHY?
HAVE YOU FOR-GOTTEN, HANAMORI?
THE NIGHT OF THE SUMMER FESTIVAL...

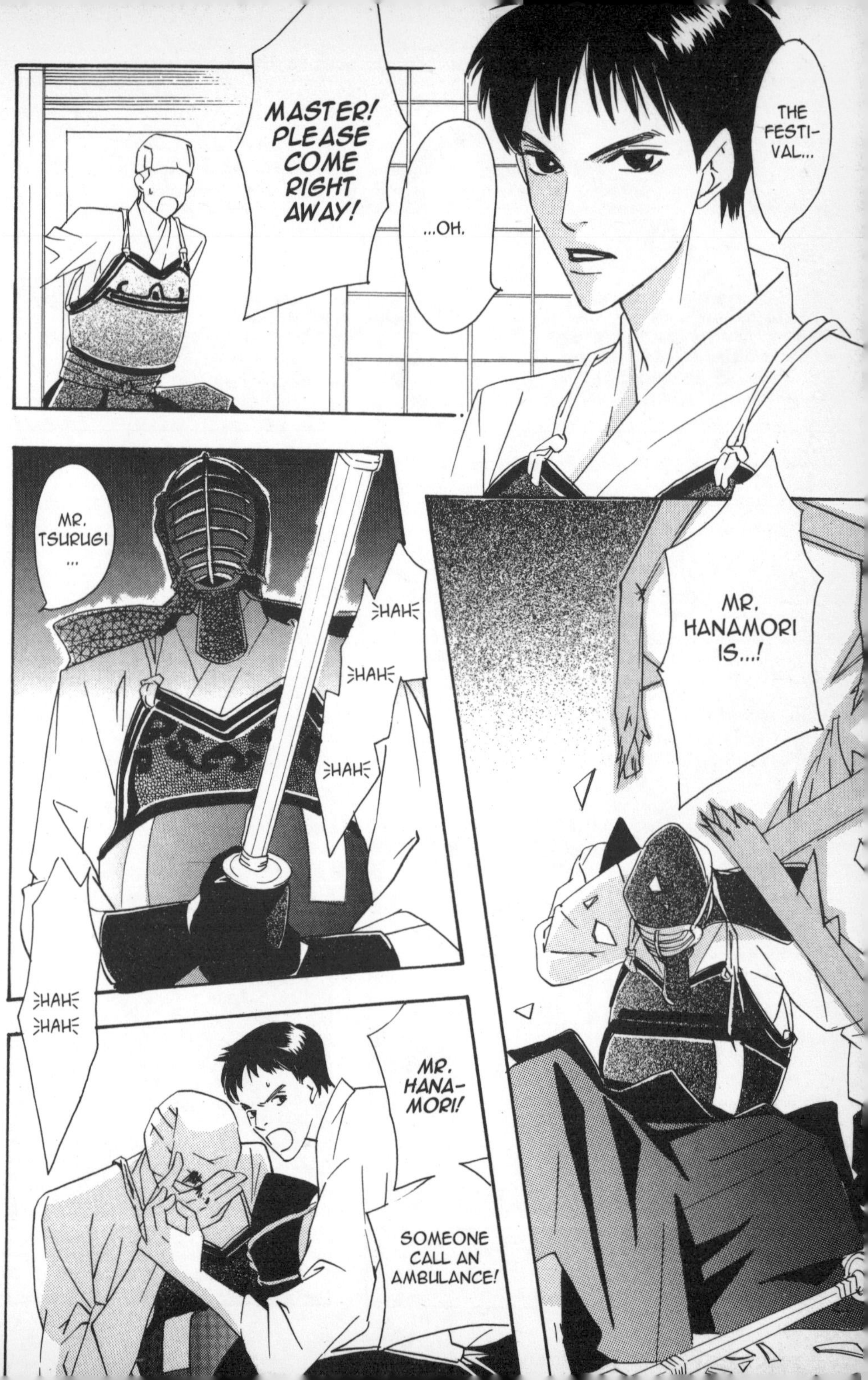
THE FESTI-VAL...
...OH.
MASTER! PLEASE COME RIGHT AWAY!
MR. HANAMORI IS...!
MR. TSURUGI ...
HAH
HAH
HAH
MR. HANA-MORI!
SOMEONE CALL AN AMBULANCE!
HAH HAH

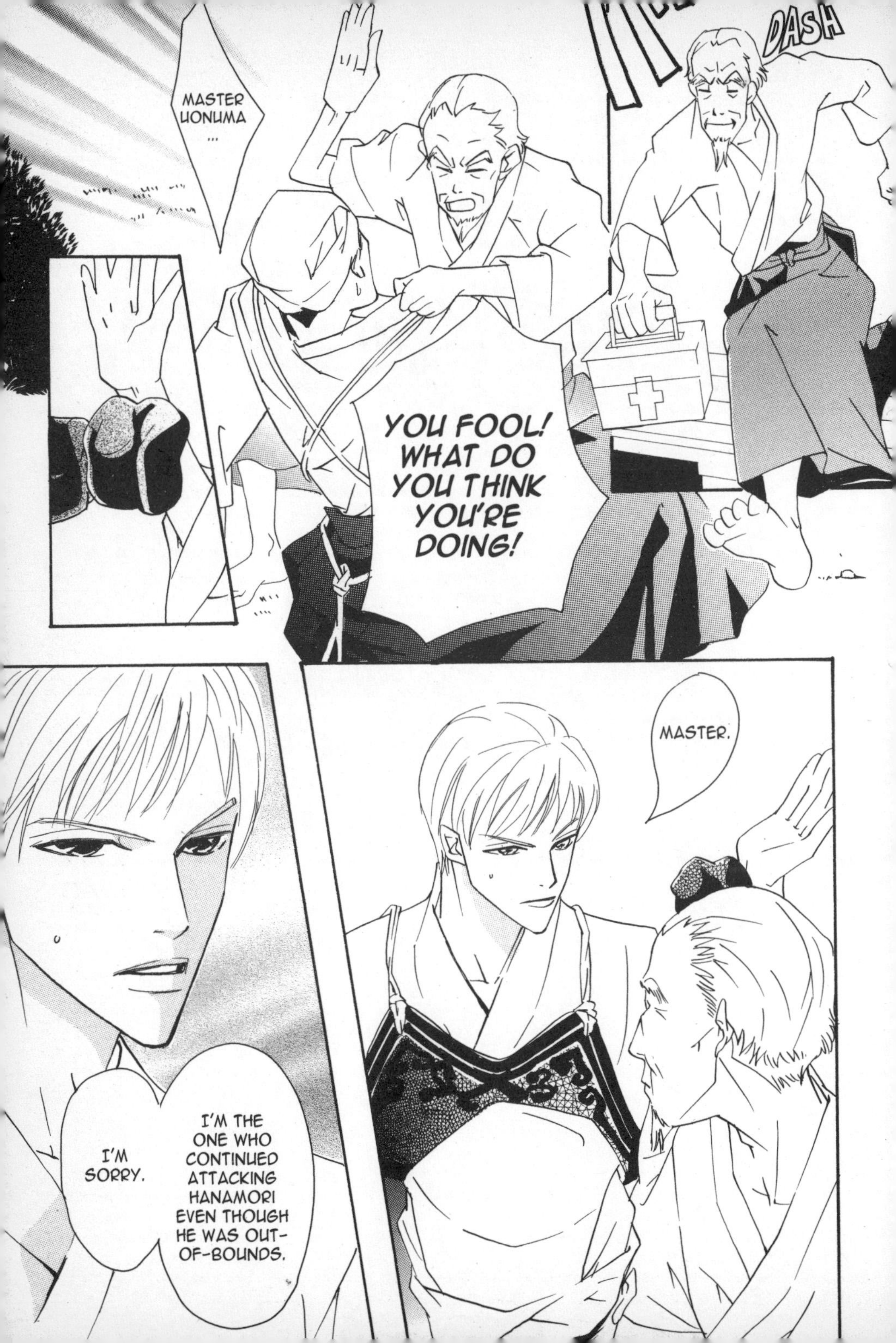
DASH
MASTER UONUMA ...
YOU FOOL! WHAT DO YOU THINK YOU'RE DOING!
MASTER.
I'M THE ONE WHO CONTINUED ATTACKING HANAMORI EVEN THOUGH HE WAS OUT-OF-BOUNDS.
I'M SORRY.

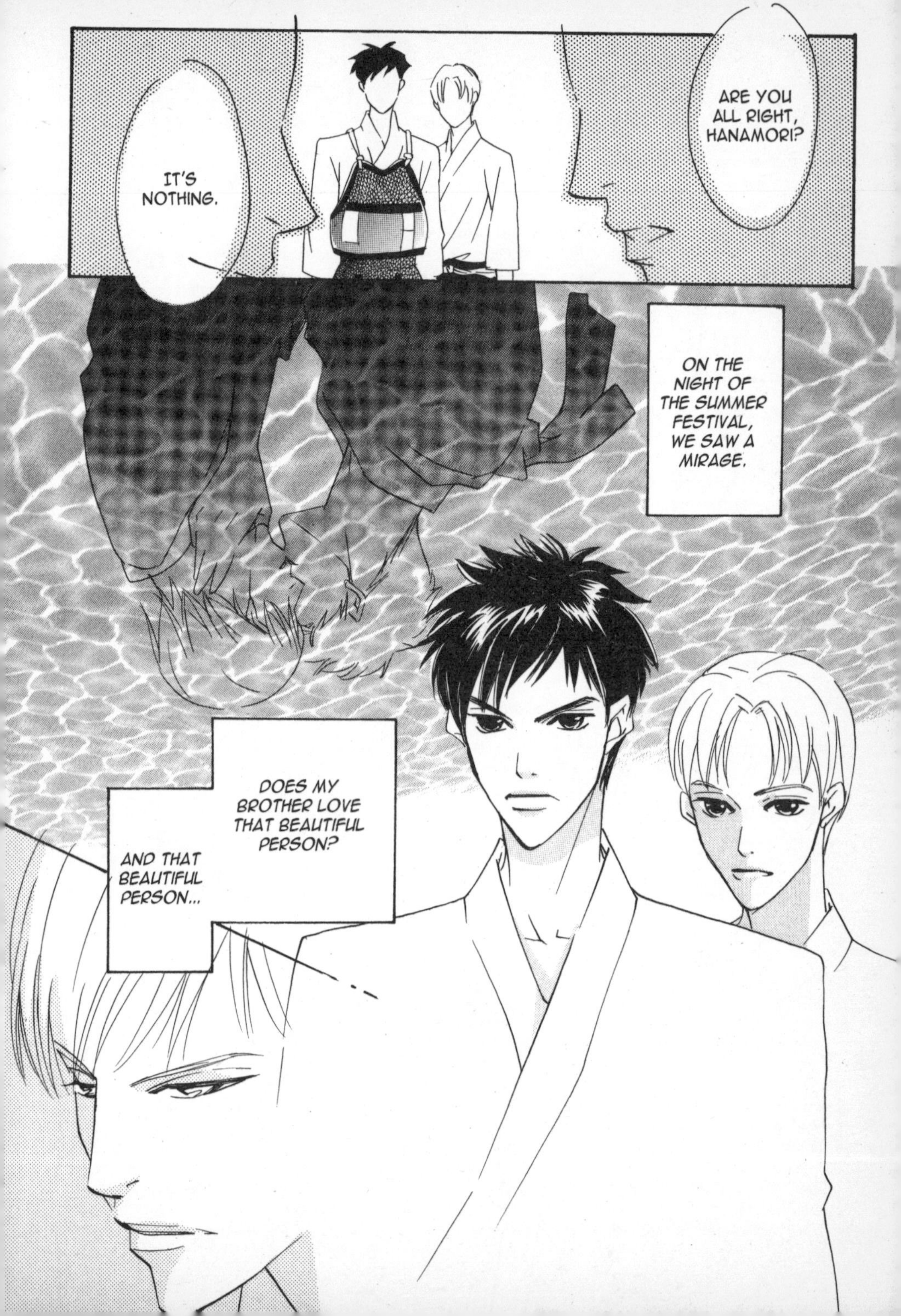
ARE YOU ALL RIGHT, HANAMORI?
IT'S NOTHING.
ON THE NIGHT OF THE SUMMER FESTIVAL, WE SAW A MIRAGE.
DOES MY BROTHER LOVE THAT BEAUTIFUL PERSON?
AND THAT BEAUTIFUL PERSON...

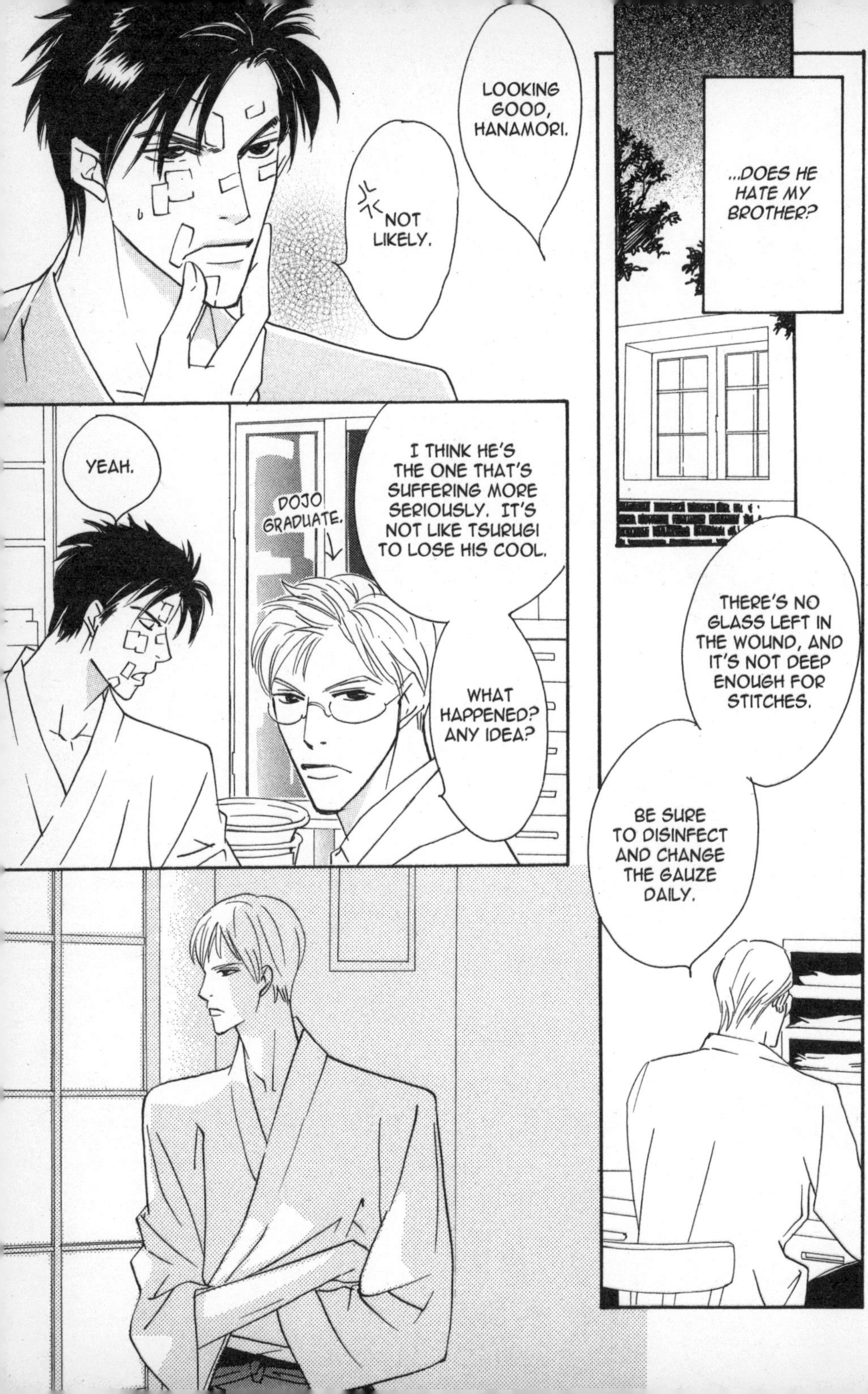
...DOES HE HATE MY BROTHER?
THERE'S NO GLASS LEFT IN THE WOUND, AND IT'S NOT DEEP ENOUGH FOR STITCHES.
BE SURE TO DISINFECT AND CHANGE THE GAUZE DAILY.
LOOKING GOOD, HANAMORI.
NOT LIKELY.
I THINK HE'S THE ONE THAT'S SUFFERING MORE SERIOUSLY. IT'S NOT LIKE TSURUGI TO LOSE HIS COOL.
WHAT HAPPENED? ANY IDEA?
DOJO GRADUATE.
YEAH.

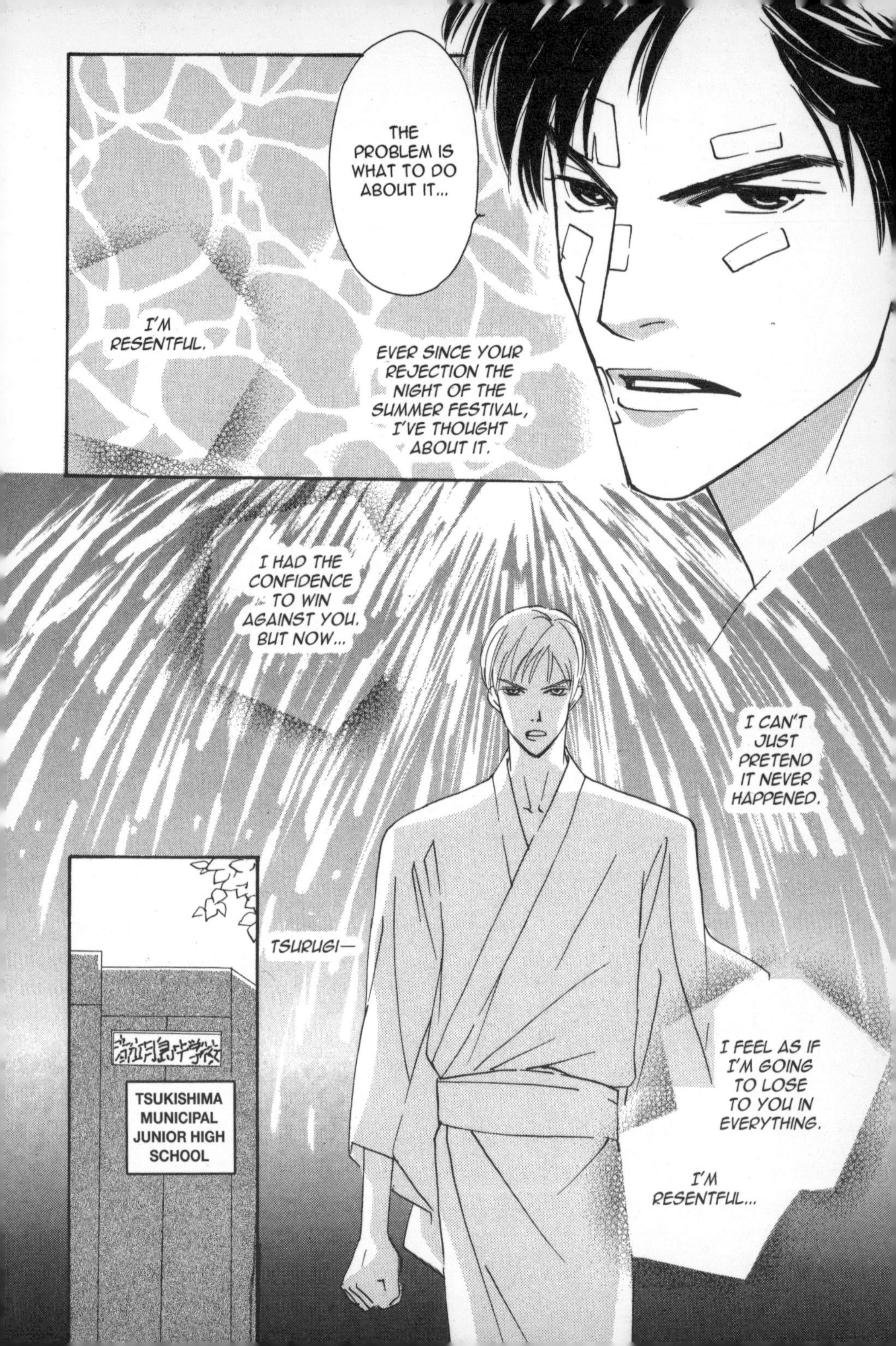
THE PROBLEM IS WHAT TO DO ABOUT IT...
EVER SINCE YOUR REJECTION THE NIGHT OF THE SUMMER FESTIVAL, I'VE THOUGHT ABOUT IT.
I'M RESENTFUL.
I CAN'T JUST PRETEND IT NEVER HAPPENED.
I HAD THE CONFIDENCE TO WIN AGAINST YOU. BUT NOW...
I FEEL AS IF I'M GOING TO LOSE TO YOU IN EVERYTHING.
I'M RESENTFUL...
TSURUGI—
TSUKISHIMA MUNICIPAL JUNIOR HIGH SCHOOL

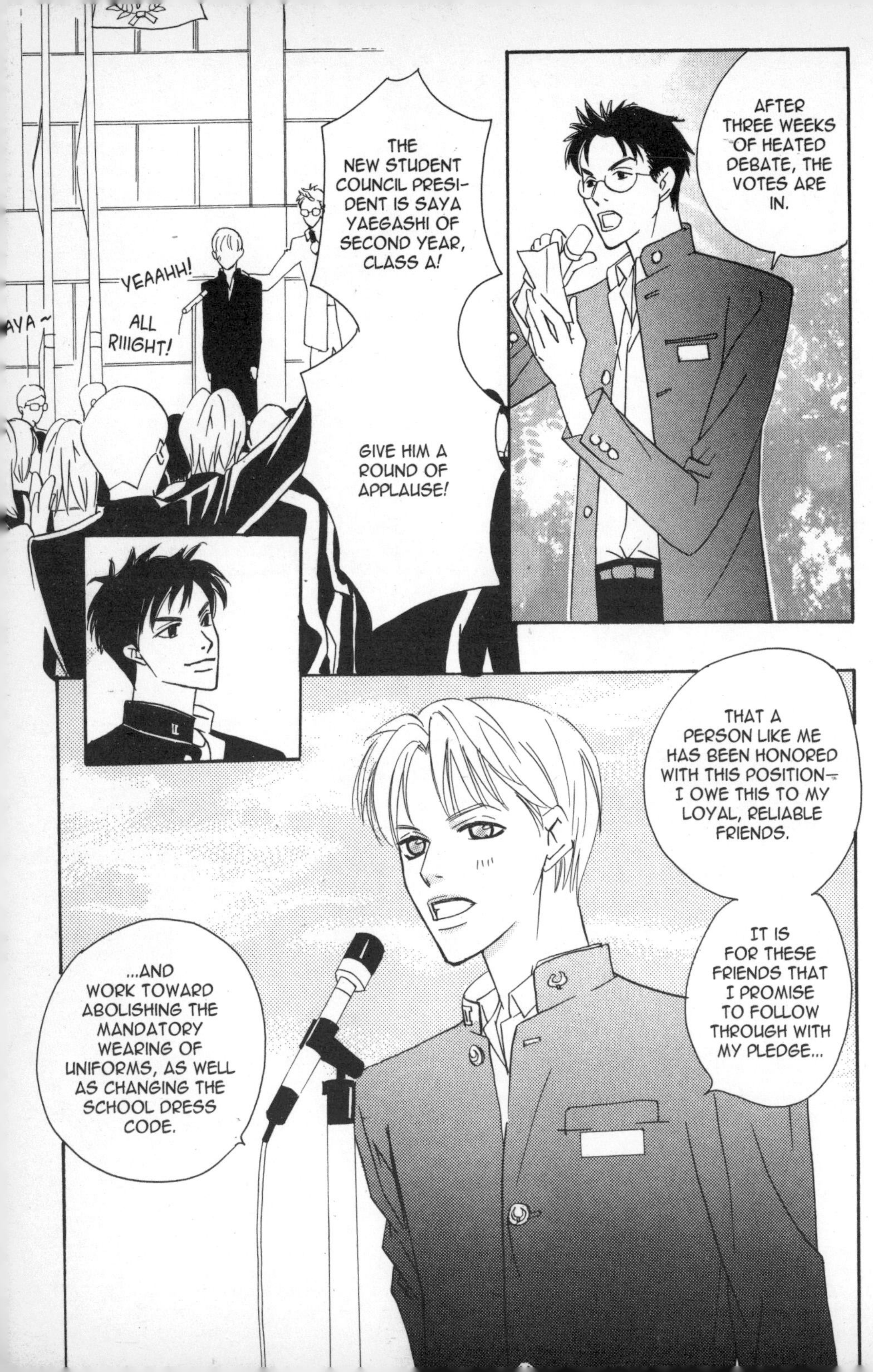
AFTER THREE WEEKS OF HEATED DEBATE, THE VOTES ARE IN.
THE NEW STUDENT COUNCIL PRESI-DENT IS SAYA YAEGASHI OF SECOND YEAR, CLASS A!
GIVE HIM A ROUND OF APPLAUSE!
YEAAHH!
ALL RIIIGHT!
AYA ~
THAT A PERSON LIKE ME HAS BEEN HONORED WITH THIS POSITION— I OWE THIS TO MY LOYAL, RELIABLE FRIENDS.
IT IS FOR THESE FRIENDS THAT I PROMISE TO FOLLOW THROUGH WITH MY PLEDGE...
...AND WORK TOWARD ABOLISHING THE MANDATORY WEARING OF UNIFORMS, AS WELL AS CHANGING THE SCHOOL DRESS CODE.

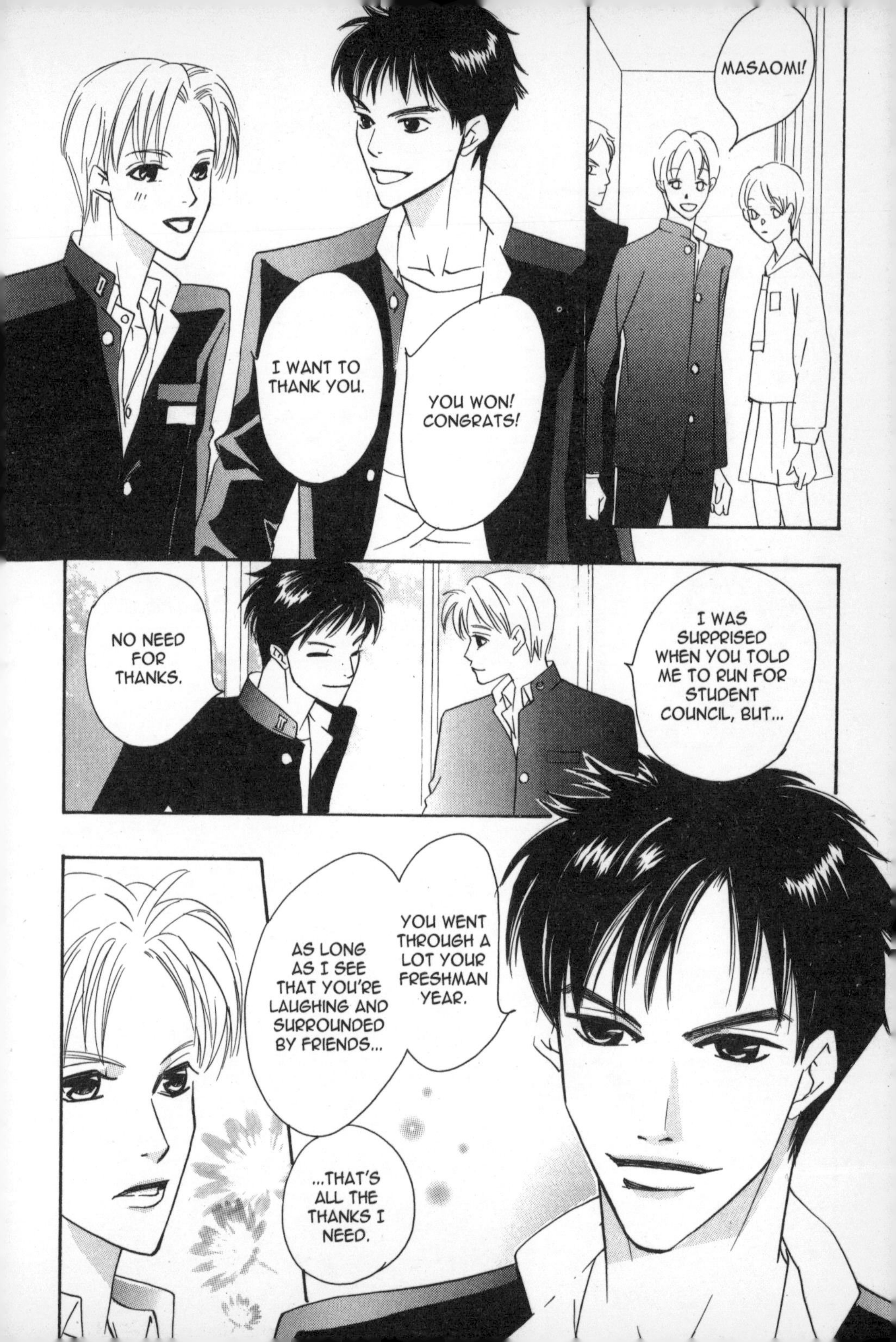
MASAOMI!
YOU WON! CONGRATS!
I WANT TO THANK YOU.
I WAS SURPRISED WHEN YOU TOLD ME TO RUN FOR STUDENT COUNCIL, BUT...
NO NEED FOR THANKS.
YOU WENT THROUGH A LOT YOUR FRESHMAN YEAR.
AS LONG AS I SEE THAT YOU'RE LAUGHING AND SURROUNDED BY FRIENDS...
...THAT'S ALL THE THANKS I NEED.

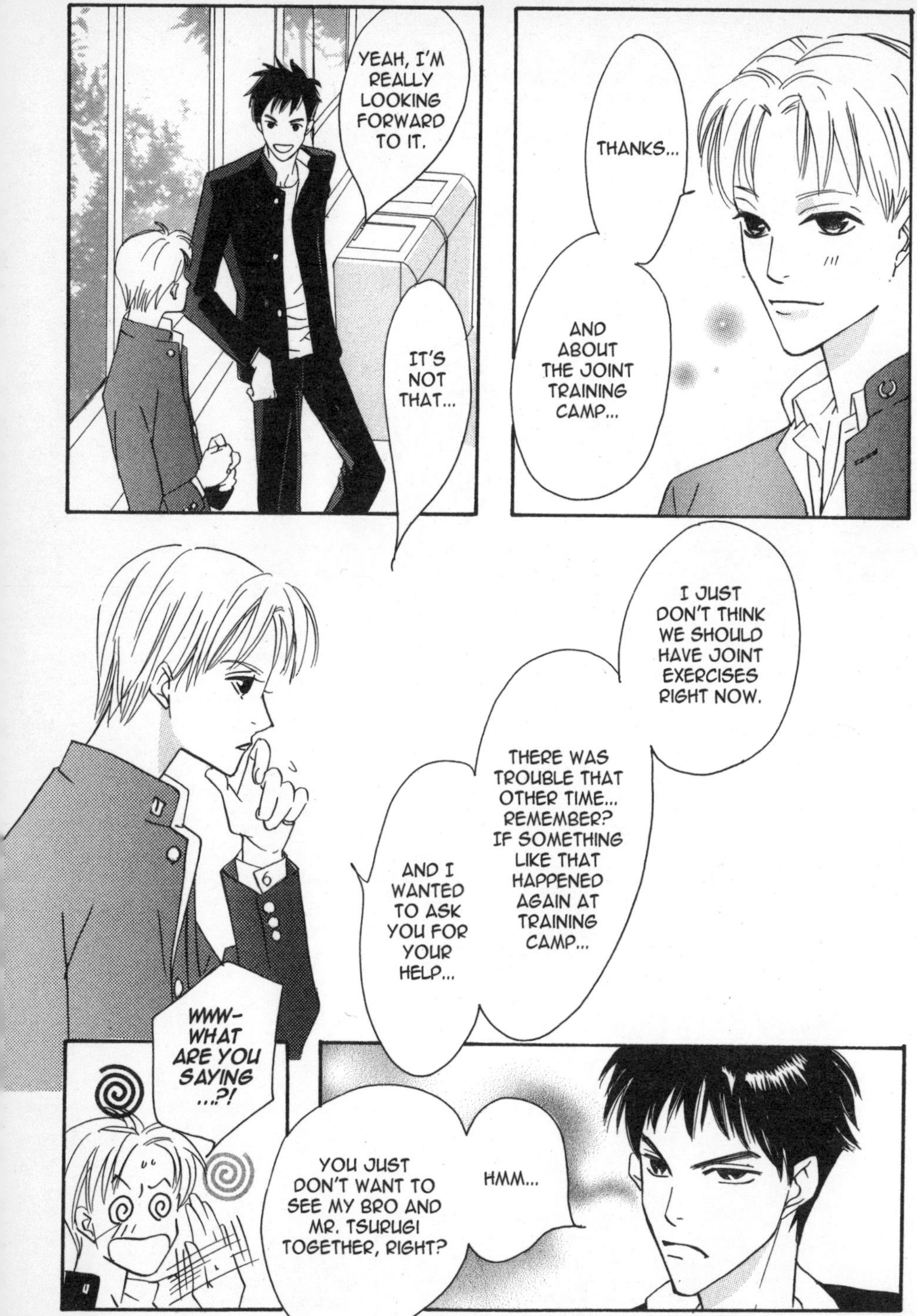
THANKS...
AND ABOUT THE JOINT TRAINING CAMP...
YEAH, I'M REALLY LOOKING FORWARD TO IT.
IT'S NOT THAT...
I JUST DON'T THINK WE SHOULD HAVE JOINT EXERCISES RIGHT NOW.
THERE WAS TROUBLE THAT OTHER TIME... REMEMBER? IF SOMETHING LIKE THAT HAPPENED AGAIN AT TRAINING CAMP...
AND I WANTED TO ASK YOU FOR YOUR HELP...
HMM...
YOU JUST DON'T WANT TO SEE MY BRO AND MR. TSURUGI TOGETHER, RIGHT?
WWW-WHAT ARE YOU SAYING ...?!

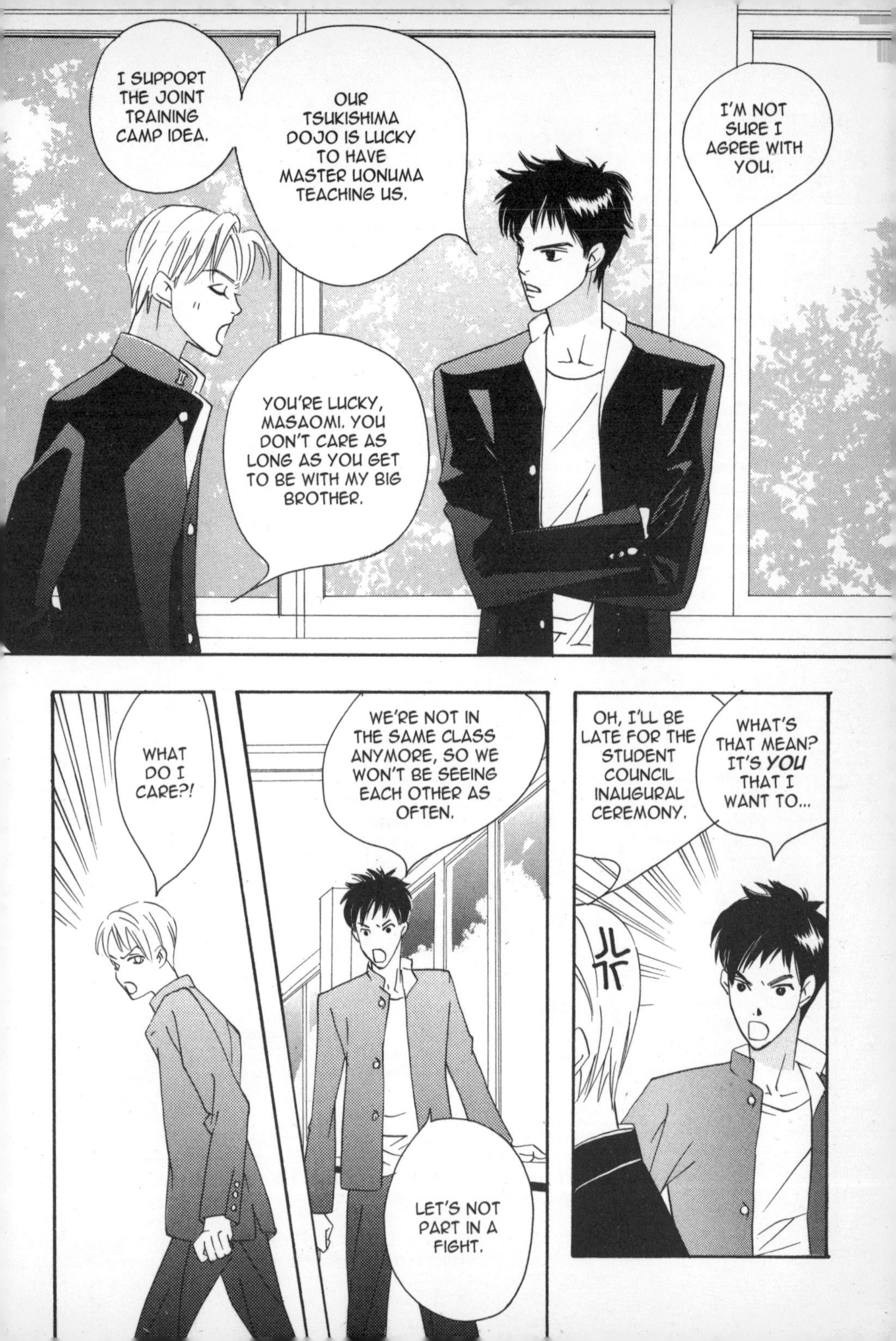
I'M NOT SURE I AGREE WITH YOU.
OUR TSUKISHIMA DOJO IS LUCKY TO HAVE MASTER UONUMA TEACHING US.
I SUPPORT THE JOINT TRAINING CAMP IDEA.
YOU'RE LUCKY, MASAOMI. YOU DON'T CARE AS LONG AS YOU GET TO BE WITH MY BIG BROTHER.
WHAT'S THAT MEAN? IT'S *YOU* THAT I WANT TO...
OH, I'LL BE LATE FOR THE STUDENT COUNCIL INAUGURAL CEREMONY.
WE'RE NOT IN THE SAME CLASS ANYMORE, SO WE WON'T BE SEEING EACH OTHER AS OFTEN.
LET'S NOT PART IN A FIGHT.
WHAT DO I CARE?!

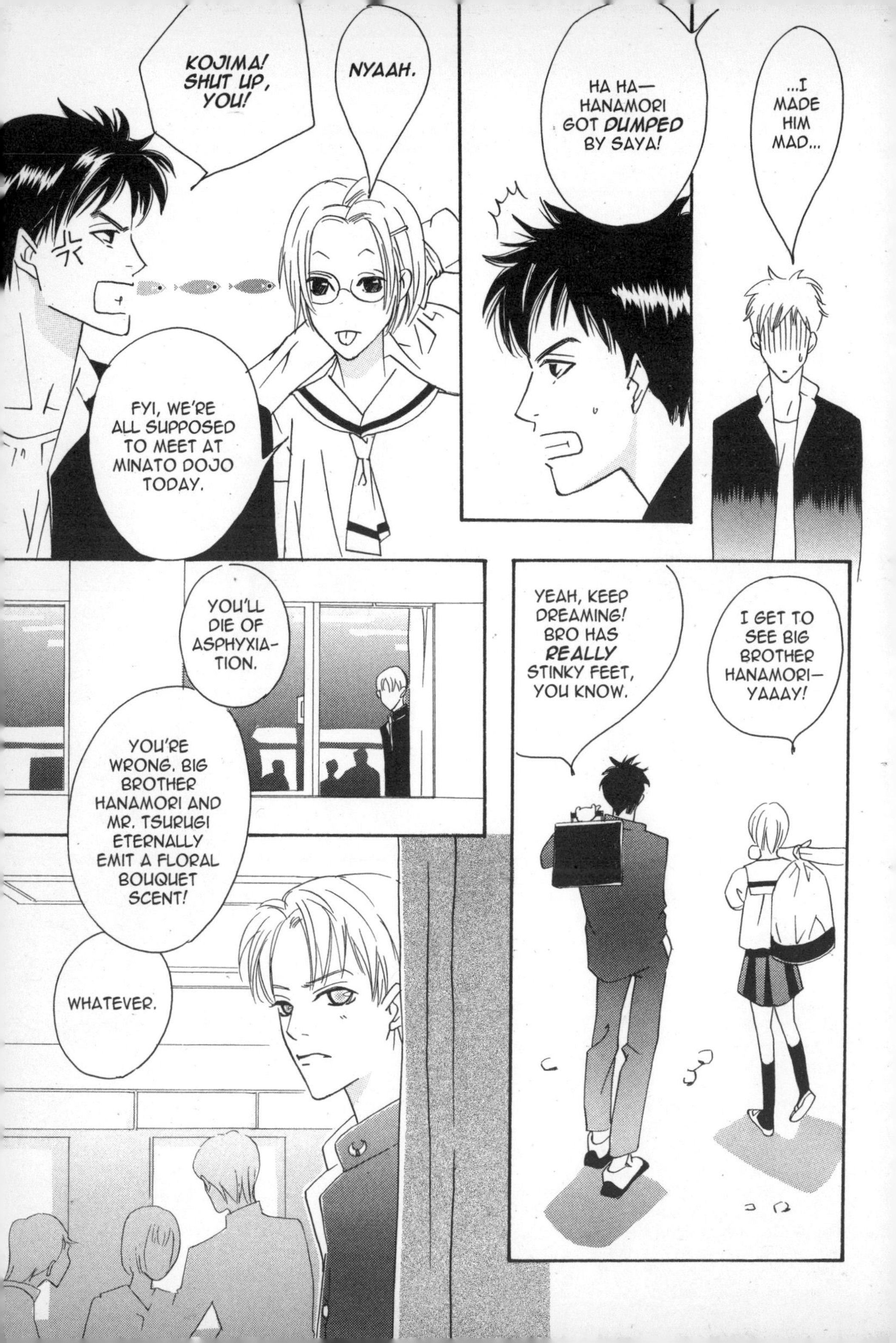
HA HA—HANAMORI GOT DUMPED BY SAYA!
...I MADE HIM MAD...
KOJIMA! SHUT UP, YOU!
NYAAH.
FYI, WE'RE ALL SUPPOSED TO MEET AT MINATO DOJO TODAY.
I GET TO SEE BIG BROTHER HANAMORI—YAAAY!
YEAH, KEEP DREAMING! BRO HAS REALLY STINKY FEET, YOU KNOW.
YOU'LL DIE OF ASPHYXIA-TION.
YOU'RE WRONG. BIG BROTHER HANAMORI AND MR. TSURUGI ETERNALLY EMIT A FLORAL BOUQUET SCENT!
WHATEVER.

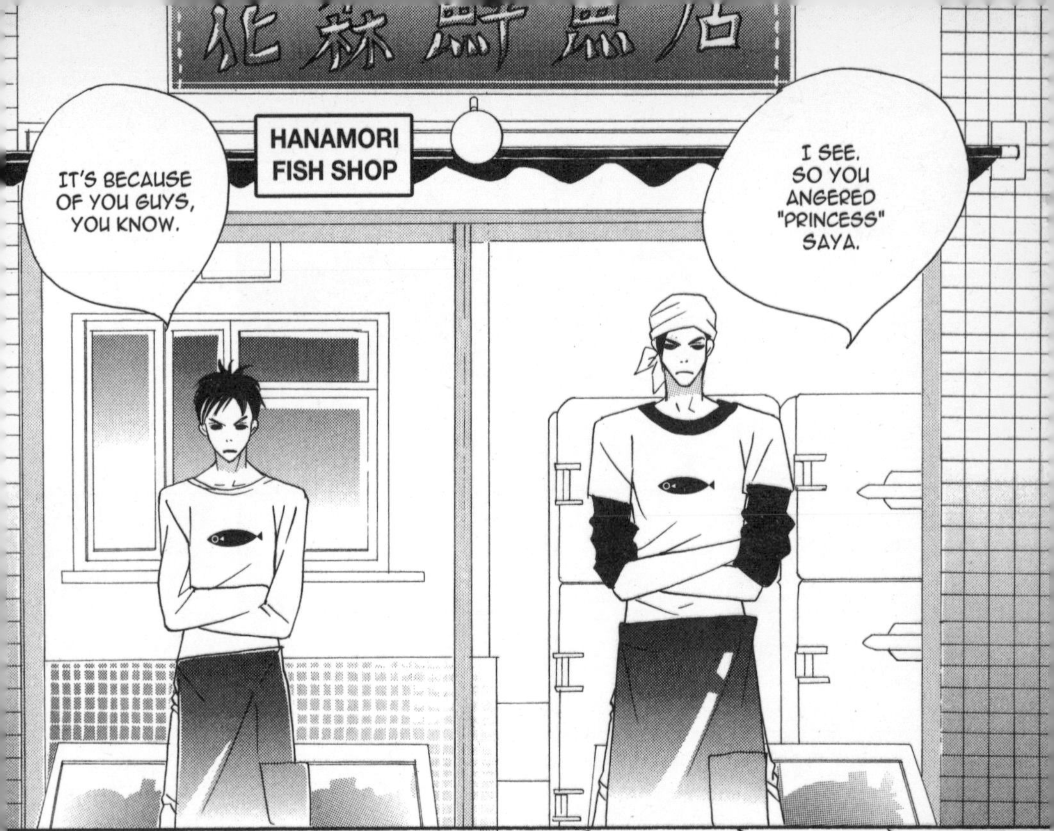
I SEE. SO YOU ANGERED "PRINCESS" SAYA.
HANAMORI FISH SHOP
IT'S BECAUSE OF YOU GUYS, YOU KNOW.
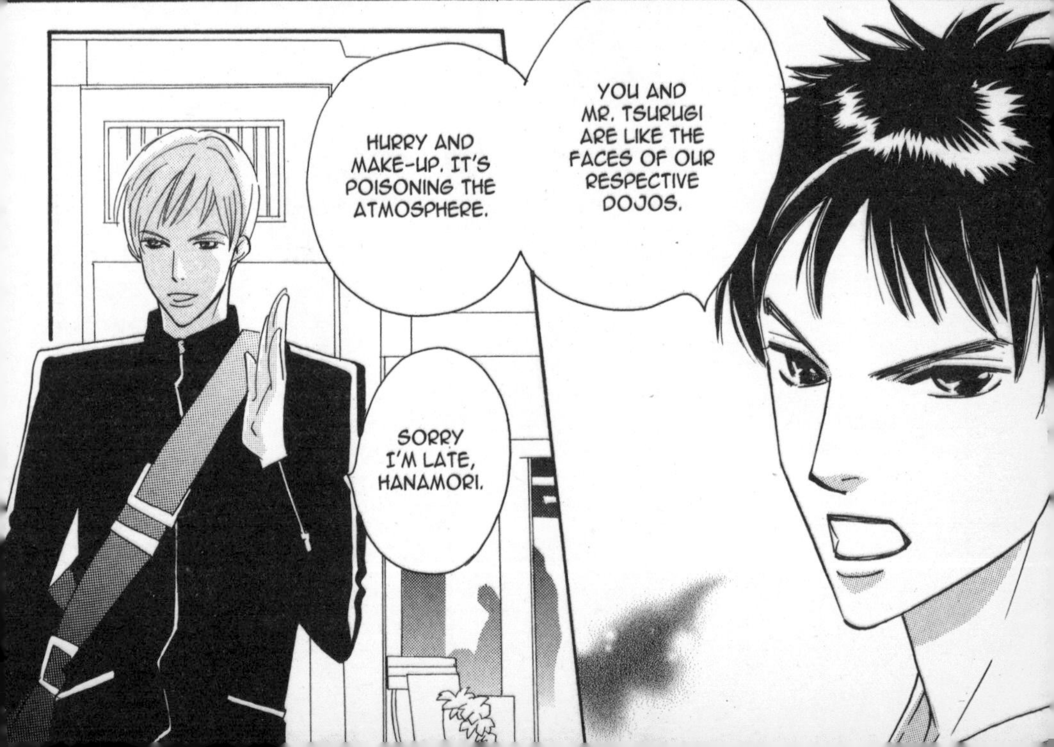
YOU AND MR. TSURUGI ARE LIKE THE FACES OF OUR RESPECTIVE DOJOS.
HURRY AND MAKE-UP. IT'S POISONING THE ATMOSPHERE.
SORRY I'M LATE, HANAMORI.

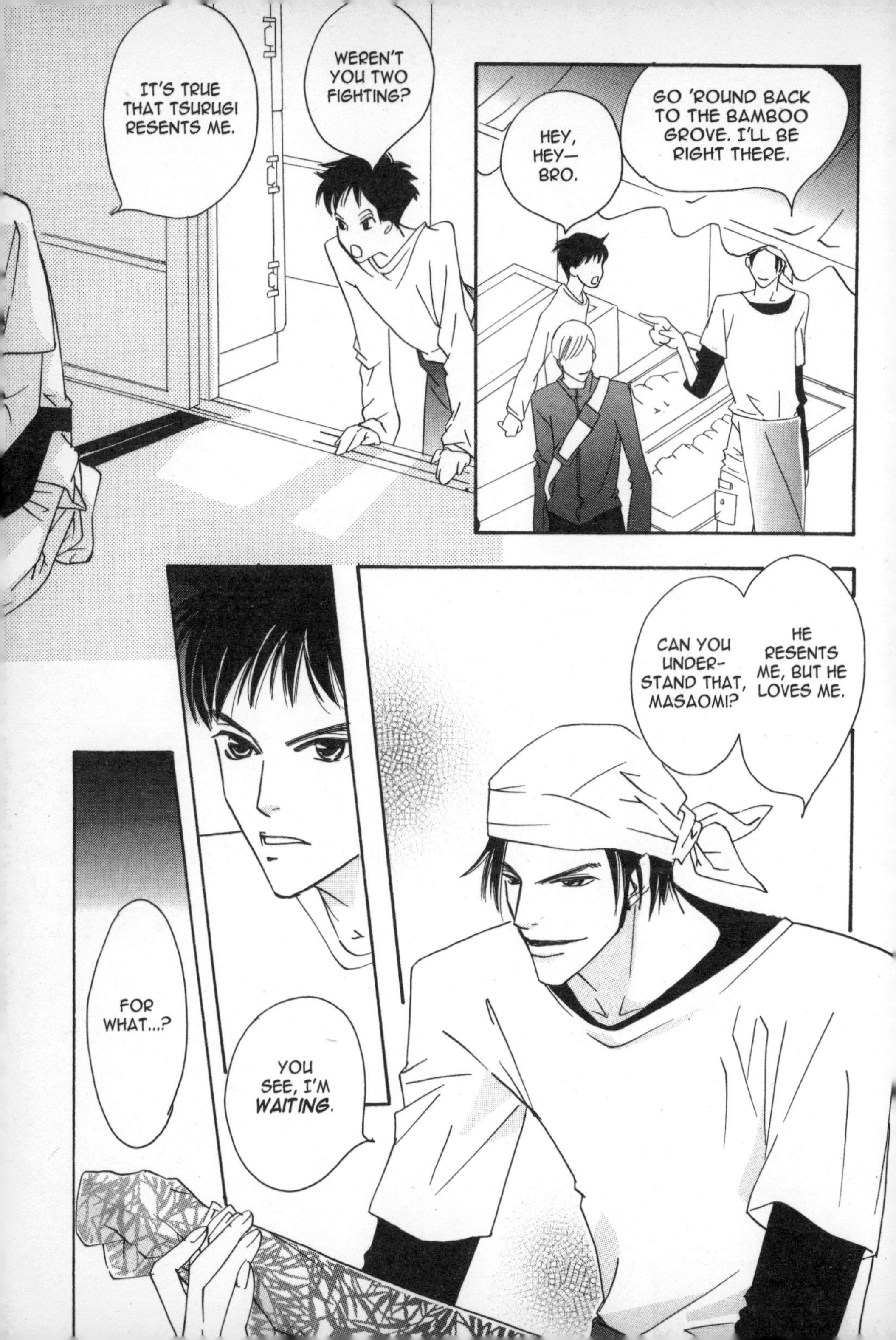
GO 'ROUND BACK TO THE BAMBOO GROVE. I'LL BE RIGHT THERE.
HEY, HEY— BRO.
WEREN'T YOU TWO FIGHTING?
IT'S TRUE THAT TSURUGI RESENTS ME.
HE RESENTS ME, BUT HE LOVES ME.
CAN YOU UNDER-STAND THAT, MASAOMI?
YOU SEE, I'M ***WAITING***.
FOR WHAT...?

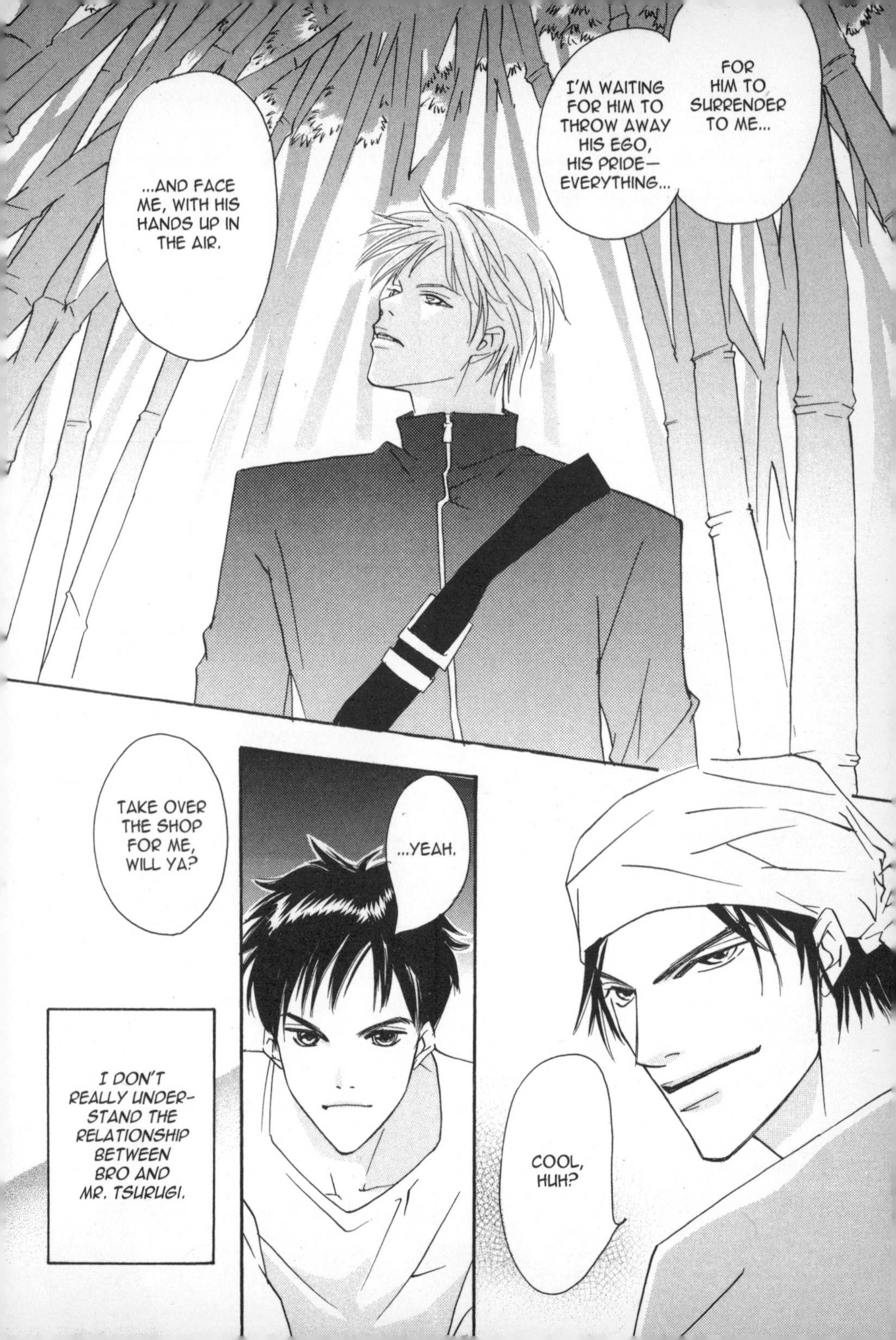
I'M WAITING FOR HIM TO THROW AWAY HIS EGO, HIS PRIDE— EVERYTHING...
FOR HIM TO SURRENDER TO ME...
...AND FACE ME, WITH HIS HANDS UP IN THE AIR.
TAKE OVER THE SHOP FOR ME, WILL YA?
...YEAH.
COOL, HUH?
I DON'T REALLY UNDER-STAND THE RELATIONSHIP BETWEEN BRO AND MR. TSURUGI.

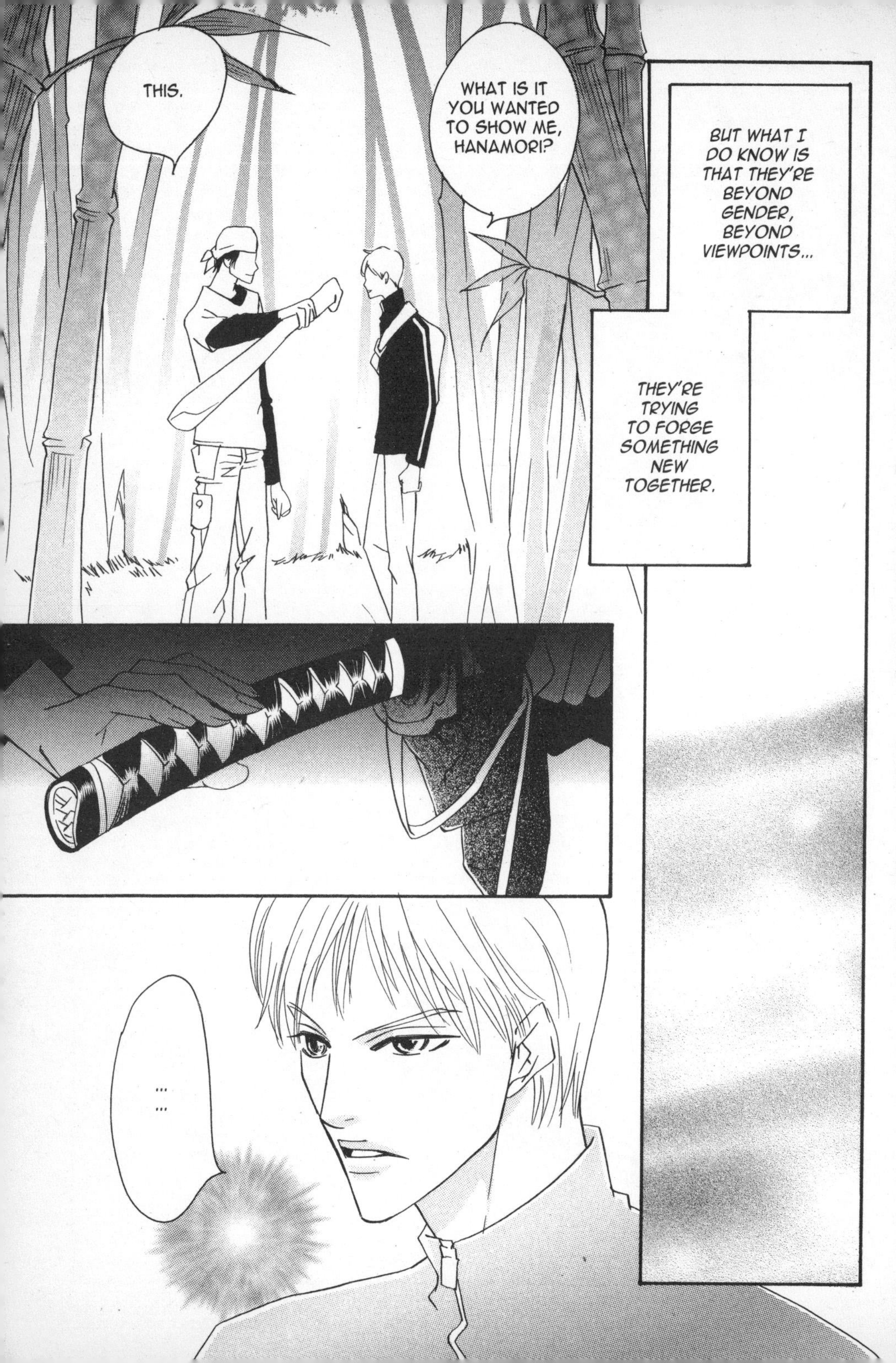
BUT WHAT I DO KNOW IS THAT THEY'RE BEYOND GENDER, BEYOND VIEWPOINTS...
THEY'RE TRYING TO FORGE SOMETHING NEW TOGETHER.
WHAT IS IT YOU WANTED TO SHOW ME, HANAMORI?
THIS.
... ...

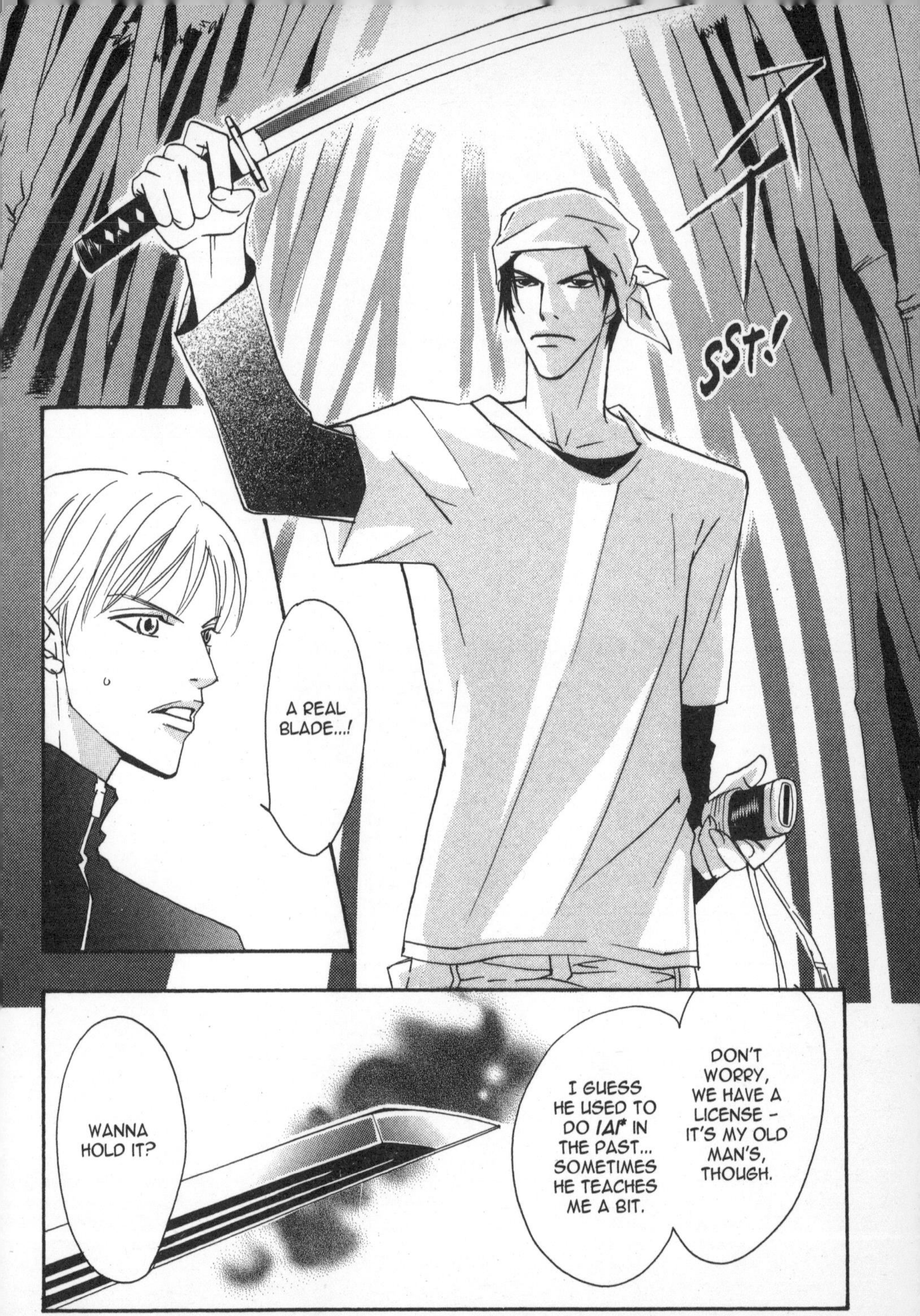
SST!
A REAL BLADE...!
DON'T WORRY, WE HAVE A LICENSE - IT'S MY OLD MAN'S, THOUGH.
I GUESS HE USED TO DO IAI* IN THE PAST... SOMETIMES HE TEACHES ME A BIT.
WANNA HOLD IT?

*NOTE: IAI IS A SWORD TECHNIQUE INVOLVING LIGHTNING-FAST SWORD REMOVAL FROM THE SCABBARD TO CUT DOWN THE OPPONENT, WITH VERY LITTLE CHANGE IN STANCE OR BODY MOVEMENT.

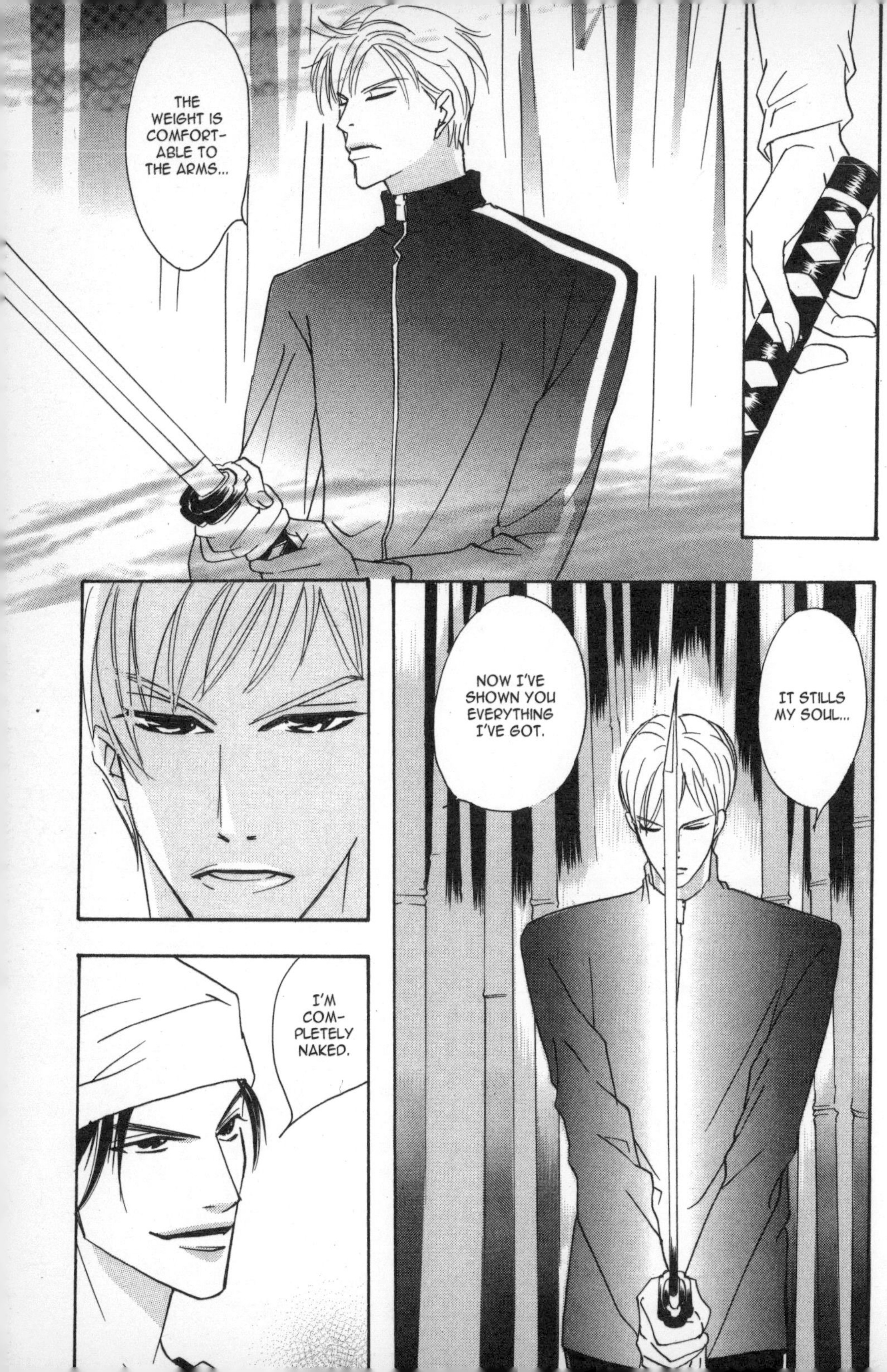
THE WEIGHT IS COMFORTABLE TO THE ARMS...
IT STILLS MY SOUL...
NOW I'VE SHOWN YOU EVERYTHING I'VE GOT.
I'M COMPLETELY NAKED.

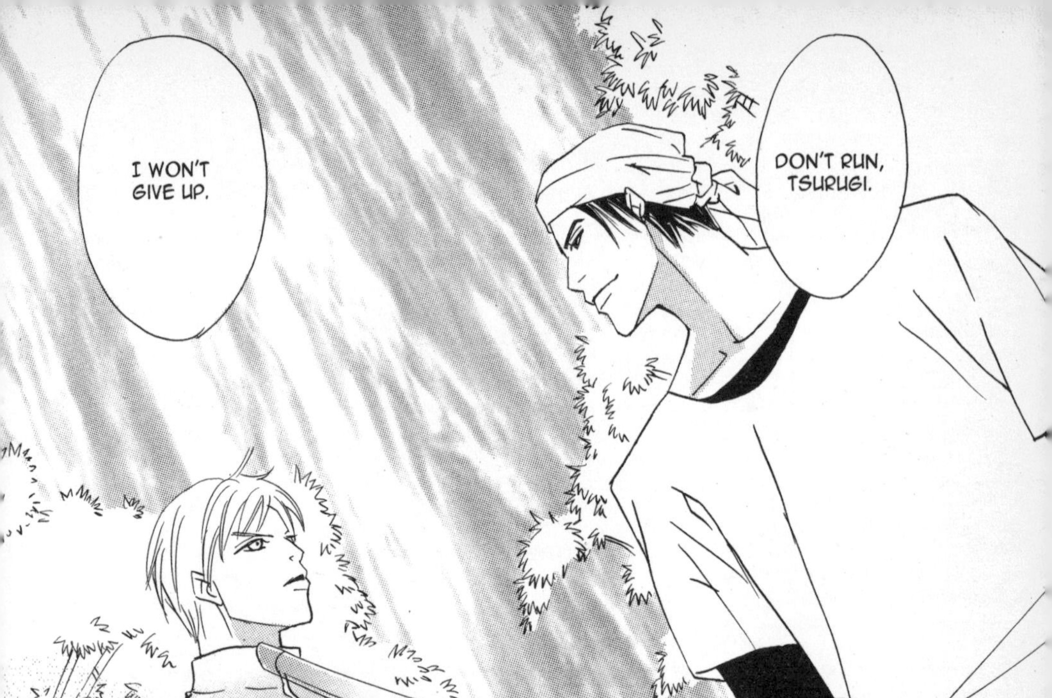
DON'T RUN, TSURUGI.
I WON'T GIVE UP.

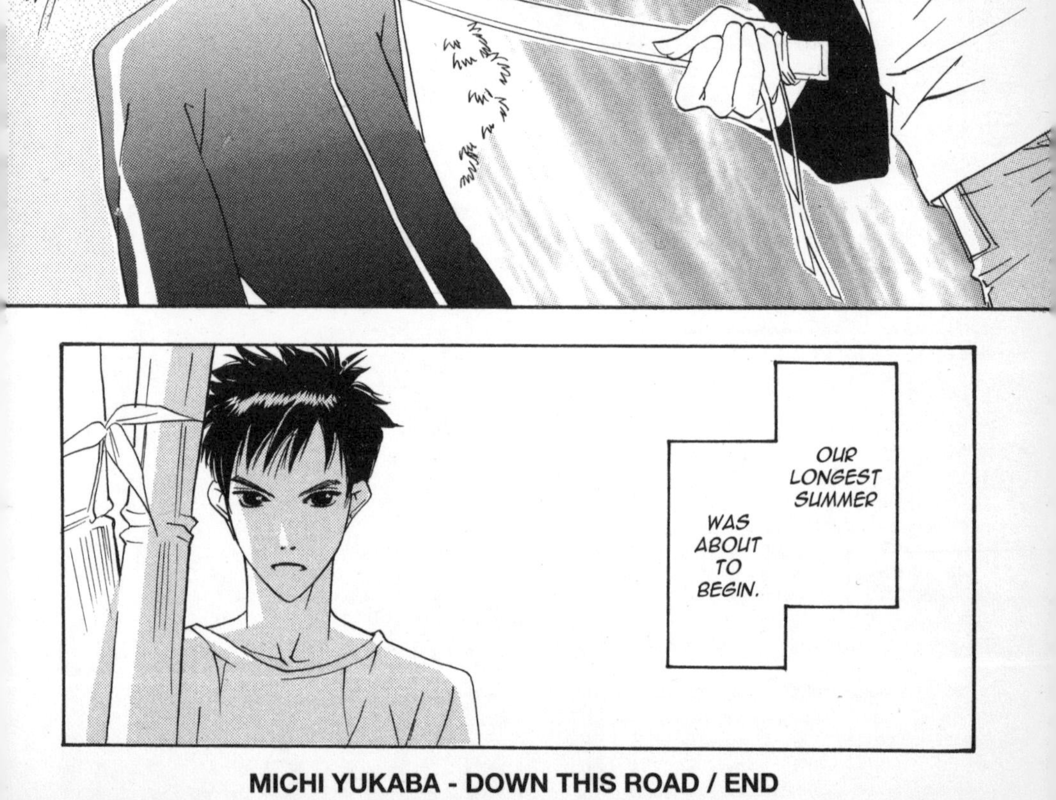
OUR LONGEST SUMMER WAS ABOUT TO BEGIN.

MICHI YUKABA - DOWN THIS ROAD / END

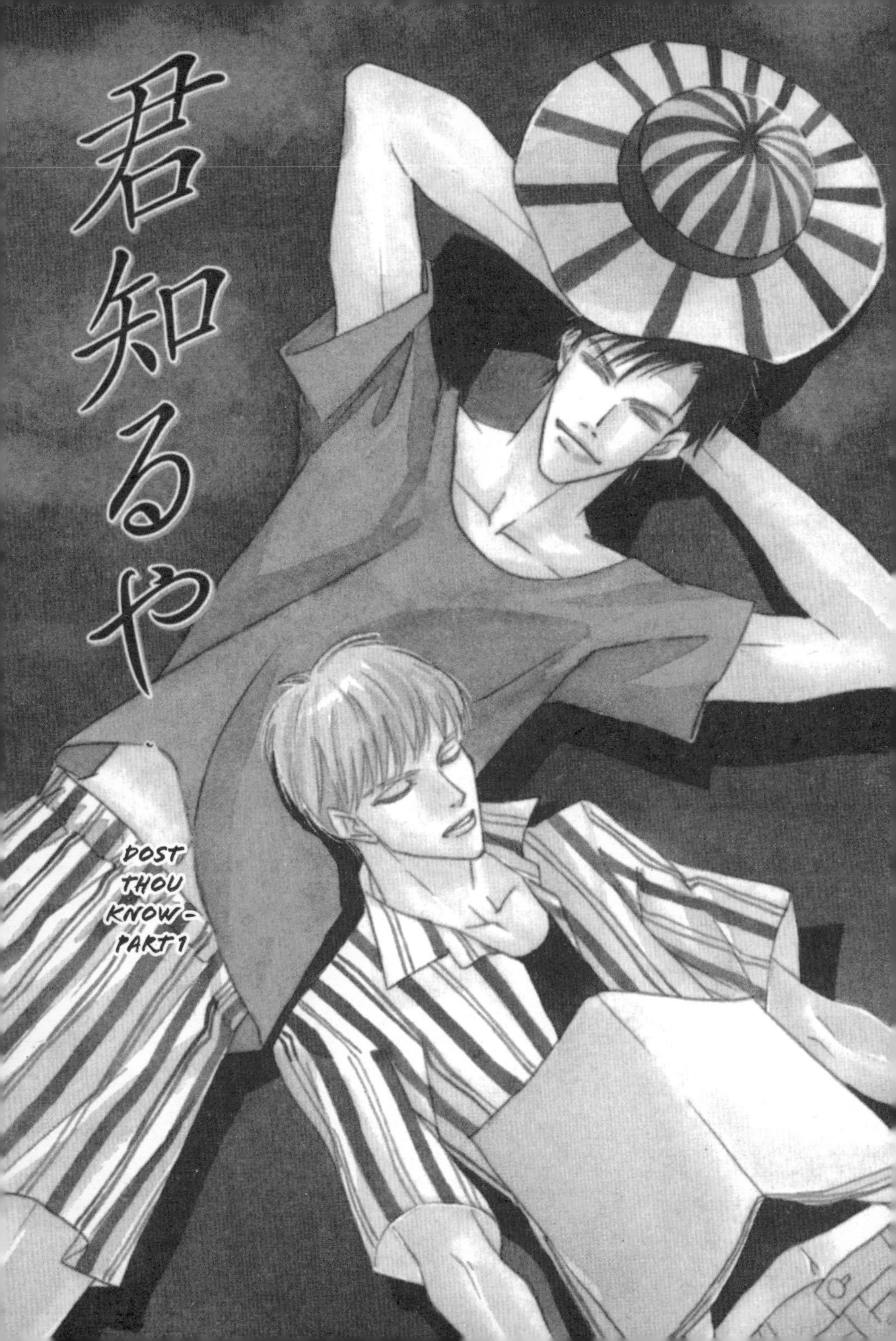
君知るや
DOST THOU KNOW- PART 1

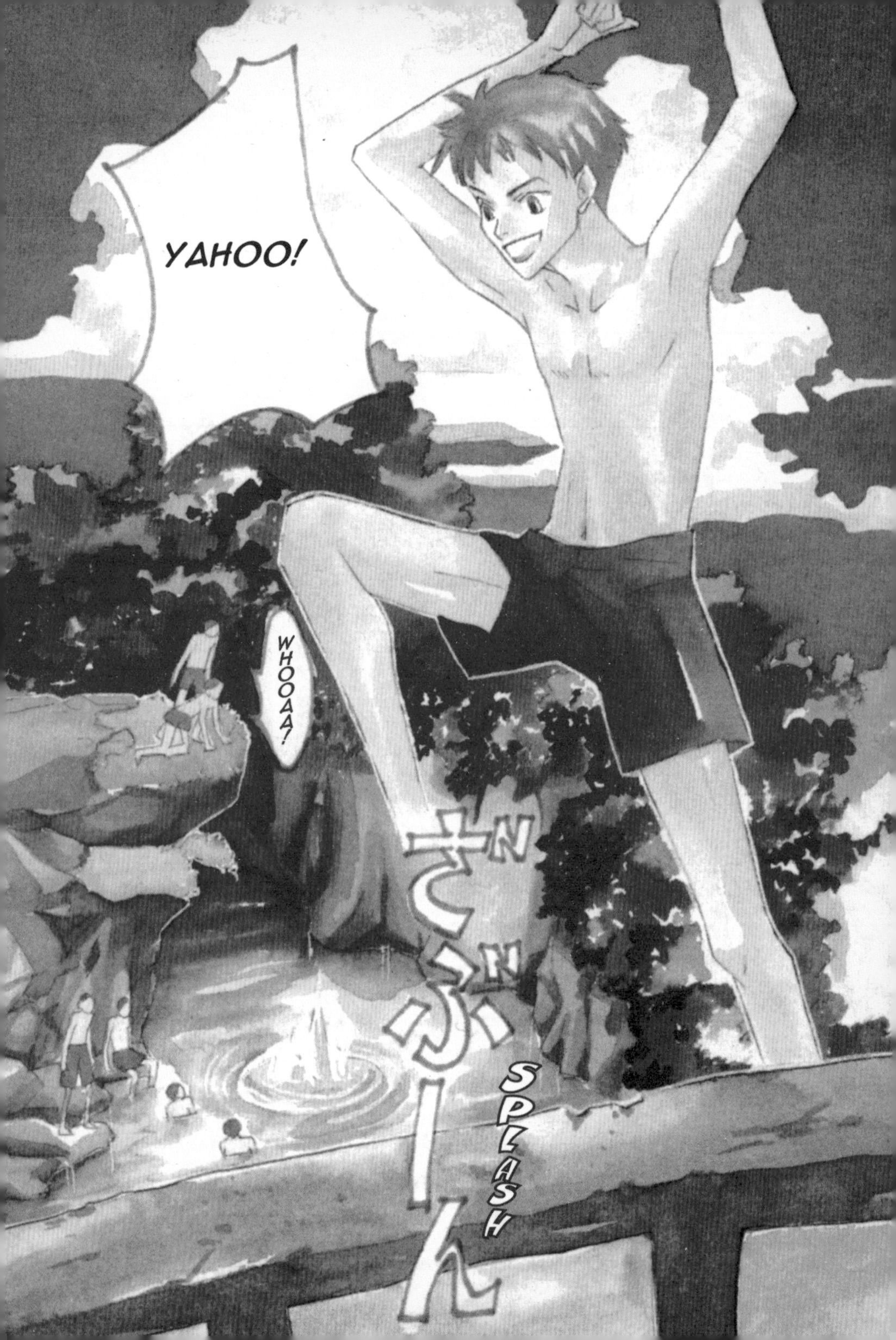
YAHOO!
WHOOAA!
ざっぷーん
SPLASH

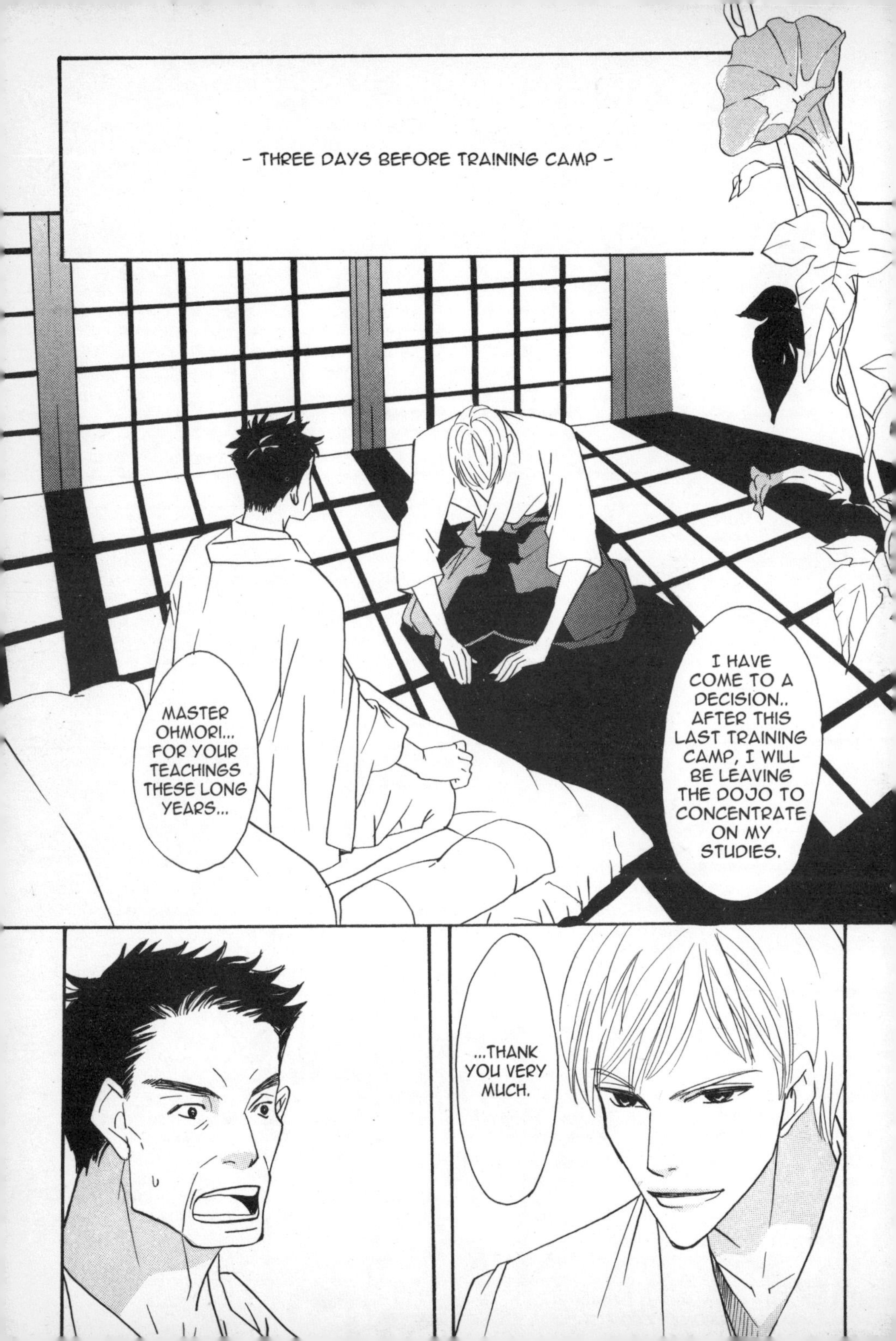
- THREE DAYS BEFORE TRAINING CAMP -
I HAVE COME TO A DECISION.. AFTER THIS LAST TRAINING CAMP, I WILL BE LEAVING THE DOJO TO CONCENTRATE ON MY STUDIES.
MASTER OHMORI... FOR YOUR TEACHINGS THESE LONG YEARS...
...THANK YOU VERY MUCH.

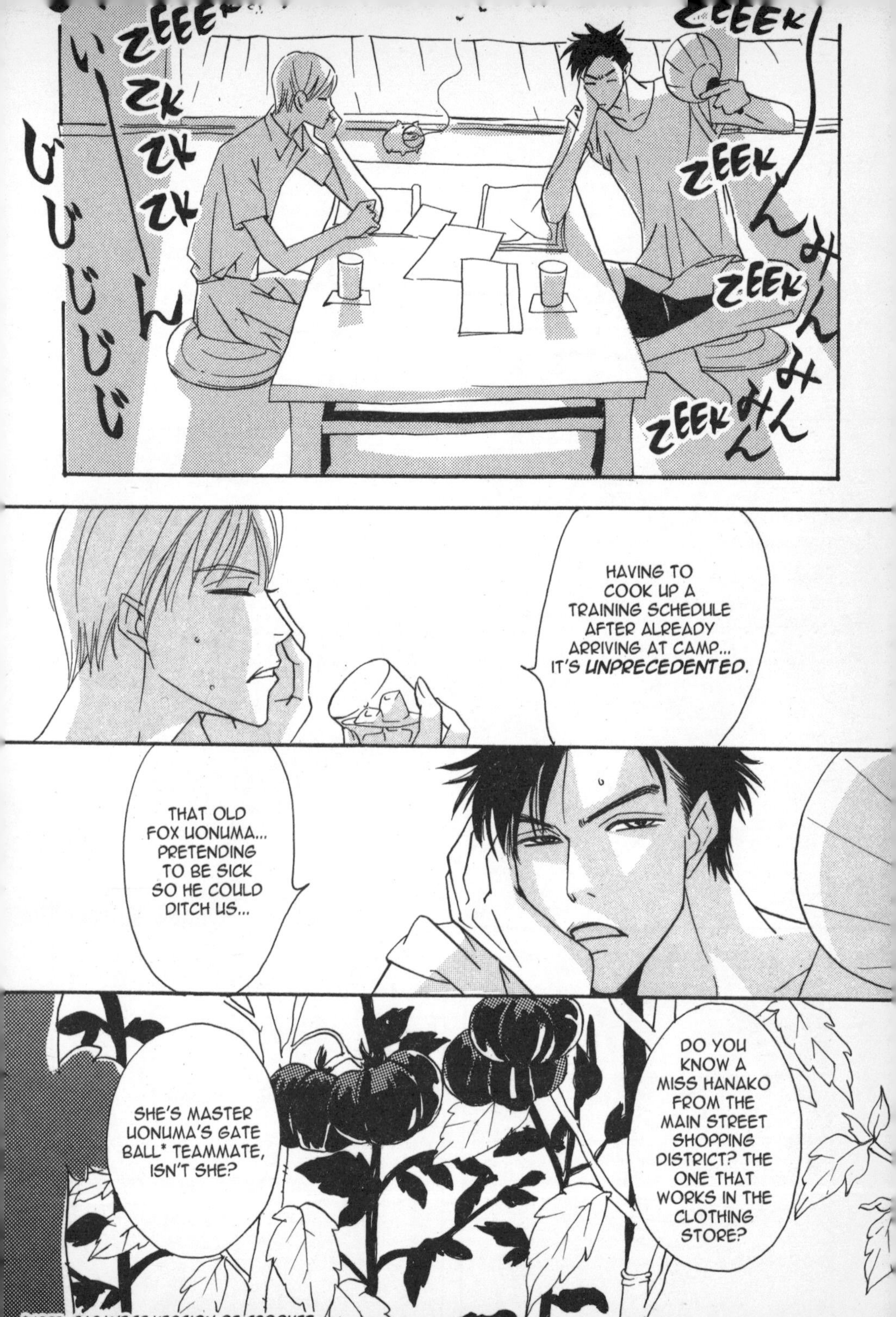
ZEEEK
ZEEK
みんみんみんみん
ZEEK
ZEEK
ZEEEK
ZK
ZK
ZK
い―ん
じじじじじ
HAVING TO COOK UP A TRAINING SCHEDULE AFTER ALREADY ARRIVING AT CAMP... IT'S ***UNPRECEDENTED***.
THAT OLD FOX UONUMA... PRETENDING TO BE SICK SO HE COULD DITCH US...
DO YOU KNOW A MISS HANAKO FROM THE MAIN STREET SHOPPING DISTRICT? THE ONE THAT WORKS IN THE CLOTHING STORE?
SHE'S MASTER UONUMA'S GATE BALL* TEAMMATE, ISN'T SHE?

*NOTE: JAPANESE VERSION OF CROQUET.

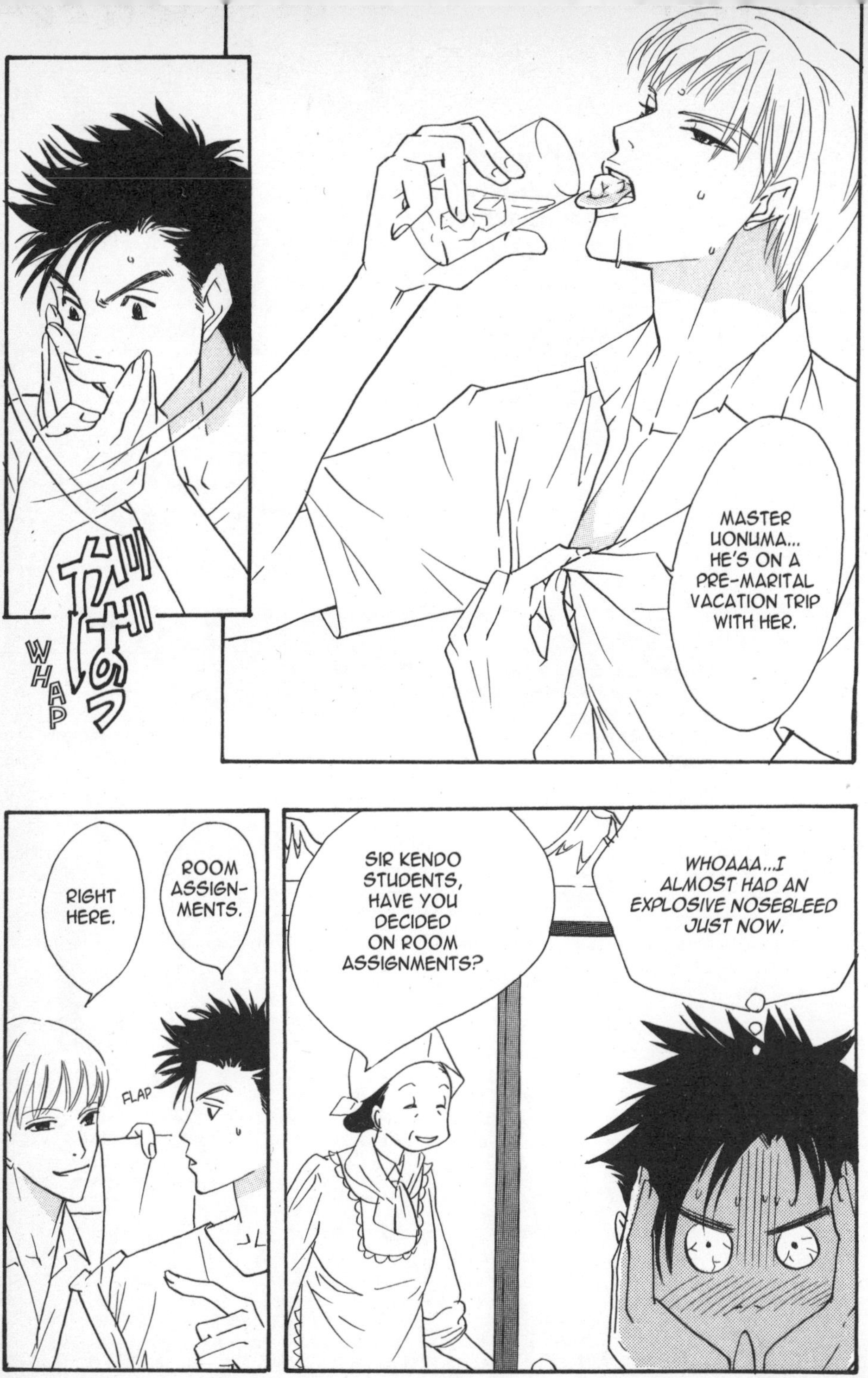
MASTER UONUMA... HE'S ON A PRE-MARITAL VACATION TRIP WITH HER.
WHAP
WHOAAA...I ALMOST HAD AN EXPLOSIVE NOSEBLEED JUST NOW.
SIR KENDO STUDENTS, HAVE YOU DECIDED ON ROOM ASSIGNMENTS?
ROOM ASSIGN-MENTS.
RIGHT HERE.
FLAP

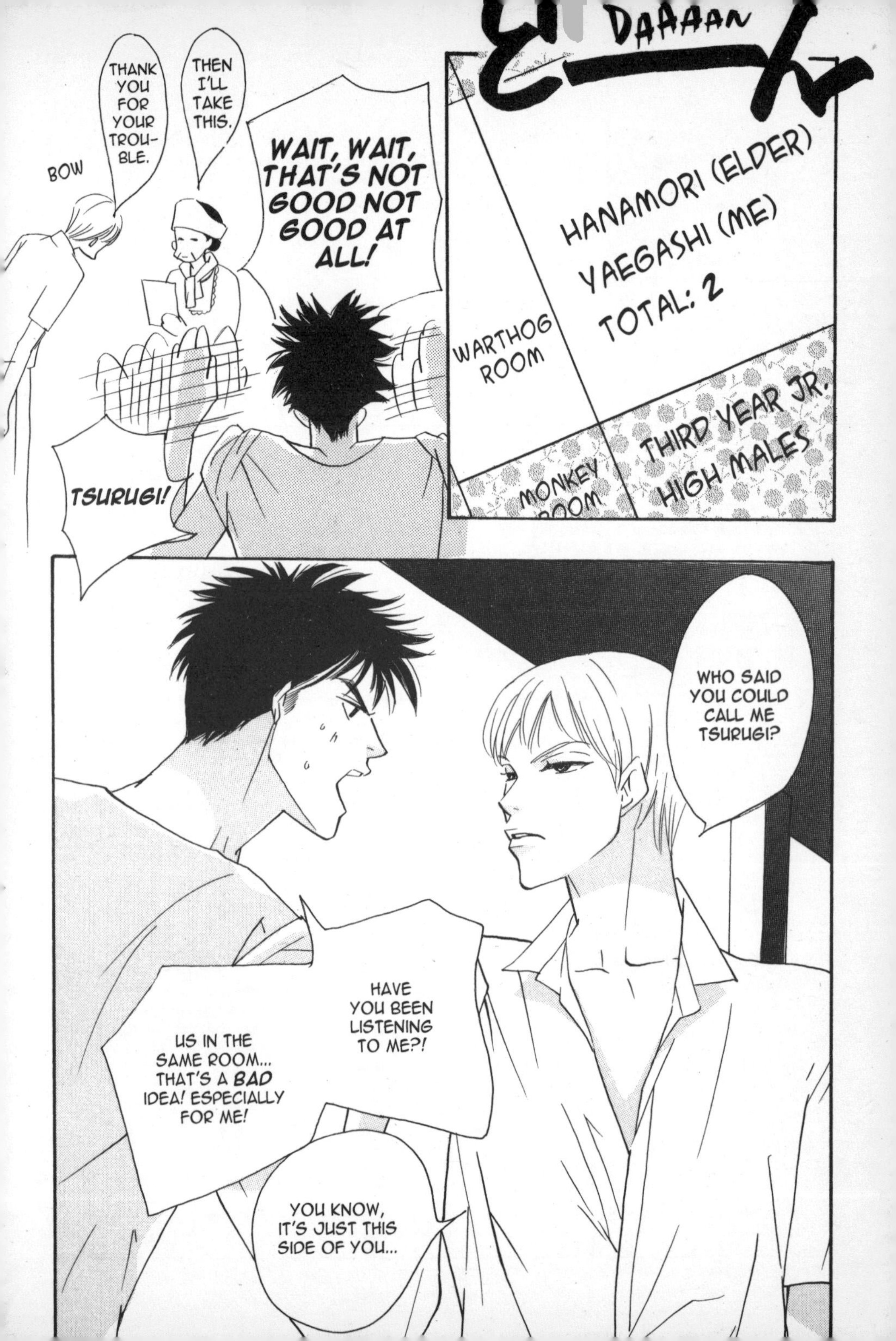
DAAAAN
HANAMORI (ELDER)
YAEGASHI (ME)
TOTAL: 2
WARTHOG ROOM
THIRD YEAR JR. HIGH MALES
MONKEY ROOM
THEN I'LL TAKE THIS.
THANK YOU FOR YOUR TROUBLE.
BOW
WAIT, WAIT, THAT'S NOT GOOD NOT GOOD AT ALL!
TSURUGI!
WHO SAID YOU COULD CALL ME TSURUGI?
HAVE YOU BEEN LISTENING TO ME?!
US IN THE SAME ROOM... THAT'S A BAD IDEA! ESPECIALLY FOR ME!
YOU KNOW, IT'S JUST THIS SIDE OF YOU...

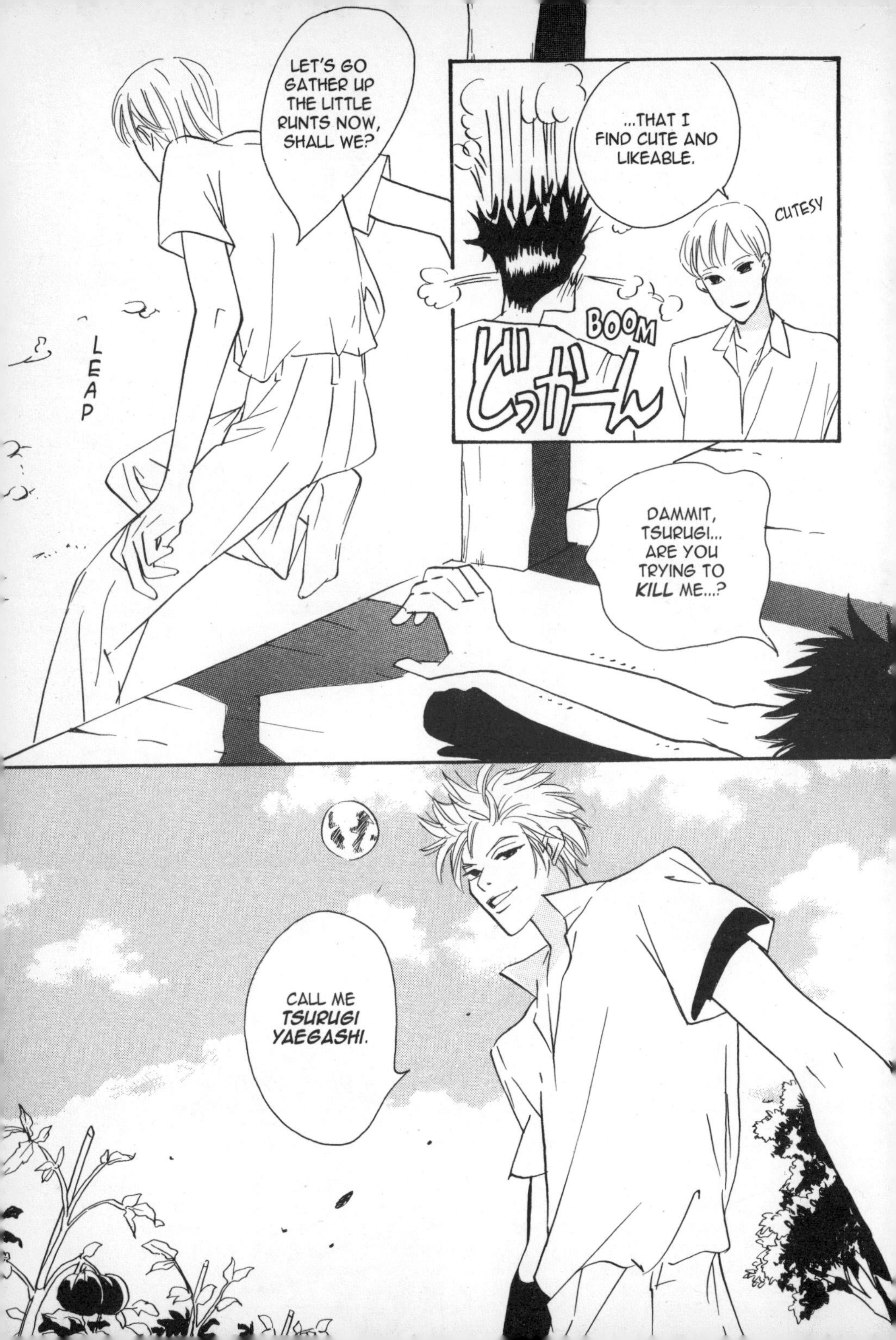
...THAT I FIND CUTE AND LIKEABLE.
CUTESY
BOOM
どっかーん
LET'S GO GATHER UP THE LITTLE RUNTS NOW, SHALL WE?
LEAP
DAMMIT, TSURUGI... ARE YOU TRYING TO KILL ME...?
CALL ME TSURUGI YAEGASHI.

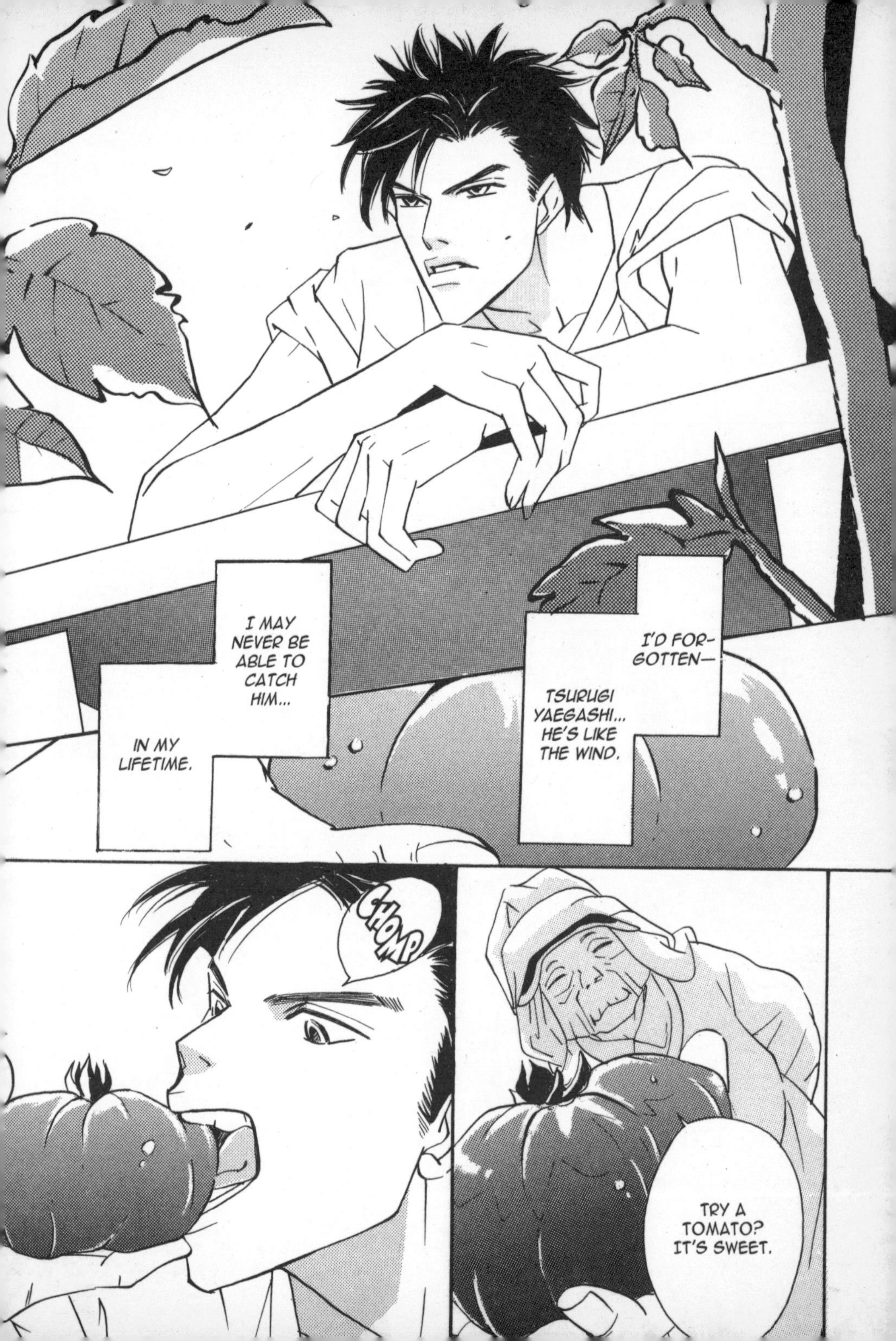
I'D FOR-GOTTEN—
TSURUGI YAEGASHI... HE'S LIKE THE WIND.
I MAY NEVER BE ABLE TO CATCH HIM...
IN MY LIFETIME.
TRY A TOMATO? IT'S SWEET.
CHOMP

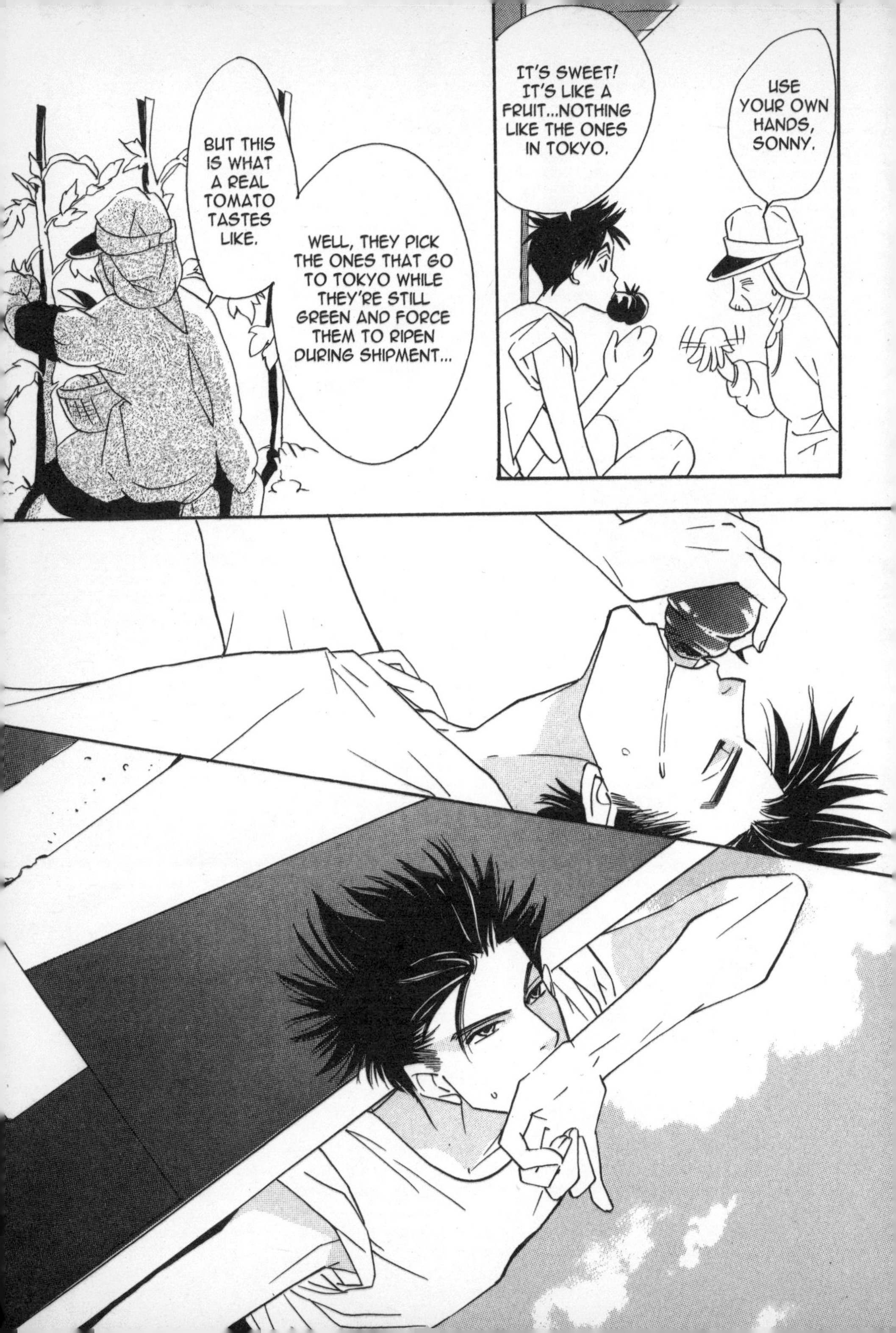
USE YOUR OWN HANDS, SONNY.
IT'S SWEET! IT'S LIKE A FRUIT...NOTHING LIKE THE ONES IN TOKYO.
WELL, THEY PICK THE ONES THAT GO TO TOKYO WHILE THEY'RE STILL GREEN AND FORCE THEM TO RIPEN DURING SHIPMENT...
BUT THIS IS WHAT A REAL TOMATO TASTES LIKE.

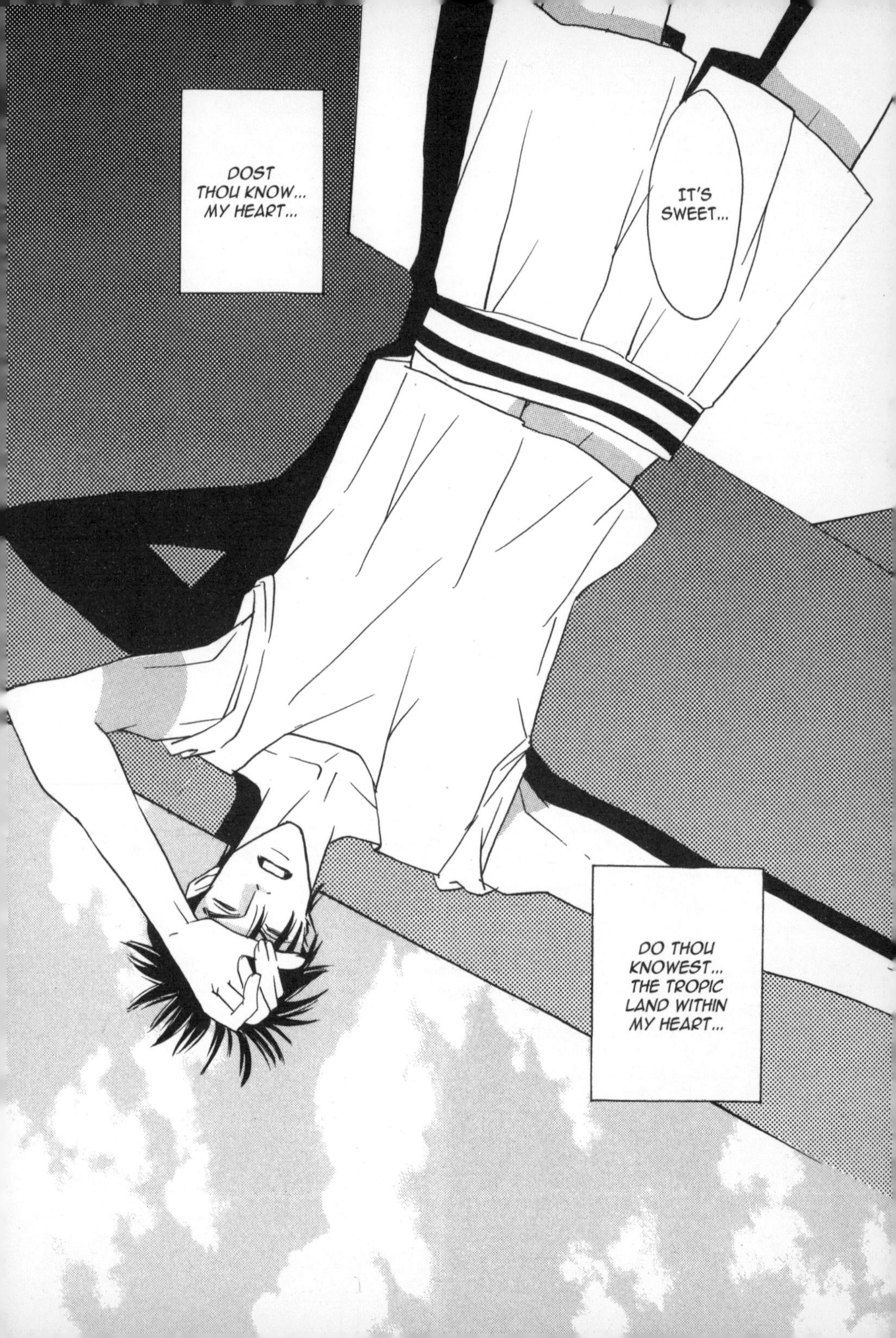
IT'S SWEET...
DOST THOU KNOW... MY HEART...
DO THOU KNOWEST... THE TROPIC LAND WITHIN MY HEART...

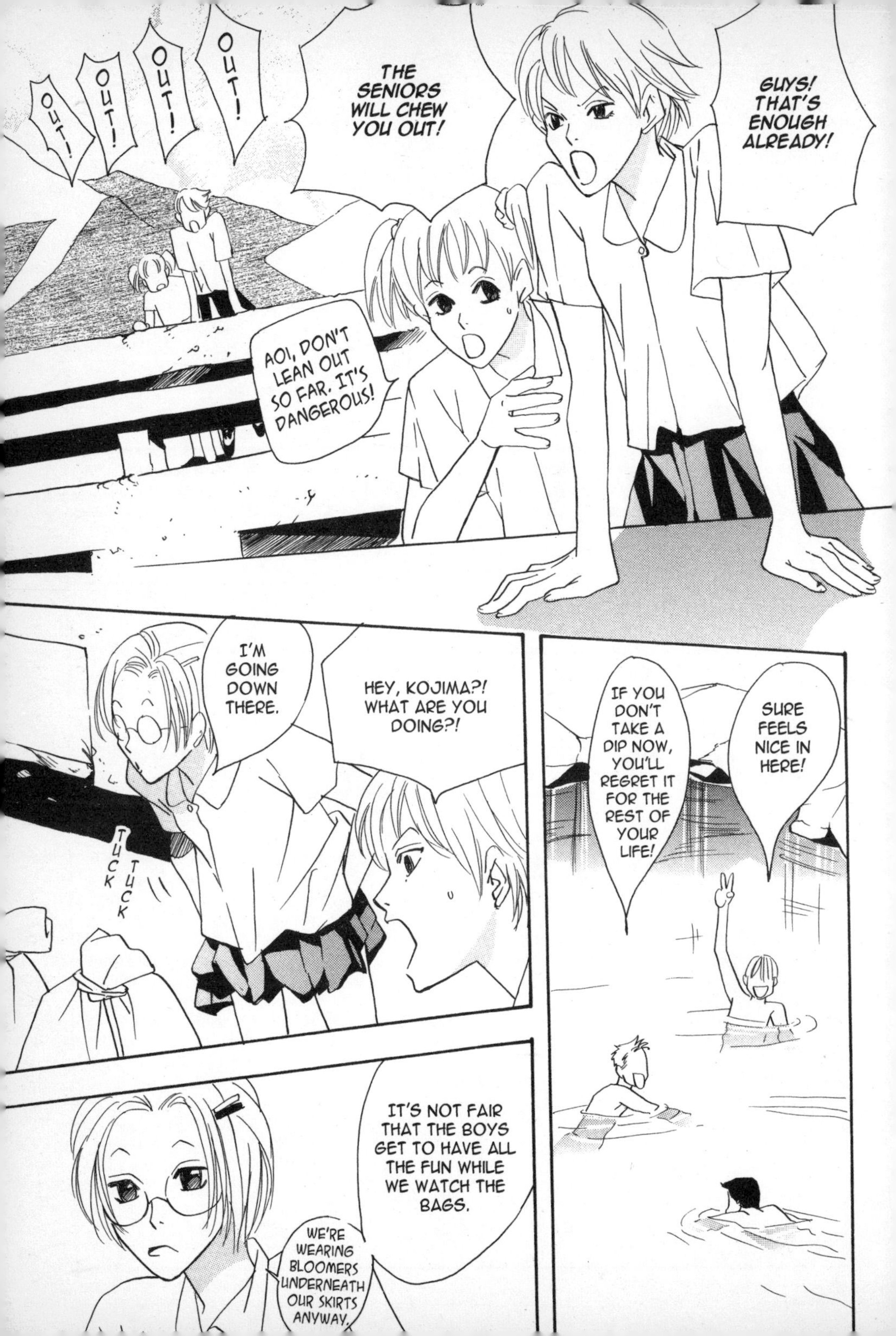
GUYS! THAT'S ENOUGH ALREADY!
THE SENIORS WILL CHEW YOU OUT!
OUT!
OUT!
OUT!
OUT!
AOI, DON'T LEAN OUT SO FAR. IT'S DANGEROUS!
SURE FEELS NICE IN HERE!
IF YOU DON'T TAKE A DIP NOW, YOU'LL REGRET IT FOR THE REST OF YOUR LIFE!
HEY, KOJIMA?! WHAT ARE YOU DOING?!
I'M GOING DOWN THERE.
TUCK TUCK
IT'S NOT FAIR THAT THE BOYS GET TO HAVE ALL THE FUN WHILE WE WATCH THE BAGS.
WE'RE WEARING BLOOMERS UNDERNEATH OUR SKIRTS ANYWAY.

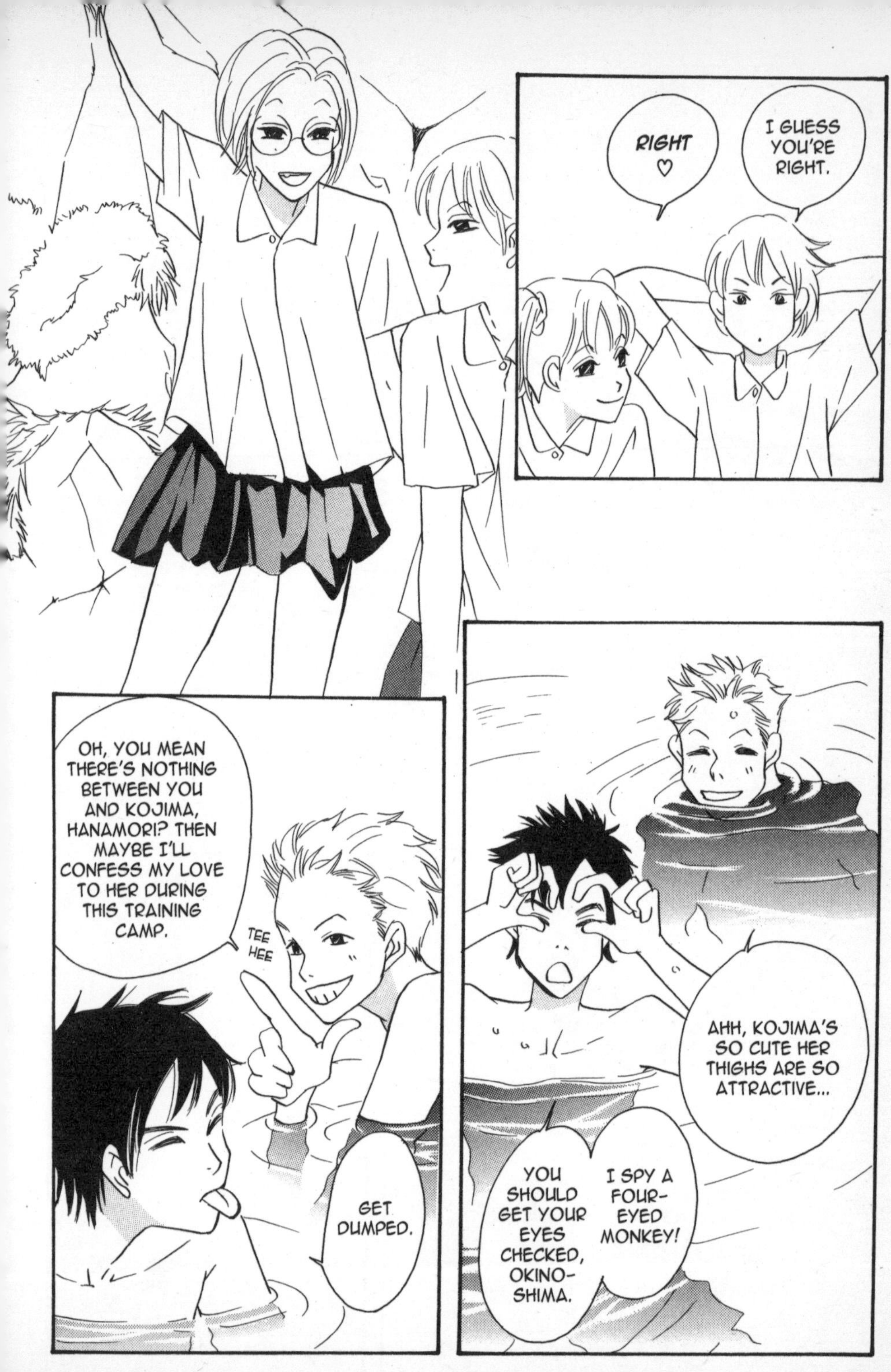
I GUESS YOU'RE RIGHT.
RIGHT ♡
AHH, KOJIMA'S SO CUTE HER THIGHS ARE SO ATTRACTIVE...
I SPY A FOUR-EYED MONKEY!
YOU SHOULD GET YOUR EYES CHECKED, OKINO-SHIMA.
OH, YOU MEAN THERE'S NOTHING BETWEEN YOU AND KOJIMA, HANAMORI? THEN MAYBE I'LL CONFESS MY LOVE TO HER DURING THIS TRAINING CAMP.
TEE HEE
GET DUMPED.

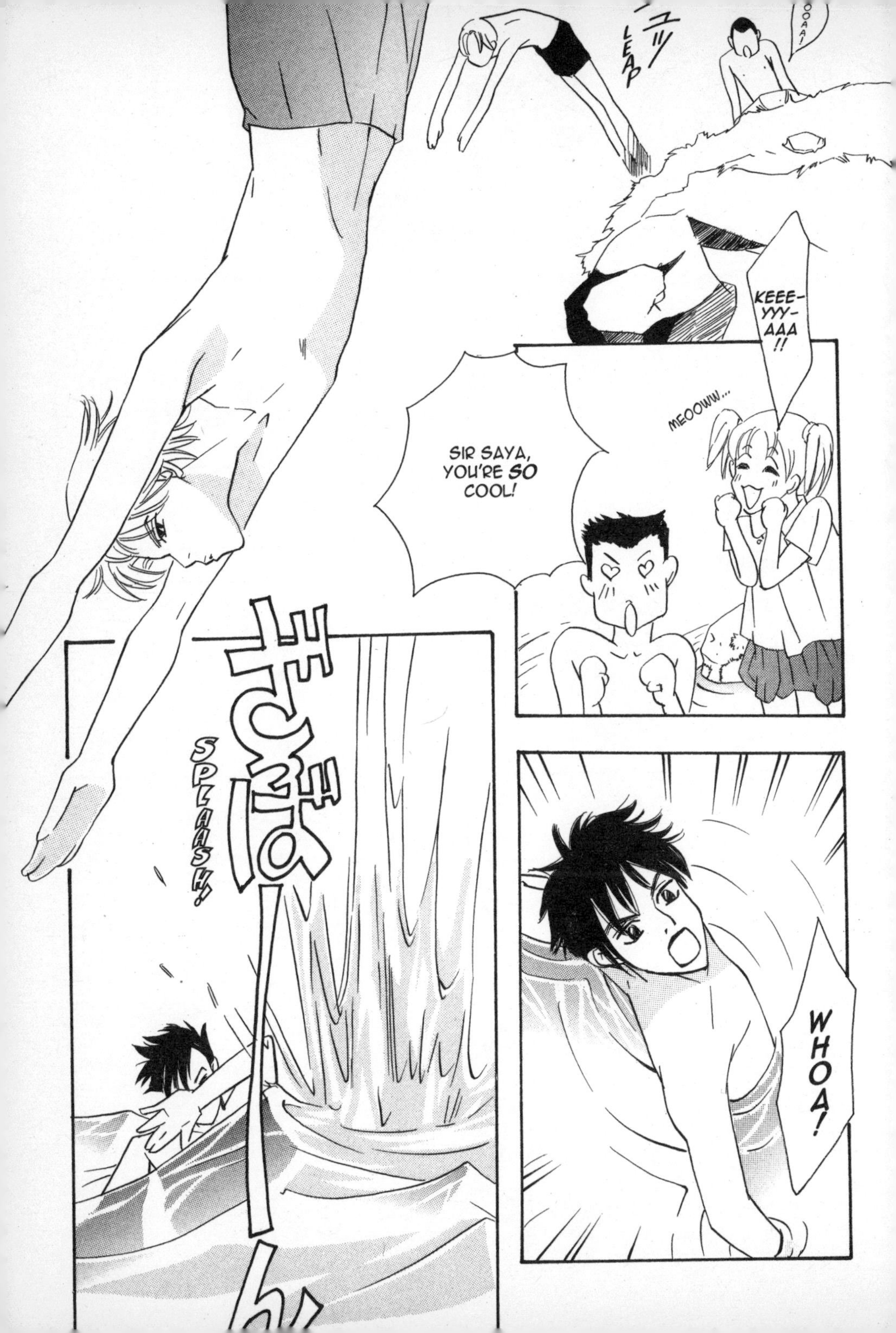
OOAA!
LEAP
KEEE-YYY-AAA!!
SIR SAYA, YOU'RE SO COOL!
MEOOWW...
WHOA!
SPLAASH!

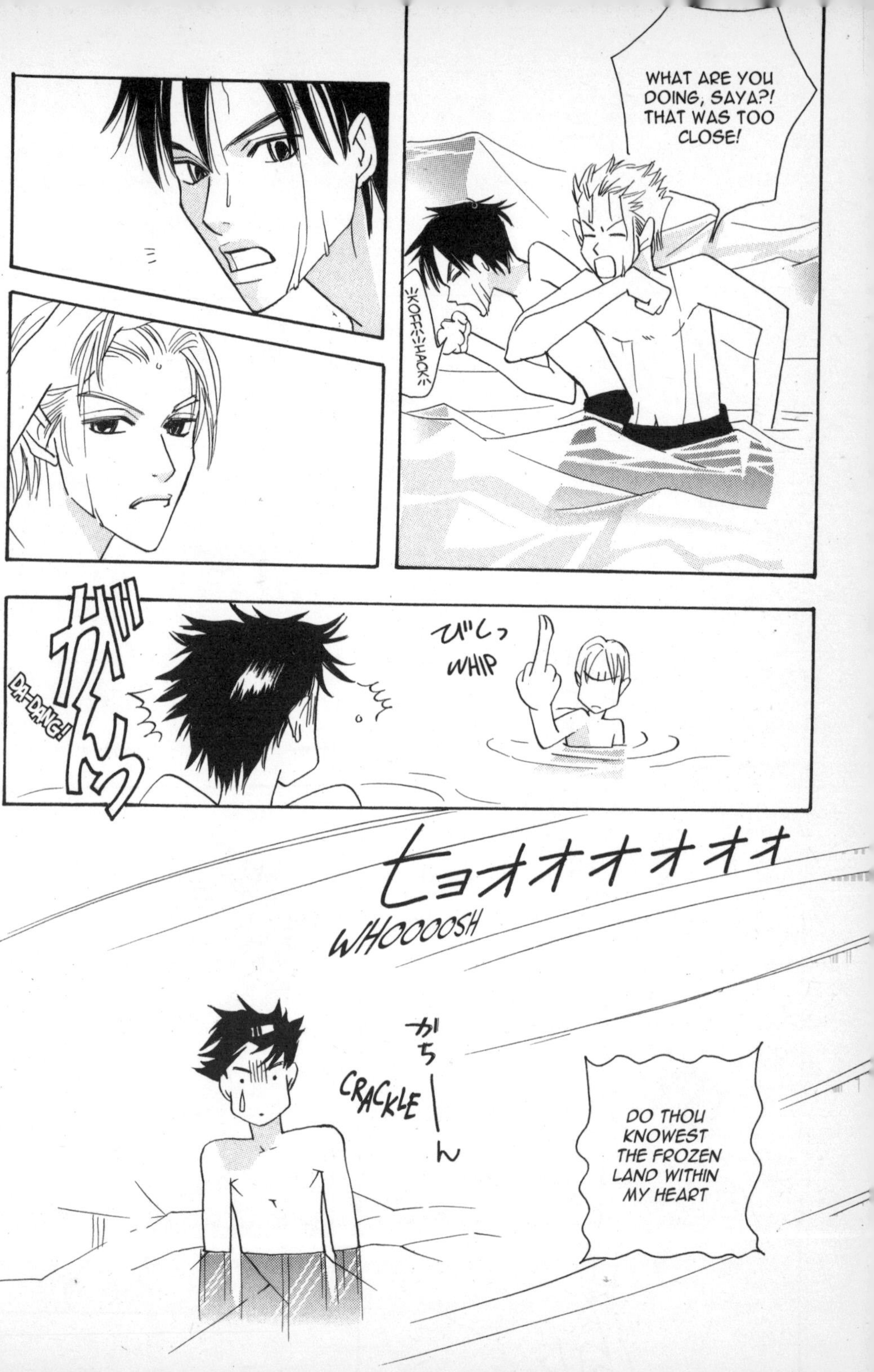
WHAT ARE YOU DOING, SAYA?! THAT WAS TOO CLOSE!
KOFF HACK
びしっ
WHIP
がん
DA-DANG!
ヒョオオオオオオオ
WHOOOOSH
DO THOU KNOWEST THE FROZEN LAND WITHIN MY HEART
がちーん
CRACKLE

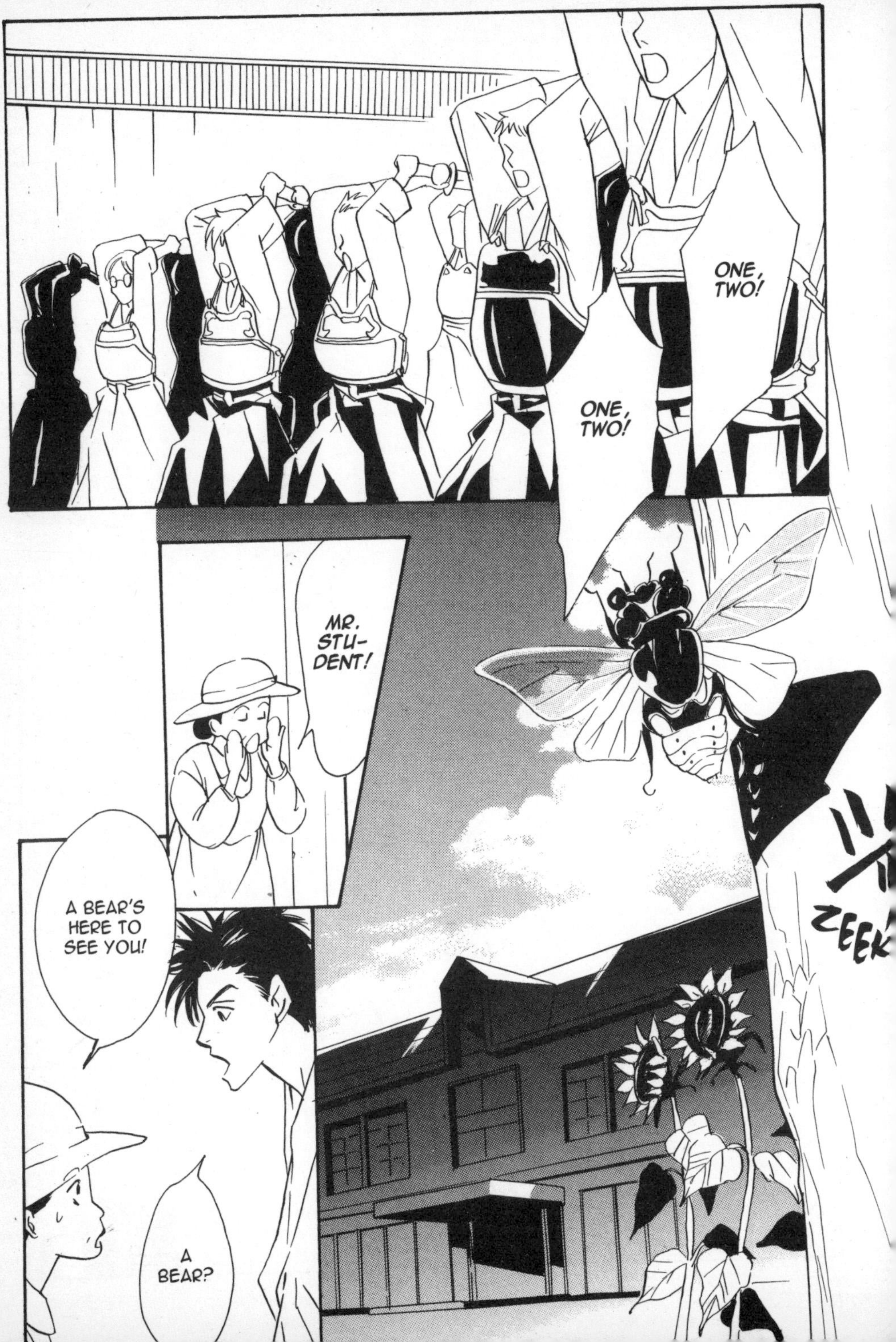
ONE, TWO!
ONE, TWO!
ZEEK
MR. STU- DENT!
A BEAR'S HERE TO SEE YOU!
A BEAR?

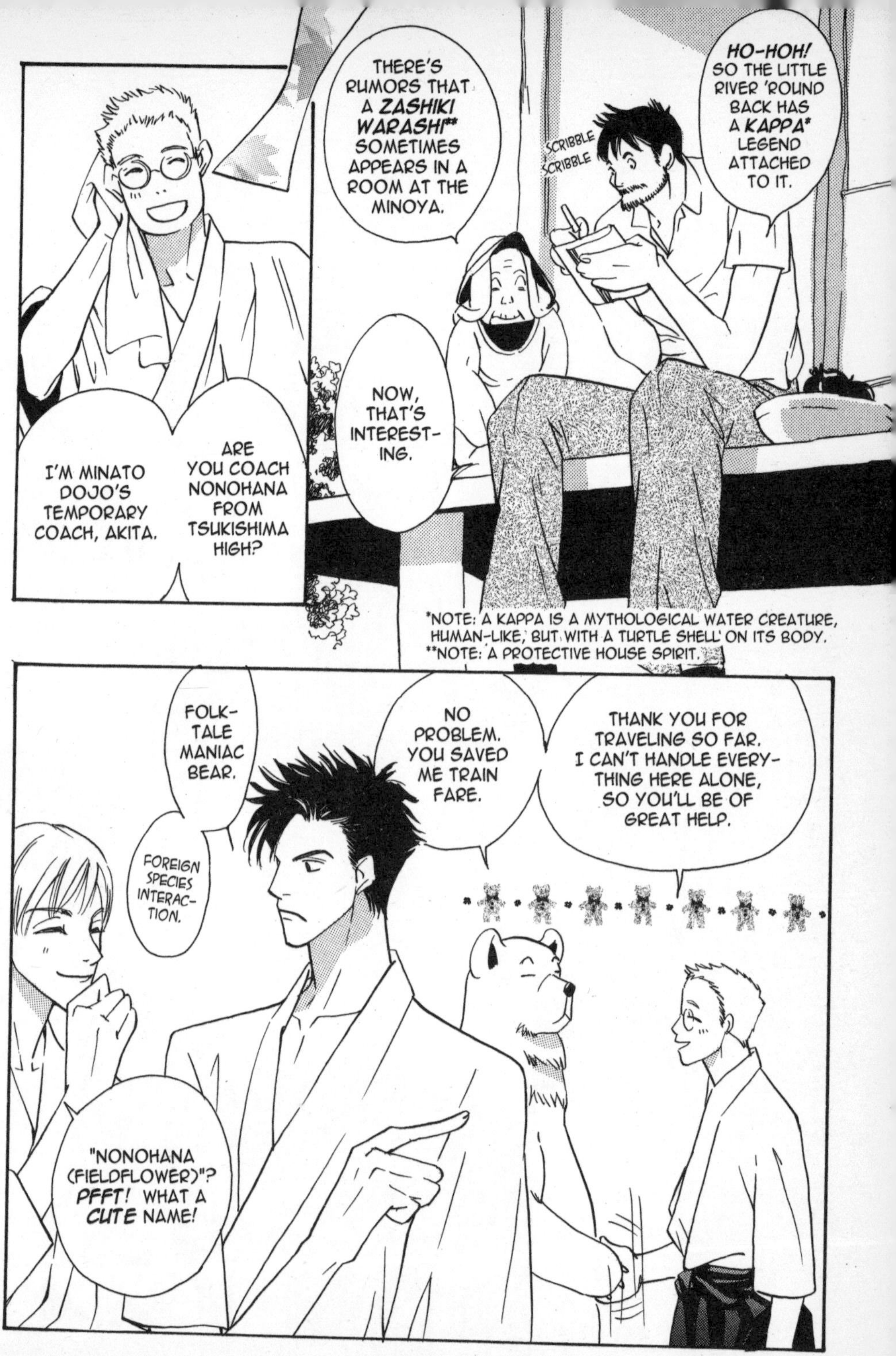
HO-HOH! SO THE LITTLE RIVER 'ROUND BACK HAS A KAPPA* LEGEND ATTACHED TO IT.
SCRIBBLE SCRIBBLE
THERE'S RUMORS THAT A ZASHIKI WARASHI** SOMETIMES APPEARS IN A ROOM AT THE MINOYA.
NOW, THAT'S INTEREST-ING.
ARE YOU COACH NONOHANA FROM TSUKISHIMA HIGH?
I'M MINATO DOJO'S TEMPORARY COACH, AKITA.
*NOTE: A KAPPA IS A MYTHOLOGICAL WATER CREATURE, HUMAN-LIKE, BUT WITH A TURTLE SHELL ON ITS BODY.
**NOTE: A PROTECTIVE HOUSE SPIRIT.
THANK YOU FOR TRAVELING SO FAR. I CAN'T HANDLE EVERY-THING HERE ALONE, SO YOU'LL BE OF GREAT HELP.
NO PROBLEM. YOU SAVED ME TRAIN FARE.
FOLK-TALE MANIAC BEAR.
FOREIGN SPECIES INTERAC-TION.
"NONOHANA (FIELDFLOWER)"? PFFT! WHAT A CUTE NAME!

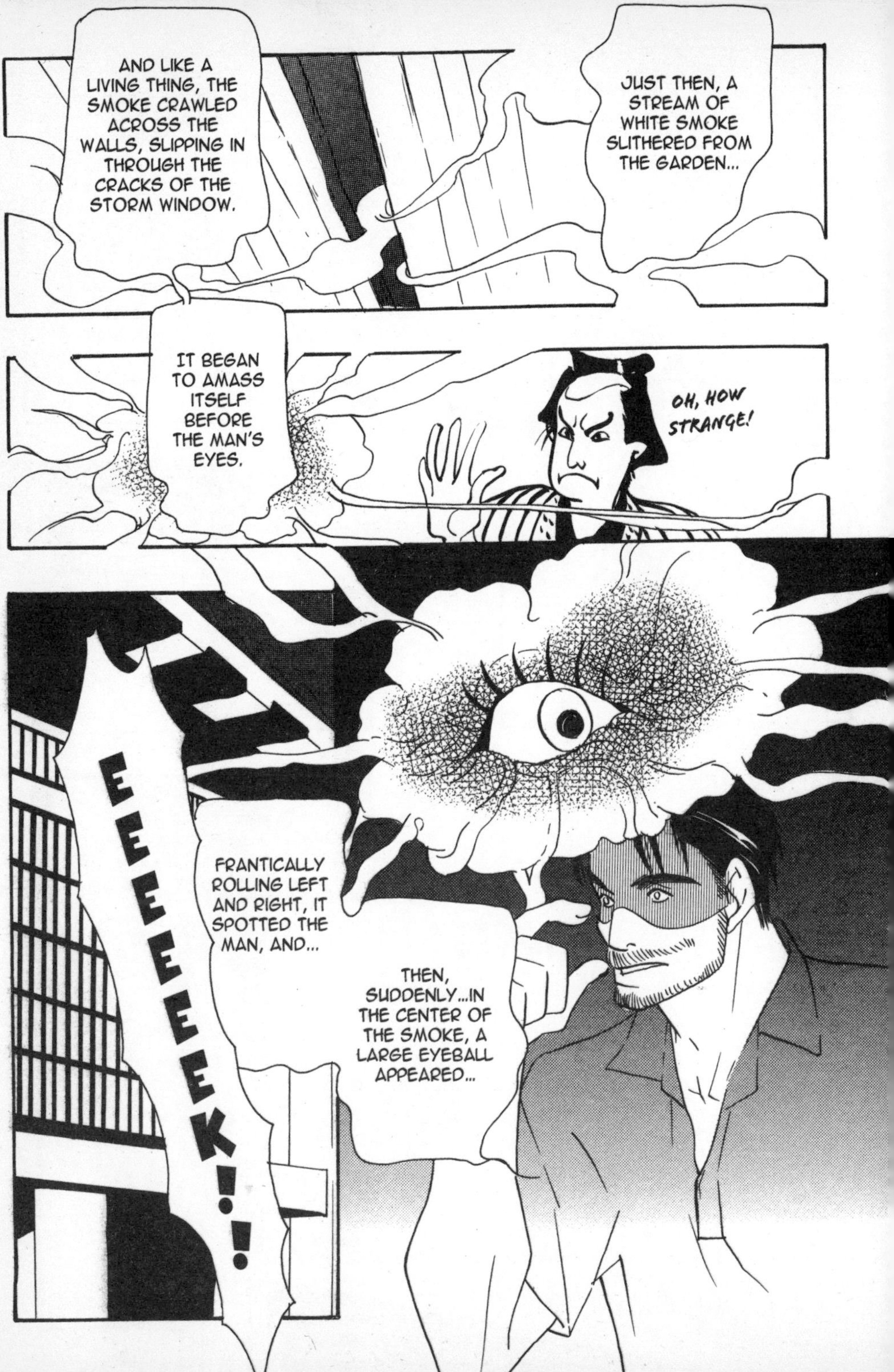
JUST THEN, A STREAM OF WHITE SMOKE SLITHERED FROM THE GARDEN...
AND LIKE A LIVING THING, THE SMOKE CRAWLED ACROSS THE WALLS, SLIPPING IN THROUGH THE CRACKS OF THE STORM WINDOW.
IT BEGAN TO AMASS ITSELF BEFORE THE MAN'S EYES.
OH, HOW STRANGE!
THEN, SUDDENLY...IN THE CENTER OF THE SMOKE, A LARGE EYEBALL APPEARED...
FRANTICALLY ROLLING LEFT AND RIGHT, IT SPOTTED THE MAN, AND...
EEEEEEK!!!

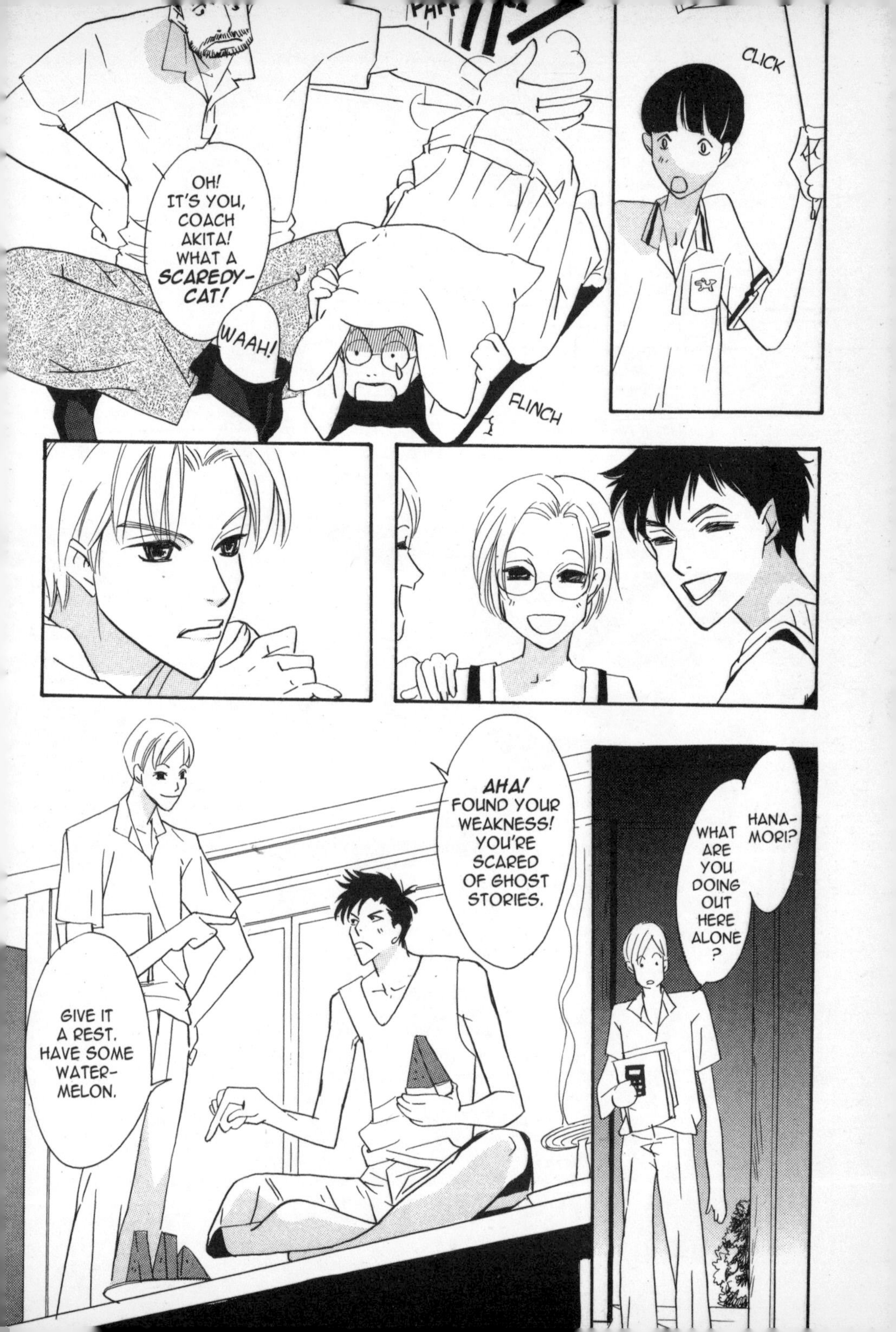
CLICK
OH! IT'S YOU, COACH AKITA! WHAT A SCAREDY-CAT!
WAAH!
FLINCH
HANAMORI? WHAT ARE YOU DOING OUT HERE ALONE?
AHA! FOUND YOUR WEAKNESS! YOU'RE SCARED OF GHOST STORIES.
GIVE IT A REST. HAVE SOME WATERMELON.

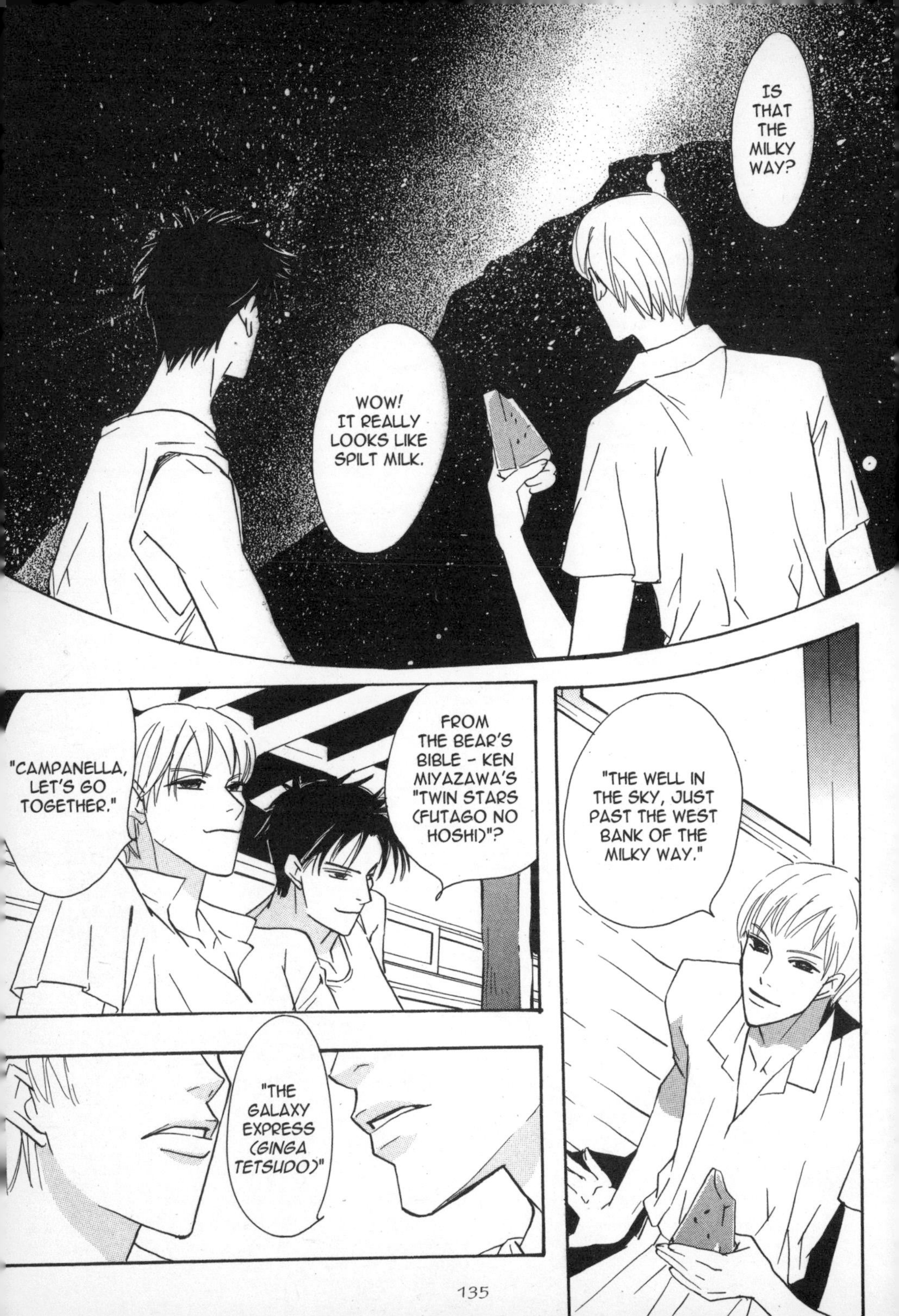
IS THAT THE MILKY WAY?
WOW! IT REALLY LOOKS LIKE SPILT MILK.
"THE WELL IN THE SKY, JUST PAST THE WEST BANK OF THE MILKY WAY."
FROM THE BEAR'S BIBLE - KEN MIYAZAWA'S "TWIN STARS (FUTAGO NO HOSHI)"?
"CAMPANELLA, LET'S GO TOGETHER."
"THE GALAXY EXPRESS (GINGA TETSUDO)"

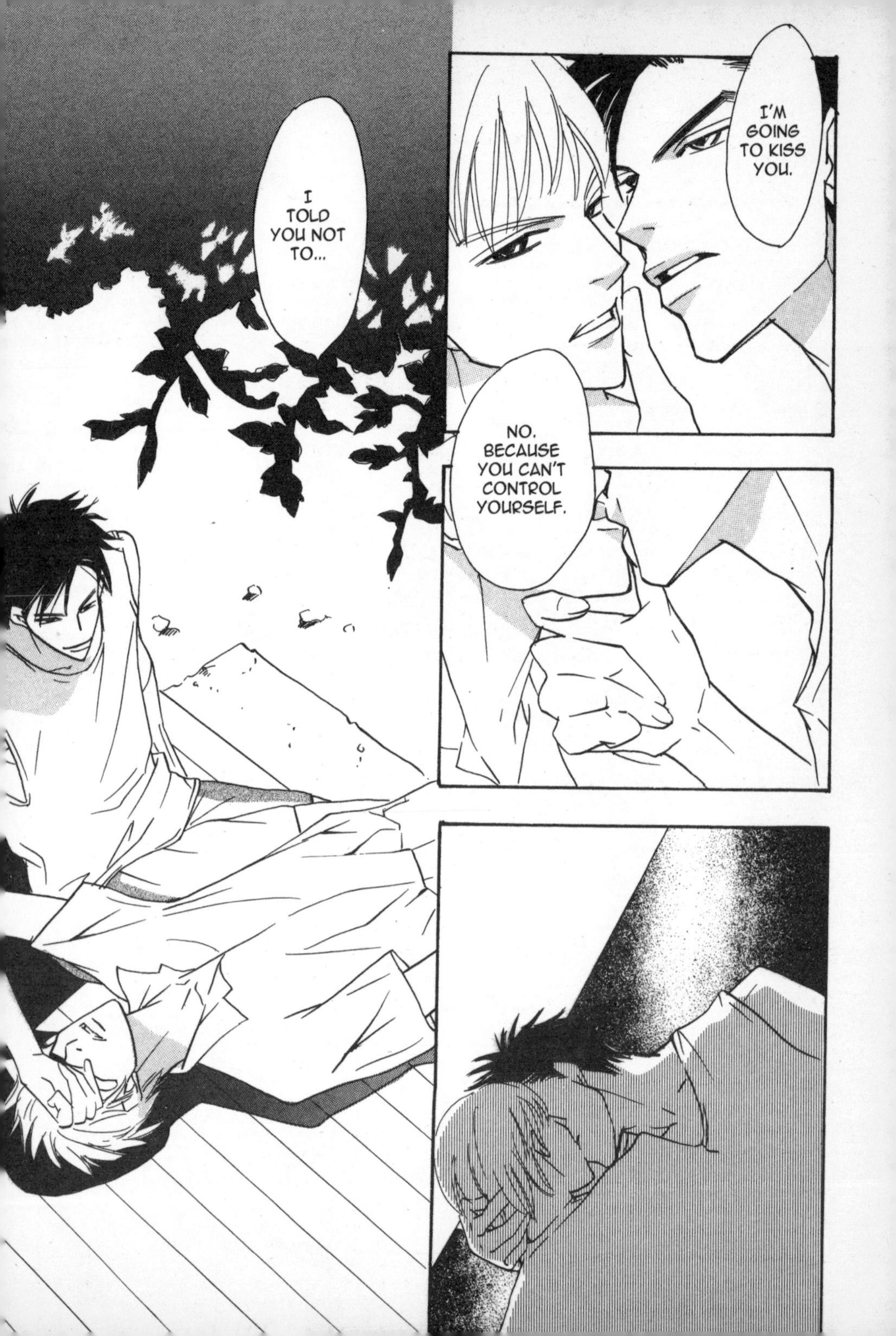
I'M GOING TO KISS YOU.
NO. BECAUSE YOU CAN'T CONTROL YOURSELF.
I TOLD YOU NOT TO...

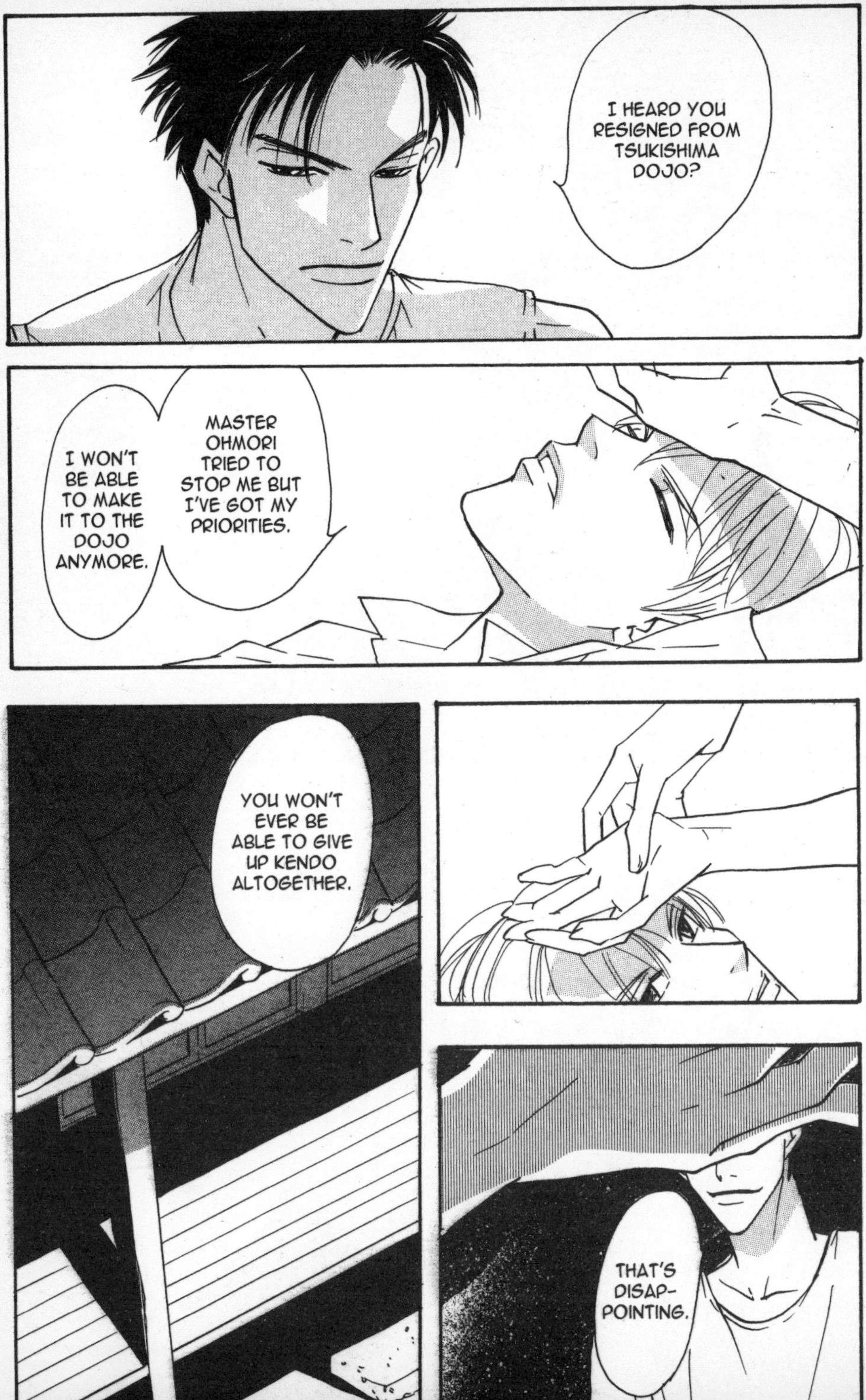
I HEARD YOU RESIGNED FROM TSUKISHIMA DOJO?
MASTER OHMORI TRIED TO STOP ME BUT I'VE GOT MY PRIORITIES.
I WON'T BE ABLE TO MAKE IT TO THE DOJO ANYMORE.
THAT'S DISAP-POINTING.
YOU WON'T EVER BE ABLE TO GIVE UP KENDO ALTOGETHER.

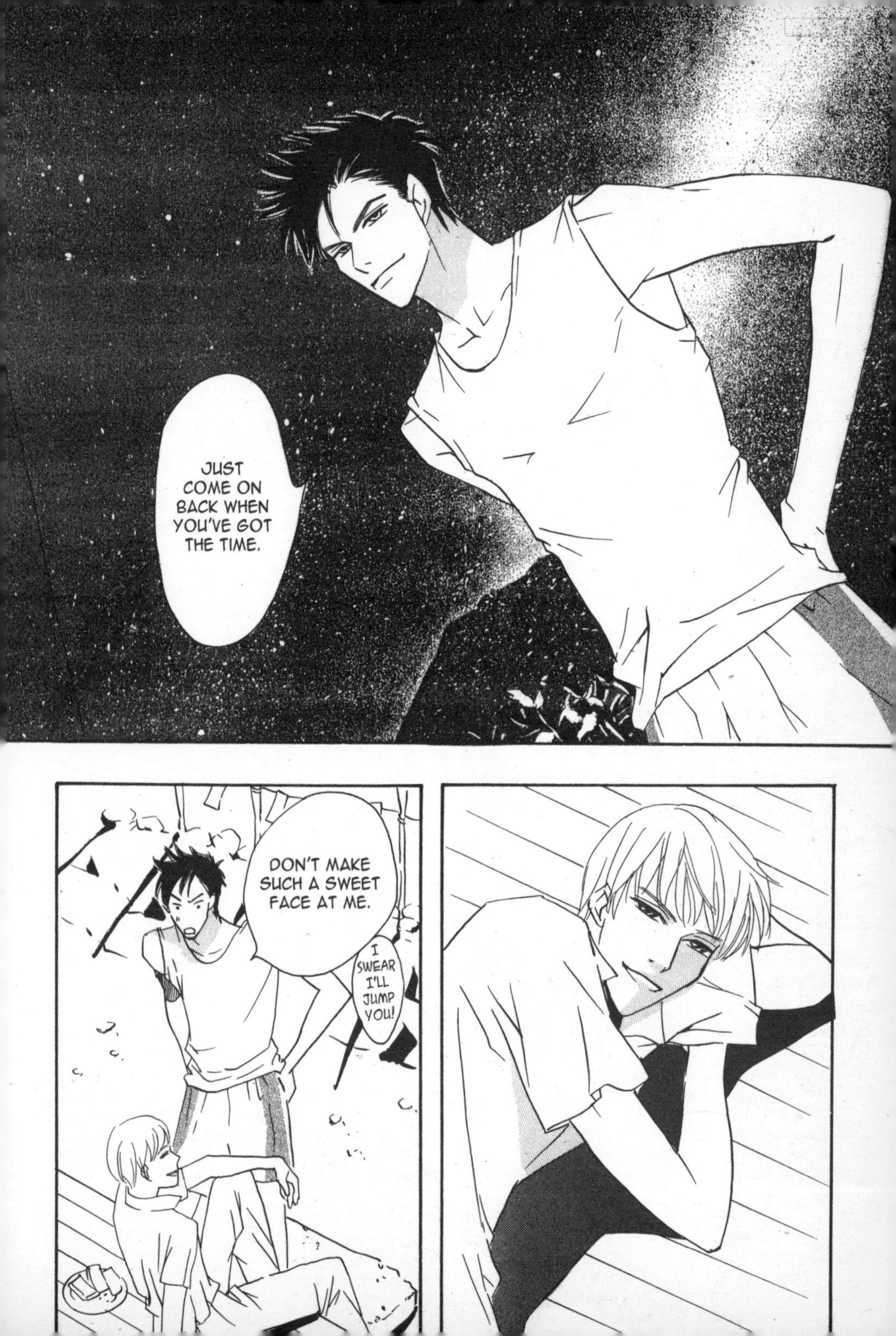
JUST COME ON BACK WHEN YOU'VE GOT THE TIME.
DON'T MAKE SUCH A SWEET FACE AT ME.
I SWEAR I'LL JUMP YOU!

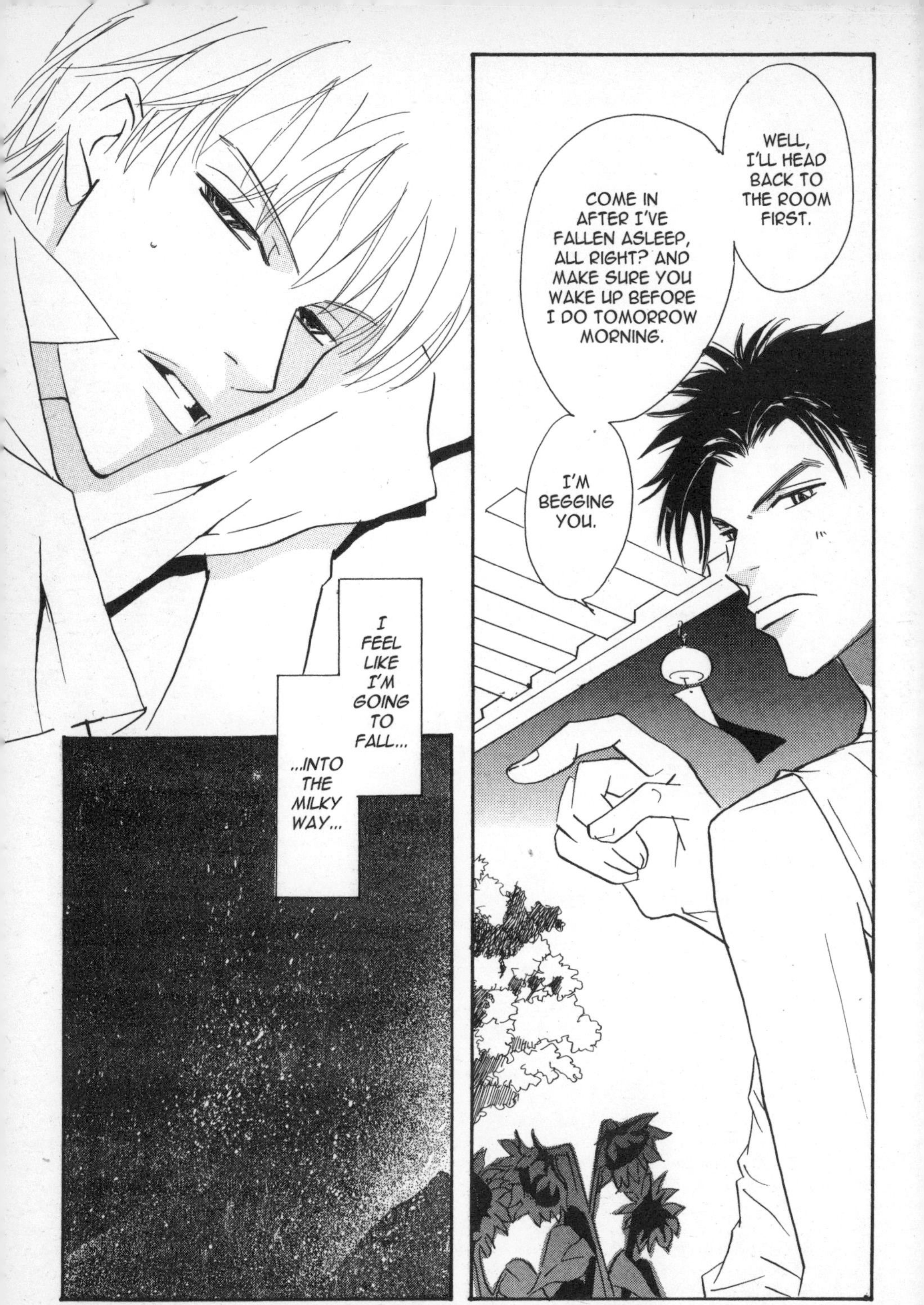
WELL, I'LL HEAD BACK TO THE ROOM FIRST.
COME IN AFTER I'VE FALLEN ASLEEP, ALL RIGHT? AND MAKE SURE YOU WAKE UP BEFORE I DO TOMORROW MORNING.
I'M BEGGING YOU.
I FEEL LIKE I'M GOING TO FALL...
...INTO THE MILKY WAY...

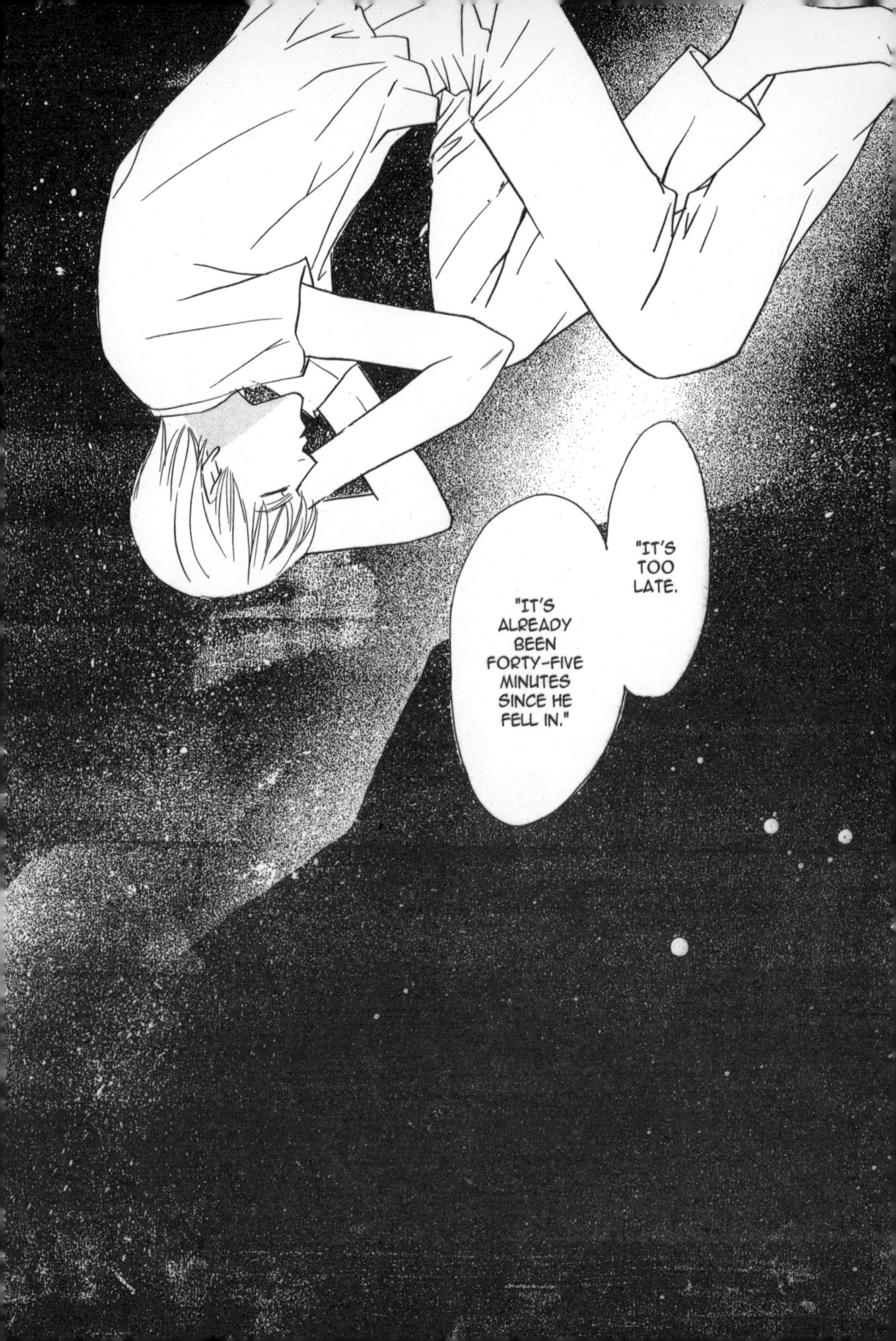
"IT'S TOO LATE.
"IT'S ALREADY BEEN FORTY-FIVE MINUTES SINCE HE FELL IN."

君知るや

DOST THOU KNOW - PART 2

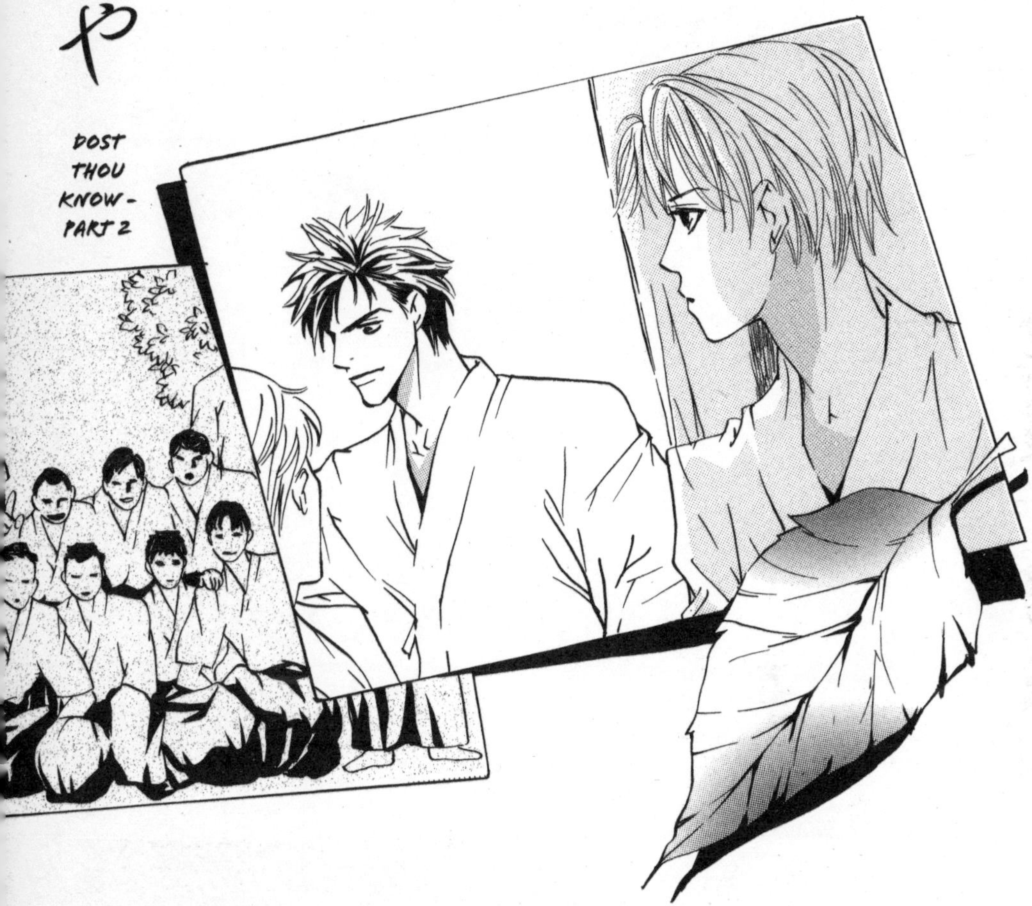

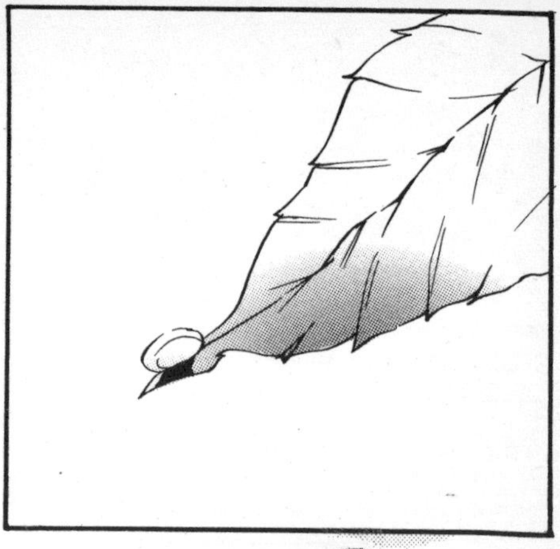

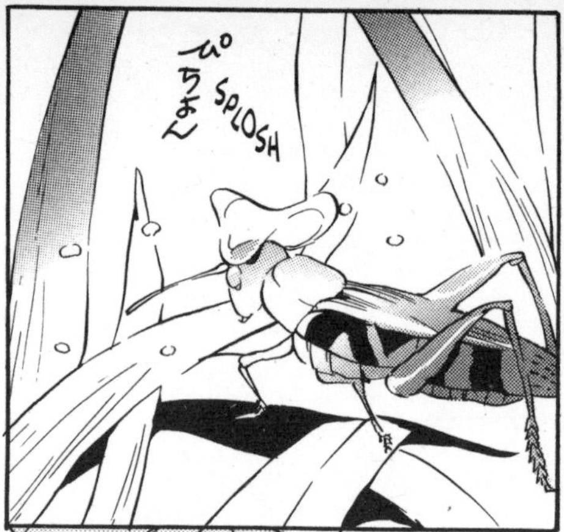
ぴちょん
SPLOSH

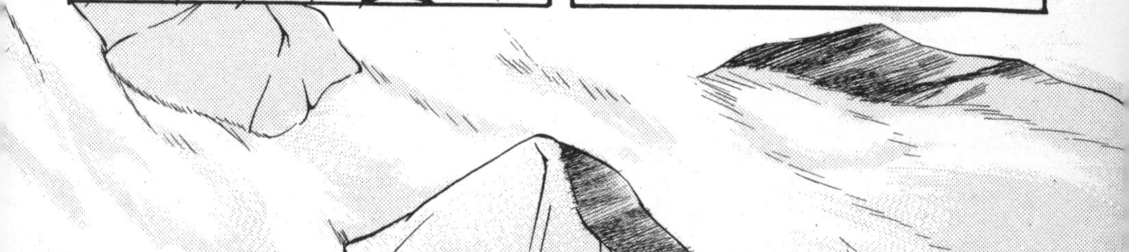

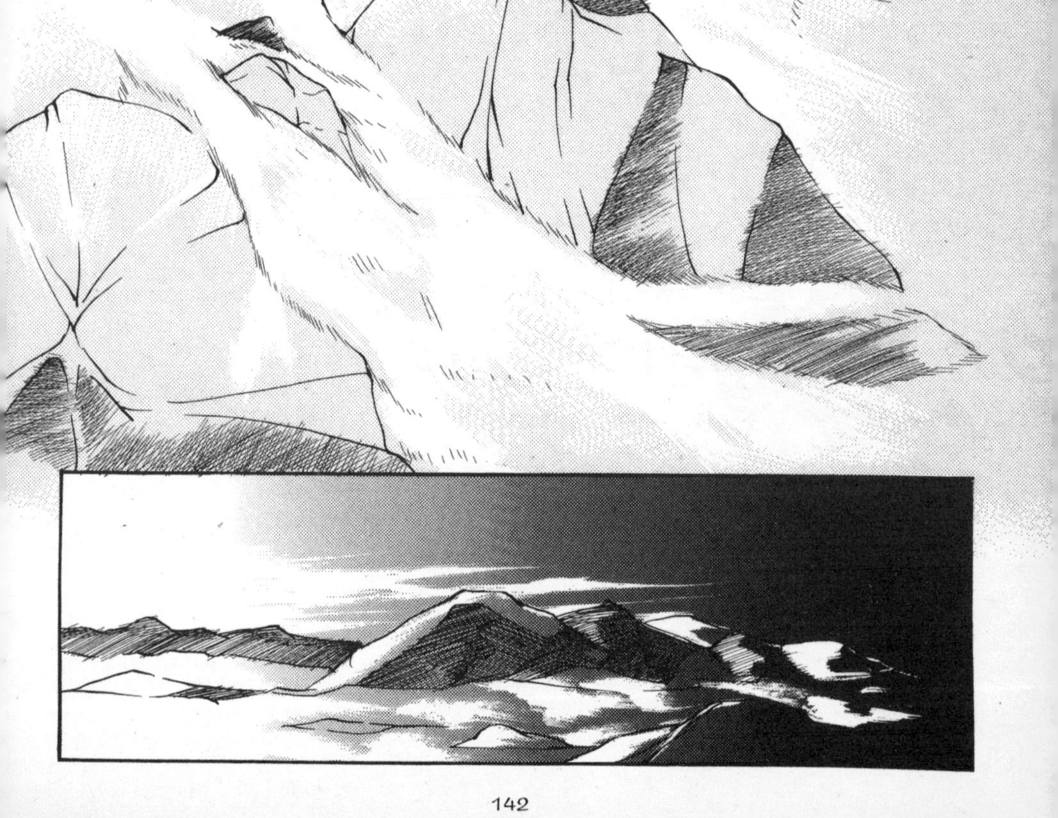

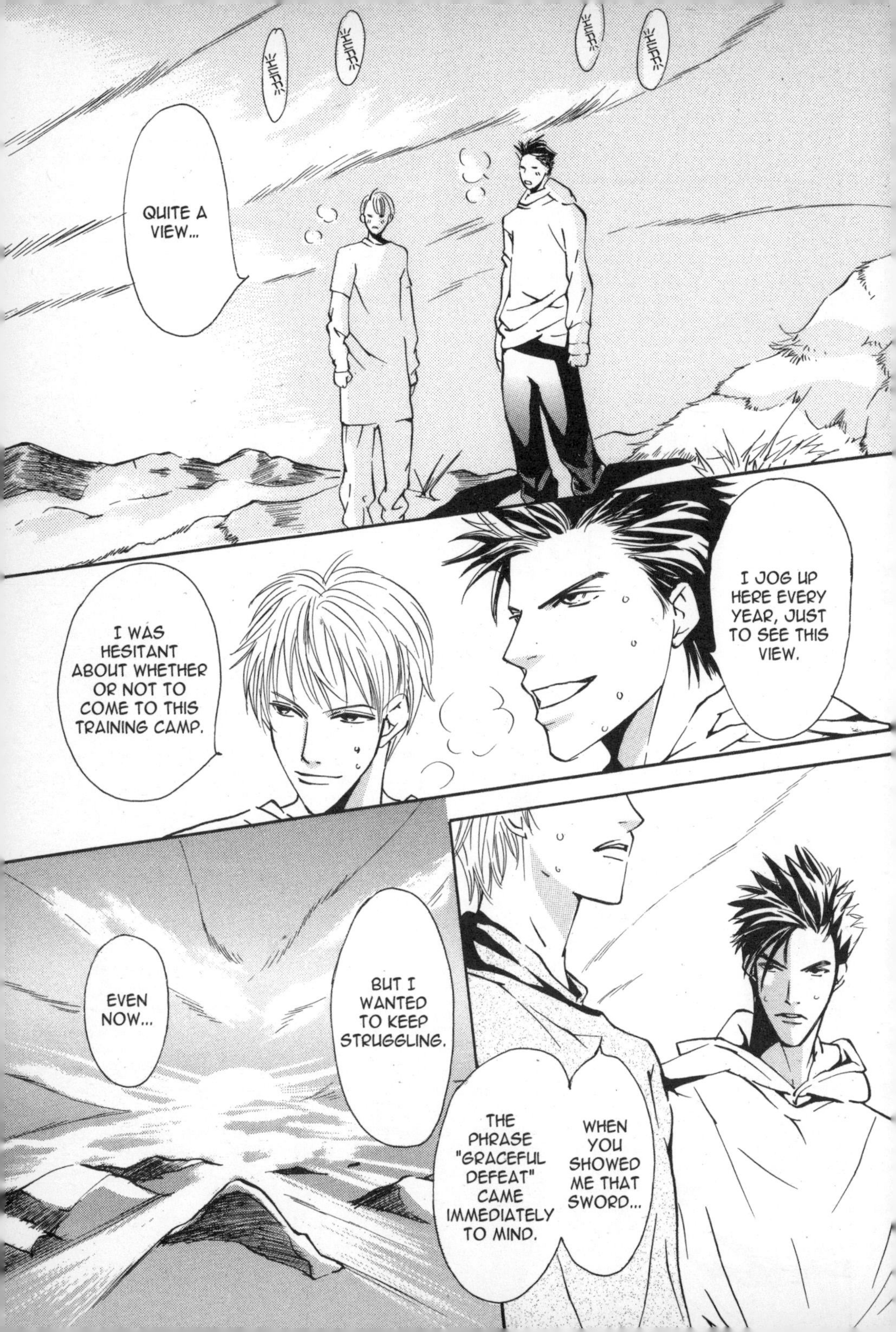
HUFF
HUFF
HUFF
HUFF
QUITE A VIEW...
I JOG UP HERE EVERY YEAR, JUST TO SEE THIS VIEW.
I WAS HESITANT ABOUT WHETHER OR NOT TO COME TO THIS TRAINING CAMP.
BUT I WANTED TO KEEP STRUGGLING.
WHEN YOU SHOWED ME THAT SWORD...
THE PHRASE "GRACEFUL DEFEAT" CAME IMMEDIATELY TO MIND.
EVEN NOW...

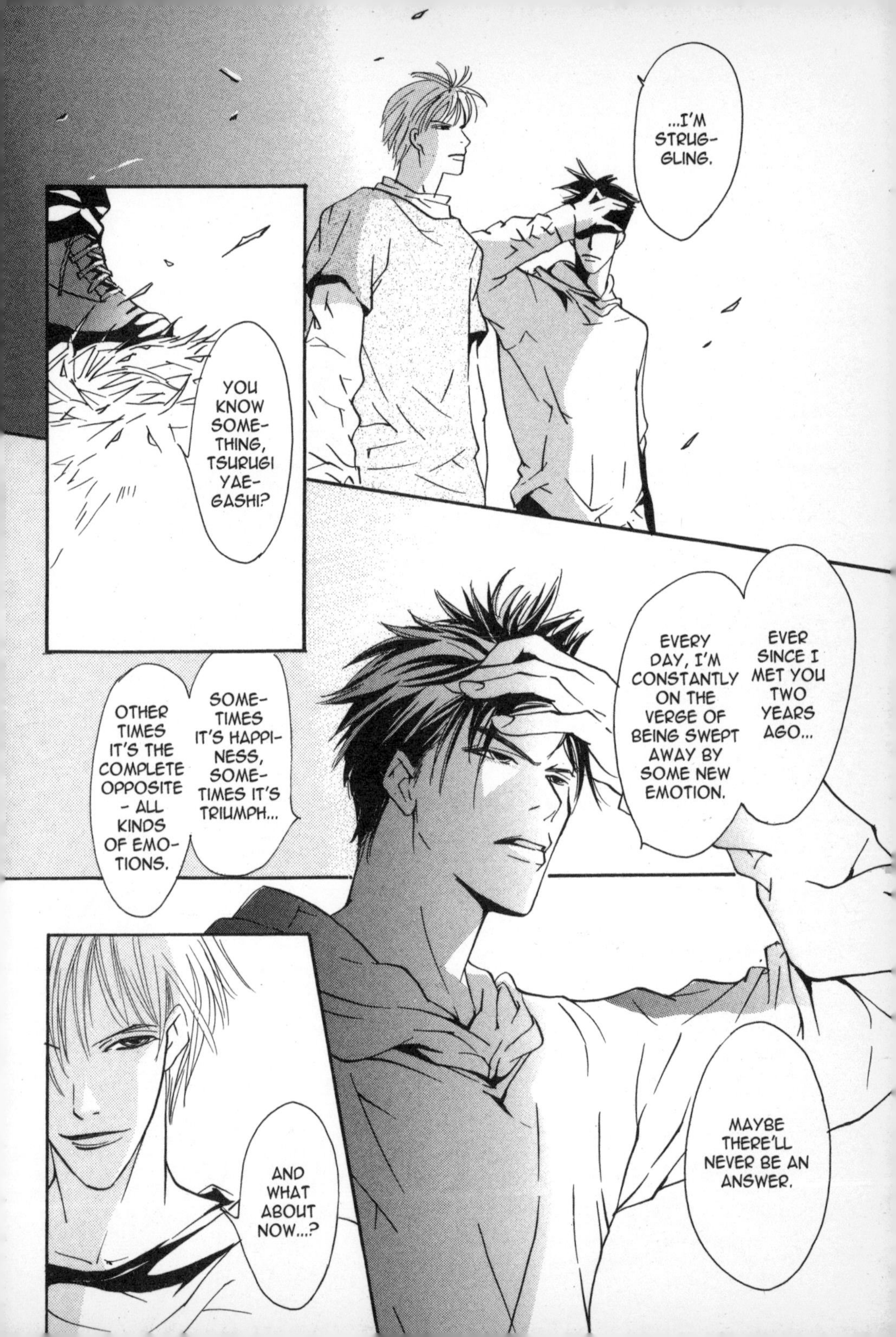
...I'M STRUGGLING.
YOU KNOW SOMETHING, TSURUGI YAEGASHI?
EVER SINCE I MET YOU TWO YEARS AGO...
EVERY DAY, I'M CONSTANTLY ON THE VERGE OF BEING SWEPT AWAY BY SOME NEW EMOTION.
SOMETIMES IT'S HAPPINESS, SOMETIMES IT'S TRIUMPH...
OTHER TIMES IT'S THE COMPLETE OPPOSITE - ALL KINDS OF EMOTIONS.
MAYBE THERE'LL NEVER BE AN ANSWER.
AND WHAT ABOUT NOW...?

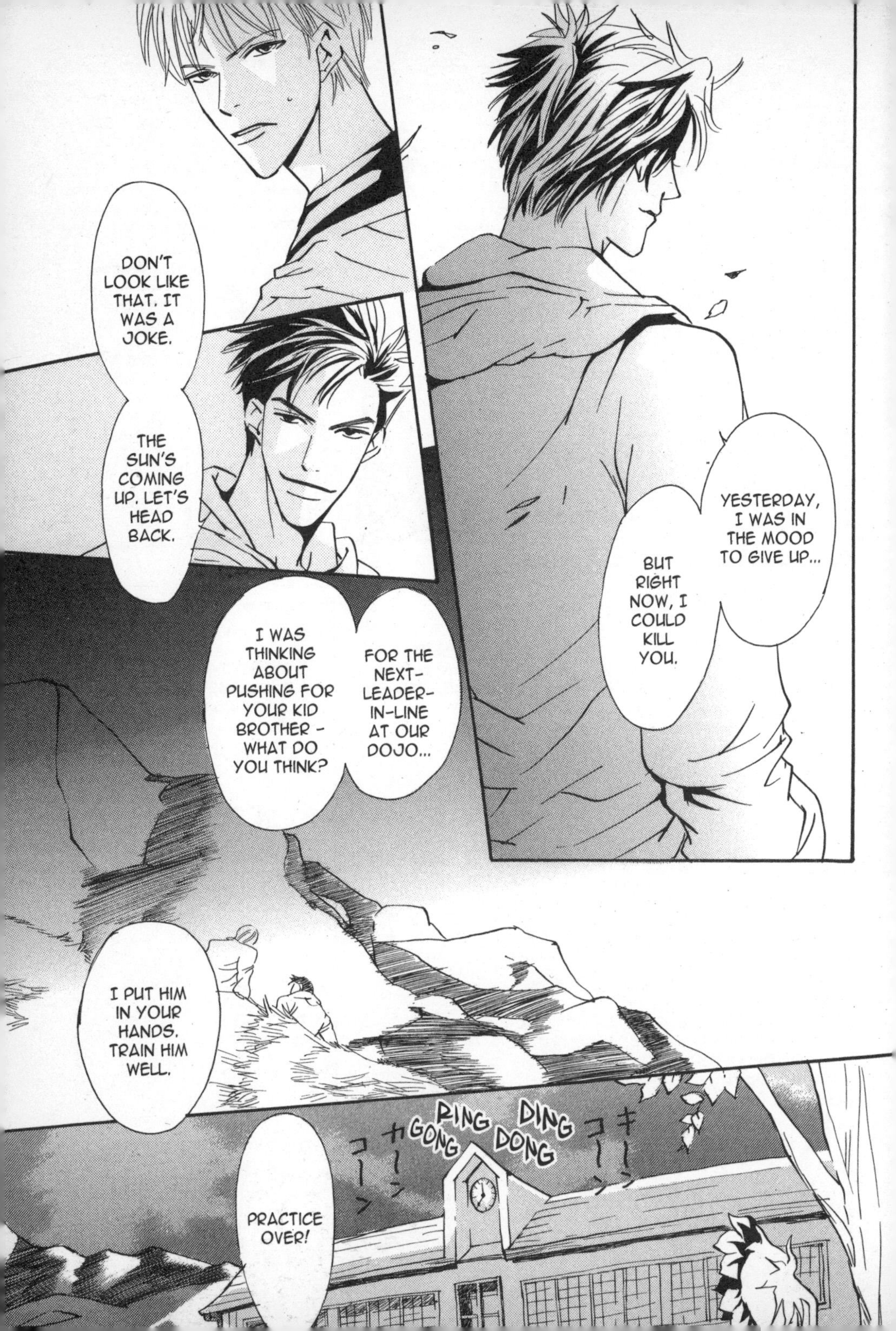
YESTERDAY, I WAS IN THE MOOD TO GIVE UP...
BUT RIGHT NOW, I COULD KILL YOU.
DON'T LOOK LIKE THAT. IT WAS A JOKE.
THE SUN'S COMING UP. LET'S HEAD BACK.
FOR THE NEXT-LEADER-IN-LINE AT OUR DOJO...
I WAS THINKING ABOUT PUSHING FOR YOUR KID BROTHER - WHAT DO YOU THINK?
I PUT HIM IN YOUR HANDS. TRAIN HIM WELL.
DING DONG
RING GONG
PRACTICE OVER!

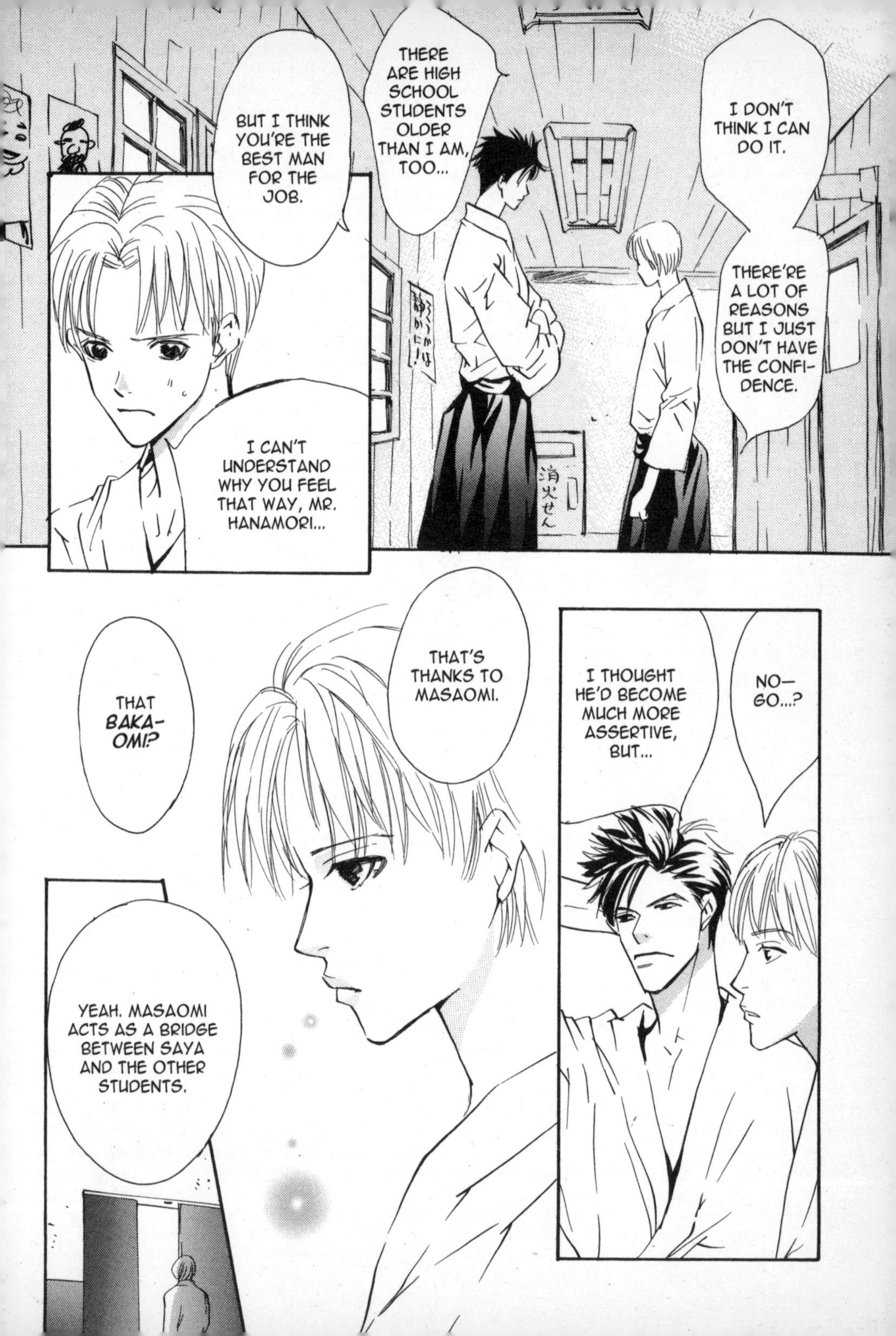
I DON'T THINK I CAN DO IT.
THERE'RE A LOT OF REASONS BUT I JUST DON'T HAVE THE CONFIDENCE.
THERE ARE HIGH SCHOOL STUDENTS OLDER THAN I AM, TOO...
BUT I THINK YOU'RE THE BEST MAN FOR THE JOB.
消火せん
I CAN'T UNDERSTAND WHY YOU FEEL THAT WAY, MR. HANAMORI...
NO— GO...?
I THOUGHT HE'D BECOME MUCH MORE ASSERTIVE, BUT...
THAT'S THANKS TO MASAOMI.
THAT *BAKA-OMI!?*
YEAH. MASAOMI ACTS AS A BRIDGE BETWEEN SAYA AND THE OTHER STUDENTS.

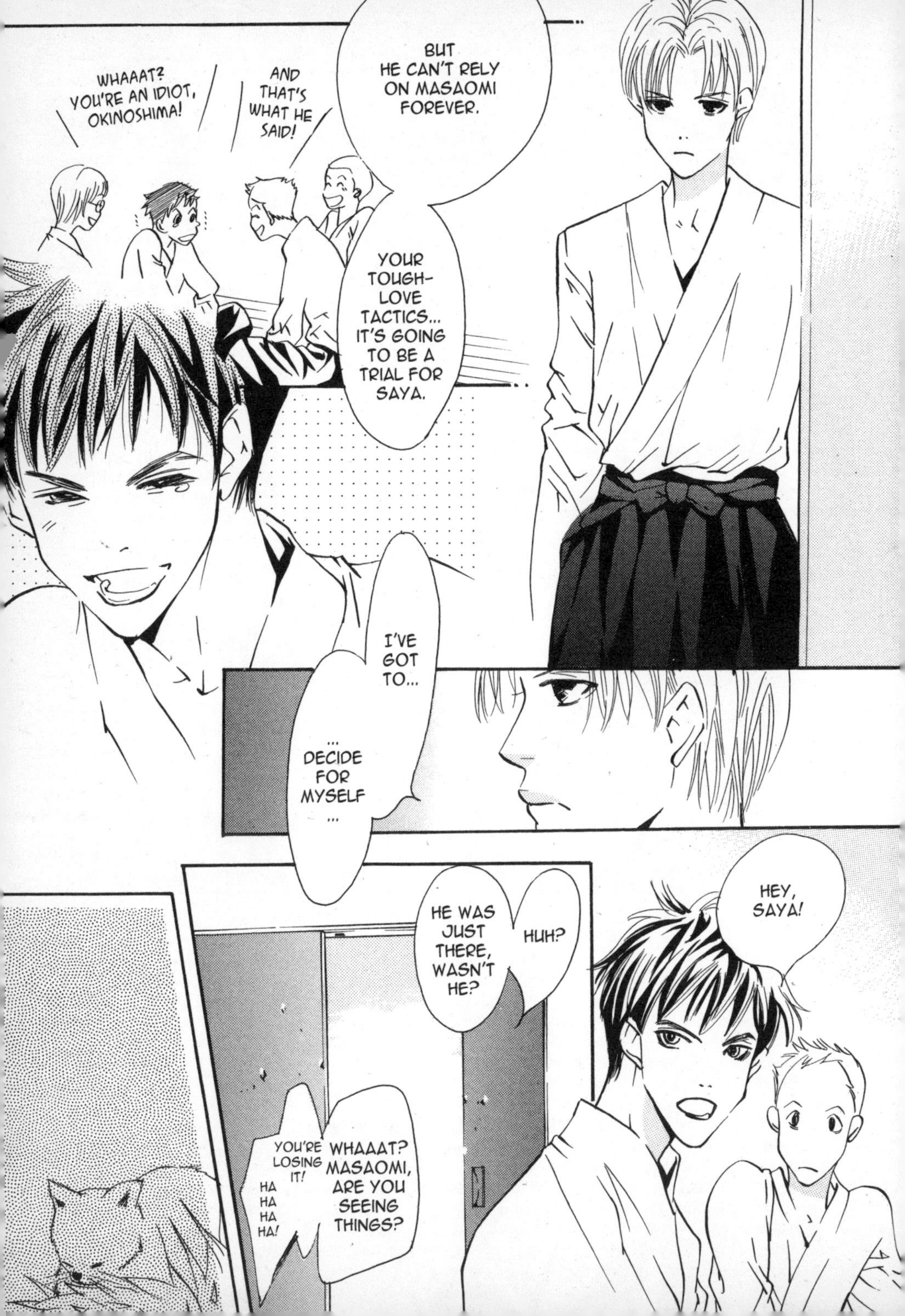
BUT HE CAN'T RELY ON MASAOMI FOREVER.
YOUR TOUGH-LOVE TACTICS... IT'S GOING TO BE A TRIAL FOR SAYA.
AND THAT'S WHAT HE SAID!
WHAAAT? YOU'RE AN IDIOT, OKINOSHIMA!
I'VE GOT TO...
...DECIDE FOR MYSELF...
HEY, SAYA!
HUH?
HE WAS JUST THERE, WASN'T HE?
WHAAAT? MASAOMI, ARE YOU SEEING THINGS?
YOU'RE LOSING IT!
HA HA HA HA!

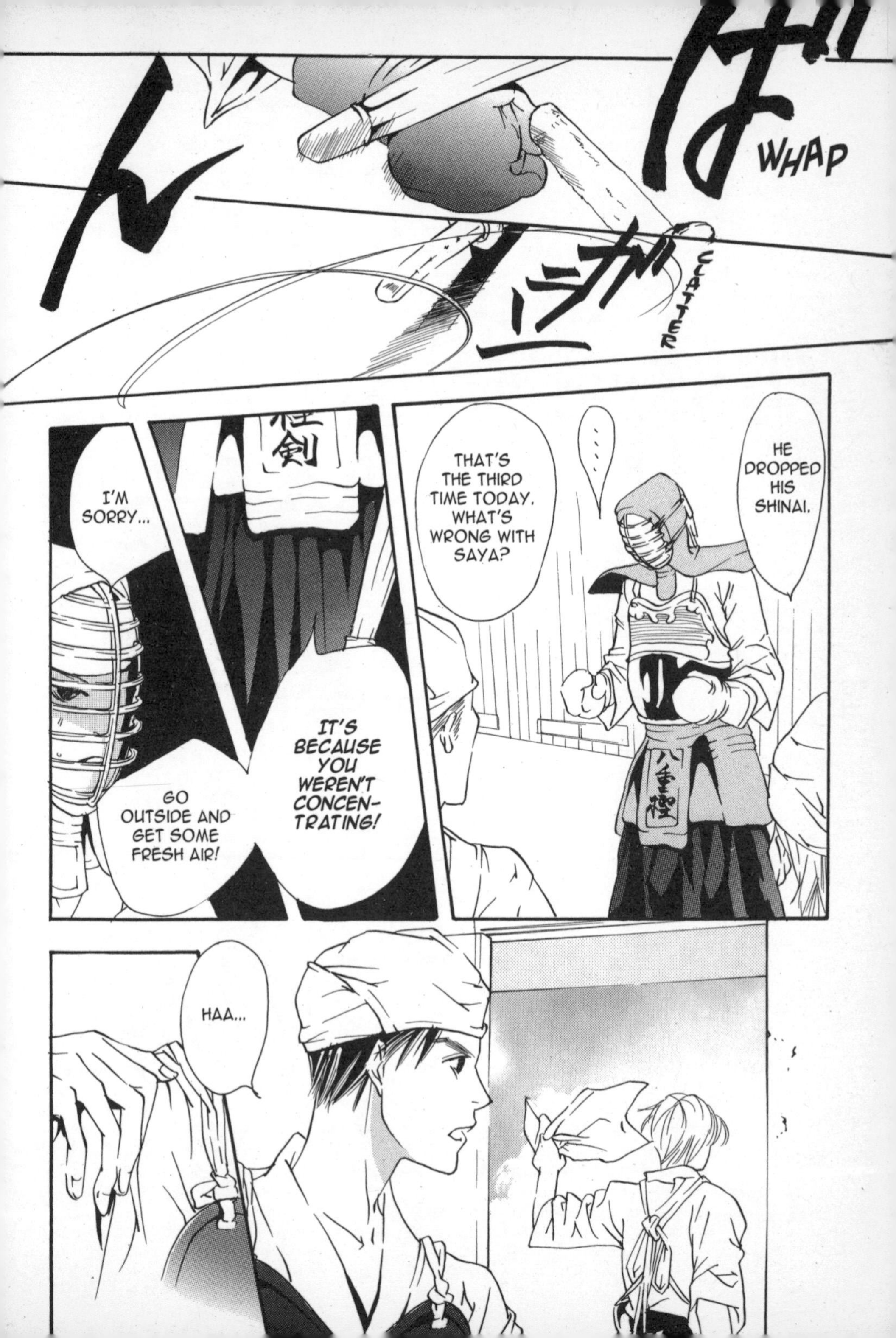

WHAP
CLATTER
HE DROPPED HIS SHINAI.
...
THAT'S THE THIRD TIME TODAY. WHAT'S WRONG WITH SAYA?
IT'S BECAUSE YOU WEREN'T CONCEN-TRATING!
GO OUTSIDE AND GET SOME FRESH AIR!
I'M SORRY...
HAA...

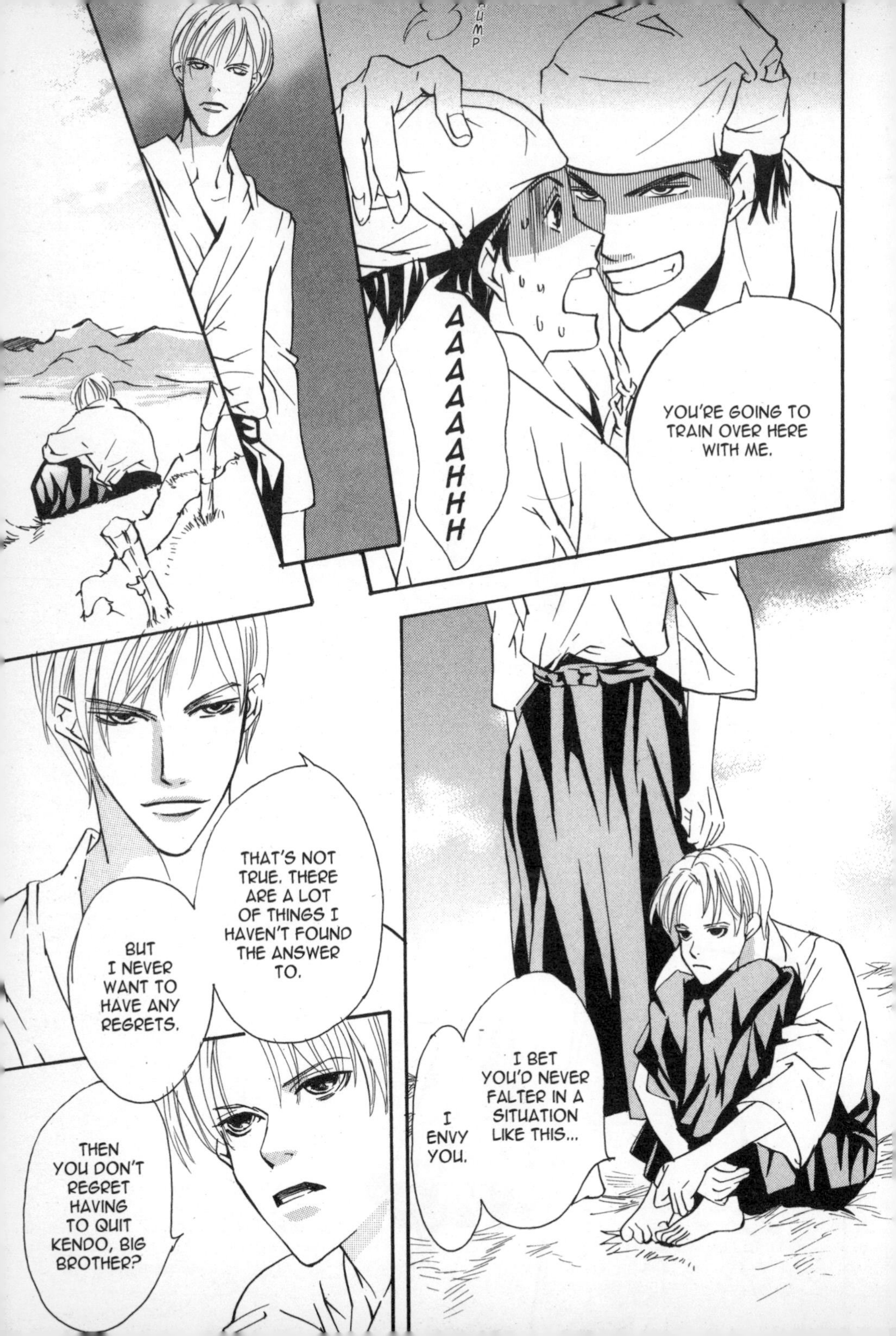
UMP
YOU'RE GOING TO TRAIN OVER HERE WITH ME.
AAAAAAAHHH
I BET YOU'D NEVER FALTER IN A SITUATION LIKE THIS...
I ENVY YOU.
THAT'S NOT TRUE. THERE ARE A LOT OF THINGS I HAVEN'T FOUND THE ANSWER TO.
BUT I NEVER WANT TO HAVE ANY REGRETS.
THEN YOU DON'T REGRET HAVING TO QUIT KENDO, BIG BROTHER?

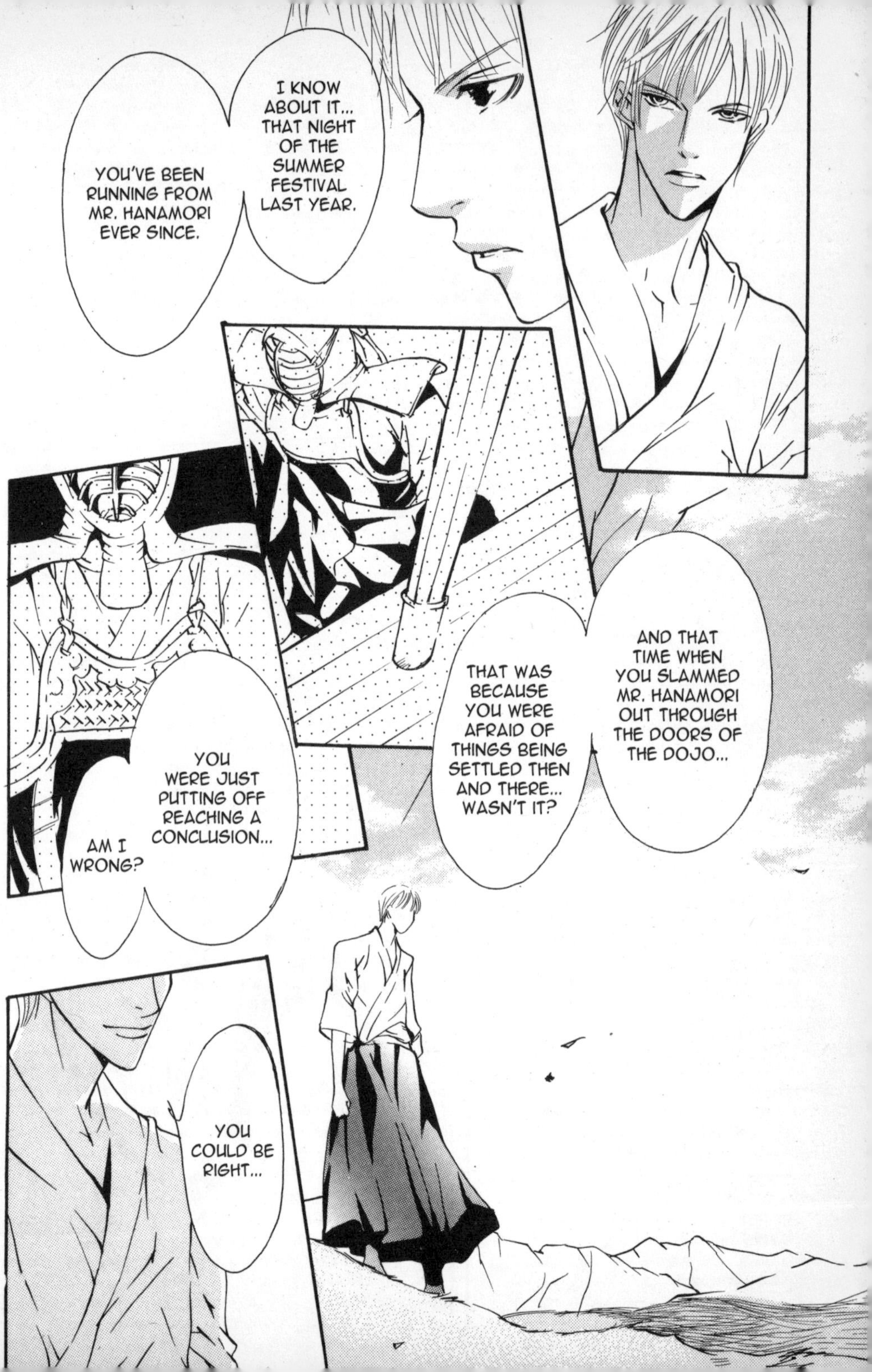
I KNOW ABOUT IT... THAT NIGHT OF THE SUMMER FESTIVAL LAST YEAR.
YOU'VE BEEN RUNNING FROM MR. HANAMORI EVER SINCE.
AND THAT TIME WHEN YOU SLAMMED MR. HANAMORI OUT THROUGH THE DOORS OF THE DOJO...
THAT WAS BECAUSE YOU WERE AFRAID OF THINGS BEING SETTLED THEN AND THERE... WASN'T IT?
YOU WERE JUST PUTTING OFF REACHING A CONCLUSION...
AM I WRONG?
YOU COULD BE RIGHT...

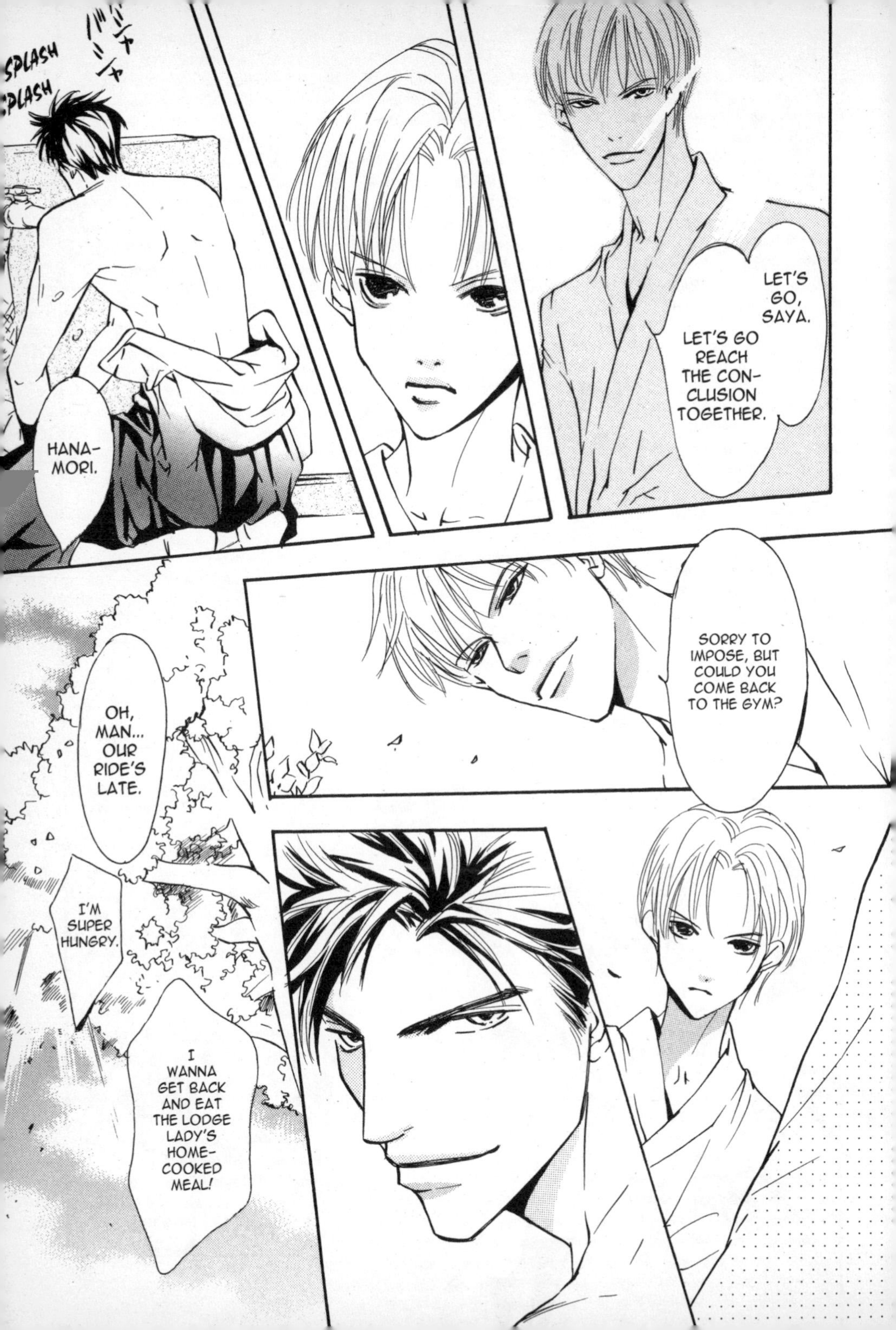
LET'S GO, SAYA.
LET'S GO REACH THE CON-CLUSION TOGETHER.
バシャバシャ
SPLASH SPLASH
HANA-MORI.
SORRY TO IMPOSE, BUT COULD YOU COME BACK TO THE GYM?
OH, MAN... OUR RIDE'S LATE.
I'M SUPER HUNGRY.
I WANNA GET BACK AND EAT THE LODGE LADY'S HOME-COOKED MEAL!

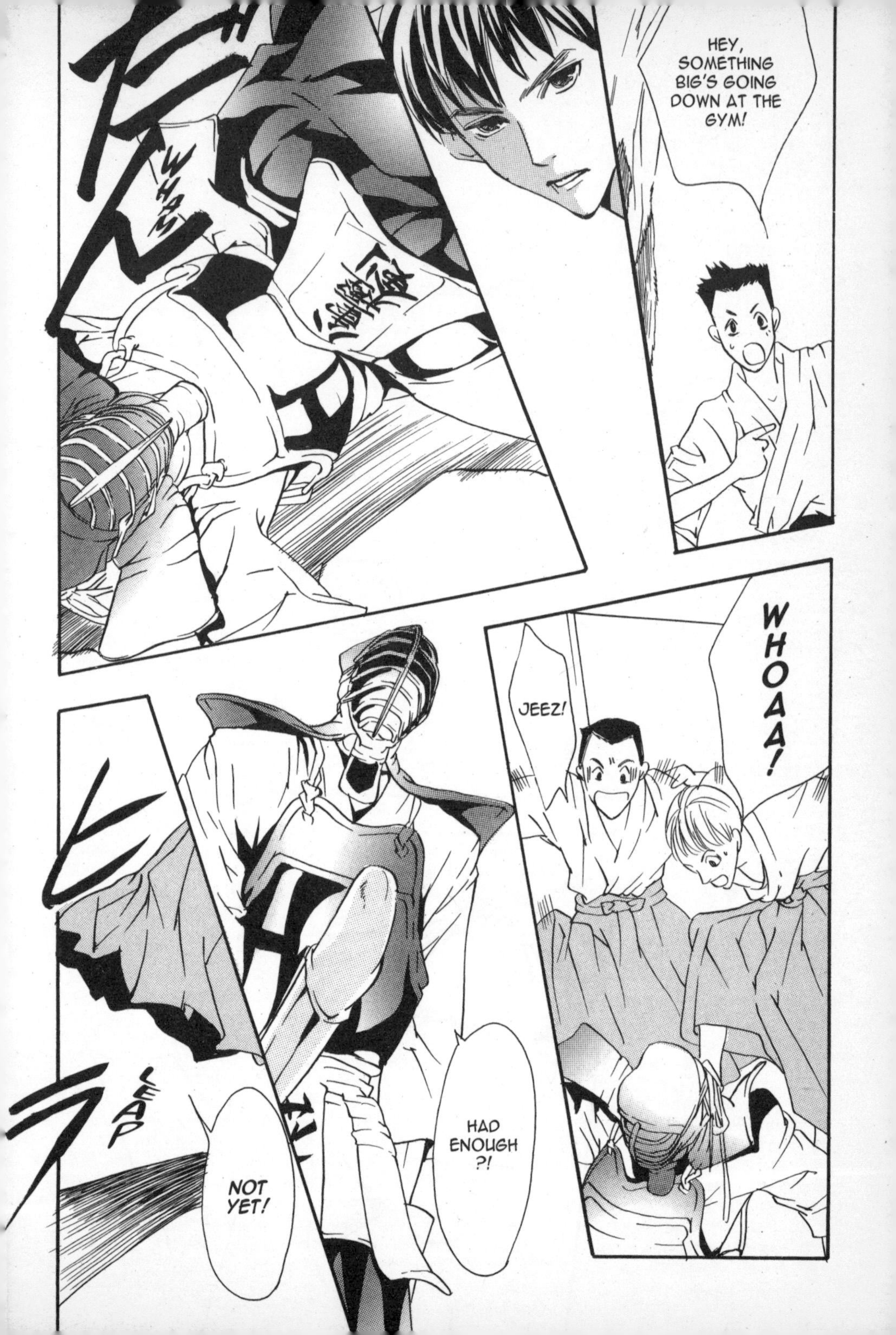
HEY, SOMETHING BIG'S GOING DOWN AT THE GYM!
WHAM
WHOAA!
JEEZ!
HAD ENOUGH?!
NOT YET!
LEAP

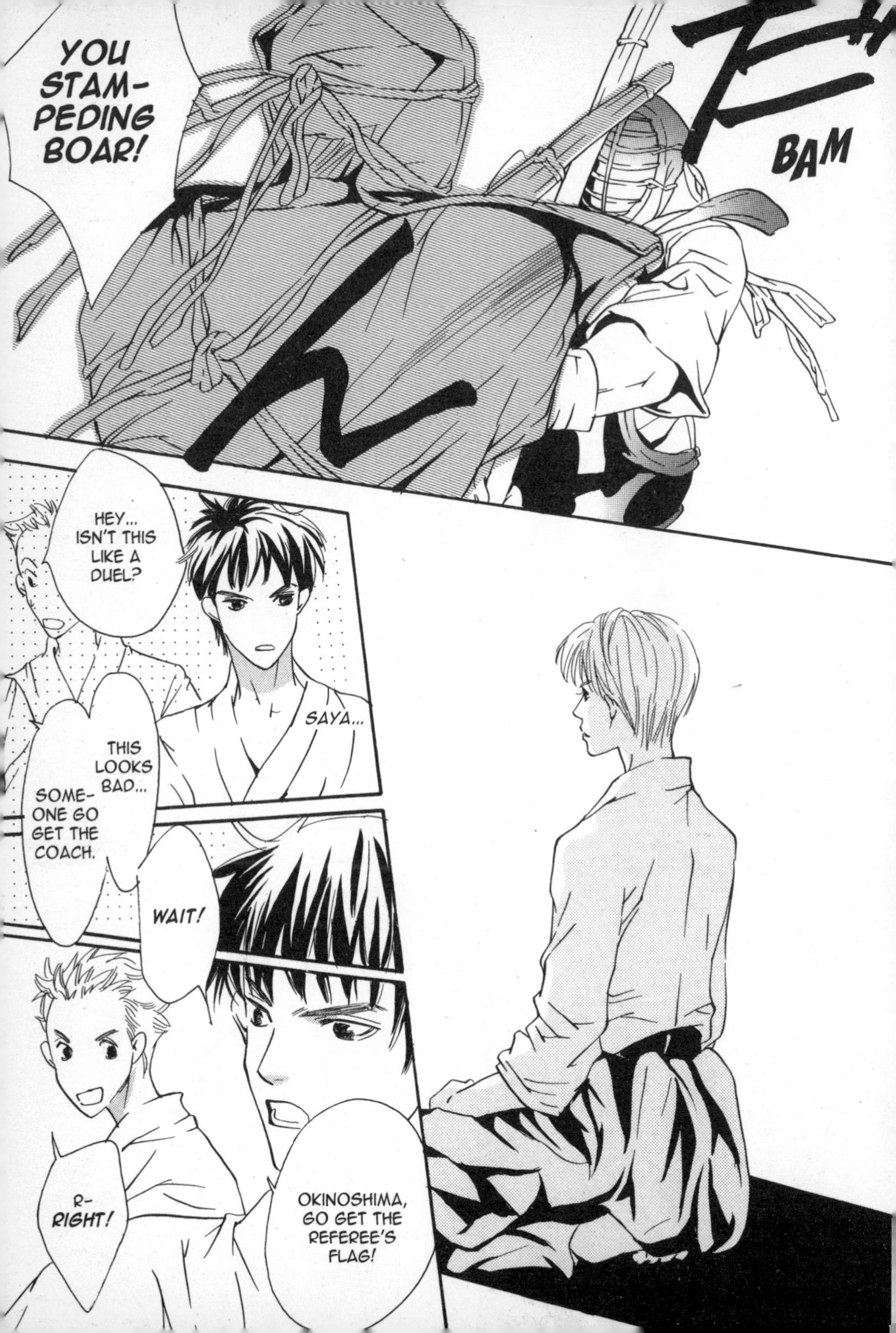
BAM
YOU STAM-PEDING BOAR!
HEY... ISN'T THIS LIKE A DUEL?
SAYA...
THIS LOOKS BAD...
SOME-ONE GO GET THE COACH.
WAIT!
OKINOSHIMA, GO GET THE REFEREE'S FLAG!
R-RIGHT!

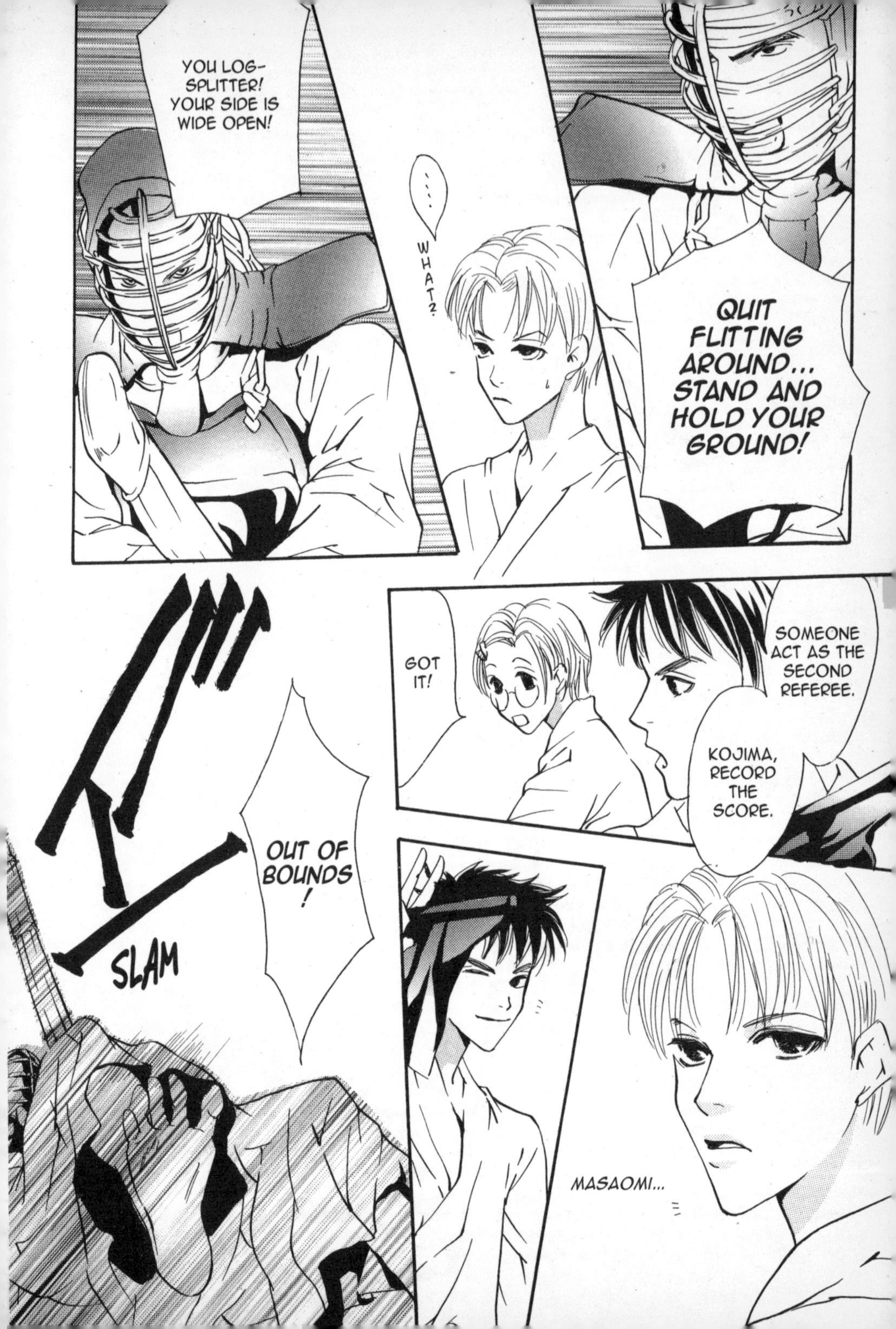
QUIT FLITTING AROUND... STAND AND HOLD YOUR GROUND!
...
WHAT?
YOU LOG-SPLITTER! YOUR SIDE IS WIDE OPEN!
SOMEONE ACT AS THE SECOND REFEREE.
KOJIMA, RECORD THE SCORE.
GOT IT!
MASAOMI...
OUT OF BOUNDS!
SLAM

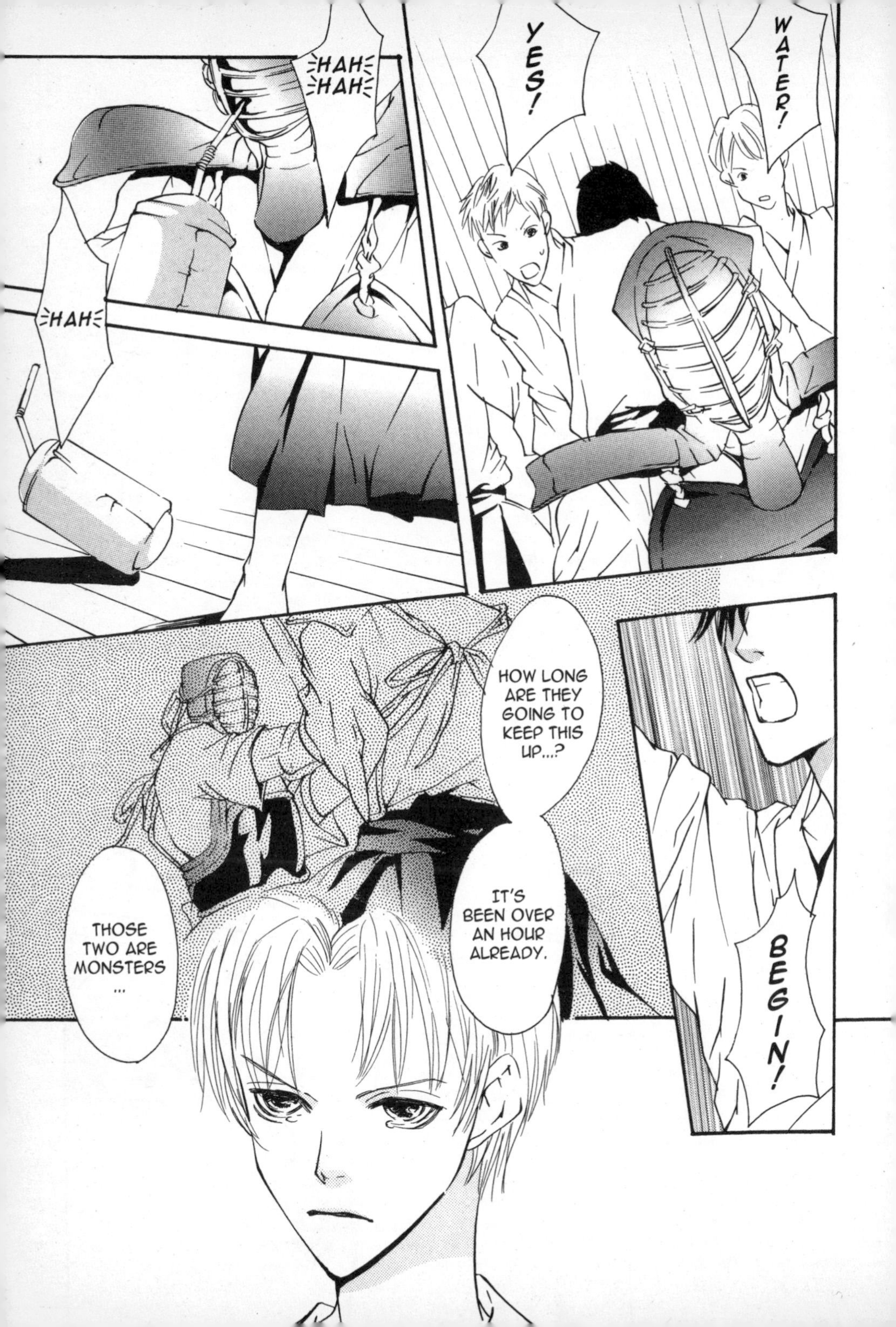
WATER!
YES!
HAH HAH
HAH
BEGIN!
HOW LONG ARE THEY GOING TO KEEP THIS UP...?
IT'S BEEN OVER AN HOUR ALREADY.
THOSE TWO ARE MONSTERS ...

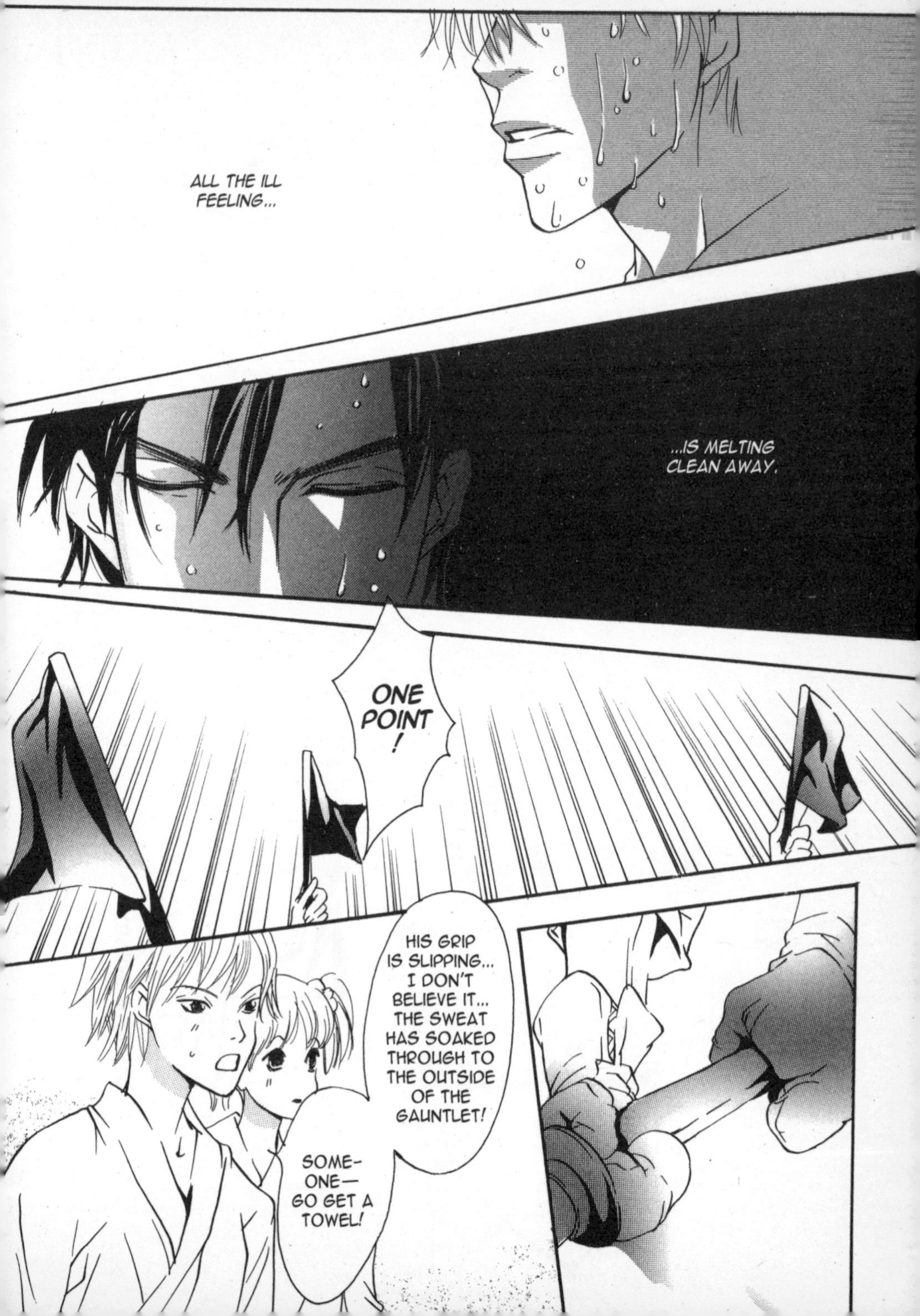
ALL THE ILL FEELING...
...IS MELTING CLEAN AWAY.
ONE POINT!
HIS GRIP IS SLIPPING... I DON'T BELIEVE IT... THE SWEAT HAS SOAKED THROUGH TO THE OUTSIDE OF THE GAUNTLET!
SOME-ONE— GO GET A TOWEL!

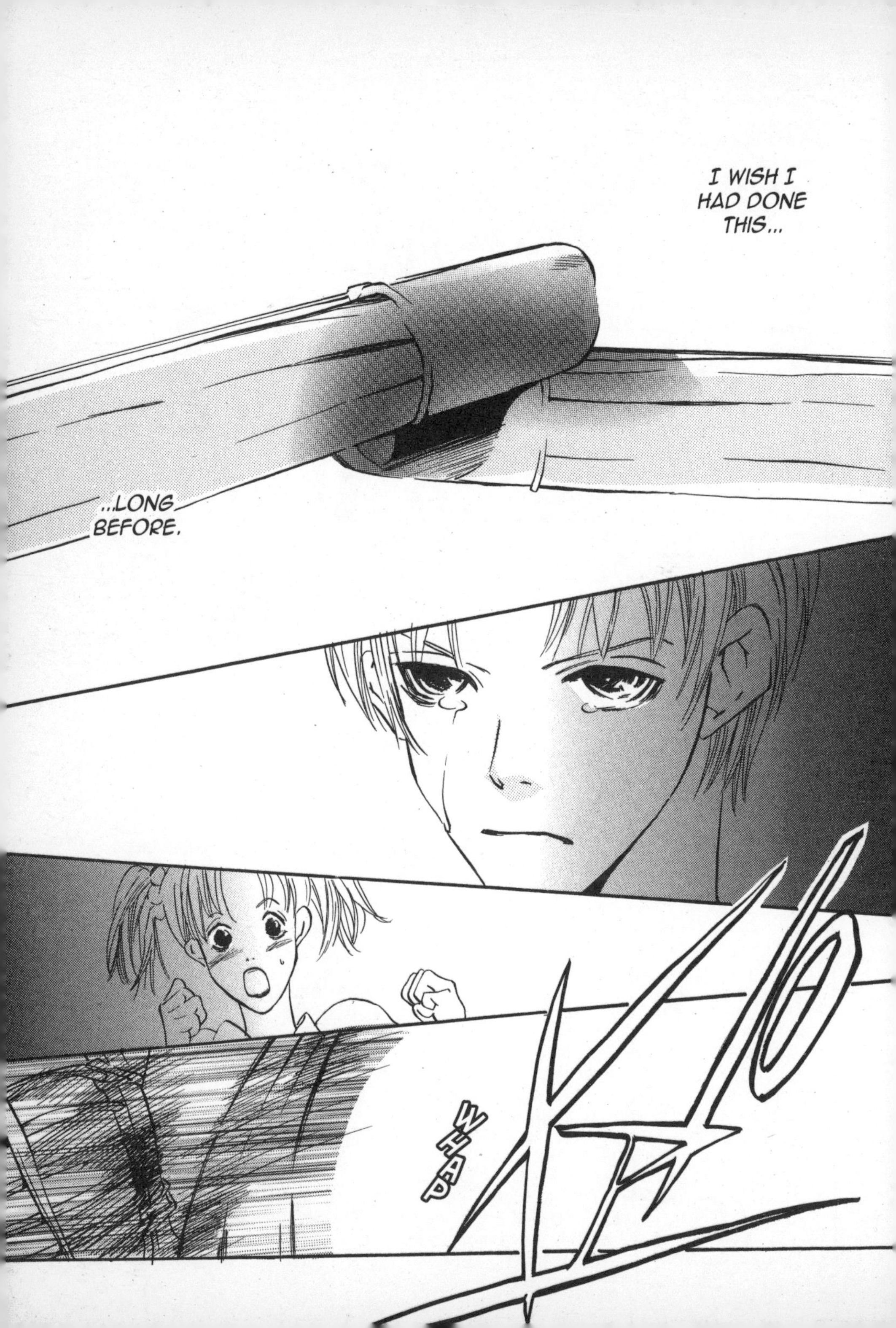
I WISH I HAD DONE THIS...
...LONG BEFORE.
WHAP

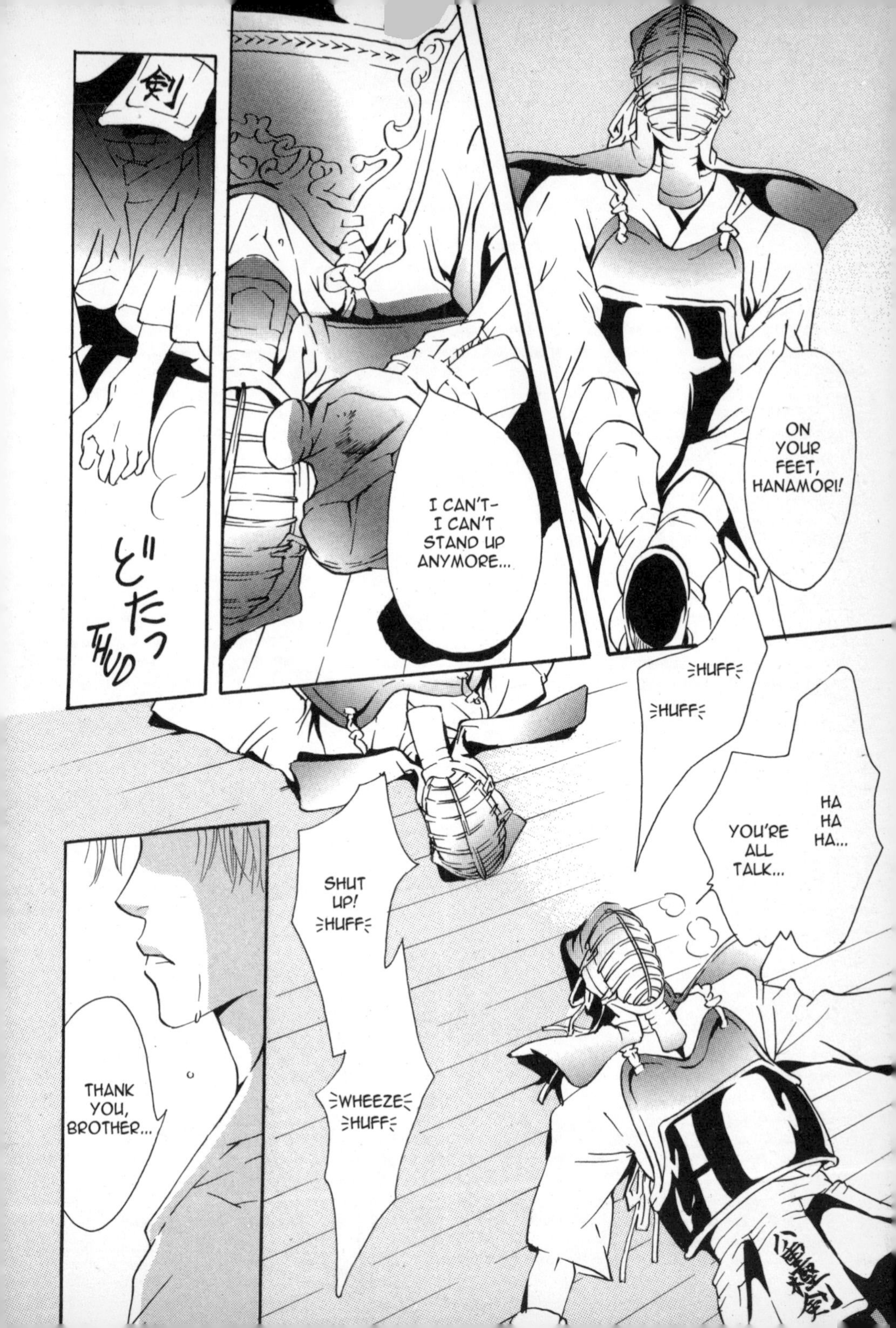
ON YOUR FEET, HANAMORI!
I CAN'T- I CAN'T STAND UP ANYMORE...
どたっ
THUD
HUFF
HUFF
HA HA HA...
YOU'RE ALL TALK...
SHUT UP! HUFF
WHEEZE HUFF
THANK YOU, BROTHER...

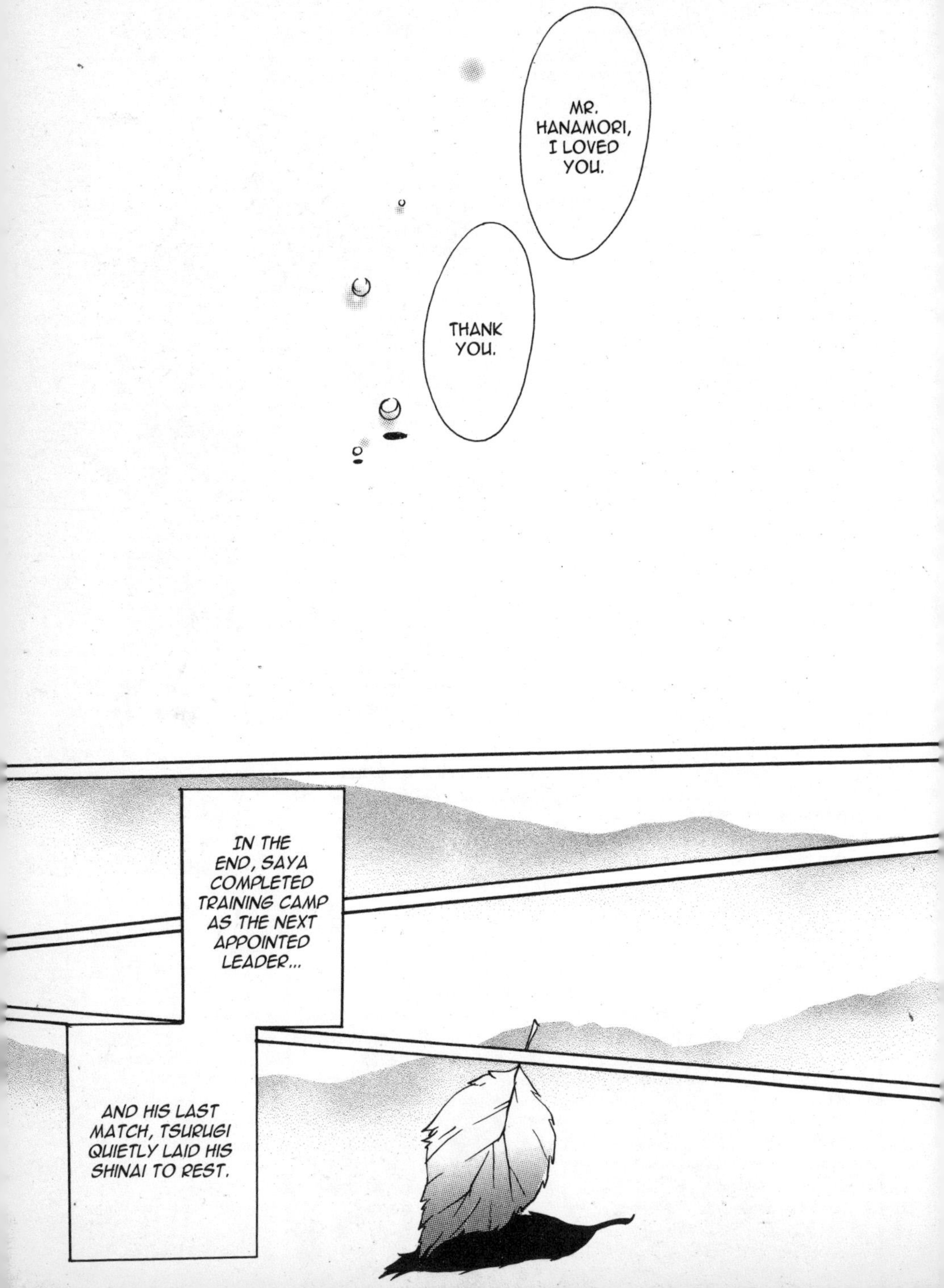
MR. HANAMORI, I LOVED YOU.
THANK YOU.
IN THE END, SAYA COMPLETED TRAINING CAMP AS THE NEXT APPOINTED LEADER...
AND HIS LAST MATCH, TSURUGI QUIETLY LAID HIS SHINAI TO REST.

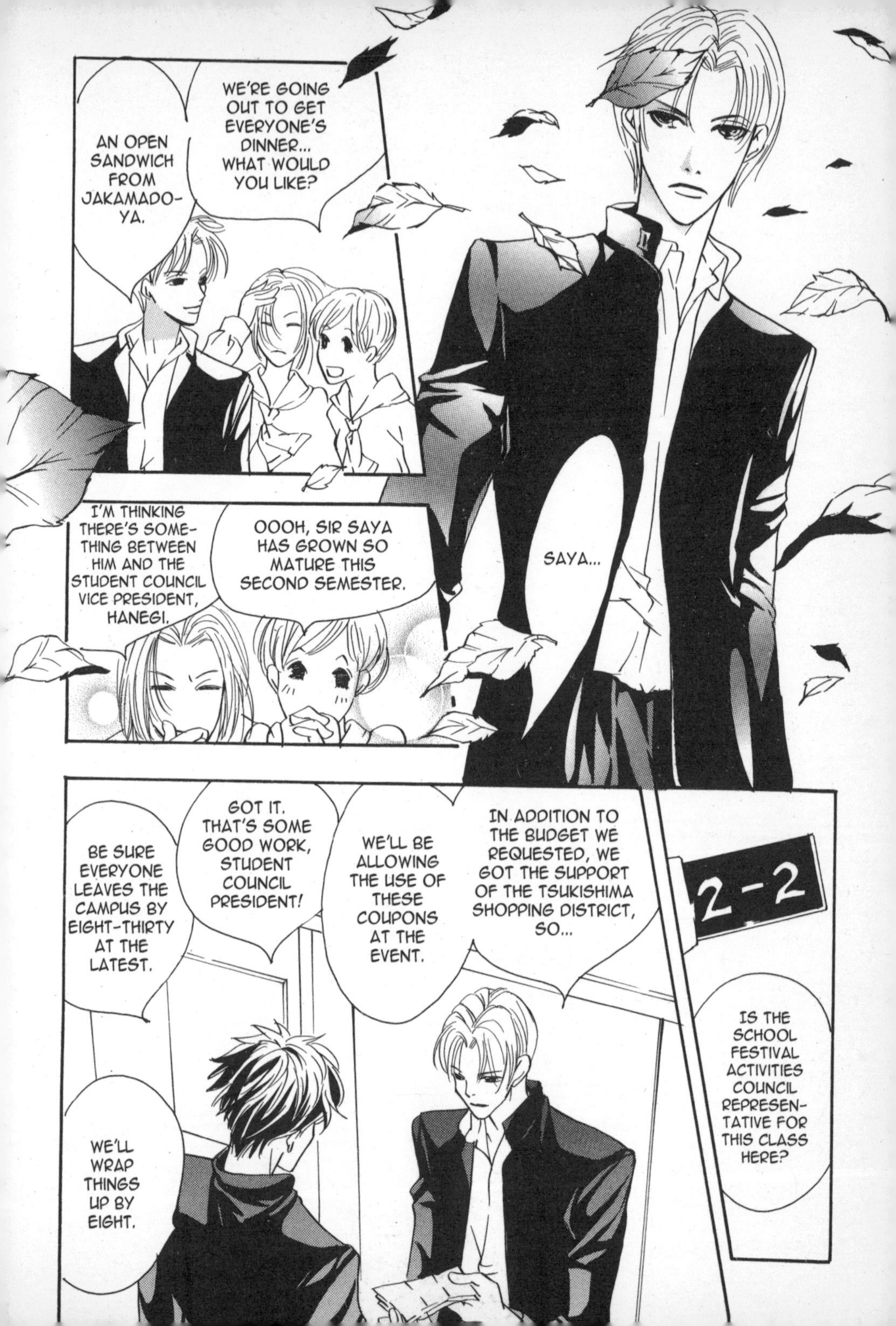
SAYA...
WE'RE GOING OUT TO GET EVERYONE'S DINNER... WHAT WOULD YOU LIKE?
AN OPEN SANDWICH FROM JAKAMADO-YA.
OOOH, SIR SAYA HAS GROWN SO MATURE THIS SECOND SEMESTER.
I'M THINKING THERE'S SOME-THING BETWEEN HIM AND THE STUDENT COUNCIL VICE PRESIDENT, HANEGI.
2-2
IS THE SCHOOL FESTIVAL ACTIVITIES COUNCIL REPRESEN-TATIVE FOR THIS CLASS HERE?
IN ADDITION TO THE BUDGET WE REQUESTED, WE GOT THE SUPPORT OF THE TSUKISHIMA SHOPPING DISTRICT, SO...
WE'LL BE ALLOWING THE USE OF THESE COUPONS AT THE EVENT.
GOT IT. THAT'S SOME GOOD WORK, STUDENT COUNCIL PRESIDENT!
BE SURE EVERYONE LEAVES THE CAMPUS BY EIGHT-THIRTY AT THE LATEST.
WE'LL WRAP THINGS UP BY EIGHT.

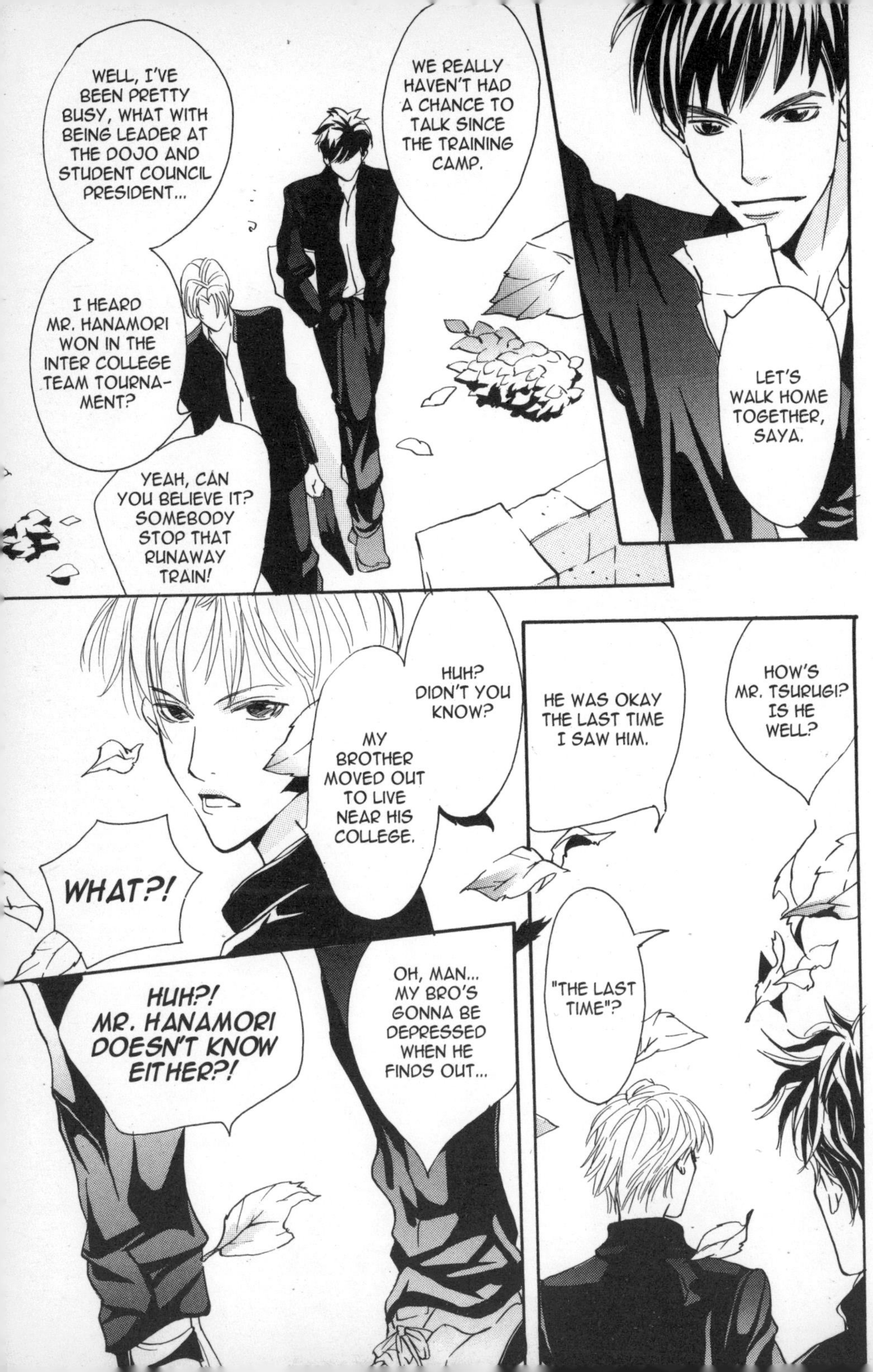
LET'S WALK HOME TOGETHER, SAYA.
WE REALLY HAVEN'T HAD A CHANCE TO TALK SINCE THE TRAINING CAMP.
WELL, I'VE BEEN PRETTY BUSY, WHAT WITH BEING LEADER AT THE DOJO AND STUDENT COUNCIL PRESIDENT...
I HEARD MR. HANAMORI WON IN THE INTER COLLEGE TEAM TOURNA-MENT?
YEAH, CAN YOU BELIEVE IT? SOMEBODY STOP THAT RUNAWAY TRAIN!
HOW'S MR. TSURUGI? IS HE WELL?
HE WAS OKAY THE LAST TIME I SAW HIM.
"THE LAST TIME"?
HUH? DIDN'T YOU KNOW?
MY BROTHER MOVED OUT TO LIVE NEAR HIS COLLEGE.
WHAT?!
OH, MAN... MY BRO'S GONNA BE DEPRESSED WHEN HE FINDS OUT...
HUH?! MR. HANAMORI DOESN'T KNOW EITHER?!

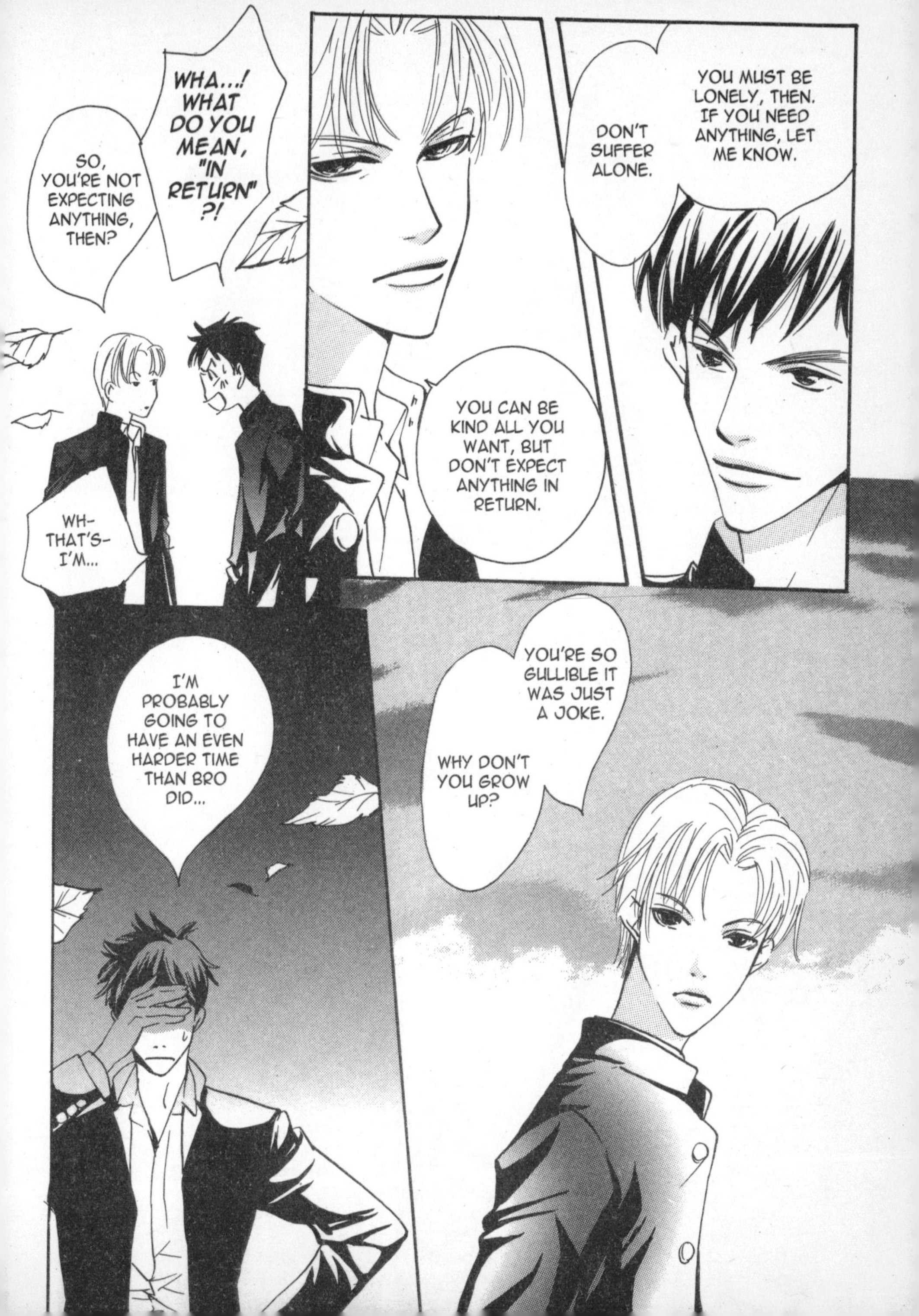
YOU MUST BE LONELY, THEN. IF YOU NEED ANYTHING, LET ME KNOW.
DON'T SUFFER ALONE.
YOU CAN BE KIND ALL YOU WANT, BUT DON'T EXPECT ANYTHING IN RETURN.
WHA...! WHAT DO YOU MEAN, "IN RETURN" ?!
SO, YOU'RE NOT EXPECTING ANYTHING, THEN?
WH- THAT'S- I'M...
YOU'RE SO GULLIBLE IT WAS JUST A JOKE.
WHY DON'T YOU GROW UP?
I'M PROBABLY GOING TO HAVE AN EVEN HARDER TIME THAN BRO DID...

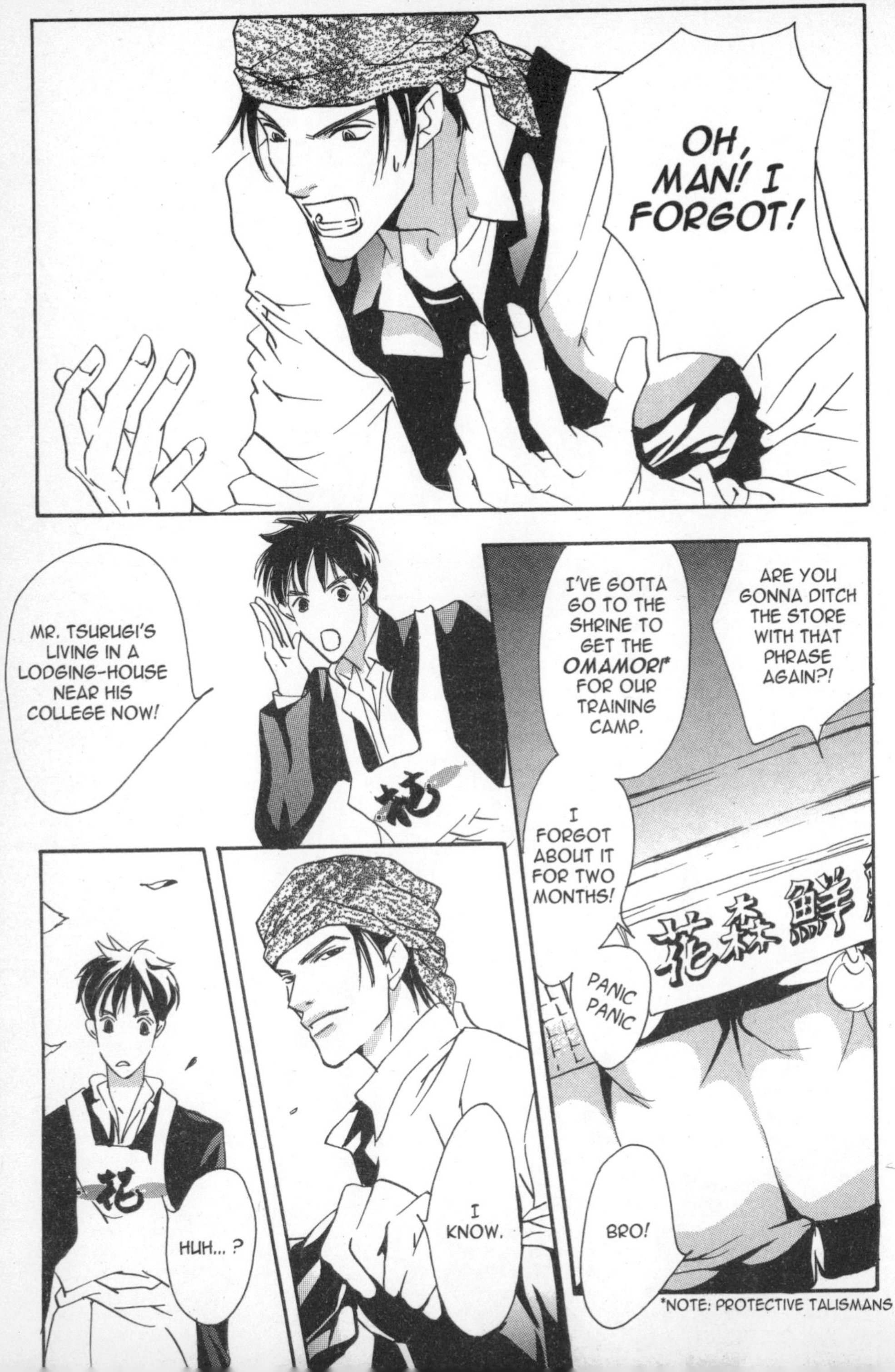
OH, MAN! I FORGOT!
ARE YOU GONNA DITCH THE STORE WITH THAT PHRASE AGAIN?!
I'VE GOTTA GO TO THE SHRINE TO GET THE *OMAMORI** FOR OUR TRAINING CAMP.
I FORGOT ABOUT IT FOR TWO MONTHS!
花森鮮
PANIC PANIC
BRO!
MR. TSURUGI'S LIVING IN A LODGING-HOUSE NEAR HIS COLLEGE NOW!
I KNOW.
HUH... ?

*NOTE: PROTECTIVE TALISMANS

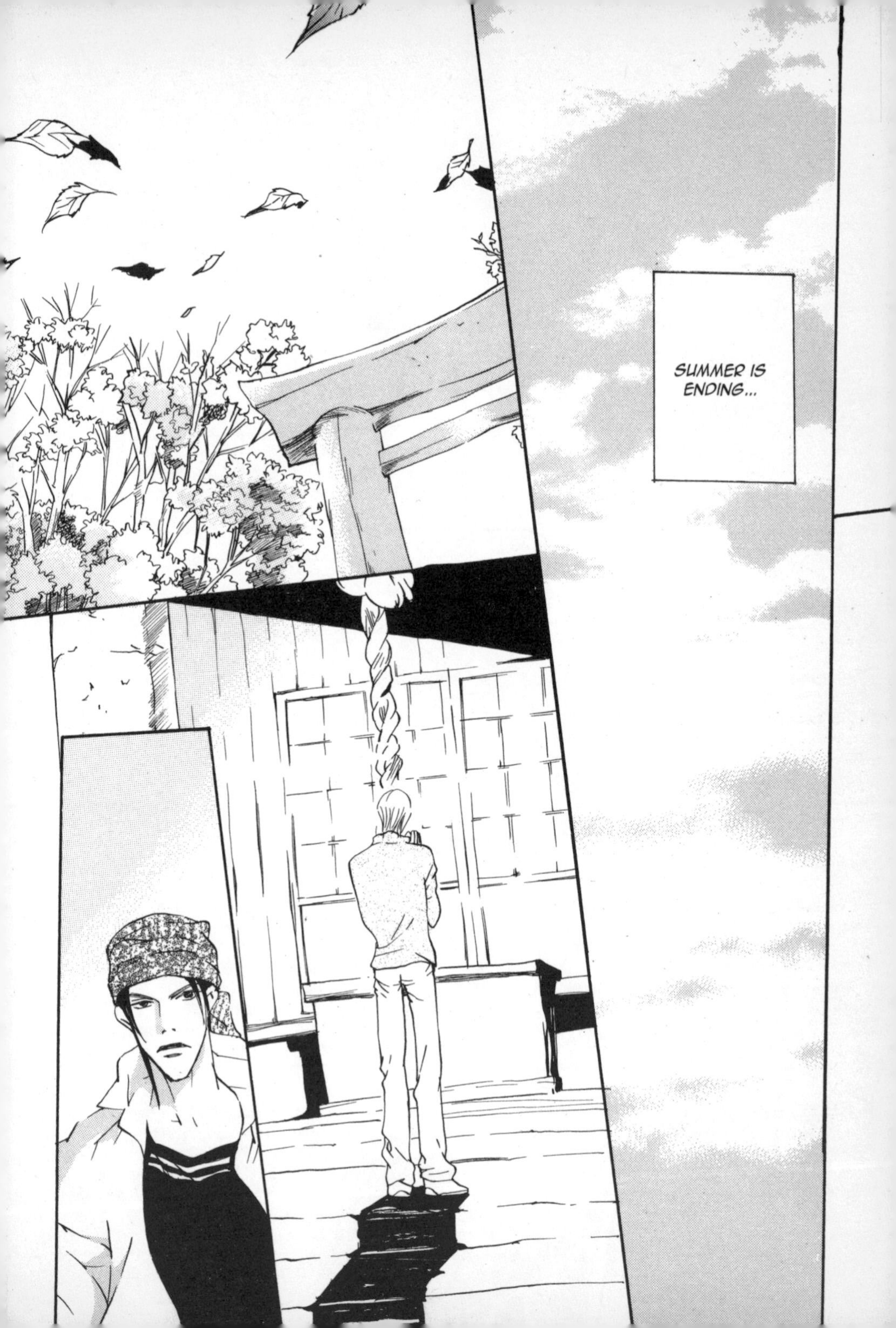
SUMMER IS ENDING...

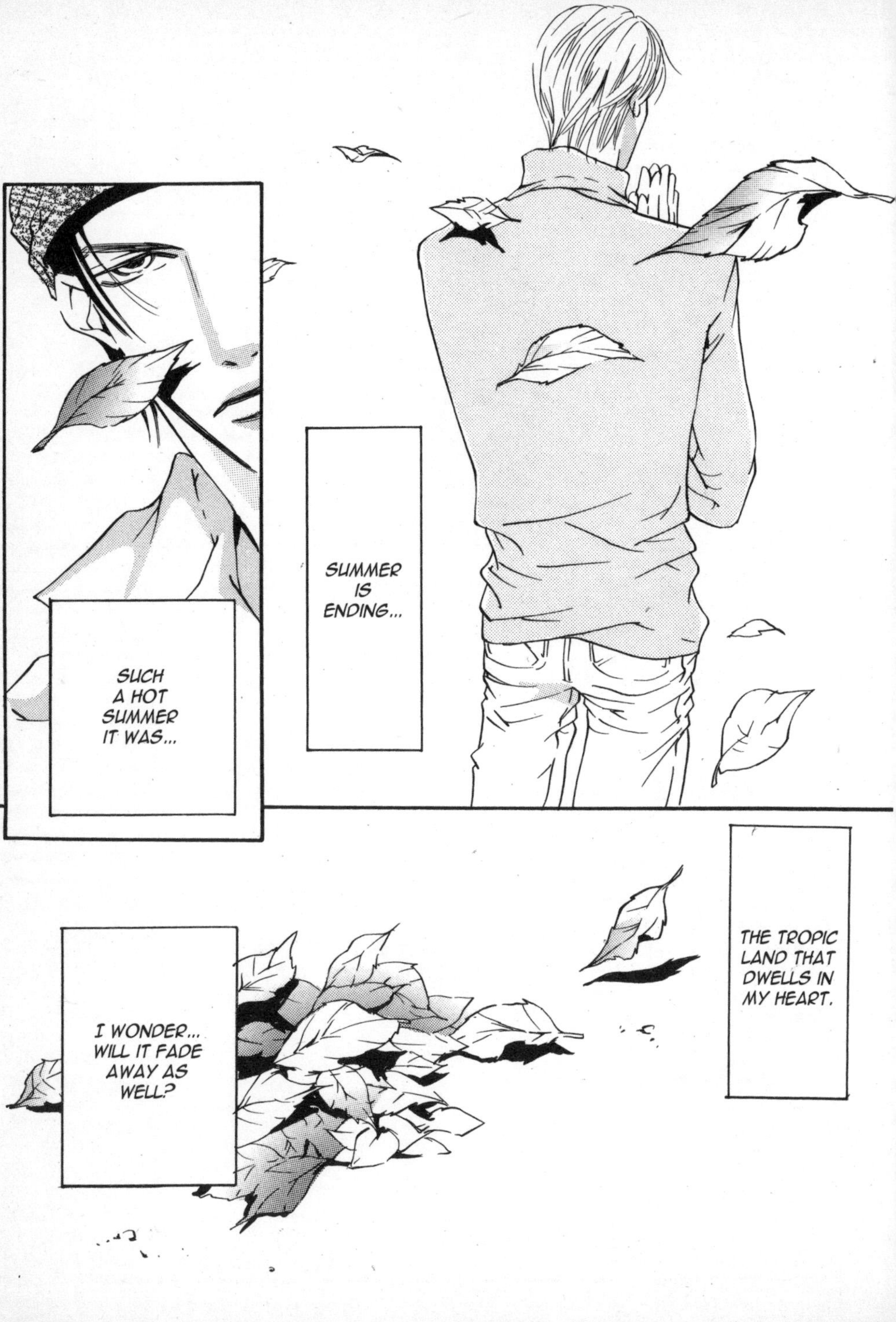
SUMMER IS ENDING...
SUCH A HOT SUMMER IT WAS...
THE TROPIC LAND THAT DWELLS IN MY HEART.
I WONDER... WILL IT FADE AWAY AS WELL?

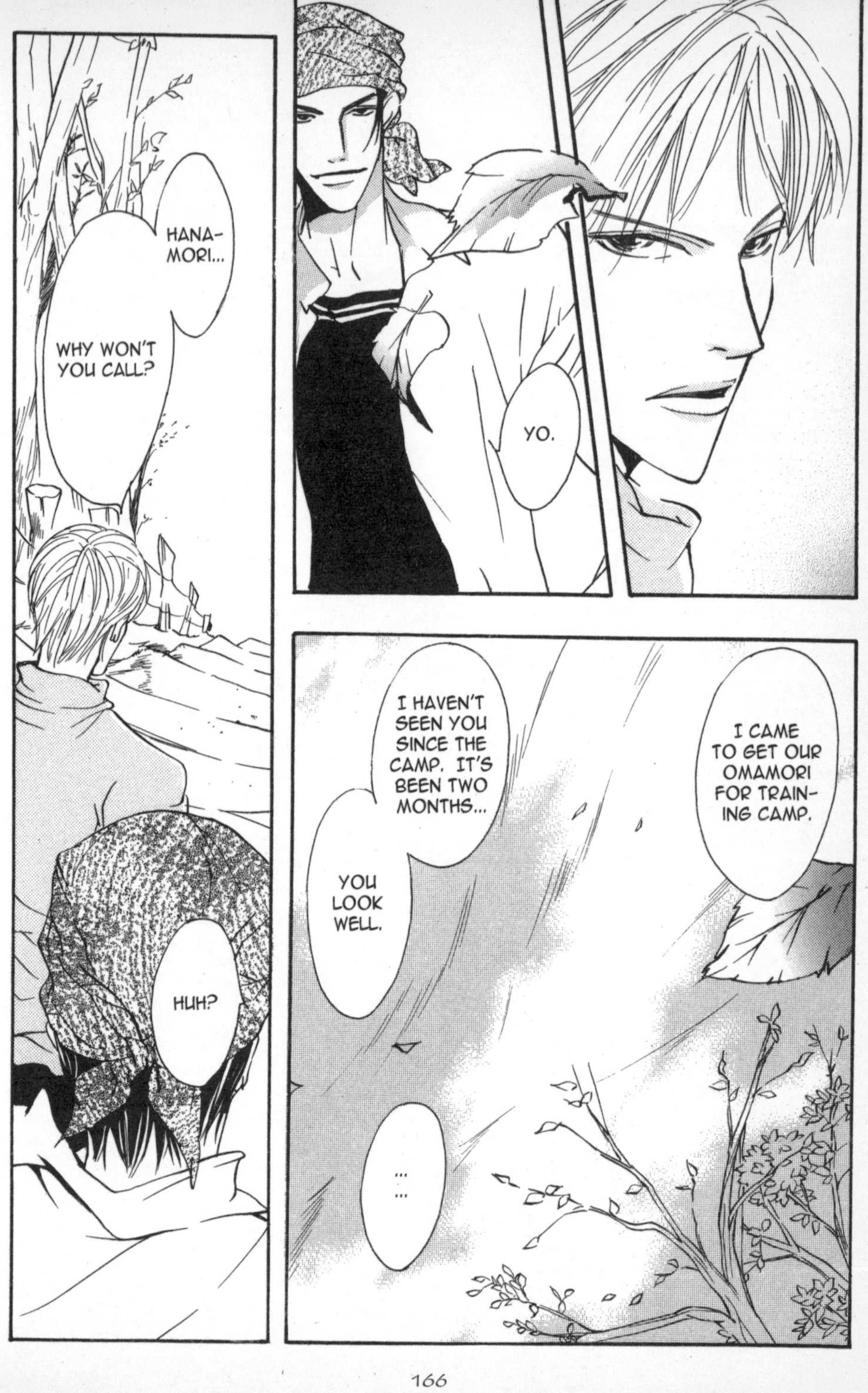
YO.
I CAME TO GET OUR OMAMORI FOR TRAINING CAMP.
I HAVEN'T SEEN YOU SINCE THE CAMP. IT'S BEEN TWO MONTHS...
YOU LOOK WELL.
......
HANA-MORI...
WHY WON'T YOU CALL?
HUH?

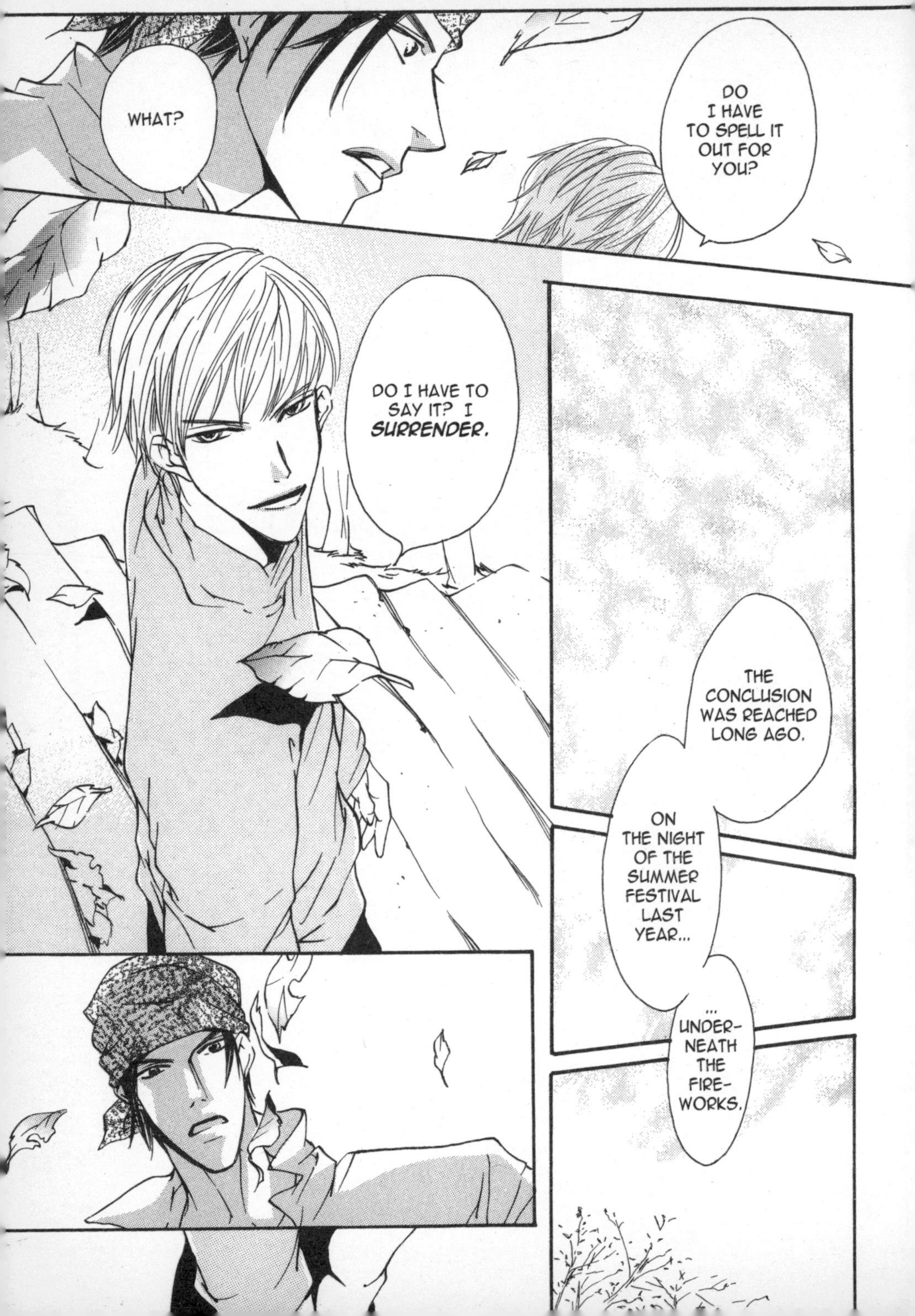

DO I HAVE TO SPELL IT OUT FOR YOU?
WHAT?
DO I HAVE TO SAY IT? I **SURRENDER.**
THE CONCLUSION WAS REACHED LONG AGO.
ON THE NIGHT OF THE SUMMER FESTIVAL LAST YEAR...
...UNDER-NEATH THE FIRE-WORKS.

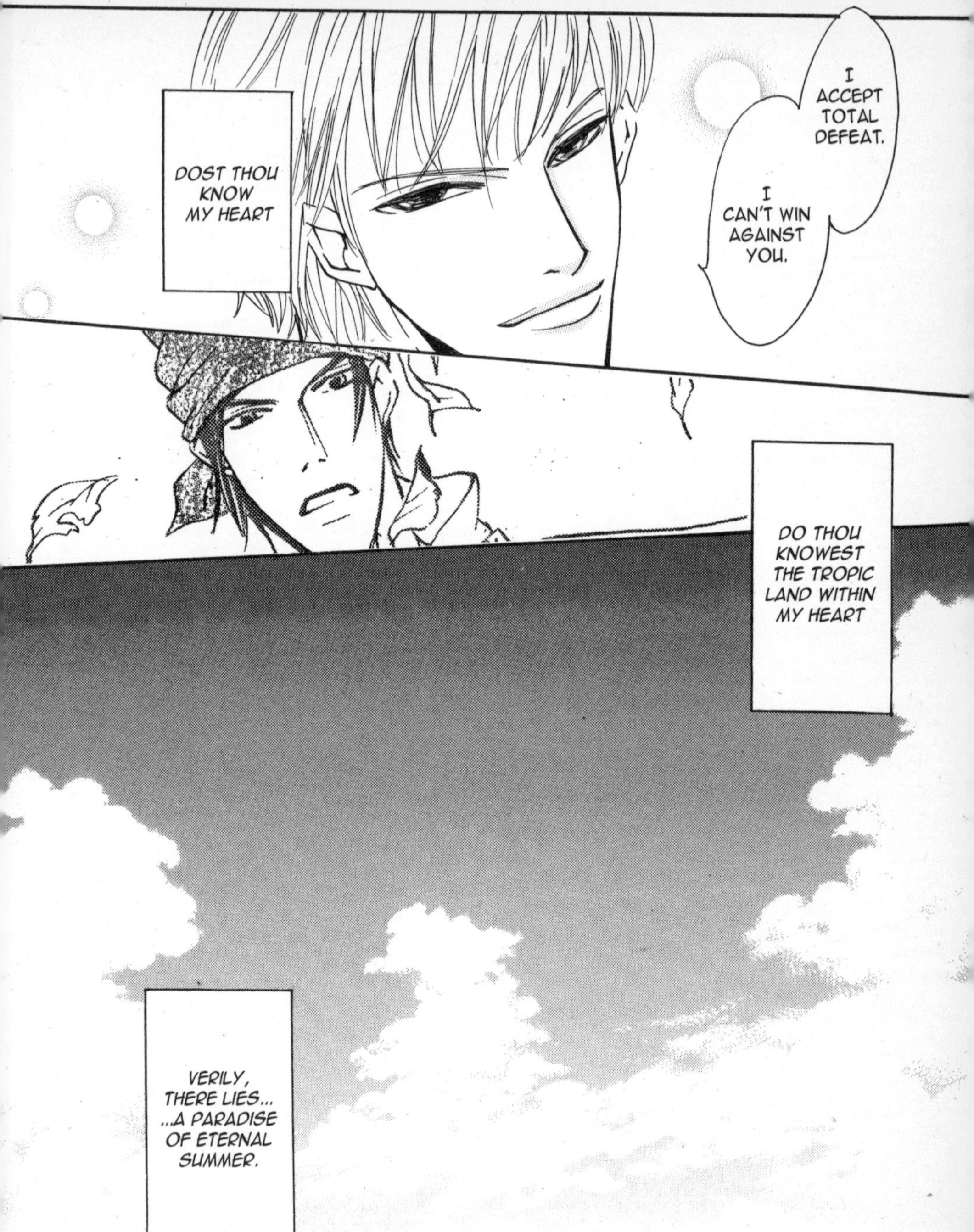
I ACCEPT TOTAL DEFEAT.
I CAN'T WIN AGAINST YOU.
DOST THOU KNOW MY HEART
DO THOU KNOWEST THE TROPIC LAND WITHIN MY HEART
VERILY, THERE LIES... ...A PARADISE OF ETERNAL SUMMER.

DOST THOU KNOW / END

HOW MANY YEARS HAS IT BEEEEEN??!!

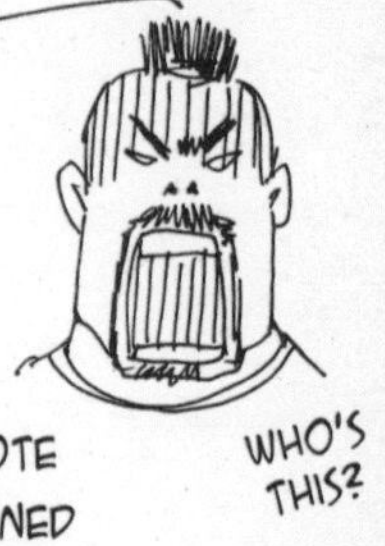
WHO'S THIS?

I CAN ALMOST HEAR THESE WORDS BEING YELLED AT ME.
IT'S FINALLY OUT - "**DOST THOU KNOW**".

ABOUT THREE YEARS HAVE PASSED SINCE I WROTE THE FIRST CHAPTER. MANY THINGS HAVE HAPPENED SINCE THEN AND EVEN GRADUAL CHANGES TO MY ART STYLE CAN BE SEEN, BUT I AM HAPPY TO HAVE SUCCESSFULLY BROUGHT THE STORY TO ITS CONCLUSION. TO MY EDITOR "T", OTHERS, AND ALL YOU READERS WHO PATIENTLY STUCK WITH ME - THANK YOU ALL VERY MUCH.
MY ORIGINAL PLAN WAS TO SEPARATE THE STORY INTO SEASONS - SPRING, SUMMER, AUTUMN, AND WINTER - BUT FOR SOME REASON, THE LAST HALF TURNED OUT TO BE ALL SUMMER. AFTER ALL, THERE ARE SUMMER CAMPS, SUMMER FESTIVALS, THE BEACH, SUMMER VACATION - ALL PRIME EVENTS FOR PASSION TO ERUPT...BUT THE REAL REASON IS THAT IT WAS SUMMER WHEN I WAS WORKING ON THIS. IT WAS SO HOT...

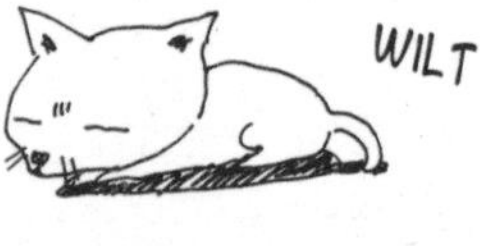
WILT

SO - I DECLARE THAT, FROM NOW ON, I WILL PUT OUT GRAPHIC NOVELS AT A PACE OF ONE EVERY FOUR YEARS.

(KIDDING).

...OR AM I...?

When a little thing like **death** gets in the way of love. A speacial ghost's affections, will come back from the **beyond**.

ISBN# 1-56970-928-9 $12.95

Beyond My Touch - Meniwa Sayakani Mienedomo © TOMO MAEDA 2003.
Originally published in Japan in 2003 by SHINSHOKAN Co., LTD

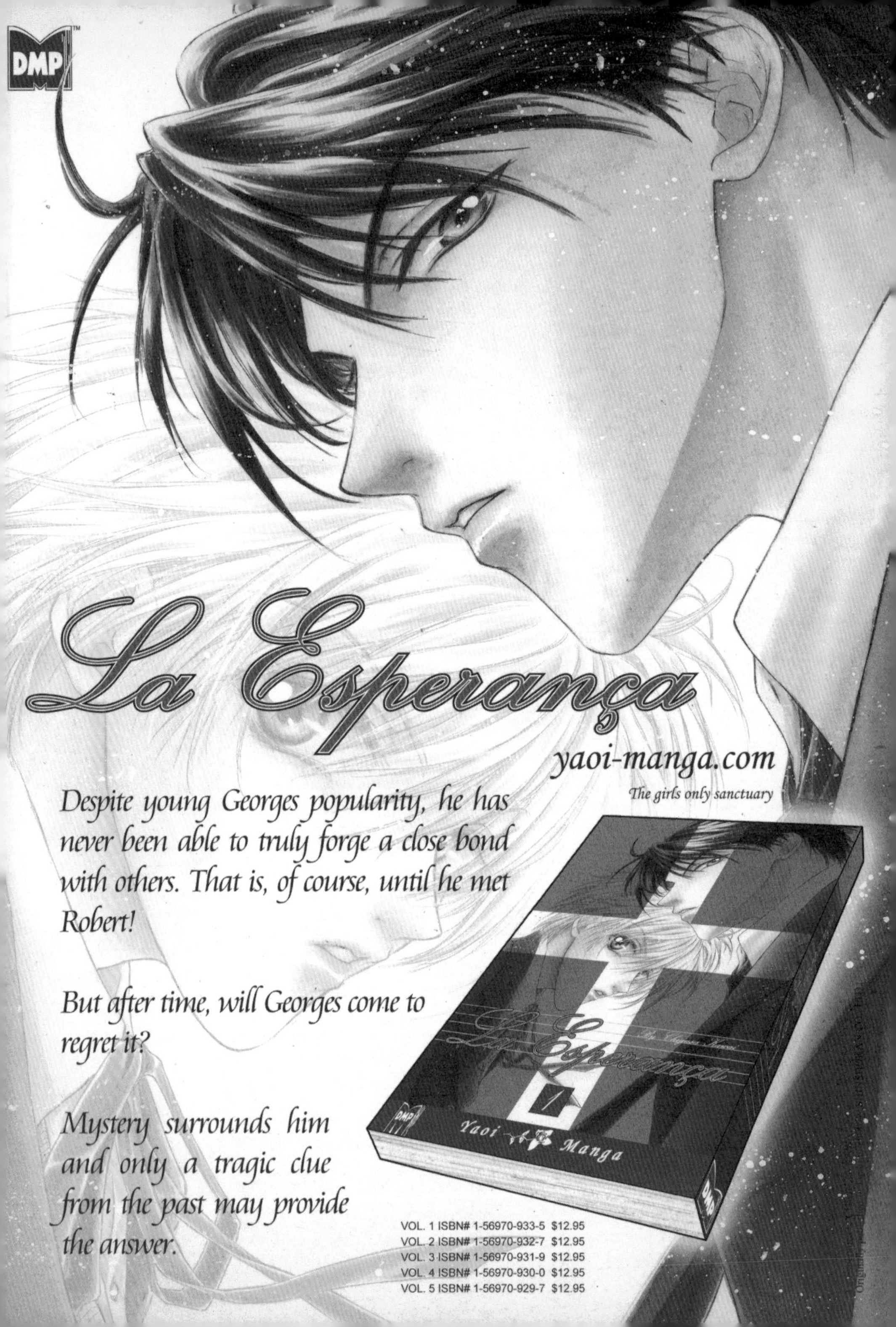
DMP
La Esperança
yaoi-manga.com
The girls only sanctuary
Despite young Georges popularity, he has never been able to truly forge a close bond with others. That is, of course, until he met Robert!
But after time, will Georges come to regret it?
Mystery surrounds him and only a tragic clue from the past may provide the answer.
La Esperança
1
Yaoi Manga
DMP
VOL. 1 ISBN# 1-56970-933-5 $12.95
VOL. 2 ISBN# 1-56970-932-7 $12.95
VOL. 3 ISBN# 1-56970-931-9 $12.95
VOL. 4 ISBN# 1-56970-930-0 $12.95
VOL. 5 ISBN# 1-56970-929-7 $12.95

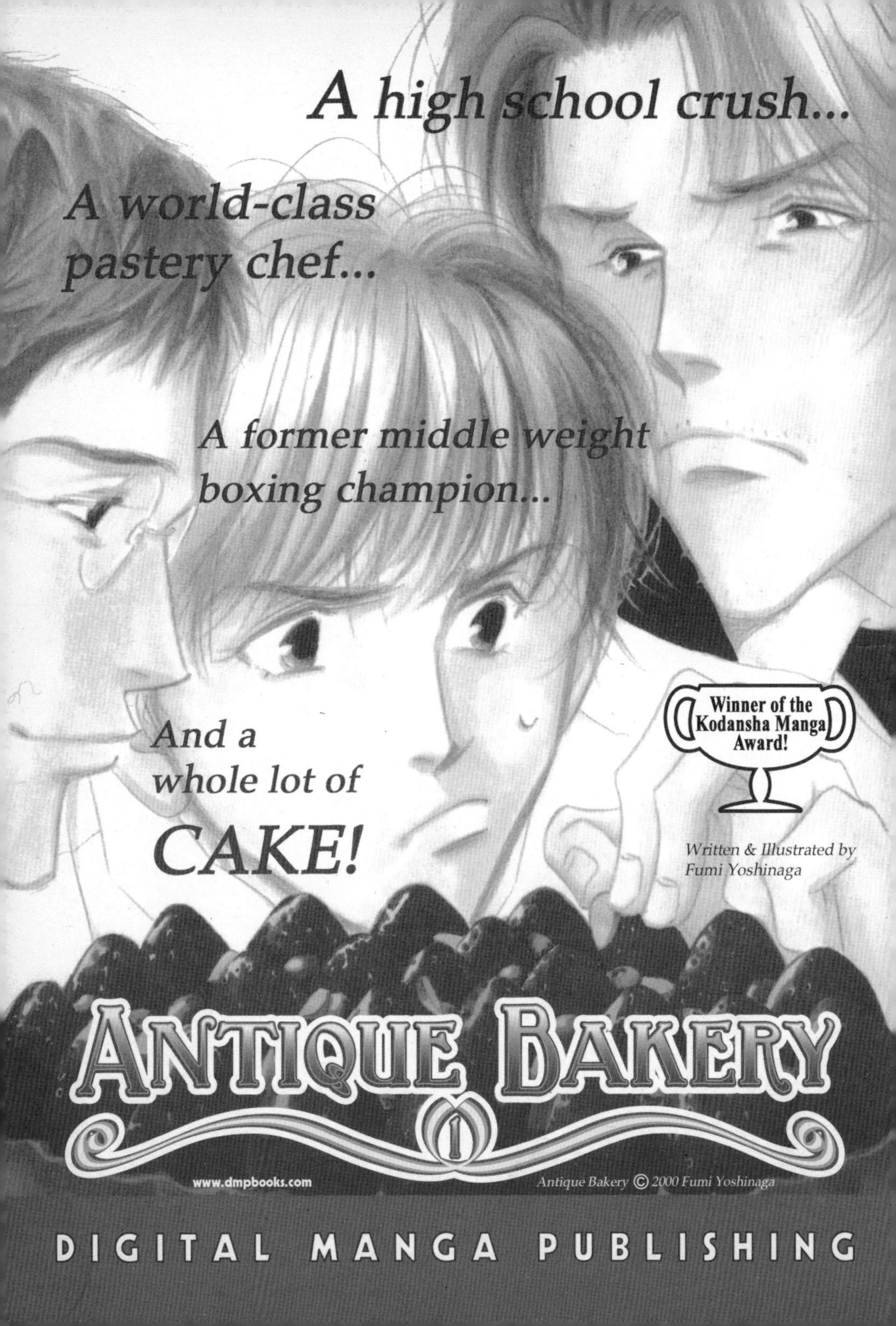

A high school crush...

A world-class
pastery chef...

A former middle weight
boxing champion...

And a
whole lot of
CAKE!

Winner of the
Kodansha Manga
Award!

*Written & Illustrated by
Fumi Yoshinaga*

ANTIQUE BAKERY

Antique Bakery © 2000 Fumi Yoshinaga

DIGITAL MANGA PUBLISHING

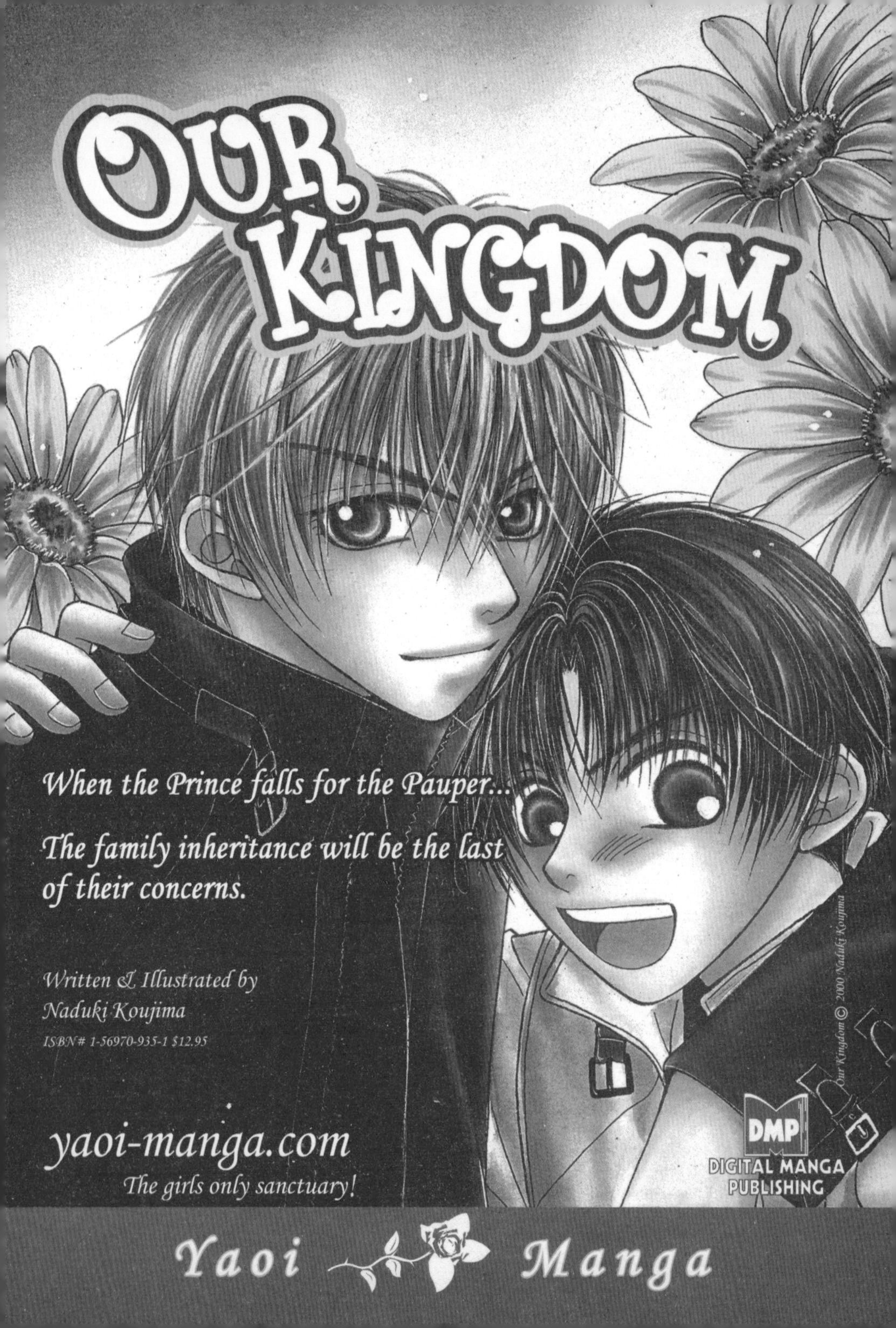
OUR KINGDOM
When the Prince falls for the Pauper...
The family inheritance will be the last of their concerns.
Written & Illustrated by
Naduki Koujima
ISBN# 1-56970-935-1 $12.95
yaoi-manga.com
The girls only sanctuary!
Our Kingdom © 2000 Naduki Koujima
DMP
DIGITAL MANGA PUBLISHING
Yaoi Manga

STOP

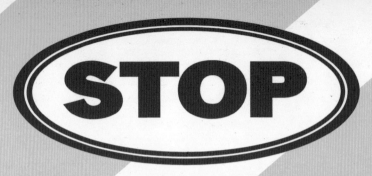

This is the back of the book!
Start from the other side.

NATIVE MANGA
readers read manga from *right to left*.

1
2
1
3
2
3
5
4
4
6
5
8
7
6

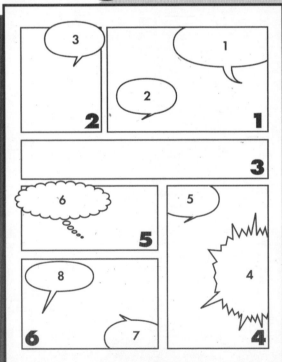

*If you run into our **Native Manga** logo on any of our books... you'll know that this manga is published in it's true original native Japanese right to left reading format, as it was intended. Turn to the other side of the book and start reading from right to left, top to bottom.*

Follow the diagram to see how its done.
Surf's Up!

NATIVE MANGA
READ RIGHT TO LEFT

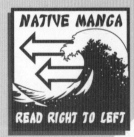